D1188232

THE LIFE OF BENEDICT XV

In Te, Domine, speravi:

non confundar in aeternum

Benedictus PP. XV

The Life of
BENEDICT XV

WALTER H. PETERS

990.1
PE

THE BRUCE PUBLISHING COMPANY
MILWAUKEE

NIHIL OBSTAT:

Patrick H. Ahern, M.A., Ph.D.
Censor deputatus

IMPRIMATUR:

✠ William O. Brady, S.T.D., D.D.
Archbishop of Saint Paul
Saint Paul, April 18, 1959

Library of Congress Catalog Card Number: 59–13565

© 1959 The Bruce Publishing Company
MADE IN THE UNITED STATES OF AMERICA

To my mother and paternal grandmother, who at the earliest dawn of my consciousness, that is, at the election of Benedict XV in 1914, through their enthusiastic and loving instruction made me aware of the joy and feeling of security which comes to the united family of Catholicism with the knowledge that it again has a Holy Father.

Acknowledgments

GRATITUDE is due first of all to His Excellency, Archbishop William O. Brady, for his scholarly interest and fatherly encouragement in this project. For priceless editorial aid I am indebted to Mr. Francis McGrade and Father Edward P. Keenan of St. Paul, and to Mr. Aloysius Croft of Milwaukee. For specialized help in research I am indebted to Fathers John C. Gruden, S.T.L., Eugene J. Moriarty, J.C.D., Patrick H. Ahern, Ph.D., Ludwig Kada, S.T.D., J.C.D., Richard J. Schuler, M.A., and David J. Dooley, B.A.

To these and countless other persons who have supplied nuggets of information, guidance, editorial and clerical help I express my gratitude and the prayer that God may show His choicest blessings on them.

Grateful acknowledgment is made to the following publishers for the permission they gave so graciously enabling the author to quote from the works indicated.

Benziger Brothers, Inc.: *The Burning Flame* by Francis Beauchesne Thornton (1952). — Burns, Oates and Washbourne, Ltd.: *Cardinal Gasquet* by Shane Leslie (1953). — Farrar, Straus and Cudahy, Inc.: *Vatican Journal 1921–1954* by Anne O'Hare McCormack (1957) and *The Life of Hilaire Belloc* by Robert Speaight (1957). — Harper and Brothers: *The Vatican, Yesterday, Today, Tomorrow* by George Seldes (1934) and *The Life of Archbishop John Ireland* by James H. Moynihan (1953). — Longmans, Green and Co., Inc.: *The House on Humility Street* by Martin Doherty (1942); *Rafael Cardinal Merry del Val* by Frances Forbes (1932); *A Papal Chamberlain* by Francis MacNutt (1936); *Leo XIII and Our Times* by René Füllöp Miller (1937). — The Newman Press: *Memories of Pope Pius X* by Cardinal Merry del Val (1951); *The Pilot*, official publication of the Archdiocese of Boston: *Recollections of Seventy Years* by William Cardinal O'Connell (Houghton Mifflin Co., 1934). — G. P. Putnam's Sons and Coward-McCann, Inc.: *Speaking of Cardinals* by Thomas B. Morgan.

Foreword

THE imagination of the world has recently been captivated by Pope John's frequent and casual appearances among his people and in the city that is his bishopric. Where Pope Pius XII stood often at a window to give a blessing, Pope John XXIII has quietly opened a door from the Vatican to the outside, assuming, and rightly so, that not only is this the place for a pope to be, but that the world is now ready to accept this re-entrance of the pope into the common affairs of men.

Few remember how startling it was when Pope Pius XI began his pontificate by standing on a balcony for a minute to give a blessing. Few recall the long and intricate negotiations between Church and State which followed that blessing and preceded an official and public appearance by a pope. Still fewer are those who recall the reasons for such long-standing restraint. Still fewer are those who know that a secret knock on a door and a secret meeting between men of the world and men of religion was all that Benedict, in his time, could authorize, afford, or effect.

Yet, the path to the balcony, the open window in the Pope's apartment and Pope John's throwing back of a door wide open are the consequences of the little thing that Benedict did privately and in secret.

A modern historian is quoted in Father Peters' book, THE LIFE OF BENEDICT XV, as saying that Benedict has suffered an "unintelligent oblivion." But the oblivion is not unintelligible.

Some men make marks because of who they are. Others make history because of what they do. A man and his accomplishments may both be worthy, but both may be overshadowed by the days in which the work is done or by the other human figures who loom larger because their personalities or their freedom from restraint allow them a more dramatic entrance or exit in their times.

Benedict has suffered by comparison with the saint who was pope before him. Benedict became Pope, but it is Rampolla, who did not, who overshadows the man he trained for an office he himself would never gain. The booming of great guns made Benedict's voice sound weak in pleas for peace, shouted down by the clamor of those who wanted no peace in principle, unwilling as they were to forego prestige and power and possible victory. Even the new warfare which Pius XI, Benedict's successor, waged for the minds of men has become more dramatic than the ravages of World War I, and has, all through the pontificate of Pope Pius XII given public concern to men and nations. Benedict, in his day, had to carry his burden much in secret and mostly in silence.

We have lived so long when millions have sought out the Pope for a blessing or consulted a Pope for advice that it is hard to imagine days when neither was welcome. Now that John XXIII has, by his charm and simplicity, captured a new affection for the person of the Pope, Benedict XV may still suffer an unintelligent but intelligible oblivion. In his day the world was not yet ready for a pope to walk among his people.

Times have changed. The Keys of St. Peter can turn many locks long rusted in the struggle of the State for the souls and bodies of men. Pope John can freely turn these keys in the hearts of even little men. Pope Benedict was refused that chance because the hearts of the mighty were bolted against him. Now the mighty have crumbled, and the popes of today and tomorrow have the chance, denied to Benedict. Benedict will not refuse them the glory of success. He will be grateful if we will remember that, true to his office, he tried, in his day, even the impossible.

WILLIAM O. BRADY
✠ *Archbishop of St. Paul*

Contents

THE LIFE OF BENEDICT XV

CHAPTER I

Birth and Childhood

NEVER had the home of Dr. Alberto Bosso known such excitement. Had the whole city of Genoa suddenly descended on him, the doctor could not have been more flustered. It was bad enough that the wealthy Marchesa Giovanna Migliorati-Della Chiesa should be brought to labor prematurely and rushed with a full complement of relatives to his home for the birth of her sixth child. But the impossible Marchese Giuseppe Della Chiesa was the last straw.[1] The birth had been extremely long drawn out and the Marchese had charged up and down the stairs like a man expecting his first child rather than his sixth. His bald head and erect carriage made him look taller than his medium height. His heavy eyebrows, which gave a piercing quality to his deep-set dark eyes, his drooping mustache, and beard, kept the maids in Dr. Bosso's house in constant fright.[2]

When the baby was finally presented to his father by Dr. Bosso, a word of sympathy seemed in order. The infant was undersized and frail. Most alarming was a bluish pallor that overspread his body. The Marchese could not help comparing the puny child with himself and his rugged health. Nor did there seem to be anything in common between the baby and the Marchesa who was renowned for her beauty. After the initial shock he agreed that his son should be baptized immediately so that he would not die before he became a son of God.

The date was November 21, 1854, and the boy was christened Giacomo Giambattista Della Chiesa.

Of all the relatives crowded into the Bosso home that day, only his mother did not share the pessimistic outlook on Giacomo's future. The Marchesa had a great devotion to Our Lady of Loving Protection, her *Madonna della Guardia,* and she was positive that Giacomo would live, even though two of her earlier children had died of childhood diseases. As a matter of fact, she did not even have to await the verdict of history, for by the next day little Giacomo himself let everyone know that he had a firm hold on life. His

strength and general progress were so noticeable by then that his
relatives took him to church for the supplying of the ceremonies
of Baptism omitted in the emergency of the preceding day.

The pastor of the Church of *La Madonna delle Vigne* (Our Lady
of the Vineyards) oddly enough, in view of future events, was Father
Cardinali. His entry in the register of Baptisms is long and detailed.

> In the year of Our Lord, 1854, the twenty-second day of November,
> at 1:00 P.M., a newborn child was brought into the Church of Our
> Lady of the Vineyards in the City of Genoa. The child was born on
> the twenty-first day of November at 9:45 A.M., in the territorial
> boundaries of this parish. The parents are Marchese Giuseppe Antonio
> Della Chiesa, son of the deceased Giambattista Della Chiesa, residing
> in Genoa, and Marchesa Giovanna Migliorati, daughter of Giovanni
> Battista Migliorati. In virtue of a precautionary measure the child was
> baptized in the house of Doctor Alberto Bosso. The name Giacomo
> Giambattista Della Chiesa was imposed. The sponsors were the
> Marchese Giacomo Spinola and Marchesa Anna Centurione, née
> Migliorati, both residents of Genoa.[3]

In the course of time, mother and child returned home. Their
summer home was in Pegli, on the Italian Riviera, a suburb of
Genoa on the Ligurian coast. This the Della Chiesas seem to have
preferred to their residence in Genoa itself, and here they spent
most of their time. In the mid-nineteenth century the principal industry of Pegli was fishing. Its ravishing scenery had made it one
of the beauty spots of the Riviera. In 1854 the most important house
was that of the Della Chiesas. From the windows on the one side,
the inhabitants could look upon the blue Gulf of Genoa. On the
other side were the peacefully towering Italian mountains. As the
Marchesa stepped from her carriage, the roving eyes of her child
may have rested for a moment on an image of the Blessed Virgin
in a niche directly above the doorway. Below the niche was in-
scribed a line from the fourth-century poet Claudianus, which, literally translated, might mean "He has more life" or "Here one has
life more abundantly." This line referred originally to an old man
who, although he never departed from his villa near Verona, always
seemed in more excellent humor, in a more serene and calm state
of mind than any of his neighbors. For such a man life surely
had more to offer. A sixteenth-century forebear of the Della Chiesa
family, who had the humanistic bent so typical of that age, took
the words of Claudianus and gave them a Christian interpretation.

What he meant to convey was that in this house Mary, the mother of God, had the place of honor, and therefore its occupants under her protection have life more abundantly.[4]

Today a new façade has replaced the one which Giacomo first saw. A wide highway passing immediately in front of the house has necessitated an alteration at the entry. A smaller niche has been carved above the door, also occupied by a statue of Mary, and the same inscription has been recarved below it. In the spacious rotunda within the house, a heavy stone ledge with a remnant of the original inscription lies as if discarded near the grand staircase. The great size of the ledge gives an idea of the impressiveness of the old entry.[5]

According to the *Golden Book of the Patrician Families of Genoa* the Della Chiesa family did not come into prominence until the sixteenth century.[6] The name, however, may be much older. Some historians claim that Della Chiesa, meaning "of the Church," was a *cognomen* or *agnomen,* ceremonially conferred by the great Saint Ambrose of Milan. The Della Chiesas, a branch of the Della Torre family, are said to have gone to heroic extremes in combating Arianism, and Saint Ambrose, it is claimed, conferred the title, *Campio Ecclesiae,*[7] "Defender of the Church," upon a member of the Della Torre family because of his efforts in defeating that heresy.[8]

The *Golden Book* also carries the coat of arms, a simple, steepled church surmounted by a large eagle, which Benedict XV later had on his papal emblems. Three members of the Della Chiesa family in the sixteenth and seventeenth centuries were distinguished senators and self-sacrificing statesmen, and left their imprint on the history of Genoa.[9]

Giacomo's mother belonged to an old family of Neapolitan aristocracy, which also had rich ecclesiastical traditions. Pope Innocent VII (1404–1406), who represented the true line of succession during the Great Schism of the West, had been Cosimo di Migliorati.[10] Because of this background it is easy to visualize Giacomo growing up in a house full of paintings and trophies which kept before his eye the glorious past of his family.

Yet, amid all this color, the greatest fascination was exerted upon him by the pageantry and drama of the sacred liturgy. His grandmother, Ersilia Migliorati-Raggi, in kindly sympathy with this interest of her beloved grandson, presented him with a miniature altar fully equipped with crucifix, candles, and tiny missal stand.[11] Here

Giacomo "played priest" as Catholic boys have done for centuries and will probably continue to do to the end. Little Giacomo's play in imitation of priestly functions did not confine itself to the Mass. He also preached.*

Carlo Montalto, the gardener at Pegli, seems to have been a mine of information for Monsignor De Waal, who has preserved for posterity so much of the story of Giacomo's early life. Carlo related that little Giacomo used to appear in one of the windows and pretend that the railed balcony was a pulpit. There he would preach with great earnestness in that beautiful, unabashed naïveté of childhood.

Anyone familiar with large Italian churches will hardly be surprised at Giacomo's choice of a window balcony for a pulpit. The pulpit is usually a large, elevated, railed platform about a central pillar in the nave of the church. Very often the priest makes his sudden appearance in the pulpit from a staircase hidden behind, or sometimes even within the pillar. In a child's mind this would help to heighten the majesty of the situation. The listeners pick up reed chairs from various parts of the church and gather about the pillar in a semicircle. There they sit with chins tilted upward, watching the expressive gesticulation to which preachers of Latin blood are especially prone.

---

* Before an anecdote concerning his early ventures at evangelization is given in detail, a word should be said about the man who unearthed these stories of Giacomo's early life. The same incidents appear in all biographical essays on Benedict XV,[12] but no credit is given to the man who preserved them for posterity. This was Monsignor Anton De Waal, for fifty years one of Rome's best known archaeologists and historians. He was the rector of the German hospice, Campo Santo, adjoining the Basilica of Saint Peter. As an archaeologist, he had the happy faculty of immersing in his own boundless enthusiasm some archaeological fact which under the treatment of another scholar would have emerged as just another dry bone of history. To have had him as a guide through the catacombs is universally agreed to have been an unforgettable experience.[13] De Waal was seventy-eight years old when Giacomo Della Chiesa ascended the papal throne. With his usual boyish enthusiasm this old man set out for Genoa and Bologna for the purpose of instituting a relentless search for firsthand information on the new Pope.[14] He was a charming conversationalist, a gift that is reflected in the witty and chatty style of his writing. Like a good archaeologist, he left no stray sentence unprobed. His fatherly face and benign manner of speaking inspired confidence and loosened the most reticent tongues. Benedict XV was elected on September 3, 1914, and by December Monsignor De Waal had a sizable biography of the new Pope in print, 174 pages of large, closely packed pages with 18 interesting and well-arranged illustrations. Except for the calendar dates marking decisive turns in Della Chiesa's life which Monsignor De Waal gleaned from newspapers, he compiled all the rest from conversations which he had with anyone he could locate who happened to have known Benedict.

Little wonder that Giacomo caught the spark of these dramatic possibilities. Carlo, the gardener, said that little Giacomo preached excellently, although he admitted that not a word ever reached his ears!

It would seem that Giacomo's elementary education was imparted by a tutor or governess. In 1862, his father had him enrolled as a day student in the *Instituto Danovaro e Giusso*,[15] a school for boys, which already offered courses of study ordinarily reserved to institutions of higher learning. The school derives its name from two priests who had evolved a system of pedagogy of their own and who were its founders and first instructors. Pietro Ansaldo, a lawyer, who had been a classmate at the *Instituto,* wistfully summarized the impression which Giacomo made in those days: "He was an example of study, of order, of precision, of obedience toward his parents and superiors, of rigorous self-discipline, in fact so much so, that no one can ever remember having seen him take part excitedly in lengthy and boisterous recreation."[16] Other former schoolmates recalled his well-regulated life. During the course of some game, he would look at his watch, and if the moment had come predetermined in his own mental horarium, he would leave, even though this might be at a most absorbing moment in the contest. To his exasperated friends he would explain that he had to go home to prepare his assignments.[17] Sometimes he incurred the derision of his companions by stealing off to visit the Blessed Sacrament, where he would remain before the tabernacle in absolute solitude.[18] He was fond of long walks and would often choose as his destination one of the two popular shrines in Genoa: that of the *Madonna della Acqua Santa* or that of the *Madonna della Guardia.*[19]

When at home, Giacomo's happiest hours were spent in reading the Italian classics. Here without knowing it he began to develop the distinguished style in his mother tongue which made his writings and discourses such a pleasure to his readers and hearers. Concerning his fondness for reading, an anecdote is related, which testifies to the invariability of a mother's reaction to a boy's apparent indolence when he is really making excellent though remote preparation for his life's work. One day as he was stretched out on a couch, his chin supported by his fists, eyes glued to a book, the Marchesa half seriously, half humorously surprised him by snatching the book away and substituting a rake, telling him to work in the garden. Like all mothers anxious about their children's health she probably bombarded him with a barrage of examples of other boys whose complexions were so much better and whose physique was so much more robust because they spent more time in the fresh air. This fact coupled with the weedy garden and the general neglect apparent in their property made for her an inescapable argument against Giacomo's staying inside to read. Glancing ruefully backward at his book, he began with his scarcely perceptible limp his descent to the garden.

There he found that his mother was right. Things were in a state of neglect. He found a palm tree which had grown up of its own accord, unnoticed on a patch of grass where it did not belong. He limped back to a garden house where he found a pot. He dug it out carefully and planted the little tree in the pot. Later he transplanted it to a vacant spot where it grew and flourished. In succeeding years when he would come home for his vacation, after meeting the members of the family, he would pay a visit to his tree.*

A crayon picture in an oval frame gives us Giacomo's appearance when he was twelve years old.[21] His arms are folded, a starched white cuff protrudes from one black coat sleeve. He is in the position of an attorney addressing a witness or the jury. The meditative expression on his face is accentuated by the slight deformity of his raised eyebrow. He wears an immaculate white collar and neatly done tie. The boy is by no means homely. In fact, there is something very winning in his appearance. He looks like a boy mentally far ahead of his years with whom older people like to converse on their own level.

Giacomo's childhood must not be thought of as unhappy. He appears to have had a more mature sense of values than most boys of his age. His beloved sister, Julia, sums up his childhood in these words: "In that sweet period of the first stage of his life he was vivacious and animated, loved by his playmates, almost festive in his attire, and never disheveled."[22]

---

* The gardener, Carlo, told Monsignor De Waal that he used to be much amused when he would secretly watch Giacomo take hold of a branch and hold it affectionately like a man shaking hands with a bosom friend whom he had not seen for a long time.[20]

CHAPTER II

Candidate for a Doctorate in Three Faculties

ONE day Giacomo met Carlo, the gardener, who saw at once that his young friend had been weeping. It did not take long for the truth to come out. Giacomo had informed his father that he intended to study for the priesthood. His father's sole comment was: "I intend that you will become a lawyer!"[1] The statement seems to have been made in such a way that any discussion or argument was out of the question. Giuseppe Della Chiesa belonged to the old-school aristocracy whose careers as well as marriages were arranged by the father.

However, when the father saw the grief and prolonged mental depression which he had caused Giacomo and Julia, the boy's sister and favorite confidante, he called his son and made a second terse announcement: "You will go to our Royal University and study law. If, after you have received your degree, you should still cling to your idea of becoming a priest, neither I nor anyone else will impede the execution of your desire."[2] These words were spoken as unhesitatingly and authoritatively as if they were a set formula pronounced by a robed judge.

When Giacomo finished his courses at the *Instituto Danovaro e Giusso,* his father made arrangements for him to study philosophy at the diocesan seminary, but simply as a lay day student. The seminarians were garbed in cassock and Roman collar, while Giacomo came in the fashionable clothes of a lay aristocrat. It may seem contradictory that the elder Della Chiesa should have taken so firm a stand against his son's studying for the priesthood, and yet have chosen for him the curriculum of a seminarian. Actually, however, there was in the decision a keen sense of discernment. Giuseppe Della Chiesa wanted for his son none of the antireligious, secular spirit that had seized Italy. He realized that scholastic philosophy imparted a rigid mental discipline which would fortify Giacomo against the poisonous and shoddy thinking of his age.

Upon the completion of his philosophy course Giacomo entered

9

the University of Genoa School of Law. To his acute analytical mind, the study of law was quite congenial. He enjoyed especially the history of law and noted with pride the great influence which Christianity had exercised upon the ancient Romans. Out of his course he obtained an integrated knowledge of the ecclesiastical and secular arms of the law.

In harmony with the politics of the time, and to insure themselves a permanent place in the Utopia of unified Italy, Genoa professors habitually spiced their lectures with barbed references to the papacy.[3] A secret political society, the Carbonari (charcoal burners), had incited Victor Emmanuel to overt persecution of the Church. In 1848, a slogan was formulated which limited the role of the pope to "praying and blessing." In 1850, the privileges of the clergy were suppressed, and, in 1855, all monasteries and convents not actually engaged in teaching or hospital work were confiscated by the State. The lawyer Pietro Ansaldo, Giacomo's classmate and intimate friend, stated later that Giacomo once made this dramatic statement in a recitation: "Human governments will fall; the Church will stand because she is immortal."[4] His professors were impressed by this student who was not afraid to expound his religious convictions.

Giacomo put himself under the spiritual direction of a relative on his mother's side, Giacomo Raggi, a Capuchin priest.[5] This erudite son of St. Francis suggested to his young charge a specialized work of the apostolate. He reminded Giacomo that most of his instructors were devotees of the "Enlightenment" which divinized the power of human reason. Since these philosophers did not believe in supernatural revelation, the Church's claims had to be pressed by arguments restricted to the field of reason. The science which governs this kind of defense of Catholicism is apologetics, and this science the Capuchin suggested that Giacomo study privately so that he might meet the members of the intelligentsia on their own level. The young student followed his mentor's suggestions and began to build up a private library of specialized works on apologetics.

The Catholic students who practiced their faith had organized a group known as The Society for the Promotion of Catholic Interests, of which Giacomo was elected secretary. Never an extrovert, he preferred the order and detail which he could fashion in the privacy of his study and upon which the success of any organization ultimately depends. In the years that he was secretary of the society, he made such an impression on university life that students in other institutions of learning began to adopt his program. It was the seed from which sprang the Federation of Catholic Students in Italian Universities, an organization which performed a service comparable to that of our Newman Clubs at secular universities.

The records of his brilliant scholastic accomplishments are still to be seen in the files of the University of Genoa. On August 5, 1875 — when he was not quite 21 years of age — he received the degree of Doctor of Laws.[6] The title of his doctoral dissertation was: *The Interpretation of Laws*. According to his father's stipulation, Giacomo would be permitted to study for the priesthood only after he had completed his legal studies with distinction. The condition had been fulfilled, but he did not immediately remind his father of the agreement. First he went on a pilgrimage to the shrine of the *Madonna della Guardia*. Thereafter, with some trepidation, he decided to approach his father.[7]

Before doing so, Giacomo discussed the problem of his vocation with his mother, who in turn tried to dispose her less pliable husband for the request.[8] It was not that he was anticlerical, but as a member of the nobility he regarded his status in its etymological sense; a nobleman should always be capable of being "known" and held in honor. At this juncture of Italian history, the priest's garb was scorned, and a nobleman wearing it could not depend on his nobility to lend him honor. No matter how poor and self-sacrificing he might be, a priest, according to the revolutionaries, was part of a conspiracy to keep the Italian people impoverished and enslaved.

When the meeting between father and son finally materialized, Giuseppe did his best to depict the beauties of being a successful lawyer and the concomitant honorable status in society. When he saw that this had no effect, the undaunted parent suggested Giacomo find a position in the juridical department of the Church. For Giacomo, however, the call to the priesthood was a call to work as a simple shepherd of souls. Throughout his life, he was to repeat again and again that the *cura animarum*, that cherished old expression which is translated so poorly by "care of souls" rather than "love of souls," was all he desired. But Giuseppe decided that his ambitions for his son could be accomplished better in Rome, and rather than irritate his father more, Giacomo agreed to attend a Roman seminary.

The Marquis Della Chiesa now turned to the archbishop of Genoa for help in executing his plans. Archbishop Charvaz assured him that he would select the place of residence and the school most advantageous to a young aristocrat aspiring to the priesthood.

The Marchesa and Julia supervised the preparation of his wardrobe, which would have to undergo some radical changes. Gone forever were the fashionable coats and cravats so artfully chosen by his sister, Julia. For the next four years his garb would be the special cassock of the seminary he was to attend, long black stockings, and knickers worn under the soutane. For formal occasions he would also wear the long pleated panel of cloth, the *ferriaiola*, which would hang down his back; otherwise the ankle-length coat known as the *grecca* would be worn over his cassock. With the loving industry of their own hands these two women sewed what they could. Many a stitch was seen through tear-blurred eyes when they visualized the long winter evenings to be spent without Giacomo. He himself, though he was now a Doctor of Jurisprudence, did not make his farewells without tears.[9]

The seminary to which Giacomo was sent by his bishop was the *Capranica*. Here a limited number of select students, from various countries, prepare themselves for the priesthood. This institution which is named after its founders, Cardinals Dominic and Angelus Capranica, two brothers who died in 1458 and 1478 respectively, was the first strictly diocesan seminary in Rome. In time, however, it became a "house of studies" — that is, a residence hall where the students had room and board, common chapel services, spiritual conferences, facilities for private study, and only such courses as homiletics, or some branch of study specifically aimed at the area of the student's future work.

For philosophy, theology, history, Sacred Scripture, and canon law, the student attended the *Gregoriana*, a Jesuit university. Here Giacomo was privileged to have as his teacher Father John Franzelin, who was to win renown by his outstanding work as the official theologian of the Vatican Council in 1870. Professor Camillo Mazella, and the famous moralist, Antonio Ballerini, were also among his teachers. Another theologian of repute was Prospero Caterini, S.J., who was wont to remark to the other fathers how impressed he was by a serious little student who always chose a front seat and with unobtrusive attention recorded the lectures in his notebook.[10] This student was Giacomo Della Chiesa. The reference to Giacomo's having chosen a front seat is interesting. It seems to indicate that the defect in hearing, which was noticeable in the days of his pontificate, went back to this very early date.[11]

One of the greatest thrills which Rome had to offer in those days was the opportunity of seeing Pope Pius IX, *il bello Papa* ("the beautiful Pope")[12] as the Italians called him affectionately. The Holy Father, himself an alumnus of the *Capranica,* enjoyed his annual visit with the students and personnel of that seminary. As each seminarian was presented to him, Pius IX, with his ready wit, was accustomed to exchange pleasantries with them.

Apparently no letter is extant in which Giacomo wrote his impressions of *Pio Nono.* There is in existence, however, a letter written by a student born in the same year as Giacomo, who had his first audience in the same year as Giacomo, and who would later become his intimate friend when Giacomo would be Pope Benedict XV. This was Ludwig Pastor, who was to become famous as the historian of the papacy. After having seen Pope Pius IX, Pastor rushed back to his chambers and wrote:

Dear Mother,
   I have just come from an audience with the Holy Father. Today I have had the most beautiful day since my first Holy Communion. Indescribable was my joy as the eighty-four-year-old Martyr-Pope appeared. . . .
   The benign appearance of the Pope, his sweet, soft eyes, will, as far as I am concerned, be unforgettable. His mien is serious, the strength of his voice incredible. No man will ever make such an impression on me as this old man adorned with the triple crown of priesthood, age, and holiness.[13]

Since the two men were so much alike in interests and temperament, it may well be that their impressions of Pius IX were very much the same.

On February 8, 1878, Cardinal Pecci, Camerlengo of the Holy Roman Church, announced, "The Pope is truly dead!" *Pio Nono* died at the age of eighty-six, after a reign of thirty-two years, the longest pontificate in history outside that of Saint Peter. Giacomo, with other students from the *Capranica,* knelt before the heavy grille of the Blessed Sacrament Chapel in Saint Peter's as a guard of honor before the remains of their distinguished alumnus.[14] With what consternation Giacomo must have received the news that, during the funeral procession to San Lorenzo, the hearse was stormed by an angry mob and the revered remains almost thrown into the Tiber.

Pius IX had so lengthy a pontificate that it was difficult to imagine the administration of the Church without him. During the conclave, the seminarians at the *Capranica* made a project of enacting a simulated conclave of their own. They studied its ceremonial and dramatized every detail. The "cardinals" were the students in their last year, among whom was Della Chiesa. Giacomo, however, was not elected in this make-believe conclave.[15]

In his last two years at the *Capranica*, Giacomo gave catechetical instructions twice a week in the Church of *Santa Maria in Aquiro*.[16] This was not an easy task in a day when no parochial schools were allowed and when religious instruction was banned in the State schools. The parents who had grown up in those days of anticlericalism were so ill-instructed that the catechist found little or no background of religious knowledge in his charges. For Giacomo, however, catechetical instruction was a labor of love. Thirty years later he was to stress the need of sound catechetical instruction as a prerequisite for effective preaching.[17]

On December 21, 1878, Raffaele Monaco-LaValetta, Cardinal Vicar of Rome, ordained Giacomo Della Chiesa to the holy priesthood in the venerable Lateran Basilica.[18] The following day he was to say his first Mass on the tomb of Saint Peter — the dream of every priest who loves the Church and its apostolic age. For this privilege there are so many applicants that a reservation must be made weeks in advance. The priest who asks for an appointment is shown a register which has a blank for every half hour at which Mass can be celebrated. He then writes his name in the blank which best suits his convenience provided it has not already been chosen by a previous applicant. Giacomo also went to the sacristan of Saint Peter's Basilica several days before his first Mass and made all the necessary arrangements. He was assured that the day and the hour would be kept open.

On the morning of his first Mass Giacomo happily ushered his family, relatives, and friends to the prie-dieus in the small subterranean chapel of Saint Peter and retired to the sacristy, only to find another priest already there fully vested. Naturally, his disappointment was great, and it is quite possible that his volatile temper flared up. In the absence of the regular sacristan who had made the initial arrangements with Giacomo, a substitute had made a rash commitment to a visiting priest for the half hour promised to Father Della Chiesa. The official in charge made a concession. Instead of making Father Della Chiesa wait until the last applicant had celebrated Mass that day, he allowed him to use the altar in the apse of the Basilica, just below the bronze chair supported by four doctors of the Church in their swirling, storm-blown raiment, known as the "Glory of Bernini."*

In a letter to a friend, Father Della Chiesa mentions an interesting detail about this Mass. He writes: "Our Joseph Migone received Holy Communion at my first Mass and he served my second Mass."[20] Joseph Migone's name will appear repeatedly in these pages. Giacomo had had three close friends at the University of Genoa, among whom was a Joseph Migone. Giacomo, however, was the only one of the four to study for the priesthood. It seems that Joseph Migone came to Rome some time after Giacomo had taken up his residence there, and he was delighted that the vocation to the priesthood, which his friend had been considering, had finally been realized. But not long after, Giacomo wrote to Ansaldo of his disappointment that he himself was the only one of these four close friends to be called to the priesthood. Giacomo's hopes were realized in Joseph Migone's son, born one year after Giacomo's ordination. Giacomo was to use his influence to favor his friend's son. As a very young priest, Father Migone was made rector of the Genoese church in Rome. When Giacomo became archbishop of Bologna, he took Joseph Migone with him as his secretary. He brought him with him to the conclave and made him his secret chamberlain when he was elected pope. Giacomo always kept a loving eye on the boy because he was the son of his close friend. This would account for the fact that even as supreme pontiff, Benedict in his lighter moods would call Migone, *Bambino*.[21]

After ordination, Father Della Chiesa remained at the *Capranica* in order to write his dissertation for the doctorate in sacred theology. This degree he received *summa cum laude* on July 13, 1879.[22]

* The holy card which Father Della Chiesa distributed as a souvenir of his ordination deserves mention. The picture has the Infant Jesus enthroned on the thorn-entwined stem of the Cross. The left hand of the divine Child holds a chalice surmounted by a radiant Sacred Host. One of the rays illuminates the Basilica of Saint Peter; further beams bathe in light the other famous churches of the world. Giacomo himself is said to have composed the prayer on the reverse side in honor of Saint Peter, Prince of the Apostles. It closes with these words: "Give me strength ever to exalt your holy and indestructible rights, and allow me ever to repel any malicious assaults of the enemies of the papacy."[19]

Since Giacomo had had formal training in civil law at the University of Genoa, his advisers at the *Gregoriana* urged him to obtain a doctorate in canon law also. Although Canon Vinciguerra, rector of the *Capranica*, was sincerely attached to Father Della Chiesa and praised him publicly, he deemed it more advantageous for him to live at the Academy of Noble Ecclesiastics. There he would have the companionship of priests training for, or engaged in, the administrative work of the Vatican. The Canon, therefore, arranged with Monsignor Placido Schiaffino, Rector of the Academy of Noble Ecclesiastics, for Father Della Chiesa to reside in the Academy.

This highly specialized school was founded by Sebastiano Valfre, "The Apostle of Turin," in 1698, in order to give priests from noble families an opportunity to pursue graduate studies in certain phases of ecclesiastical learning. Later it was converted into a school training priests for service in the diplomatic corps of the Church. Pius VI had placed it under the immediate supervision of the Holy See. Such great figures as Consalvi, Pacca, Leo XIII, Rampolla, Merry del Val, and Pius XII are among its alumni.

In 1880, Father Della Chiesa received his doctorate in canon law, the third in his series of academic distinctions. He was now the Reverend Giacomo Della Chiesa, LL.D., S.T.D., J.C.D. The new pope, Leo XIII demanded that every Thursday one student in residence at the Academy deliver an address on some point of law or aspect of papal diplomacy. At the conclusion of the address, questions from the floor were invited. Very often objections were leveled at the student, and he had to prove his ability to think on his feet, and like a true diplomat to reply to his objectors suavely and logically but without any display of petulance or rancor. As the number of students was about twenty, Della Chiesa's turn came frequently enough. The Pontiff requested that the cardinal protector or some distinguished prelate designated by him be present at this weekly seminar.[23] Among those sent to represent the Pope was the distinguished Monsignor Mariano Rampolla del Tindaro. His sharp eye and keen mind followed Giacomo. Henceforth Rampolla del Tindaro was to be the guiding star in Giacomo Della Chiesa's life.

Giacomo's early devotion to literature, which we have noted, left him with an appreciation of the beauties of language. His elegance of speech and facility of pen were noted and admired in these seminars. Without further preparation he was chosen to occupy the chair of Diplomatic Style at the Academy.[24]

CHAPTER III

In the Service of the Holy See

GIUSEPPE DELLA CHIESA's ambitions for his son — that he should be in the direct service of the Holy See — were soon realized. With Monsignor Rampolla, one of the most remarkable figures in the modern history of the Church, Giacomo's life and personality were destined to merge.

The story of the association of the two goes back to the year 1877 when Giacomo was still a seminarian.[1] The *Capranica* celebrated alumni day with a *pranzo*, that is, a sumptuous banquet. Among the guests was a distinguished alumnus whose stature, large and boldly sculptured face, leonine head of hair, and piercing look combined to inspire awe. Like Michelangelo, he had what the Italians call *terribilità,* a psychological trait which inspires a spontaneous awe. The German newspapers were wont to refer to him as *der scharfblickende Prälat,* the prelate with the piercing look.[2] This was Mariano Rampolla del Tindaro, whom Pius IX had just recalled from Nuncio Simeoni's office in Madrid. On the day of the festivity at the *Capranica* he was asked to recount some of his experiences in Spain, which the Italian of that era regarded as an exotic land of Moorish mystery. The sharp eyes of the Monsignor noticed a delicate-looking student in a position of almost ecstatic immobility. This attentive listener, he learned, was from the noble family of Della Chiesa in Genoa. This banquet with the accident of Giacomo's attracting the notice of the great Rampolla was one of the most significant occurrences in young Della Chiesa's life.

Mariano Rampolla del Tindaro was born of a wealthy and noble family on August 17, 1843, at Polizzi in Sicily. In 1856, he entered the Vatican Seminary, and, in 1861, he transferred to the *Capranica.* Five years later, after ordination, he entered the Academy of Noble Ecclesiastics. In 1875, Pius IX made him a Canon of Saint Peter's, but within a few months sent him to the nunciature at Madrid. Two years later he was recalled by Pius IX to become secretary of the Propaganda for Oriental Affairs. It was at this juncture in Rampolla's life that Giacomo Della Chiesa saw him for the first time.

17

From time to time, Monsignor Schiaffino, rector of the Academy of Noble Ecclesiastics, discussed with Monsignor Rampolla the merits of Doctor Della Chiesa. In 1882, Rampolla obtained for the young priest the position of *apprendista* in the Congregation of Extraordinary Affairs, of which he himself was now secretary. The position of *apprendista* carries much the same meaning as its English cognate, "apprentice." On December 8 of that same year, Mariano Rampolla was consecrated titular archbishop and was given the coveted appointment of nuncio to Spain. In private audience Leo XIII gave him the privilege of choosing anyone he wished as his secretary, promising to ratify the choice by an official appointment. Without any hesitation the Archbishop asked for Giacomo Della Chiesa. To give the young secretary prestige in Spain, the Pope created him a papal chamberlain with the title of "Very Reverend Monsignor."

Monsignor Della Chiesa did not embark for the Iberian Peninsula unprepared. He hastily acquired the rudiments of the Spanish language and strove to acquaint himself with Spain's history and topography. His interest in mysticism, already noted in his university days at Genoa, made him curious as to why Spain brought forth such prayerful souls as Teresa of Avila, John of the Cross, and Ignatius of Loyola, all of whom established remarkable intensity of union with God. In his study of theology he had learned to admire the subtlety of the Spaniards, Suarez, Molina, Vasquez! Ever interested in law, he wanted to see the sites of Isabella's circuit courts where at times questionable and peremptory justice was said to have been meted out, and where that stumbling block to prospective converts to the Catholic Faith, the Spanish Inquisition, had come into being. Lover of literature that he was, he wanted to see the land that had inspired Lope de Vega, Cervantes, and Calderon. He remembered Horace's observation concerning the intellectual superiority of the ancient Spaniard — *"Me peritus discet Hiber,"*[3] "The learned Spaniard will instruct me." As a keen student of antiquities, he hoped to have ample opportunity to see a multicolored mosaic of ancient lore preserved in the inhabitants of Spain now amalgamated into one people.[4]

On February 2, 1883, Archbishop Rampolla and Monsignor Della Chiesa presented their credentials to Alfonso XII at the Court of Madrid. As private secretary to the Nuncio, the Monsignor soon attracted attention because of his wide education and culture, his consummate tact, his cool and unerring judgment.[5] He was not long in Spain when he asked the pastor of the Church of San Pedro in Madrid to appoint him to a regular confessional. Certainly no task of the priest is so physically and nervously fatiguing as the work of the confessional. Yet Monsignor Della Chiesa, whose work in the nunciature would have excused him from pastoral duties, asked for the canonical faculties for hearing confessions so that he might not lose contact with his first priestly love, the *cura animarum*.[6] Soon he also mounted the pulpit and preached in Spanish — a tribute, certainly, to his ability as a linguist. Such an avocation did the Spanish language become for him that until his death he wrote notes and private memoranda in Spanish.[7]

Because he always gave two copper coins to everyone who asked, at least until his purse was empty, the beggars of Madrid gave him the nickname *el cura de las dos pesetas*, "the priest of the two coins."[8]

In Spain, the prestige of the Church grew tremendously during Rampolla's tenure. Credit for this fact is due, at least in part, to Monsignor Della Chiesa, who saved the hotheaded Nuncio from many an undiplomatic outburst of rage, and from more than one precipitate decision.[9] Giacomo himself lived by the watchword, *Suaviter in modo sed fortiter in re*, "Suavely in manner but bravely in action."

In the winter of 1884 a great earthquake left shambles and devastation throughout the provinces of Malaga, Granada, and Andalusia. Almost immediately after the calamity, Archbishop Rampolla and his faithful secretary were on the scene directing rescue operations. The international ambulance service of the Red Cross was well organized in Geneva and in Paris, but time was needed to bring personnel and equipment into Spain. Meanwhile, the inhabitants, stunned by the disaster, gladly followed the direction of the Holy Father's representatives in their country.

In 1885, an attack of cholera ravaged the provinces of Spain with ghastly fury. The moans and misery of disease filled the cities and the stench of unburied dead lay heavy on the air. It was as if the livid rider on the pale horse of Saint John's *Apocalypse* had come at last. During this period of calamity the Archbishop and his secretary observed long, grueling hours in the nunciature, allocating the relief fund of 40,000 lire from the personal resources of Leo XIII and an additional 25,000 lire collected from the members of the College of Cardinals. After office hours, Nuncio and secretary with aprons of the male nurse over their cassocks could be seen in the wretched hovels of the poor or in the overcrowded hospitals, feeding the hungry and giving drink to the thirsty. Concerning this work, a contemporary wrote:

> His Excellency, Nuncio Rampolla, with his trusted secretary, Monsignor Giacomo Della Chiesa, hurried to the hospitals, to the infirmaries, and there took care of the most loathsome patients. With their own hands they freshened the soggy mattresses, they cleaned the beds so disgustingly soiled, they served food and administered medicines. They were heroically solicitous that nothing should be wanting to the stricken.[10]

Yet from Giacomo himself there is no mention of heroism, no complaint concerning his arduous labors. From this period only one letter is extant, written to Ansaldo, his boyhood friend in Genoa:

> I am enjoying good health in spite of the pestilential crisis which has traversed Spain. For about a week the number of the stricken has tripled itself, and the number may even increase because we are having weather conditions favorable to the multiplication of the microbes. At one time we believed an immunizing medicine had been found; however, it was soon perceived that its inventor merely caused the ranks of the charlatans to grow.[11]

To illustrate the impression made by Monsignor Della Chiesa on the Spanish people, a native writer of that period, Pedro Louis, recounted that on one occasion his father was standing on a balcony conversing with a bishop when the small figure of the limping Monsignor Della Chiesa chanced to cross the square below. Looking down, the bishop said, "In that priest the prudence of a diplomat stands in absolute harmony with Christian simplicity."[12] This is perhaps the best brief appraisal of Della Chiesa's character ever made.

March 14, 1887, brought to a close the interesting life at Madrid. Leo XIII recalled his Nuncio to name him Secretary of State and to invest him with the scarlet robes of a cardinal. As might be expected, the new Secretary of State petitioned the Holy Father to recall Monsignor Della Chiesa also.

Upon his return to Rome, the Monsignor took up temporary residence at the Academy of Noble Ecclesiastics. Since he was told that he would not receive an appointment immediately, he decided to take a vacation. He visited his family at Genoa, stopped awhile at Loreto and then at Bologna where he was invited to celebrate Mass at the high altar, never dreaming that twenty years later he would be installed archbishop of that see at that very altar.[13]

After this holiday, he was appointed *minutante* in the secretariat of state. A *minutante* must read all reports on a given question, summarize them, and integrate them into one trenchant *precis*. The cardinal secretary of state is like a field marshal who receives from his subordinates maps and reports shorn of all superfluous verbiage. To him, of course, goes the credit for his diplomatic victories, but much of the work is done by the *minutante*.*

From 1887 until 1901 Della Chiesa lived in obscurity. His name appeared in no newspapers; his superiors, Leo XIII and Rampolla, were not men who showered praise on subordinates. It is said that, in this period his mother tried to hasten the progress of her son's career — an attempt that is not entirely without precedent, even in the pages of Holy Writ.[14] The story is that at a State reception, Giacomo proudly presented his mother to the great Rampolla. While her son's attention was momentarily diverted by the greeting of an old friend, the Marchesa, to Giacomo's horror, as he returned to rejoin the group, was telling Rampolla that in her opinion her son's talents were not being sufficiently recognized. The lion's head turned, the eyes blazed and looked beyond time and space, the stentorian voice said without annoyance, though with great precision, "Madame, your son will take only a few steps, but they will be gigantic ones."[15]

The friendship between mother and son was very close. Evidently Giuseppe Della Chiesa, Giacomo's father, had never given his son much companionship. The strictness with which he governed his household, although coming undoubtedly from the best of intentions, seems to have left Giacomo psychologically inhibited. Very likely the motto "Children should be seen and not heard" had been the rule. As a result, among his equals or superiors Giacomo was always shy, silent, and subdued. His father died on May 25, 1892, while Giacomo was still *minutante* at Rome. No details of his death are recorded. A letter written to the bishop of Piacenza contains this personal paragraph.

---

* The late Pope Pius XII, still gloriously reigning when these pages were written, was a *minutante*, and to the end reflected this training in his amazing ability to comprehend a situation almost instantly.

I am grateful to your Excellency for the part it pleased you to take in my domestic misfortune, above all I thank you for the prayers and the Mass offered for my deceased father. Of course, he was sick for a long time, and his demise did not come unexpected, yet the departure has not been less cruel. I hope the good Lord will have counted as his purgatory the many sufferings endured by my poor father. Nonetheless, I beg that you will choose to keep him present in your prayers. In this sorrowful circumstance, I am by no means only a little comforted by Your Excellency.[16]

In these lines, at least, there is no hint of any close friendship or intimacy.

Della Chiesa had rented an apartment in *Palazzo Brazza* not far from the Academy of Noble Ecclesiastics and across the street from the Church of San Eustachio. He invited his widowed mother to live with him. These were pleasant days for Giacomo. Men like him, who labored in the Curia, led colorless and lonely lives, but now he had his own household and he could approximate a happy family life. His sister Julia stayed with them from time to time. Francis MacNutt, the renowned American convert to Catholicism and chamberlain on active duty at the Vatican, left us a fleeting impression of this loving household:

My relations with him were unbrokenly good. His mother, a charming, dignified old lady, Marchesa della Chiesa, had, during my student days, an apartment near the Piazza in Aquiro, where I was invited, and met his sister. To be thus received in the family circle of that particular class of Italians, people of good ancestry and title, but not of the fashionable world, signified more than some of my readers may realize.[17]

Every day, promptly at the stroke of 6 a.m., Giacomo appeared in a choir stall in the sanctuary of the Church of San Eustachio. Someone relates how, as a boy coming to serve Mass, he would find the little priest at his place every morning. At a distance he could see the glow of only one little lamp, under which Monsignor Della Chiesa was peering at his meditation book.[18] At 6:30 he said Mass with dignity and great devotion. After Mass, having completed his thanksgiving, he would step into the confessional. People from various parts of Rome wishing to live a spiritual life under close supervision, approached him for direction. Then he would hurry to the *Palazzo Brazza* to have breakfast with his mother. At nine o'clock he was at his desk in the Vatican.

some bit of news to the press, someone was almost sure to rema
"Before we go ahead with this, we had better see what *il piccolo*
thinks about it."[22] He does not seem to have been ignorant of
label given him. Once, as Pope, he was recounting an incident ab
a certain well-meaning group whose members had blundered int
very delicate situation. Over his otherwise so fastidious lips
following remark slipped out: "They would have been in a fi
mess, if *il piccoletto* hadn't stepped in and pulled them out."[23]

On April 15, 1901, Leo XIII elevated Giacomo to the rank
domestic prelate with the title "Right Reverend Monsignor," and
acceding to Cardinal Rampolla's request appointed him *sostituto,*
i.e., undersecretary of state.

The new appointment brought a change to Della Chiesa's domestic
arrangements, since his new duties required him to live at the Vatican. His mother, however, continued to live in *Palazzo Brazza,*
where he visited her several times a week and always on Sundays.
He wanted her to be happy and when he came for Mass at San
Eustachio, his first greeting was to his Lord and Master, the second
to his mother. When he was due at some ecclesiastical function
before her rising time, he would send up a half sheet of paper on
which he would have scribbled, *"Buon giorno, Mamma!"* or a little
family joke written in French or something humorous in the Genoese dialect, such as, "To my waking little Marchesa!" If he received a souvenir booklet, an artistic place card, an extraordinary
post card or holy picture, he would bring it to his mother on his
next visit.[24]

The attention which Giacomo tendered his mother may seem at
first sight to savor of pure sentimentality. In the light of his
whole life, however, one may see it as the result of the supernatural
gift of understanding for the exercise of which he was known both
as ecclesiastic and as pope. He could see how much his mother was
aging and how pathetically her interests were retreating into the
past, fixed on the insignificant things of bygone days. Her mind
went back to a period in her life when, as a young mother, she had
enjoyed daily the refreshing simplicity of her growing children. Her
delight in his little tokens of affection pleased him and he was happy
to have been able to afford her this temporary illusion that the
hands of time had been turned back.

Upon those who met him casually, and who knew nothing of the
rich life of the spirit which he was leading under an unimposing

Outside the time spent in the office, Della Chiesa engaged i
voluntarily assumed pastoral duties. If one of his penitents becam
ill and would leave word at San Eustachio, the little Monsigno
would call upon the sick person as soon as possible. He enjoyec
preaching the word of God and volunteered to take his turn foi
sermons in San Eustachio.*

Giacomo belonged to the Archconfraternity of San Rocco, and
at their public functions wore the members' rough garb known as
"the sack." He was an officer in the Priests' League for Nocturnal
Adoration, and took his turn at the appointed church, without ever
allowing his night of vigil to interfere with his scrupulous punctuality at the office in the Vatican.[19] As a Tertiary of Saint Francis, he
made a monthly day of recollection at the Church of San Nicola in
Tolentino. He enjoyed preaching retreats and days of recollection
to nuns. At two convents, Giacomo gave weekly conferences of a
spiritual-archaeological nature on the vigorous Christianity of apostolic times.[20] He was also president of the Society of Saint Jerome,
which had for its purpose to spread a love of Sacred Scripture. The
society placed a copy of the New Testament into any home which
would welcome it. Monsignor Della Chiesa loved to accompany a
priest on a sick call, or to carry the white *ombrellino*, a sort of
miniature canopy, behind one who was bearing Holy Viaticum to
a dying person.

That Pope Leo knew of these hidden pastoral functions can be
gleaned from his words when he sent Monsignor Della Chiesa on
the first of his two secret missions to Vienna. "I am really sorry,"
said the Pope with his customary enigmatic smile, "that this new
task will take you away from your pastoral functions to which you
seem to have dedicated yourself with so much love."[21]

Although Monsignor Della Chiesa worked unostentatiously and
apparently made no great impression, he was highly respected for
his diplomatic instinct. In clerical life nicknames from college and
high school days often endure. Behind his back Monsignor Della
Chiesa was still frequently referred to as *il piccoletto* — roughly,
"the little fellow." When questions would come up among prelates
or diplomats as to whether some matter should be mentioned to the
Pope or his secretary of state, or whether it was politic to release

* After his death the parishioners donated a beautiful pulpit with panels of multicolored marble which bears an inscription testifying to his zeal as a preacher:

"Lest it be forgotten that on this spot Benedict XV, Supreme Pontiff, exercised
his priestly functions for a long time, this pulpit was erected in 1937."

some bit of news to the press, someone was almost sure to remark: "Before we go ahead with this, we had better see what *il piccoletto* thinks about it."[22] He does not seem to have been ignorant of the label given him. Once, as Pope, he was recounting an incident about a certain well-meaning group whose members had blundered into a very delicate situation. Over his otherwise so fastidious lips the following remark slipped out: "They would have been in a fine mess, if *il piccoletto* hadn't stepped in and pulled them out."[23]

On April 15, 1901, Leo XIII elevated Giacomo to the rank of domestic prelate with the title "Right Reverend Monsignor," and acceding to Cardinal Rampolla's request appointed him *sostituto,* i.e., undersecretary of state.

The new appointment brought a change to Della Chiesa's domestic arrangements, since his new duties required him to live at the Vatican. His mother, however, continued to live in *Palazzo Brazza,* where he visited her several times a week and always on Sundays. He wanted her to be happy and when he came for Mass at San Eustachio, his first greeting was to his Lord and Master, the second to his mother. When he was due at some ecclesiastical function before her rising time, he would send up a half sheet of paper on which he would have scribbled, *"Buon giorno, Mamma!"* or a little family joke written in French or something humorous in the Genoese dialect, such as, "To my waking little Marchesa!" If he received a souvenir booklet, an artistic place card, an extraordinary post card or holy picture, he would bring it to his mother on his next visit.[24]

The attention which Giacomo tendered his mother may seem at first sight to savor of pure sentimentality. In the light of his whole life, however, one may see it as the result of the supernatural gift of understanding for the exercise of which he was known both as ecclesiastic and as pope. He could see how much his mother was aging and how pathetically her interests were retreating into the past, fixed on the insignificant things of bygone days. Her mind went back to a period in her life when, as a young mother, she had enjoyed daily the refreshing simplicity of her growing children. Her delight in his little tokens of affection pleased him and he was happy to have been able to afford her this temporary illusion that the hands of time had been turned back.

Upon those who met him casually, and who knew nothing of the rich life of the spirit which he was leading under an unimposing

Outside the time spent in the office, Della Chiesa engaged in voluntarily assumed pastoral duties. If one of his penitents became ill and would leave word at San Eustachio, the little Monsignor would call upon the sick person as soon as possible. He enjoyed preaching the word of God and volunteered to take his turn for sermons in San Eustachio.*

Giacomo belonged to the Archconfraternity of San Rocco, and at their public functions wore the members' rough garb known as "the sack." He was an officer in the Priests' League for Nocturnal Adoration, and took his turn at the appointed church, without ever allowing his night of vigil to interfere with his scrupulous punctuality at the office in the Vatican.[19] As a Tertiary of Saint Francis, he made a monthly day of recollection at the Church of San Nicola in Tolentino. He enjoyed preaching retreats and days of recollection to nuns. At two convents, Giacomo gave weekly conferences of a spiritual-archaeological nature on the vigorous Christianity of apostolic times.[20] He was also president of the Society of Saint Jerome, which had for its purpose to spread a love of Sacred Scripture. The society placed a copy of the New Testament into any home which would welcome it. Monsignor Della Chiesa loved to accompany a priest on a sick call, or to carry the white *ombrellino,* a sort of miniature canopy, behind one who was bearing Holy Viaticum to a dying person.

That Pope Leo knew of these hidden pastoral functions can be gleaned from his words when he sent Monsignor Della Chiesa on the first of his two secret missions to Vienna. "I am really sorry," said the Pope with his customary enigmatic smile, "that this new task will take you away from your pastoral functions to which you seem to have dedicated yourself with so much love."[21]

Although Monsignor Della Chiesa worked unostentatiously and apparently made no great impression, he was highly respected for his diplomatic instinct. In clerical life nicknames from college and high school days often endure. Behind his back Monsignor Della Chiesa was still frequently referred to as *il piccoletto* — roughly, "the little fellow." When questions would come up among prelates or diplomats as to whether some matter should be mentioned to the Pope or his secretary of state, or whether it was politic to release

---

* After his death the parishioners donated a beautiful pulpit with panels of multicolored marble which bears an inscription testifying to his zeal as a preacher:

"Lest it be forgotten that on this spot Benedict XV, Supreme Pontiff, exercised his priestly functions for a long time, this pulpit was erected in 1937."

external appearance, Monsignor Della Chiesa was likely to leave a negative impression. Cardinal O'Connell of Boston for one, was singularly unimpressed by him. In his autobiography he writes:

I had known Monsignor Della Chiesa quite well during the days of my Rectorship of the American College, between 1895 and 1901. Nearly every morning his frail figure, clothed in the simplest clerical garb, might be seen, walking from his apartment along the narrow streets which led to the Vatican, where he held the position of Under-Secretary with Cardinal Rampolla, his chief, as Secretary of State. He might well pass unnoticed for any impressiveness of appearance, for his figure was rather angular and he walked with something of a limp. His complexion was sallow and his head, generally tilted to one side, gave no indication of the very fertile brain within it. Not once, but several times, meeting him on my way toward the office of the Maggiordomo with whom I had freqeunt business, I joined him in the walk, but as he was a person of most extreme reticence, conversation was mainly about the weather.[25]

Another indication of Monsignor Della Chiesa's lack of impressiveness can be gleaned from a remark made by Archbishop Michael A. Corrigan (d. 1902) of New York. An article defending certain policies of Archbishop Ireland of Saint Paul had appeared anonymously in *L'Osservatore Romano*. Archbishop Corrigan made a relentless probe as to the identity of the author of the article. When he learned that it was Giacomo Della Chiesa, he dismissed him in these devastating lines:

. . . a gentleman without any influence whatever in theological circles, and whose name consequently if published would carry absolutely no weight with it. I have direct and reliable information that Mgr. Della Chiesa wrote the article, and the estimate of his standing is also beyond question.[26]

The rooms used as offices for the secretariat of state were very old-fashioned until they were somewhat modernized by Cardinal Pacelli. "Under the leads" was Vatican jargon for those offices immediately under the heavily leaded roof. Two hundred and ninety-four steps had to be mounted to arrive at "this swallow's nest" from Saint Peter's Square.[27] Giacomo's living quarters were a dingy apartment between the Sistine Chapel and the Basilica of Saint Peter. Very often at midnight and after, the windows of this room yielded the solitary light.[28]

Practically everything had to pass through Della Chiesa's hands. True, he had many secretaries, apprentices, and *minutanti* working for him. But it was his duty to review the drafts, and lay them before the stern Rampolla del Tindaro. The Cardinal would issue various instructions for each nuncio, ambassador, archbishop, head of a congregation, etc. The undersecretary would have letters prepared which would contain these instructions in diplomatic language, and then present these to the Cardinal for signature.

On days when the Cardinal Secretary of State was engaged with distinguished visitors, the Undersecretary had to appear before the Holy Father. Monsignor De Waal conjectures that when Giacomo made his first appearance alone before Leo XIII, he must have had that cold, congested feeling experienced by all conscientious men when they make their initial appearance in holy precincts.[29] At this time, Leo XIII was ninety years old. One must see him in the mind's eye to appreciate the sensation of being alone with him for the first time. There was the large hairless skull which converged suddenly beneath the prominent cheekbones. The skin was like old parchment, shiny, dry, and yellow. As the head turned one could see why he was thought of as a reincarnation of the classical Roman eagle. His piercing beady eyes and beaklike nose were indeed impressive. The long thin lips parted, and prominent yellow teeth became visible. One expected a hoarse, quavering voice from the distant buried past, but, instead, the voice rang young and rich.[30]

In those years Giacomo had an opportunity of meeting almost all the bishops who came to the Vatican on business. Their problems fell within the competency of some one particular Roman congregation, office, or tribunal. Owing to an understandable ignorance of the intricacies of the Roman Curia in the days before Pius X and the Code of Canon Law, a bishop might come, wait for hours or even days to see the secretary of state, only to find that he should have spent his time waiting for the secretary of the Holy Office or of the Consistory or of some other congregation. Visitors from foreign lands, who, because of inability to speak the language and general ignorance of procedure were timid, experienced a welcome reassurance when they arrived at the office of Monsignor Della Chiesa. It was his custom to leave his desk, limp hurriedly to the guest, and kiss his ring. This was noted because Vatican officials, surrounded, as they are, by prelates and their insignia of office, do not usually snap to attention at the sight of a ring on some groping, timorous prelate from a foreign land.[31]

Archbishop Ireland of Saint Paul, for example, expressed great joy when he heard of the election of Cardinal Della Chiesa. He remarked that he entertained most pleasant memories of the courtesy and fine counsel which had always been shown him by Monsignor Della Chiesa on the American Bishop's many visits to the secretariat of state.[32]

During his tenure of office Giacomo also met the great world figures whom Divine Providence set on one of the myriad roads that lead to Rome. Some of these meetings paved the way for the important diplomatic strokes which he was to make during his pontificate. Notable in this connection was the last of the three visits which William II paid Leo XIII who had an inexplicable attraction for the German Emperor. After his audience with the Pope, the Kaiser repaired to the residence of the German ambassador where a banquet was served. After the meal, in continental fashion, the guests, among whom were Cardinal Rampolla and his Undersecretary, stood about in the drawing room with liqueur and coffee. It was noticed how Della Chiesa absorbed the Emperor's attention, quite probably with talk of Roman or German antiquities, of which both made a hobby. As a consequence of this pleasant meeting, Cardinal Rampolla was admitted to the Order of the Black Eagle, and Monsignor Della Chiesa was decorated with the Great Cross of the Order of the Crown.[33] In 1917, Archbishop Pacelli, special envoy of Benedict XV, visited the same Emperor at Kreuznach. In his memoirs, William II wrote favorably of Eugenio Pacelli, who in profile, quality of voice, intelligence, and dignified demeanor was reminiscent of Giacomo Della Chiesa.

At about this time, Giacomo came very close to becoming the cardinal archbishop of his native diocese. The cardinal of Genoa had died and the see was vacant for several months. One day in 1902 Monsignor Della Chiesa entered Leo XIII's study on routine business and when he arranged the sheaves of paper on the Pope's desk, Leo did not begin to affix his signature to them but said slyly, "Well, you ought to be happy now because we have named your new archbishop."

"I do not know a thing about it," said Giacomo. "Could I perhaps know his name?"

"It is Bishop Pulciano of Navara."

Giacomo was sincerely happy because he counted Pulciano among his closer friends. Therefore he exclaimed almost melodramatically: "Genoa is indeed well favored!"

"Actually," said Leo, "another was considered for the position and we almost sent him to Genoa. The new archbishop of Genoa was to be you, but *the Cardinal* opposed it." "The Cardinal," of course, was Rampolla. It was a matter of general amusement that Leo XIII invariably referred to Rampolla as *il Cardinale* as though there were but one genuine cardinal and the other members of the apostolic college had the title only in a broad sense.[34]

Despite appearances Cardinal Rampolla was not being selfish in his request that Leo XIII should not promote his undersecretary at that time. E. J. Dillon, a British journalist, known for anything but his sympathy with the Vatican, broke a precedent by writing the following words about Monsignor Della Chiesa:

> It is asserted that at times the powerful Cardinal, when desirous of taking a step to which Leo XIII was known to be opposed, was wont to send his secretary to clear the ground, prepare the Pontiff for what was coming, and disarm his opposition. We are also assured that success invariably crowned his efforts.
>
> "Has the cardinal given you his view on this matter?" the pope would ask.
>
> "No, Holy Father, he reserves that for your ears."
>
> "Then you do not know how he regards it?"
>
> "I do not know, Holy Father, but if I may venture to draw an inference from his judgment on kindred questions which are essential elements of this one, I should say that he would look upon it somewhat in this way."
>
> And then followed a masterly *exposé* of the problem set in the light of a whole coherent system, and a closely reasoned plea for the decision to which his chief had come. And before he left the audience chamber he had broken down opposition and achieved his purpose. It remained for Rampolla only to knock at an open door.[35]

A glimpse into the day's routine of Cardinal Rampolla will show what manner of man Giacomo Della Chiesa chose for a model. Monsignor De Waal reports that once when he was entertaining the distinguished Dr. Ernst Lieber[36] at the hospice of Campo Santo, where he was rector, he was anxious to present his visitor to Cardinal Rampolla. Late in the afternoon the Monsignor and his guest went to the Cardinal's reception room and found it filled. The hours passed, and at nine o'clock Monsignor De Waal finally asked the secretary when Cardinal Rampolla would close his office to visitors.

"It will remain open as long as there is someone here who wishes to speak to him," was the brief answer.

Further conversation with the Cardinal's receptionist revealed interesting details of Rampolla's strictly disciplined life. He had no definitely determined hour for dinner. He dined only when the business of the day was over, which was sometimes as late as 11 o'clock at night. He always rose promptly at 5:30, said his breviary, made his meditation, and offered Holy Mass which he never completed in less than three quarters of an hour. At 9 he ate his breakfast standing while arranging the agenda to be laid before the Pope in the morning's audience which usually lasted two hours. Then followed reception of visitors so that lunch was seldom eaten before 2 o'clock. He never took a siesta but employed the afternoon hours in formulating answers to be sent by wire. His only recreation was a daily ride to his titular church, St. Cecilia, where he made a holy hour which he terminated with the first stroke of the Angelus. He never took a vacation, and in the whole time that he was secretary of state, he was absent from the Vatican for only one night — when he was summoned to the bedside of his dying mother.[37]

This was the man whom Giacomo served and whom he imitated in his own life and routine.

CHAPTER IV

Restoring All Things in Christ

DURING the summer of 1903, there were frequent rumors that Pope Leo XIII, now ninety-four years of age, was at death's door. Each time he rallied, and even took another ride in the Vatican Gardens.[1] On Sunday, July 19, it was reported that the Pope was really in his last agony. Monsignor Della Chiesa now had his first opportunity of observing how popes yield their soul to God. Like royalty, a pope must die in public — his bed is a stage.[2] Giacomo knelt and added his clear voice to those begging God to accept this noble soul to His divine bosom.[3] Occasionally the murmur of prayers would rouse the Pontiff who would then with the greatest exertion possible attempt to trace his blessing.

The Pope did not speak until Monday morning when his smile, made so famous in the oleographs and photographs of the twenty-five years of his pontificate, presaged a pronouncement. Suddenly, the shrewd eyes still bright and penetrating, rested on the papal physician, Doctor Lapponi. With the old enigmatic sense of humor he said very distinctly: "This time, Doctor, you will not win your valiant battle against death."[4] Then he lapsed into his former immobility as though he meant to conserve his strength for the final struggle.

Suddenly toward 4 o'clock in the afternoon, as he caught sight of his *camerlengo*, Cardinal Oreglia, entering the room, he said loudly and clearly: "To you, *Eminenza*, who will soon hold the reins of supreme command, I entrust the Church in these difficult times." In that last show of strength which nature supplies in time of need, he held out his hand to be kissed by the five cardinals about his bed. Then he dropped his hand in exhaustion and sighed:

"This is my last greeting to you!" A few minutes after 4 o'clock that afternoon, Leo returned his soul to the hand of its Maker. The grand penitentiary absolved him once more, and Cardinal Oreglia was heard to say:

"The Pope is really dead."

Giacomo passed by the bed with the rest and gazed upon the deceased Leo. Twenty-five years before, he had knelt in Saint Peter's Basilica looking through the grille of Blessed Sacrament Chapel at the body of Pius IX. He looked at the eagle's head now stamped with the signet of death. Those beady, luminous eyes which had awed him so thoroughly in the past were now closed. The ancient, yellow hand, dry and emaciated, lay inert upon the crimson cushion. All knelt and kissed the ring upon it. Giacomo, who for the past two years had kissed that ring almost daily upon entering and leaving the papal presence, might well have written as a courtier did after performing this same act of protocol at the death of King James I: "It was not so hard a hand when we touched it last nor so cold a hand when we kissed it last."[5]

When Leo had spoken his last words he was convinced that he had left the governmental machinery of the Church in the best of order. However, something had happened of which the dying Pope was not aware. About three hours before the Pope's death, Monsignor Volpini dropped dead from a heart attack just outside the Pope's room. The death of any man is a tragedy and leaves a void, but Monsignor Volpini was a most important cog in the mechanism of transferring supreme authority from the deceased Pontiff to the pope to be elected. Monsignor Volpini was the secretary of the Consistorial Congregation and, as such, would automatically become the secretary of the conclave in complete charge of assigning lodgings to the cardinals, arranging the schedule, appointing cardinals to various duties, and the like. The *camerlengo* was in a quandary as to what to do, when he chanced to meet the young rector of the Academy of Noble Ecclesiastics, Archbishop Merry del Val. He said to Merry del Val, "Monsignor, I have something serious to tell you. The first duty of the cardinals after the death of the Pope will be to appoint a successor to poor Monsignor Volpini, for we must have a secretary for the conclave. I shall, therefore, at our first assembly, propose to the cardinals two names — Monsignor Gasparri's and your own."[6]

The cardinals, however, nominated the *Sostituto*, Monsignor Della Chiesa, in place of Gasparri.[7] A vote was taken, and Archbishop Merry del Val was chosen. A reporter perhaps oversimplified the reason for the choice, when he wrote, "Merry del Val was handsome while Giacomo Della Chiesa was short, stoopish, and surly."[8] This apparently insignificant election was a decisive event which did much to change the history of the papacy in modern times. It set in motion a remarkable chain of circumstances. In that very hour Giacomo's star began to wane, and for almost a decade its light as an influence on world affairs was to be all but totally extinguished.

From the moment that the names of Rafael Merry del Val and Giacomo Della Chiesa were first proposed for the position of secretary of the conclave, the lives of these two men were to be intimately associated.

In 1887, while Giacomo was still in the nuncio's office in Madrid, Leo XIII had elevated a seminarian not yet in major orders to the dignity of papal chamberlain with the title of "Very Reverend Monsignor." The recipient of this title was Rafael Merry del Val, son of the Spanish ambassador to Great Britain. While the appointment caused a good many raised eyebrows,[9] it was not entirely without precedent. Pope Gregory XVI had made Giaocchino Pecci (Leo XIII), while he was still a seminarian in minor orders, a domestic prelate, who enjoys even higher rank than a papal chamberlain.

The peculiar family name, Merry del Val, needs some explanation. Students and friends affectionately called him "Merry," so that many thought that "Merry" was his Christian name, and "Del Val" his family name. Even Archbishop Ireland of Saint Paul, who in that era had a reputation for "knowing his way about Rome," refers to him in his earlier correspondence as "Monsignor Del Val," and only later seems to have become aware of the fact that his full family name was Merry del Val.[10] Actually his Christian name was Rafael.

In 1887, after his return from Spain, Giacomo made the Academy of Noble Ecclesiastics his temporary home. Here he had the opportunity of meeting the Monsignor who was not yet a priest. It must be remembered that Giacomo had gone to Spain with great enthusiasm for that country's culture, lore, and language. So now, on his return to Italy, he was delighted to find in residence at the academy a distinguished student, who came not only from the upper strata of Spanish society but also from a family of diplomats who would certainly have a thorough knowledge of the internal affairs of Spain. No friendship, however, sprang from this meeting. Without meaning to be haughty or rude, Merry del Val could be icily reserved to those who sought him out. It has been thought that this attitude was really due to timidity. It seems that Giacomo's enthusiastic questions were met with this characteristic aloofness.

Although no camaraderie developed from the meeting of these two men, they had a great deal in common. Both were of noble birth. Both were capable of great intellectual achievements. Both were sensitive and refined. Both, contrary to the world's mental picture of "ecclesiastical diplomats," in an eminent degree cherished the riches of the interior life, the life of the soul. Both had attracted the attention of Leo XIII. Both, at least in the early years, were in the best of graces with Rampolla del Tindaro.

Nevertheless, these similarities were superficial. Fundamentally, their characters were radically different. To understand the years which led to the pontificate of Benedict XV, it will be of great help to understand this vital difference.

Giacomo Della Chiesa is a perfect example of the man who had been cheated by Nature but dowered by the Spirit. Merry del Val was extraordinarily favored by Nature but strove all his life, and not without success, to capture the riches of the Spirit.

That Nature had copiously endowed Merry del Val can be seen from his remarkably winning appearance. A reporter who saw him for the first time said, "Had he not become famous, he would have made famous any artist by merely sitting for his portrait, so arresting were his features."[11] As he grew older, he became ever more handsome and distinguished in appearance.[12]

His melodic voice and gift for tongues accompanied by his charming smile were but further evidences of Nature's fondness for him. Pilgrims to Rome during the pontificates of Saint Pius X, Benedict XV, and Pius XI found their greatest thrill in having been addressed by Cardinal Merry del Val. Thomas B. Morgan expressed it thus: "While he spoke English with the finish of a professor of philosophy, yet he spoke it with an authoritative rhythm and in the hypnotic aura of a cosmopolitan."[13] A historian of the North American College in Rome recalls the Cardinal's visits to the college: "He spoke to us in flawless and fascinating English. His words were musical entities that danced delightfully on the auricular nerves. And the dance they danced was a Viennese waltz. His sentences were as finely cut and exquisitely proportioned as the sculpture of a mediaeval master craftsman."[14]

Furthermore, Merry del Val's prowess in athletics shows how wholesomely Nature throbbed in every fiber of his being. His brothers remember him in his boyhood as one who "loved dancing, swimming, and shooting; he was an excellent shot and a fearless rider."[15] He kept himself physically fit all his life. For reasons of the rigorous asceticism which he practiced, he ate but sparingly. His apostolic work with the underprivileged youth in the Trastevere region of Rome forced him into regular walks and helped to preserve his trim figure.

As an aging man, he still delighted in going to the American College and challenging the best tennis players in residence there. The seminaries which had facilities for swimming were his favorite haunts in summer. Here he would amaze all with his gigantic strokes or feats of endurance.[16] In the back yard of the *Palazzina Santa Marta* where he lived after his retirement from the office of secretary of state, he would place the smallest of Italian coins in the crevices on the ledge of his garden wall, and with a rifle shoot them off one by one with a calmness which would have aroused the envy of Buffalo Bill's "sharpshooters."[17]

Giacomo Della Chiesa found for himself no acclaim in these fields. When he was *minutante* and undersecretary of state, his friends would remonstrate with him for his tireless and uninterrupted routine of work. They pointed out to him the many recreations which he could take legitimately and with the greatest propriety. Giacomo would peer wistfully through his heavy lenses and with a gently melancholy smile would answer: *"Per il mio temperamento va bene cosi"*[18] — "For my temperament, it's all right this way." He may have envied men like Merry del Val who could engage in all these feats of the body, but he knew that similar attempts on his part would be greeted with derision. "Yearning for Nature," a term coined by Schiller,[19] was within him, but the very revealing qualification in his response, "For my temperament," showed that he was resigned to the fact that indulgence in the gifts of Nature was not for him.

Father Leo Schlegel tells of a pilgrim to Rome, who after returning from an audience with Benedict XV, was at a loss how to begin his description of the Pope, and he said that there was *etwas schmächtiges* about him.[20] Etymologically the word has a meaning of "slender" or "emaciated" but with the added idea of something pathetic almost to the extent of arousing embarrassment. In fact, employing a favorite German expression, the same writer said: "He impressed me as a man who had been treated by Nature in a rather stepmotherly fashion."[21]

Giacomo was not unaware of Nature's "stepmotherly" treatment of him. It is for this reason that he shunned the camera. As Benedict XV, he is said to have appraised his own physical appearance in a picturesque phrase, "I am but an ugly gargoyle on the beauties of Rome."[22] If it is true that he uttered these words, it might explain why he shunned public appearances and frequently delegated to members of the apostolic college his place at the papal altar in Saint Peter's. Two pictures appear in print[23] of Archbishop Della Chiesa on horseback, prepared for a visitation of certain parishes in Bologna accessible only by tortuous mountain passes. His whole face seems to show his lack of relish of this situation which to many others would have been most enjoyable.

Unless Giacomo knew people well, he was unable to enter a room filled with persons and feel at ease. When he was still undersecretary in the pontificate of Saint Pius X, he, in the absence of Cardinal Merry del Val, attended Cardinal Gotti's golden jubilee as the Pope's official representative. The priest who had to meet the guests describes the unpretentious entry of Giacomo:

> We exchanged the compliments of the occasion, and then came the difficult task of finding for him a place in the front of the hall through the dense crowds. He leaned on my arm with his slender frail person, gripping my right hand while I ushered him in with such a sort of childish, trustful yielding, and with such a pure, good smile, that it was revealed to me all at once how, under the habit of the expert and cautious diplomat, behind the impassive face almost stiffened through a life of routine work, and a mind used to look at men only as categories of ecclesiastical affairs, there survived a rich amount of human sympathy, which only demanded an occasion to be set free.[24]

Rafael Merry del Val, on the other hand, became the focal point of admiring glances in any hall which he chanced to enter. Without intending any irreverence, the Anglican Rector in Rome, Walter Lowrie, remarks concerning his first meeting with Merry del Val that he was "then a man about town, very popular."[25] Yet it is absolutely true to say that, had Merry del Val, with the world at his feet, been confronted with making a choice between the acclaim of the world and the highest ecclesiastical preferment, on the one hand, or the humblest position in the Church but with a guarantee

of the close friendship of Saint Pius X, on the other, he would not
have hesitated an instant in choosing the second alternative. So
intent was he on learning the "science of the saints," that when his
days of power ended with the death of Saint Pius X, and his
enemies maligned him, he weighed in the balance the worth of the
magnificence which had been his over against the detraction and
calumny which he was now suffering, and he deemed his poignant
sufferings an easy premium to pay for the pearl of great price, the
paternal love of Saint Pius X.[26]

If one reads his letters, one realizes that no saintly hermit ever
had greater detachment from the things of this world.[27] For his own
devotion he wrote the beautiful *Angelus in Gethsemane*[28] and his
Litany of Humility in which he begs his Lord and Master to be
delivered from the slightest desire of being praised or consulted,
from the fear of being humiliated or repulsed.[29] One chapter of
appreciable size in Professor Cenci's life of the Cardinal comprises
a list of quotations which Merry del Val had jotted down in notebooks or on sundry scraps of paper — all of them showing his
relentless yearning for the spiritual.[30]

To see Merry del Val say Mass was an experience never to be
forgotten. A distinguished visitor to Rome once remarked that to
have heard Merry del Val chant the *Pater Noster* was sufficient to
convince him of the Cardinal's sanctity.[31] Frances Forbes quotes
the words of another who attended Merry del Val's Mass:

> If you could see how he celebrated Holy Mass — especially when
> he came to the words *fiat voluntas tua*. They seemed to come straight
> from the depths of his soul and to go straight up to the throne of God.[32]

So great was Merry del Val's reputation for sanctity that the
late Cardinal Hayes wrote after Merry del Val's death, "Is it too
presumptuous to pray and hope that . . . one day not far distant,
another Saint Raphael may be raised to the Altars of the Church?"[33]
The Archbishop of New York had penned these words less than
a decade after Merry del Val's death in 1930, and on July 24, 1956,
the Sacred Congregation of Rites met for the so-called *revision of
the writings* of the "Servant of God," Rafael Merry del Val, one
of the first steps towards beatification.[34]

Rafael Merry del Val's first preferment over Giacomo Della
Chiesa occurred on that day in 1903 when the cardinals elected a
secretary of the conclave to replace Monsignor Volpini. The state-

ment, "Merry del Val was unanimously elected pro-secretary of the sacred college,"[35] is most probably a somewhat exaggerated version of the event. It must not be forgotten that Rampolla had proposed the name of Giacomo Della Chiesa, and the cardinals who favored Rampolla are most likely to have favored his candidate. Nevertheless, the fact remains, Merry del Val was elected, and the duties of this office brought him into immediate contact with the new Pope who had to learn papal procedure from him.

When the conclave opened, the only cardinal whom Merry del Val did not know was Sarto. Since he had appointed the cardinals to their cells and chairs, he reasoned that the benign white-haired prelate must be Cardinal Sarto, the patriarch of Venice.[36]

When the infamous veto of Francis Joseph against Rampolla was presented by the Polish Cardinal Puszyna, and the votes began to accumulate in favor of Giuseppe Sarto, it was Archbishop Merry del Val who had to summon the unhappy Cardinal from the Pauline Chapel in order to ask him to accept.[37] Sarto, whose life had always been one of delightful simplicity, felt very old and helpless in this swirl of grandeur and diplomatic protocol. He was indeed shocked that so crude an action against Rampolla should have been undertaken by a member of the sacred college at the behest of a layman.[38] To this feeling of shock was added embarrassment at the fact that it was the great Rampolla whom he was asked to replace. However, the confident tones of Merry del Val's rich voice, the eyes glowing with sympathy, the youthful vigor which created the impression that he was in control of every situation, made the white-haired Sarto feel less alone in this maelstrom into which he was being pushed so much against his will.

When Saint Pius had to vest for the imparting of his first blessing and the various cases of pectoral crosses were presented, the newly elected Pontiff looked at the servants holding them up to him, but their noncommittal, impassive faces gave him no help in making a choice. It must have been a pathetic sight to see the bewildered Sarto as he turned away from the sparkling array of gold and precious stones to seek the eye of Merry del Val in order to ask with childlike simplicity, *"Monsignore, which shall I choose?"* *Monsignore,* as usual, rose to the occasion. His deft hands touched one of the velvet-cushioned trays and held the cross up to the new Pontiff's lips, put the chain over his head, and latched the cross to a buttonhole. Years later, Pius X explained why he had a prefer-

ence for a particular pectoral cross. It was the one chosen for him
by *Monsignore* Merry del Val.[39]

In his own memoirs, Merry del Val tells of his official visit to
Pius X's room on the night of his election in order to obtain his
signature. He found Pius saying his breviary. The secretary of
the conclave apologized for the interruption, but the new Pope
welcomed this first break in the solitude which henceforth would
be an inseparable adjunct to his office. As Merry del Val came out
of the Pope's room, he met a little monsignor who stopped him to
see the signature. He wrote in his memoirs:

> On returning to my room I met Monsignor Della Chiesa, who was
> particularly eager to see the Pope's signature and pointed out its
> resemblance to that of Pius IX. How far he must have been then
> from imagining that the next Pontiff to sign similar documents would
> be himself as Benedict XV![40]

Biographers seem to be afraid to mention Benedict XV and Pius
X's *prima creatura* (the first cardinal created) in the same book.
Since Merry del Val inserted this charming incident in his memoirs,
it is quite evident that much of the animosity which writers hint at
existed only in the minds of those who craved the sensational.[41]
In the same *Memories of Pope Pius X* he expresses his gratitude
to Benedict XV for the unselfish and glowing words which the
latter spoke in praise of Pope Pius X on the occasion of the promulgation of the Code of Canon Law.[42]

To Saint Pius it was an unceasing miracle to see Merry del Val
walk down a corridor and speak in perfect English to one bystander,
equally perfect French to the next, superb Spanish to a third, excellent German to another. His Italian was so correct that few
adverted to the fact that he was not an Italian.[43]

Merry del Val was asked to act as pro-secretary of state, and
about six months later was promoted to secretary. In the first consistory held by the new Pope he was created a cardinal. His church
was Santa Prassede which Browning immortalized in *The Bishop
Orders His Tomb at Saint Praxed's Church.*

It is interesting to speculate on the "might-have-beens" had
Della Chiesa been elected secretary of the conclave. It is safe to conclude that although he might have brought greater efficiency to
the work of the Curia than Merry del Val did, he would not have
inspired the same sense of pleasant security in the saintly old man

whose heart craved the consolations of a small parish and the intimacy of a loving family. Someone has well epitomized Della Chiesa's character: "Ironic, reserved, distant, he was not made for facile friendships."[44] In fact, as archbishop of Bologna, he hurt some of the older clergy by his strict "chancery" etiquette when these old men who had "borne the burden of the day's heat" thought that they might combine their business visit with a leisurely chat.[45]

For himself, however, Giacomo seems to have shown no disappointment at Merry del Val's preferment. It was he who, on November 9, 1903, had to read aloud to the papal court the document appointing Merry del Val to the office of secretary of state. No correspondence or anecdote indicates whether Monsignor Della Chiesa knew Cardinal Sarto before the latter's election to the Chair of Peter. Since, as has been said, bishops on business in Rome were always happy to confer with the deferential undersecretary, it is quite possible that Sarto also received favors from Giacomo. Previous acquaintanceship would explain, although not conclusively, Pius' immediate confirmation of Della Chiesa in his position in the secretariat which he had held under Leo. After Della Chiesa's first visit to Pius X after the conclave, he wrote to a priest friend in a letter dated August 27, 1903: "The new Pontiff is a sweet delicacy (una pasta di zucchero). If it were possible to sin by an excess of charity and amiability, then I think the new Pope would be guilty of that fault."[46]

December 21, 1903, was to mark the twenty-fifth anniversary of Giacomo's ordination to the priesthood. He decided to observe his silver jubilee on Sunday, December 20, so as not to be absent from his office in the secretariat.[47] The truly papal gift which Pius presented to him on this occasion clearly demonstrates his love for the humble Sostituto. One must remember that Pius was elected in August and that the gift about to be described was something not purchased on the spur of the moment. As Merry del Val attests, Saint Pius X "loved beautiful things"[48] and especially Venetian glass and lace. He gave Giacomo a pair of cruets of exquisite Venetian glass, trimmed with bands of gold and silver, set on a silver platter with a lacelike rim, in the center of which a papal tiara was delicately engraved. To match these objects was a delicately wrought silver bell. All these were attractively boxed in a large leather case lined with white satin.[49] With the gift came a handwritten note from His Holiness in which he referred to Giacomo as *Nobis devictissimus* (most loyal to Us). He wished him "the best of health and the Lord's favor for many years to come." He concluded the letter by granting him permanently his papal blessing and a plenary indulgence to him and to all who would attend the solemnities of the occasion. There are few notes from Saint Pius X in which he speaks so intimately.

Less than a year later, on July 4, 1904, Marchesa Giovanna Della Chiesa, Giacomo's mother, died while visiting Genoa and Pegli. Father Vistalli divines the grief which must have been Giacomo's. "That summer there was no more vacation for him. The death of his mother constituted a tremendous misfortune, from which, in spite of his philosophical and calm temperament, it took a long time for him to recover. He missed her as the dearest thing he had in life, as a necessary and essential element. Poor monsignor! To his friends, who visited him at Pegli or at Rome, he was incapable of observing silence about his deep sorrow. He would point out objects which had belonged to his mother or which bore some sign of her special affection."[50] Again the gentle hand of Saint Pius X reached out for note paper and quill. This time he wrote a letter of sympathy which could well be included in an anthology of noteworthy letters.

July 10, 1904

Dear Monsignor,

I share very keenly in your grief and that of your dear ones because of the loss of that best of mothers, and I wish to all the sweet consolations of the Faith as a source of strength. And your dear ones certainly will not be wanting in them, if they but think of the undefiled life of your saintly mother, who, having been summoned to receive the reward for her virtues, now from heaven above is watching over them and is blessing them.

With this holy thought it is a delight for me to impart to you, to your brothers, to your sister, and to all your relatives the Apostolic Blessing.

Pius Pp. X[51]

There is little official information available concerning Giacomo's relationship with Saint Pius X for the next three years. Count Sforza intimates that when Giacomo cautioned Cardinal Merry del Val, Cardinal Vives y Tuto, secretary of the congregation of the inquisition, and Cardinal De Lai, prefect of the congregation of the consistory, against some of their very stringent and precipitate meas-

ures, it was arranged that there would be fewer and fewer occasions for him to be received by the Pontiff in private audience.[52]
Giacomo's elevation to the see of Bologna and his removal from
the sphere of Vatican diplomacy were construed by many as an
execution of the ancient principle: *Promoveatur ut amoveatur* ("Let
him be promoted so that he can be removed.")[53] This may not be
entirely untrue. Even the most cautious writers of the time betray
their belief in statements like: "This [Della Chiesa's appointment
to the see of Bologna] proved, after all, a blessing in disguise."[54]

What was the policy on which Giacomo's caution was considered
as out of harmony with the aims of the pontificate? This question
can be answered only in tracing the history of intellectual speculation within the sacred sciences during the pontificates of Leo XIII
and Pius X.

CHAPTER V

Modernists and Integralists

BEFORE 1870, the popes had been able to move actively among the people and to make immediate decisions on particular situations brought to their attention. The scholarly Leo XIII, following the policy of voluntary imprisonment in the Vatican inaugurated by Pius IX, made his pontificate one of intense study. As a guide for those who feared that the progressive development in science, history, and philosophy would lead to a vast triumph of reason over faith, Leo wrote a series of encyclicals which were like the blows of a mighty hammer.

In *Aeterni Patris* (1879), the encyclical which reinstated Saint Thomas Aquinas as the prince of Catholic philosophers, Leo had written, "And if we find in the scholastic doctors any useless subtlety or weakly grounded thesis or anything that is unacceptable for any reason whatsoever, it is evident that we must not teach such things to our contemporaries."[1] In *Immortale Dei* (1885) he stated clearly and boldly the Church's concept of government. In *Providentissimus Deus* (1893) he encouraged new approaches in biblical studies. In 1883 he opened the doors of the Vatican Library to all scholars who might wish to come and browse. In 1884, in an address to the German Historical Circle, he invited its members to search to their hearts' content among the time-yellowed parchments in the Vatican Library, saying, "Draw as much as possible on the sources. It is for that purpose that I have opened the Vatican archives. We are not afraid to let the light come in on them."[2] Pope Leo's rule for historians was: "The first law of history is: may it never dare to tell a falsehood; the second is: let it not presume to suppress the truth, and may it not reveal so much as a suspicion of favor or of animosity."[3] A historian of Modernism described the ensuing situation in these words:

> It was an epoch of religious, intellectual, social, and political turmoil
> characterized by a concerted effort of the Catholic Church under the
> influence of a leader like Pope Leo XIII to recognize contemporary
> realities, to grasp them, and to adapt herself to them in so far as

adaptation was compatible with the living tradition of Catholicism. As always, this work of adaptation inevitably carried with it vents of spleen, excesses, and veritable errors.[4]

Many scholars, who in the course of time found themselves under ecclesiastical censure, had begun their research in the best of faith, zealous to comply with the requests of Leo XIII. The saintly Father Lagrange, founder of the *École Biblique* in Jerusalem, was an example of this type of scholar. Others, however, moved away from the light of faith and treated divine revelation as though it were mere folklore. They seized upon the revolutionary principles of Spencer[5] and Hegel,[6] and applied them to the Bible and the Church, leaving no room for divine guidance. They applied their principles to political science and ruled out the influence of the Church.[7]

The spirit which prompted these ideas was termed Modernism. However, it would be unfair to leave the impression that Modernism did not exist before Pope Leo XIII. In fact, his predecessor, Pius IX, had watched it develop. With acute anxiety he condemned it in his famous *Syllabus*. Under each of the pontificates Modernism took a different turn. Under Pius IX it was politico-liberal; under Leo XIII it was social; under Pius X it became principally theological.*

In the year 1907 Pius X mobilized his forces against Modernism, which he branded in an allocution of April 17 as the "synthesis of all heresies."[9] On July 3, the Congregation of the Holy Office, of which the Supreme Pontiff himself is the prefect, issued the decree, *Lamentabili* condemning a catalogue of sixty-five errors.[10] On September 8, Pius X issued the encyclical, *Pascendi*,[11] which condemned Modernism in most unequivocal terms, and was actually a detailed commentary on *Lamentabili*. The encyclical carried a threat of excommunication to all who would continue to hold these condemned doctrines and demanded special vigilance by bishops and superiors of seminaries lest candidates tainted with these tendencies be promoted to Holy Orders.

No sincere lover of the Church has ever questioned the worth or the timeliness of this action of Pius X. The criticism which arose from loyal Catholics was directed only against the methods employed in maintaining the vigilance which the saintly Pontiff had so stringently and so rightly enjoined.

---

* The name itself is believed to have been coined by Jean Jacques Rousseau in a letter dated January 15, 1769.[8]

That Giacomo Della Chiesa heartily approved of the condemnation of Modernism is evident from the fact that he himself as pope clearly and fully affirmed Pius X's censure in his first encyclical, *Ad Beatissimi*.[12]

Even before the turmoil arose, however, Giacomo Della Chiesa was referred to as "the pope's right hand in combatting Modernism."[13] In fact, there is evidence that even in the days of Leo XIII, Giacomo had kept a prudent and vigilant eye on the new tendencies. The first mention of Della Chiesa in the diaries of Ludwig Pastor occurs in the entry for March 15, 1902. Since Pastor worked daily in the Vatican and attended many of the ecclesiastical functions, he undoubtedly knew the Undersecretary of State by sight, but this date seems to have marked their first meeting. The German scholar was working in his usual alcove in the Vatican Library, when Monsignor Della Chiesa suddenly stood at his side to ask him whether in his opinion Albert Erhard's *Catholicism and the Twentieth Century in the Light of Ecclesiastical Development of the Modern Era* should be submitted to the Congregation of the Index for possible condemnation. From the Undersecretary's question Pastor could not divine his opinion on the matter. Pastor's carefully worded answer was also noncommittal. From the comments he added in this day's entry of his diary one can sense the reputation for shrewdness which Giacomo enjoyed at this time. Pastor gives the impression of taking some pride in his own evasive answer, feeling that he had parried very successfully with an expert in the art of verbal fencing.[14]

The incident really shows the care with which Giacomo formed his judgments. Monsignor Della Chiesa enjoyed so great a prestige as a man of universal knowledge with sundry facts stored in his orderly mind that he was frequently consulted on a wide range of subjects. In the present case he may have read Erhard's work himself or had heard it discussed and may have questioned the competency of the ecclesiastic who was planning to condemn it. Since Giacomo realized that he himself was no trained historian, he sought the opinion of an expert whose reputation was definitely on the side of orthodoxy. It is interesting to note that Erhard's work was not placed on the Index.

In the early years of Pius X's pontificate a secret organization came into being which took the name *Sodalitium Pianum* (Sodality of Pius) in honor, not, as many supposed, of Saint Pius X, but of St. Pius V, who, as supreme pontiff from 1566 to 1572, was an uncompromising reformer. The purpose of the *Sodalitium Pianum* was to bring hidden Modernists to light. It was because of Giacomo Della Chiesa's disagreement with the methods employed by this organization that he was considered by the zealots to have outlived his usefulness in the secretariat of state. At the time of his transfer to Bologna, the fact that he himself was an object of attention on the part of the *Sodalitium* was not yet known. In fact, the methods employed to ferret out and to punish alleged offenders were not ascertained for some years after the death of Pius X. What was known was that Catholic authors wrote with great trepidation because from time to time they were amazed to learn that their colleagues, writers of hitherto unimpeachable doctrinal orthodoxy, had been forced to withdraw their works from circulation or to present documents retracting certain views. The situation is well summed up in a letter of the Dominican Genocchi to Baron Von Hügel, dated November 5, 1906: "Rome is swarming with spies watching the 'Modernists.' *To be a friend to suspected persons is a crime.*"[15]

It may be easier to grasp the methods of the *Sodalitium* if the reader learns how its inner composition and method of procedure came to light. In the occupation of Belgium in World War I, a lawyer's house in Ghent was raided. Among the officers participating in the raid was a German priest, a member of a religious congregation.[16] One filing cabinet contained coded documents which seemed to have no political implications, but which were so completely absorbed with ecclesiastical matters that they aroused suspicion. The papers contained a variety of names like *La Sapinière*, Michael, Michaelis, Michelet, George, Ars, Charles, Gus, A.I.R., plus much apparent light gossip about some aunts and nephews. It seemed to those inspecting these files that the co-ordinator of this information had worked in Rome; but that owing to some threatening storm the files had been transferred to Belgium for safety.

As a precautionary measure the contents of the filing cabinet were confiscated and transferred to Cologne where the Germans promptly decoded all the documents. Before returning them, however, they made photostatic copies of every scrap of paper in those files. It was only after World War I, when the information from the confiscated files became generally known, that the mosaic of a potentially dangerous movement could be pieced together.

The zealotical phase of the anti-Modernism campaign revolves around one scholarly ecclesiastic and his career. A brilliant Italian priest, Monsignor Umberto Benigni, formerly professor of History and Diplomatic Style in the Academy of Noble Ecclesiastics, obtained a position in the secretariat of state on May 24, 1906.[17] It is worth observing that Benigni was a native of Perugia, the see held by Cardinal Pecci before the latter became Pope Leo XIII. Leo may have recognized Benigni's great intellectual endowments, but he was careful not to invite him to serve in any official capacity in the Vatican. His talents were put to use in teaching, and it is of further interest to note that he took over the chair of Diplomatic Style in the Academy of Noble Ecclesiastics when it was vacated by Giacomo Della Chiesa. The latter was still undersecretary of state when, in 1906, Merry del Val invited Benigni to join the staff of the secretariat. One year later, May 23, 1907, Monsignor Benigni released the first number of his *Correspondenza Romana,* a periodical which was to aid in ferreting out Modernists. In 1908 this journal was replaced by a periodical bearing a French title, *La Correspondance de Rome.* This paper had several satellite sheets, such as *La Critique du liberalisme, Paulus,* and others, to which *La Correspondance de Rome* sent confidential reports. Monsignor Benigni was the director of all these activities. This little priest with the heavy glasses and closely cropped hair was known to go on many journeys to France and Belgium and various parts of Italy, but the Roman clergy did not suspect the magnitude of his operations.

His code to ensure secrecy shows that he was not without a sense of humor. The *Sodalitium Pianum* was designated as *La Sapinière,* an anagram, in which the initial letters *S.* and *P.* were retained. Pius X was designated by derivations and variants of Michael, such as Michelet, Michaelis, or Lady Micheline. Cardinal Merry del Val was George or Monsieur Georges. Benigni referred to himself by about a dozen names, among which were: "Ars, Charles, Arles, Charlotte, Lotte, Kent, Jerome, Lady Friend of O.," and so forth. His paper was lovingly called "Nellie." Bishops were called aunts; priests were designated as nephews. A specialized clearinghouse of information was the *Agence Internationale de Rome* which was termed the A.I.R.

The way in which Benigni reported a situation in code can be seen from the following incident. It seems that in 1912 Cardinal Merry del Val was becoming aware of the massive proportions to which Benigni's operations had grown and of their precarious implications. Consequently, he must in some way have censured the ruthless tactics of Benigni's paper, *La Correspondance de Rome*. Fully conscious of the power which he had accumulated, Benigni seems to have insisted that *La Correspondance* continue to receive reports and be free to print them. In code, the story appeared thus: "In spring, Charles threatened Michael and George that Nellie would die for want of freedom. Monsieur Georges in his infinite prudence has been putting continual pressure on poor Nellie so that she is in danger of dying from anemia."[18]

When someone was reported to the director of *La Sapinière* as being imbued with Modernism, a few quotations would be printed and the impression created that they represented consistent samplings from the cross section of the victim's writings or addresses. In reality, these citations might be lifted out of all context, or abbreviated, or sometimes falsified and even invented, but they were always steeped in a commentary of invective which warped their meaning completely.[19]

In fairness to Benigni it must be said that the finger of guilt did not fall on victims in entirely arbitrary fashion. Usually they were persons who had shown agreement with liberal elements on some point on which there might or might not be legitimate freedom of opinion. But once a man was touched by the ruthless finger of *La Sapinière*, his name was never secure again. It was churned over and over in a solution of denunciations and criticisms, generously seasoned with subtle contradictions and incredible exaggerations, until in the mind of every reader the name in question became that of a dangerous character. These blasts would be published in small periodicals with very limited circulations. The strategy was to send an issue of one of these insignificant monthlies to a large paper or magazine which for a "filler" would summarize or partially reprint the article and give it a sensational headline, such as SEMINARY PROFESSOR QUESTIONS DIVINE ORIGIN OF CHURCH. Most readers would never have heard of an obscure periodical like *La Chiesa Vera*, but with the public's reverence for print, they would conclude that it must be the erudite publication of some learned society. The denunciations then would suddenly find corroboration in anonymously written pamphlets which would continue the "smear campaign." Chancery offices, the desks of religious superiors, the Vatican itself would be flooded with these brochures so that the immediate superior of the victim would be forced to take action. To aid the Holy See in carrying out the principles of *Lamentabili* and *Pascendi,* certain ecclesiastics wrote their exposition of Catholic truth in the framework of very conservative orthodoxy. In itself this was most laudable. They called themselves "Integral Catholics" or "Integralists." In other words, they were "wholly" Catholic. In the field of politics in France "integral" Catholicism took the form of *Action française* which Pius XI condemned sharply. The common denominator present in the many forms of integralism was the tendency to defend the past against the present, to be on the side of unbending authority against even legitimate liberty. Politically the movement showed a dread of democracy.[20] Commenting on the way certain French political writers deviated from the well-meant intention of the original integralists, Monsignor Joseph C. Fenton aptly says,

> Since some of these specifically political views were unfortunate, the men who supported them brought a certain amount of discredit upon their doctrinal attitudes, and caused the name of integralism to be stretched to cover fields quite distinct from that which it originally served to designate.[21]

It was, therefore, the distortion of the original good intention, and the reckless means employed which caused the storm.

Because of his prestige, Cardinal Rampolla alone dared to raise his voice in protest against this excessive rigorism.

> Words cannot describe the sad impression which has been made on me by the agitation continually growing among Catholics, by these intolerable polemics, by this confusion of ideas, and above all by this lack of respect and of obedience to the Holy Father. I regard this the worst of all the damage, and I offer most ardent prayers that this come to an end. For us Catholics the name of the Pope is sacred and untouchable. The confusion which dominates minds, the doubts which arise from it, the judgment of the press, sometimes so unjust, and finally, the outbursts of emotion constitute a state of affairs which is deplorable. It behooves all of us to pray to God that some remedy be found.[22]

Needless to say, Monsignor Della Chiesa likewise was made very unhappy by this state of affairs. A number of times he advised caution and charitable deliberation.[23] Not only was he not listened to, but he also was suspected of liberal tendencies. His unswerving loyalty to Cardinal Rampolla contributed not a little to this reputation.[24]

Night after night, with his peculiar halting gait, Giacomo could be seen making his way to the *Palazzina di Santa Marta* ("The Little Palace of St. Martha") behind St. Peter's, to visit the old Cardinal. The former secretary of state, who had guided the Church's diplomacy through one of her most difficult periods in history, had to see himself ignored and his advice repudiated. As a matter of fact, many even regarded Giacomo's visits as "bad diplomacy."[25] But Cardinal Rampolla del Tindaro had made him what he was. The fear of jeopardizing a possible career meant nothing to Giacomo if the alternative was to withhold gratitude and affection from an old man who had been severely hurt.

Monsignor Della Chiesa saw that little could be gained by open denunciation of the personnel of *La Sapinière*. Carefully organized, they would strike back secretly and insidiously. Even as Archbishop of Bologna, especially in the first years, he followed a course of reserve and veiled vigilance, a course which disappointed the people of his see. The newspaper sketches of Della Chiesa, printed when his appointment to Bologna was first announced, pointed to his apostolate among the students of Genoa during his own student days. Bologna, said the Catholic journalists, had long needed a learned and progressive bishop who would understand the problems of students at a secular university in united Italy. And there was truth in what they said. Cardinal Svampa, the congenial predecessor, had contented himself with uttering innocuous platitudes. However, when the eagerly awaited Archbishop arrived, and was invited to participate in youth rallies, he showed himself somewhat frigid and aloof. This attitude of cold reserve he maintained on purpose. He realized that *La Sapinière* was watching him continually, and that public addresses to organizations of this kind would offer special opportunities for misquotation and misrepresentation.[26]

On one occasion, however, the Archbishop's patience reached the breaking point. On December 2, 1913, a notice appeared in *L'Osservatore Romano* that certain newspapers like *Il Messagero Toscano* of Pisa, *Il Momento* in Turin, *Il Corriere d'Italia* in Rome, and *L'Avvenire d'Italia* in Bologna left much to be desired in measuring up to the norms laid down in a letter of Pius X to the bishops of Lombardy, July 1, 1911. The notice in *L'Osservatore* stated flatly that religious were not to read them without the written permission of their superiors. In normal times this would have been accepted as applying to the religious orders only, even though one might have felt that the matter would have been better handled through a letter to the superiors concerned. In that time of tension, however, a printed notice was not easily dismissed. Other papers at the request of *La Sapinière* began to beat the drums, with the result that scrupulous lay persons felt that the warning was at least indirectly meant for them, and thus a grave burden was laid upon the conscience of the public. One of the Catholic journalists brought the matter up in conversation with Cardinal De Lai, prefect of the Congregation of the Consistory, who promised to speak to the Supreme Pontiff about it when occasion arose. Archbishop Castelli of Fermo felt that a matter which was causing so much confusion could not wait. He visited the archbishops of the sees in which the accused newspapers were printed, and obtained from the editors a written expression of regret for having caused offense in the past and a promise to adhere firmly to the directives of the Holy See in the future. In an anonymously published article the four archbishops were attacked as having shown themselves especially credulous and gullible. The article said that Archbishop Castelli had entered the affair entirely on his own initiative, without any approval of the Holy See. Archbishop Della Chiesa was attacked with special venom because he had written the editor of *L'Avvenire d'Italia* of Bologna a letter of praise for his humble submission.[27] What the accusing integralists did not know was that on the very day that Archbishop Castelli had visited Bologna, Archbishop Della Chiesa had written to the Vatican demanding an unequivocal answer as to whether Castelli had approval for his action. The answer came that the Pope had personally approved the plan.

Archbishop Della Chiesa sent a copy of this letter to the little periodical which, in line with the usual tactics of certain members in *La Sapinière*, had attempted to sully his good name.[28] This flagrant disregard of the Pope's approval of a policy and the contumacious continuance of an opposite policy by *La Sapinière* clarifies what Cardinal Rampolla meant when he deplored the tactics of the integralists as "this lack of respect and of obedience to the Holy Father."

What judgment should be made concerning Monsignor Benigni? Father Schmidlin's verdict seems unduly harsh. After discussing *La Sapinière* he opens his treatment of Benigni with this sentence: "The soul and embodiment of this anti-modernistic and at the same time anti-reformatory conspiracy and organization was a fat little gentleman with a spying eye, a man in perpetual motion, the Italian prelate Benigni."[29] Elsewhere he refers to him as "the pious Judas."[30] The *Enciclopedia Cattolica* is more cautious in its judgment of Benigni: "It is entirely too early as yet, and too difficult to give a fair and definitive judgment on the multiplicity of aspects in his life and of the multiform and at times unclear activities."[31]

There are those who defend him. For example, a recent biographer of Saint Pius X writes:

He [Pius X] met its [Modernism's] cloak and dagger implications by the toleration and mild encouragement of an anti-modernist society known as the *Sodalitium Pianum*. This originally was directed by Monsignor Benigni and it functioned all over the Christian world. It too was a secret society. Its members were known only to each other and Monsignor Benigni. Their purpose was to ferret out and denounce to the Holy Office priests or students who wore any of the multiple masks of Modernism.

Benigni was a man of towering talent and devoted his entire energies in assisting Pius X in combatting the heresy. . . .

The truth of the matter is that Giuseppe Sarto *tolerated* the work of the *Sodalitium*. Benigni received a yearly stipend of a thousand lire, which was scarcely enough to pay for his paper and stamps. The secret machinations of Modernism had to be fought with an instrument capable of meeting surreptitious activities with its orthodox counterpart.[32]

In other words, Benigni's defenders say that since Modernism progressed in secret, it was only logical to fight it in kind. The charge of secrecy may, indeed, be true, but it is not true that Modernism was an organized movement. There was never any suggestion of a conspiracy. Modernists were always individualists and had sharply differing views.[33]

It is difficult to say how much Pius X knew about the methods of *La Sapinière*. He received its members annually and gave them praise and encouragement.[34] To his knowledge it was an organ of the Sacred Congregation of the Consistory under the prefectship of Cardinal De Lai, a learned and highly respected prelate, in whom the Pontiff had the greatest confidence. Cardinal Merry del Val, however, was better informed than the Pope, and when he realized the unrest which *La Sapinière* was causing, he suppressed *La Correspondance de Rome* in 1913.[35] When Benigni left the Vatican very suddenly in 1912, the *Postzeitung* of Augsburg — followed by the *Kölnische Volkszeitung* — launched a reckless campaign of calumny against him. They charged him with having betrayed the

confidence of the Vatican to the Russians and with being a Free-
mason. Merry del Val stanchly defended him and lodged an official
complaint against the newspaper through the bishop of Augsburg.
L'Osservatore Romano branded the attack so scurrilous as not to
merit an answer. In referring to these slanders a few days later,
Ludwig Pastor, who recorded the whole dispute in his diary,[36]
asked Pius X whether Benigni might not have been more prudent
in his polemics. The Pope did not say a word against Benigni* but
maintained that the newspapers were now getting their revenge
because of certain discoveries Benigni had made which were embarrassing to them.

While a criticism of integralism is easier today when the movement can be viewed in calm retrospect, contemporary criticism from
orthodox sources was not lacking. For example, an address by Archbishop Csernoch of Gran, primate of Hungary, was quite outspoken.
In the last year of Pius X's pontificate, Archbishop Csernoch addressed the General Assembly of the Society of Saint Stephen. After
stressing the necessity of Catholic leaders in the intellectual field,
the Archbishop continued:

> In the ardour of their work they may make mistakes, they may
> even have need of the friendly remonstrances of the competent eccle-
> siastical authorities, but they do not deserve to be treated with a
> pitiless criticism, and least of all a malevolent interpretation of their
> intentions from their brethren. They will have the strength to obey
> the maternal exhortations of the Church, and even in the observations
> that she will make to them they will see that their work is appreciated.
>
> By the *hateful* and *quarrelsome criticism* of their brethren, they may
> easily *be driven away from the field of their labours,* and thus *the
> Church is deprived of men of merit.*
>
> In these latter times, especially abroad, we have seen with the utmost
> pain the ravages made by criticism aimed directly against the most
> active Catholics and coming *from persons who claim to be not only
> Catholic but Integral-Catholic.*
>
> I should be profoundly distressed if I were obliged to conclude, from
> certain indications that have appeared that this Integral-Catholic
> criticism is about to begin its negative action in our country also. I

---

* Without any doubt Monsignor Benigni was "a man of towering talent."[37] His
scholarship was of extraordinary breadth. He contributed more articles to the
Catholic Encyclopedia than any other collaborator in that monumental work. His
articles are well written, and the matter is outstanding for its precise and logical
organization. With his activities in the *Sodalitium,* his newspaper work, his writing
for encyclopedias, he found time to write a *Social History of the Church,* the last
volume of which appeared in 1933. He died in Rome in 1934.

must seriously admonish the Catholics of our country that they should hold in high esteem those workers, already so numerous, who are labouring for the Catholic cause and that they should enthusiastically help them.

If faults are committed we must settle matters among ourselves. But let us *instead of seizing on an ill-chosen word or an unhappy phrase* remember the true lines of conduct of Catholic action and the intense work of Catholic life of these workers, and especially the good, the excellent fruits that have been derived from their work.

The Integral-Catholics do not stand for that — irresponsible as they are, *from under cover they spy out the workers to wound them in a moment of distraction with the shafts of criticism.* And yet these same workers are good, unwearying, noble men who have been impelled to action by the love of Christ and who are fighting against Christ's enemies.

A man is not showing himself Catholic, still less integrally Catholic, by displaying the zeal of a conspirator and arrogantly distinguishing himself in judging others and casting suspicion on them.

. . . Let us be on our guard, then, against any such action, and let us all be Catholics, children of the Church, affectionate brothers full of life and enthusiasm in action.[38]

With that admirable ability of the French mind for clarity of statement, Adrien Dansette has summarized the content of the critics of integralism by showing that the program involved a twofold danger, intellectual and tactical. The first danger is *intellectual* because (a) the impression is given that routine constitutes tradition; (b) the progress of science and of Catholic thought is impeded; (c) there is a refusal to separate pure doctrine from the commentaries of a bygone age which impose upon that doctrine conformity with the thought of a past epoch. The second danger is *tactical* because there is the tendency to keep the faithful enclosed in a walled tower against the world and to keep Catholic savants in a state of impasse so that they are forced to give up their intellectual pursuits, or what is worse, it presents the temptation of leaving the Church.[39]

The thread of the story of integralism will be resumed in the chapter outlining the first encyclical of Benedict XV, in which he expressed his mind on integralism with resolute firmness but without vindictiveness. Suffice it to say, that after the publication of *Ad Beatissimi*,[40] *La Sapinière* seems to have become inactive. Very quietly at Benedict's request the Congregation of the Council declared the *Sodalitium Pianum* defunct in December, 1921.[41]

CHAPTER VI

Archbishop of Bologna

ON THE morning of October 4, 1907, Monsignor Della Chiesa found himself in the office of Saint Pius X on routine business. He had always liked the relaxed atmosphere of an audience with the new Pontiff, so different from the cold protocol which governed all contacts with Leo XIII. Giacomo never felt that he was in an executive's office. The Pope's desk was littered with stacks of papers, letters, sketches of addresses, periodicals, newspapers, clippings — some of them yellow and brittle with age. On a ledge behind him were more papers, folio notebooks, books of reference and of the spiritual life. One always felt as though he had just entered the cluttered "lived-in" sanctum of some country village pastor. So often this pastor was smiling as if lost in some secret amusement. Giacomo had to concentrate on the white cassock to remember that he was in the presence of the Pope.

When the business of this morning was done, Pius groped about in the upper strata of his papers and found a newspaper folded in the usual small oblong packet. As he was shaking open the paper, he asked Giacomo with a smile: "Did you see *Il Messagero* today?" He handed the Italian daily to the Monsignor and with his well-rounded index finger pointed to a caption: *Decreto Vaticano,* under which the paper stated that on the preceding day Monsignor Giacomo Della Chiesa had been appointed Nuncio to Madrid. The appointment had been rumored for some time and would have been most welcome to Giacomo. He replied, however, that this unauthorized publicity annoyed him. Here the Pope interrupted, saying:

"I too am irked because I was going to ask a favor of Monsignor Della Chiesa."

"Just voice your command, Holy Father," said Giacomo. "It is not a question of favors on my part."

"Yes," replied the Pontiff, "you would be doing me a real kindness *(una carità)*. I know that Monsignor Della Chiesa will do well wherever he is sent. The Cardinal Secretary of State told me you

The Giuseppe Della Chiesa family. Giacomo is at the extreme left and Giulia at the right.

St. Pius X consecrates Giacomo Della Chiesa in the Sistine Chapel on December 22, 1907.

Della Chiesa at the
time of his consecra-
tion as Archbishop of
Bologna, December,
1907.

Della Chiesa as
Cardinal-Priest of
Quattro Coronati,
May, 1914.

Benedict XV in summer
mozzetta, about 1915.

Cardinal Rampolla, Giacomo's
patron and model.

would be an excellent nuncio at Madrid, but I have to think of the dioceses too; I want to have good bishops. I should like very much if Monsignor Della Chiesa would go to Bologna."

"Holy Father," said the Undersecretary of State, "I am overwhelmed by the kindness of Your Holiness, but, on the other hand, the difficult situation at Bologna just now is a terrifying thought to me. However, I am ready to do whatever Your Holiness commands."

"No," said the Pope once more. "I am not demanding absolute obedience. I am only expressing a desire and am asking whether you would not prefer the life of the sacred ministry which yields so many consolations."

"Oh, I have always felt inclined toward the active ministry to souls. But as to Bologna, the difficulty of the situation does frighten me. It was so far from my thoughts. I shall not hide the fact from Your Holiness that the Spanish ambassador hinted that Madrid would probably be my destination, but I surely never thought of Bologna. It just occurs to me that in Bologna at this very moment they are celebrating the feast of Saint Petronius, the titular saint of the cathedral. I really regard this as a good omen."

Saint Pius X thanked the bishop-elect with all sincerity and humility, then added a trifle mischievously, "I am sure that Cardinal Rampolla would be more than willing to do it, and Cardinal Merry del Val would certainly do it for his undersecretary. But no! The consecration of Monsignor Della Chiesa the Pope is reserving for himself."

This dialogue can be trusted as being practically a verbatim account. The very next day, while it was still fresh in his mind, Giacomo Della Chiesa, known for his prodigious memory, wrote it faithfully to his brother.[1]

The date of consecration should have been December 21, the feast of St. Thomas the Apostle. Since bishops are to be consecrated on the feasts of Apostles, a dispensation must be obtained if the rite is to take place on another day. Giacomo asked the Holy Father for a Sunday so that the Papal Curia would not have to sacrifice a working day. The consecration, therefore, took place on Sunday, December 22, in the Sistine Chapel. Coconsecrators with Saint Pius X were Archbishop Balestra of Cagliari and Bishop Valfré de Bonzo of Vercelli. Cardinals Rampolla, Gotti, Respighi, and Merry del Val were in special places to the right of the papal throne. Many bishops, monsignori, members of the diplomatic corps, and naturally members of Giacomo's family witnessed the memorable occasion. His mother, the "Little Marchesa," was not present in body, but, in the words of Pius X, "she watched from heaven."

The consecration Mass was a low Mass. The Sistine choir sang under the direction of Perosi. There is a photograph in existence showing the part of the ceremony in which the newly consecrated Bishop Della Chiesa sat on a faldstool before the altar, facing the congregation. He wore his miter and held his crosier. The picture alone would indicate why the world in its superficial judgment would forget Benedict XV and remember only his predecessor. Saint Pius X is standing before his throne on the Gospel side. Despite his seventy-one years, he retained a fine, robust figure. Giacomo sits on the edge of the faldstool looking very uncomfortable, as if his slippered feet are reaching the floor only with difficulty.[2]

Few newly consecrated bishops can boast of having had the pope at their consecration breakfasts. Giacomo had that distinction. Since under ordinary circumstances the pope must eat alone, a special table arrangement must be made when he eats with others. The table and chair of Pius X were somewhat more elevated than the rest. The new Archbishop sat on his right. The four cardinals were also present. In the afternoon the Pope received the members of Giacomo's family and the delegations from Genoa and Bologna in private audience.[3]

De Waal says that in his half century spent in Rome he never saw so many gifts. Among them was that of Saint Pius X, a crosier and ring. Merry del Val's was a chalice with statues on the base, rich in their symbolism.[4]

As was the case with Bishop Sarto, both at Mantua and Venice, there was an annoying delay in the execution of the *exsequatur*, a ratification of his appointment by the King of Italy. Since the application had been made in October, it was thought that January 8 could safely be set as the date for the installation. A postponement was made until January 28. When another delay ensued, no further date was set. At long last, on February 9, the document with the King's signature arrived.[5] De Waal surmises that Della Chiesa was *persona non grata* for no other reason than that he had been the understudy of the iron-willed Rampolla. On February 10, 1908, the Archbishop's pastoral letter left the Vatican. This document, like the first encyclical which he was to issue as supreme pontiff, could serve as a blueprint of action for himself — as a written pledge of what his people might expect of him.[6]

The new Archbishop explained that his appointment meant for him a radical change in his field of activity. God will help those whom He has chosen for a special task. He admits that he has begged God earnestly to inspire him to know what He wishes from him. God had deigned to infuse in him a sort of gentleness. Should he not show that to his charges? He quotes Saint Gregory the Great: "If you like being called father, then keep the name in honor and by your conduct carry out what it implies." His reference to Mary is touching: "O Virgin, if you blessed my cradle from the mount that adorns and crowns my first home, then, O Maria della Guardia, bless also from the hill which hovers above my second home, the new field of my activities, and, if all the other archbishops of Bologna always experienced your protection, grant it now in a very special manner to him who now joins their rank not only the last in point of time but in merit." This pastoral letter is striking because of its sentiments and style.[7]

Della Chiesa chose as his secretary Monsignor Migone, rector of the Genoese Church in Rome,[8] the archbishop of Genoa agreeing to release him out of deference to the new Archbishop of Bologna. Archbishop Della Chiesa was, from this time forward, always to have him at his side. On February 10, the day of departure, he worked in his office up to a few minutes before train time.[9] No one would deny that he was very conscientious about his duties in the Curia, but it is quite possible that this extraordinary diligence was his means of preventing an emotional breakdown. He had come to Rome thirty years before, and he knew and loved the ancient city. To leave it was not easy.[10]

The new Archbishop went first to Genoa, where the learned Columbus Society, of which he was a member, presented him with an episcopal ring. The next stop was Pegli where he administered the sacrament of confirmation for the first time.[11] On February 17, he arrived in Bologna and took solemn possession of his see on Sunday, February 23. Della Chiesa had sent 2000 lire to the religious houses for the aged poor, a considerable sum in those days of monetary stability. It was intended for a banquet, so that the poor might have some part in the festivities.[12]

The following morning the new Archbishop said Mass in the shrine of Our Lady of Protection on the hill, and afterward repaired to the cemetery to offer public prayers at the tomb of his predecessor, Cardinal Svampa.[13] Every day he visited schools and attended receptions of various organizations. At each gathering he gave an interesting and instructive address.[14]

The feast of Corpus Christi in 1908 marked the opening of Archbishop Della Chiesa's great project, the *Sacra Visita*, a canonical visitation of every parish in the archdiocese, which would take four years to complete.[15]

The visitation has a ritually fixed ceremony which is studied and rehearsed by the clergy, altar boys, and choir members in the respective parishes. Sacred vessels are regilded, sacristies are scrubbed, vestments are cleaned and mended. When the ceremonial part has been carried out with all solemnity, the parochial records of baptisms, marriages, and burials are inspected. The minutes of the trustees' meetings are read and countersigned.

In Bologna, as in other Italian sees, details prescribed by old statutes had been allowed to go unobserved because of a sustained lack of supervision. Cardinal Svampa, Archbishop Della Chiesa's immediate predecessor, had been a kindly, smiling old gentleman who relied upon the old saw: "Problems will solve themselves." However, in Monsignor Della Chiesa's many years of dealing with bishops from all over the world, he became ever more aware of the etymological root of what it meant to be a bishop (Greek, *episkopein* means "to supervise," "to be an overseer"). Without insinuating that Svampa was culpably responsible Giacomo felt that Bologna would not have fallen into its domestic difficulties had a stronger hand guided it. He knew too that the regal-looking and congenial Svampa would be hard to follow especially by one as ill-favored in stature and appearance as he was. Vistalli describes the situation well when he says: "When the people saw the official entry made under the canopy which had once welcomed the majestic, imposing figure of the eminent Cardinal Svampa, Della Chiesa's immediate predecessor, they did not appear to be fully satisfied. 'The eye did not get its money's worth.' "[16]

The new Archbishop had received his training at a desk under the indefatigable Rampolla, relentless with himself and his subordinates. Here, in the mountainous province of Bologna, much of which can be reached only on horseback, he would also drive himself relentlessly. Many a dangerous mountain path he would climb to visit some small village nestled about a little church.[17] And he in turn would impose this same spirit of work upon his clergy.

About his own person, his room, and his office Della Chiesa had been scrupulously neat and clean. In the pastoral letter announcing the visitation he made special mention of cleanliness which he wanted to see even more accentuated in the house of God. To be fair to the clergy, it should be said that most Italian churches are built of stone to keep out the summer heat. There is no central heating. Hence the moisture collects, and neither the sun nor furnace ever dries them out. The vestments used for every day, which unlike the festive *paramenta* are not put away in special covers, became dull and moist. Without our modern methods of dry cleaning, everything had a tendency to become moldy. Della Chiesa realized how easy it is, under these handicaps, for the clergy to fall into a groove and assume a defeatist attitude. He was going to be very thorough in his inspection. The tours were to be so arranged that he would not be absent from his chancery for more than ten days at a time. He had, however, provided for every eventuality in his absence. Upon his arrival he made the auxiliary bishop, Vincenzo Bacchi, his vicar-general. He ratified every action and pronouncement which his auxiliary made in his absence. A good ruler knows how to delegate authority and in a time of crisis to ratify the decisions of his deputies.

Besides the inspection of the church and the records already mentioned, he would ask pointed questions concerning the pastor's preaching, teaching of the Christian doctrine, and visiting of the sick. He would scan the pastor's bookshelves to see what theological, pastoral, and spiritual books were in his modest library.[18]

He insisted that no special cooking be done because of his visit not only to avoid unnecessary work, but also to enable himself to have the simple home-cooked food which he enjoyed. He wanted to spend the evening with the pastor at his hearth under the green-glass lamp shade — universal equipment in the clerical studies of Italy. He would lead the pastor into those channels of conversation about which the priest liked to talk, and thus he would form an accurate opinion of his character and ability.

It is a mistake to think that *Sacra Visita* primarily affected the pastor. Quite to the contrary, one day of the visit was to be regarded as a feast day for the parishioners. He requested that the people be prepared by a novena or triduum of special prayers. He himself said the community Mass and distributed Holy Communion. He also preached, trying to adapt his speech to the intellectual level of his audience. He announced that he would hear confessions during a certain period so that he could give any necessary absolution from reserved sins. He appeared on the parish property under the open sky so that anyone could meet and speak to him. On the last day there would be a dinner to which the neighboring clergy were invited. On this occasion, alone with his priests, he would throw off completely the stiffness and frostiness which ordinarily seemed so essential a part of his character. However, those priests who were foolish enough to think that his remarks were but idle chatter were quite mistaken. In a spirit of persiflage he would interweave some criticism so that soon the little Latin phrase, *ridendo docet* ("he teaches with a smile"), began to be applied to him by his clergy.[19]

An example of this is the following. One day, when the Archbishop was on a visitation tour, his car (which had been given him by the people of Bologna) rounded a bend with such speed that a young priest on a bicycle had all he could do to get out of the way of this metal monster without even a thought of avoiding being seen by the episcopal occupant. The rider saluted, smiled, and pedaled away. However, at this time there was an old diocesan statute forbidding priests to ride bicycles. At the dinner table of the rectory where the visitation was held, the pastor of this young priest was present. Suddenly directing the conversation to him, the Archbishop said, "Our auto almost collided with your assistant's bicycle."

"Yes," said the pastor. "I know. He was on his way to the Capuchin monastery where he makes his weekly confession."

"He looked very stately on a bicycle in all his priestly garb," said Della Chiesa, without a change of mien, "so much so, that if I were ever to relax the law, I would certainly have to cite your assistant as a model."[20]

At the conclusion of each visitation, the pastor was given a card on which the Archbishop had noted what stood in need of improvement. A copy of these notes was filed with the dean of the district. Two months later, the dean was to inspect the parish regarding these particular items and to report to the Archbishop whether they had been corrected. Archbishop Della Chiesa was pleasantly surprised at the conscientious spirit in which his mere suggestions were accepted; however, the priests appraised their Ordinary by means of a provincial proverb: "Upon the heels of the Father (Svampa) follows the master (Della Chiesa)."[21]

On December 13, 1913, he held a solemn *Te Deum* service in the cathedral to celebrate the completion of his personal visitation of 392 parishes, including the chapels, convents, schools, and hospitals connected with them.[22] So thorough and systematic a visitation was unique in the history of Italian sees.

Saint Pius X was so gracious as to send him a letter written in his own hand regarding his splendid work in the *Sacra Visita:*

> I congratulate you heartily on the completion of your strenuous pastoral visitation, and with the blessing that I am imparting with particular affection to you personally, to the clergy, and to the people of your archdiocese, I am happy to assure you that I am,
>
> Your most grateful,
> Pius Pp. X[23]

The many reforms which he set in motion and the specialized societies which he founded are too numerous to mention. For instance, although he had no ear for music and chanted the liturgical texts woefully,[24] he was insistent that Pius' famous *motu proprio, Tra le Sollecitudine,* be carried out to the letter.[25] Catechetics constituted another of his prime interests. From his own experience in catechizing in Santa Maria in Aquiro, while he was still a seminarian in Rome, he concluded that there was a serious necessity for a catechetical reader which would contain interesting collateral material to illustrate the terse, dry questions and answers of the catechism. At the same time, he considered the catechism absolutely necessary for precise formulation of the truths of faith. The reader which he sponsored was later adopted by other dioceses.[26] Annually he held a catechetical convention at which priests and catechists could exchange views and arrive at a uniform method for solving their common problems.

In 1910, he founded *Il Bolletino,* a monthly, which at the end of the year constituted a volume of about 500 pages. This periodical was inaugurated by the Archbishop himself who wrote the leading article in the first issue. His beautiful pastoral letters were published in it. When political matters needed clarification, the vigilant "overseer" was never lax in supplying an authentic interpretation. People waited for *Il Bolletino,* and in its pages found solutions to their perplexities.[27]

He influenced his flock to hold Saint Francis De Sales in high esteem and recommended him to every family as the saint who

would foster the word of God in their homes.[28] In the see of Bologna
he anticipated what Pius XI was to do for the universal Church,
when one year after Benedict's death, on January 26, 1923, he
declared Saint Francis De Sales patron of journalists and of the
Catholic press. Perhaps no pontiff ever had a successor who carried
out his every inclination with such fidelity as did Benedict's successor, Pius XI.

In his chancery office Archbishop Della Chiesa was courteous,
but brief and businesslike. Some of his priests resented this at first,
contrasting him with his predecessor, who prolonged every interview into a long amiable chat.[29] At times priests would forget that
their new Archbishop had behind him years of training in the capacity of *minutante*, and could not be beguiled from incontestable
facts by a barrage of affability. Some, for instance, would attempt
to maneuver him into giving them a written permission by insinuating that on a previous occasion, some months before, he had
promised the concession orally. In such a situation the volatile
temper of Della Chiesa would flare. He would leap up from his
desk and stand before his amazed visitor and reconstruct almost
word for word the dialogue of that previous meeting.[30] Cardinal
Rampolla's parting words to him had been, "You just go to Bologna
to be the archbishop, and tell everyone that you are the archbishop."
In cases like this his priests were not left in doubt as to who their
archbishop was.

To Bologna, too, Giacomo carried his great regard for punctuality. In the first year of his incumbency one of the older and
revered priests arrived several minutes after the time stipulated for
an appointment. When he entered the Archbishop's private office,
Della Chiesa rose to welcome him, smiled amiably, looked at his
watch, and said, "Evidently one of our watches does not keep accurate time. Undoubtedly it is mine." Then, with an allusion to the
theme never out of vogue in any age — that things are no longer
made as well as they were in the past — he took up the business on
which his visitor had come.[31] It was merely another instance of
ridendo docet.

The nonchurchgoing people in the politically seething city at first
regarded him with cool aloofness. Moreover, basing their judgment
on his unimposing figure, they drew a too hurried conclusion that
the new Archbishop would be quite without influence. When besides, they found that he confined himself to the internal and

strictly ecclesiastical affairs of his see, they breathed a sigh of complete tranquillity. Their judgment was correct only insofar as he did not compete for popular favor. However, whenever they encroached upon the rights of the Church, they found at once that they were dealing with an expert in the field of civil and canon law. In every altercation of this kind, they ended up by retreating, attempting to give the impression that their withdrawal was in accord with predetermined tactics. Soon they learned to move with extreme caution, for they could not risk any loss of prestige.[32]

As time went on, however, the attitude of the people changed. An appraisal of their estimation can be made from the following incident. One day, that very remarkable automobile of his collided with a streetcar. The impact was great, Monsignor De Waal assures us, and bystanders were certain that the accident would prove fatal to their Archbishop. However, without as much as a bruise, he emerged nimbly from the other side of the auto, and seeing a statue of Saint Anthony of Padua enshrined in a niche above a doorway, he uttered a public prayer of gratitude for the vigilant care accorded him by the Franciscan saint. All day, telegrams of sympathy poured into the chancery office. Such a crowd of people gathered outside his residence that he had to make a personal appearance in order to dispel the rumor that he had been injured. A little plaque commemorating the incident and expressing thanks to San Antonio was fixed beneath the niche.[33]

His love of ancient things found expression in the restoration of the old and forgotten churches of Bologna which were in a sad state of dilapidation.[34] The most beautiful church in the city is that of the Sacred Heart. It had been begun by Cardinal Svampa, who, true to his personality, had enthusiastically envisioned a majestic church but had not given much thought to the details of ornamentation. This was fortunate for Della Chiesa because it allowed his good taste to be exercised in the work of completing the church, the favorite project of his years in Bologna.[35] He dedicated it on October 15, 1912. From his own limited resources he donated the money for the mosaic of the Holy Redeemer above the main portal. He also arranged for the transfer of the remains of Cardinal Svampa from the cemetery to a richly wrought sarcophagus in the basilica itself. This was his own idea and shows his usual delicacy and respect for the deceased.[36]

The building of the new seminary was also a project which interested him keenly. The old diocesan seminary was on a busy thoroughfare. Cardinal Svampa had long felt that the noise and distractions of the city were not conducive to the quiet and study so essential to the life of the aspirant to the priesthood. The good, serene Cardinal bequeathed the problem to his successor. The Holy See gave Archbishop Della Chiesa permission to build, and authorized this seminary to be the *Seminario regionale per la Romagna,* i.e., a seminary for all the neighboring sees also. On November 5, 1912, he laid the cornerstone.[37] For its dedication, however, he could not be present because he was already "the prisoner of the Vatican." But the new seminary remained close to his heart, and on the very day of his election to the papacy amid the hundreds of minutiae which he alone could settle, he asked how much there was in the Vatican's treasury for charitable disbursements. He wanted his expression of love toward Bologna to take the tangible form of a gift to his beloved seminary.[38]

Not long after his arrival in Bologna he made changes in the seminary curriculum by increasing the number of courses in jurisprudence and canon law. He presided at the oral examinations and learned the name and appraised the personality of every student for his diocese. He spoke to them so freely and intimately that he became acquainted with their intellectual interests and avocations. When a seminarian became so ill as to be hospitalized, the Archbishop was among the patient's first visitors.[39]

The aspirants to the priesthood were not the only recipients of the Archbishop's attention. The diocese of Bologna had a hospice for retired priests, whom he visited frequently. They had generously spent their strength in the service of the diocese and deserved the gratitude of their bishop. He pontificated there twice a year, on the feast of St. Vincent de Paul and on the feast of St. Augustine to whom the adjoining church was dedicated.[40]

In a pastoral letter dated April 28, 1913, he invited the people of his diocese on a pilgrimage to Loreto. Six hundred responded, thrilled at the thought that their Archbishop would lead the pilgrimage and be their companion on the trip.[41] However, just before the determined date, the Archbishop was alerted by a message from the Vatican that Saint Pius X was very ill. To his great disappointment and that of his flock he could not accompany the pilgrimage that he had organized to pray for the ailing Pope. He organized another which was to go to Lourdes on August 5. On this journey he was able to go. He had inherited Cardinal Rampolla's love for France and he enjoyed his visit to the full. En route the train stopped at Tarbes. Monsignor Migone and the Archbishop's nephew, Giuseppe Della Chiesa, stepped out on the platform for a cup of coffee. A shabby old lady stood on the platform and kept on chattering: "Is it true that the future pope is on this train? Is it true . . . ?"[42] On September 3, 1914, Giuseppe Migone and Giuseppe Della Chiesa were to remember her.

Saint Pius X had been criticized because he had never set foot out of Italy. *Extra Italiam nulla est vita* ("Outside of Italy there is no life") was a quip coined about him in parody of *Extra ecclesiam nulla est salus* ("Outside of the Church there is no salvation"). In fact, Saint Pius X always felt extremely sorry for Italians who decided to emigrate.[43] This could never be said of Della Chiesa. He always had some vague hope of seeing the Western Hemisphere, especially Mexico, but that dream was never to be realized.[44]

Archbishop Della Chiesa, who had spent over thirty years of his adult life in Rome and who loved every stone in it, went to the Eternal City but seldom. He obtained a dispensation from making even the required *ad limina* visit.[45] In November, 1908, he did preach in the Church of San Agostino in Rome, but the invitation had been accepted over a year before — before his appointment to Bologna.[46] Some interpreted this abstention from the City as a sign of injured feelings at his sudden transfer. Vistalli interprets it as an indication of his rigid sense of duty.[47] Whatever his reason, he was in fact following the example of Saint Pius X. When the latter was bishop of Mantua, he had gone to Rome but once after taking possession of his see. That was when the Holy Father, Leo XIII, personally invited him to be present for his golden jubilee as a bishop and silver jubilee as Pope.[48] One of his biographers called Saint Pius X a rigorous observer of the law of residence.[49]

One might think that Della Chiesa would have sought opportunities to visit his friend and prototype, Cardinal Rampolla. In reality, he did see the Cardinal repeatedly, but it was Cardinal Rampolla who came to Bologna. After being relieved as secretary of state, the Cardinal went every summer to the Benedictine Monastery of Ensiedeln in Switzerland where he became enamored of the library so rich in documents pertaining to the history of the medieval Church. Rampolla, who had never permitted himself a vacation while in the employ of Leo XIII, now combined research with the enjoyment of Switzerland's scenic beauties.[50] He arranged his journey so that he would pass through Bologna where the train would halt for several hours during the night. Advised beforehand as to the time of arrival, the Archbishop would board the train and visit with his old friend until the railway switching operations were completed. When Rampolla passed through Bologna in 1911, the Archbishop expressed concern that his friend was not looking well. The Cardinal closed his tired eyes and said, "I desire to be dissolved and to be with Christ" (Phil. 1:23).

"Oh, no, no, no!" interjected Della Chiesa. "Do not say that, Your Eminence, your health is precious to the Church!"

"Very well," said the sharp-witted Cardinal. "If Saint Paul does not please you, allow me to speak in Saint Augustine's words: 'Yea, Lord, let me die that I may see You; I desire to die that I may see Christ; I am willing to forego living so that I may live with Christ.' "

Durante closes the incident with his own comment which is justified indeed: "What a sublime and holy conversation between two persons whom some chose to identify with the sarcastic term, the *Politician Prelates*."[51]

When Della Chiesa was in Rome, he did indeed hurry first to the *Palazzina di Santa Marta* to visit Rampolla. In the summer of 1913 when the illness of Saint Pius X summoned him to the Eternal City, he found the "prelate with the eyes of fire" in excellent health, poring over books on archaeology and immersed in his many other interests. In December the seventy-year-old Cardinal suffered a slight indisposition which was attributed to the winter weather and was expected to disappear in a day or two. The end came so suddenly that in Rome, proverbially said to teem with priests, one was found with difficulty, and he arrived just in time to administer the last sacraments.[52] Rampolla died on December 16, 1913.

Archbishop Della Chiesa was notified and left for Rome at once. Many passed by the bier in the *Palazzino* but no one knelt there so long and wept so bitterly as he. The Cardinal had not forgotten his beloved disciple. He bequeathed to him his vast collection of precious medals and decorations which had come to him in his long diplomatic service. Many of these were collector's items.[53] Like his model, Archbishop Della Chiesa always said Mass with the greatest possible devotion and recollection, but those who saw him at the altar next to the bier of his old friend will never forget his tear-stained face and choked voice.[54]

CHAPTER VII

The Cardinal

THE diocese of Bologna is a so-called cardinalitial see. From time immemorial its archbishops have been cardinals. As a matter of fact, notice of elevation to the Sacred College has in some instances accompanied the bull of appointment as archbishop of this see. While this was not the case when Giacomo was appointed, it was felt that he would be nominated at the very next consistory. Seven years later, however, in 1914, the little Archbishop was still in his purple robes instead of the expected scarlet. Venice, Milan, Florence, Naples, Genoa, all had the prestige of a cardinal's coat of arms, but Bologna looked like the stepchild of the Holy See. This slight appeared to come to it only with the appointment of Archbishop Della Chiesa.

At Rome, at least, the blame was laid at the door of the Cardinal Secretary of State, Cardinal Merry del Val.[1] Outside of Rome the same suspicion was rife. Canon William Barry, in his beautiful obituary article on Benedict XV's death insinuated that his not having become a cardinal was without precedent. He closed the passage with the words, "Why his promotion to the cardinal's title of Quattro Coronati was delayed until May 25, 1914, the general public has never learned."[2] That Merry del Val and Della Chiesa disagreed sharply on integralism was no secret to their contemporaries. Shane Leslie, however, writing in the present day, deserves commendation for having injected humor into the situation, thus taking the sting out of the bitter truth. He relates the story in such a way that Merry del Val does not appear as the scheming manipulator pictured by the secular press of his day, but rather as the *cooperator non obstans,* that is, the man in theological terminology, who sees a course of events rushing on to a certain evil but does nothing to impede the wrong from taking place. And so Shane Leslie writes: "Gasquet's Cardinalate was a matter of tremendous congratulation from Merry del Val, who prided himself on having pointed out the merits of the abbot to Pius X. In the same batch was Cardinal Della Chiesa, whose merits *poor Merry had signally failed to point out to the Holy See on successive occasions.*"[3]

Many thought that as long as Cardinal Rampolla was isolated and placed "in cold storage," as De Waal picturesquely describes the situation, there was no fear of a return of the liberal policies of Leo XIII. Should Della Chiesa be made a cardinal, it was felt, these two would form a nucleus impeding the program of the pontificate. However, Cardinal Rampolla died on December 16, 1913.

Among the anecdotes which biographers of Pius X relate in order to exemplify the Pontiff's ready wit, there is one which tells of a delegation which suggested that "a certain ecclesiastic" receive the red hat. Saint Pius smiled and answered, "You know, of course, that I am a tailor and not a hatter." The Italian word for tailor is *Sarto* — the family name of the Pope.[4] According to Monsignor De Waal, that "certain ecclesiastic" was Giacomo Della Chiesa, the Archbishop of Bologna.[5]

Francis MacNutt, who for many years had been a papal chamberlain on active duty, after his departure from Rome kept himself *au courant* of events in the Pope's *anticamera*. He avers that a delegation from Bologna importuned Saint Pius to make Della Chiesa a cardinal.

> Astonishment gave way among the Bolognese to indignation, and the general resentment at the inexplicable slight offered their city and province resulted in a group of representative citizens appearing before Pius X, to whom they more or less baldly declared that if Archbishop Della Chiesa was not worthy to be a member of the sacred college, neither was he worthy to be Archbishop of Bologna; either he should receive the Hat, or he should be transferred elsewhere.[6]

In the spring of 1914, Saint Pius rose before his assembled cardinals of the Curia and read the names of those whom he meant to raise to the cardinalate. The list from which he read was written in the flowing hand of his secretary of state, Merry del Val, except for one name — that of Giacomo Della Chiesa. This had been written in between others by the Pontiff himself.[7]

Late in April, the Cardinal Secretary of State informed Archbishop Della Chiesa of the Holy Father's intent. The date for the consistory was set for May 25, 1914, the feast of Saint Gregory VII. Cardinal-designate Della Chiesa arrived in Rome several days before the determined date and sought lodging at his favorite home in

Rome, the Academy of Noble Ecclesiastics.[8] Monsignor De Waal reports that the newly named Cardinal had brought with him a picture of Cardinal Rampolla, which had the place of honor on his table. The incident furnishes an interesting insight into the character of Della Chiesa. His loyalty was peerless.

Giacomo had missed Rome more than anyone could realize.[9] He walked the old familiar streets and renewed old memories. He paid a visit to *Palazzo Brazza* where he had lived so contentedly with his mother. Strangers now occupied the apartment, but he called on the caretaker who had a small cobbler's shop off the main courtyard. Giacomo noted how much the man had aged. He ordered two pairs of cardinal's slippers. This made the old cobbler so happy that he reached for his leather and thread immediately, shouting to all passers-by of his great commission.[10]

On May 25, the Pope met with the cardinals where he had two amazing revelations to make. The first was the appointment as patriarch of Lisbon of Antonius Mendez Bello whom he had created cardinal *in pectore* (in his heart) almost three years before, in the consistory of November 27, 1911, but had not proclaimed. This Archbishop was living in exile from his see and Saint Pius X did not wish to aggravate the bitter relationship between Portugal and the Holy See by announcing the elevation of Mendez Bello in 1911.[11] The second amazing revelation was the announcement of the new *Camerlengo*, that is, the cardinal who rules the Church between the death of the pope and the election of the new pontiff. It is a very important position, and supreme pontiffs select the *Camerlengo* with great care. For example, Leo XIII, as Cardinal Pecci, had been the *Camerlengo* of Pius IX. Pius XII, as Cardinal Pacelli, was the *Camerlengo* appointed by Pius XI. The newspapers had taken for granted that the office would go to Merry del Val. Cardinal Della Volpe, however, was appointed.

The newspapers meanwhile continued their unkind speculation as to why the red hat had been so long in coming to Della Chiesa. The editor of *Rome* printed a vindication of the Vatican's procrastination in the case:

Not only during the last six months but during the last six years the name of Mgr. Della Chiesa has been before the public as a probable cardinal, and various weird explanations have been given by baffled prognosticators for the failure of their horoscope. The explanation in reality is simple enough. Mgr. Della Chiesa who was born at

Pegli in the diocese of Genoa on November 21st, 1854, and ordained to the priesthood in 1878 . . . received a noted promotion when on December 16th, 1907, Pius X appointed him to be archbishop of the important see of Bologna. Less than seven years of prudent administration there have won for him a place in the sacred college. He will not be sixty years of age until next November, which is about the average age for cardinalitial "creations."[12]

The explanation is edifying but unconvincing, especially in the light of the fact that the same Pontiff had created Merry del Val a cardinal at the age of thirty-seven years and that in the very consistory in which Della Chiesa was made a cardinal, Archbishop Piffl of Vienna was elevated at the age of forty-nine.

Now the Pope began to read the list of the new cardinals; including the cardinal *in petto* there were fourteen. Then the rich voice of Pius X asked, *"Quid vobis videtur?"* The cardinals raised their scarlet zucchettos as a sign of acquiescence. The *biglietti* of nomination were handed to the secretary of the *Cancelleria* who accompanied the secretary of Cardinal Merry del Val to the various places where the newly appointed cardinals were in residence. This part is, of course, mere ceremony. The new cardinals had known for a month about their elevation, but only now did they receive their official appointment. In response to the *biglietto* read to him, Cardinal-designate Della Chiesa gave one of the most moving speeches of his career:

Although the official notification of the highest dignity to which the Holy Father has wished to elevate me, was made to me a month ago, and consequently does not come as a surprise to me, my heart is nevertheless both oppressed and exhilarated. I feel oppressed because I do not find in myself the merits which the august honor of cardinal presupposes. I feel oppressed because I did not render to the Church those remarkable services for which the honored scarlet is a recompense. On the other hand, I am joyful when I reflect that lack of merit in a person as negligible as I am, has been covered over by the goodness of the Holy Father. This illustrious pontiff has already given me so many proofs of his paternal beneficence, whether it was that he himself with his anointed hands imparted to me the fullness of the priesthood, whether it was that almost daily by multiple proofs of encouragement he sought to strengthen me in the rule of the diocese which he had entrusted to me. But today he has reached the zenith in paternal favors by elevating me to the highest ecclesiastical dignity. To him is due gratitude, to him is due an expression of my filial reverence, to him is due my promise to dedicate myself with the greatest zeal, with all my strength to the service of the Church and the salvation of the souls whom he has entrusted to me.[13]

On May 28, the new cardinals received their red hats at a public consistory in the Hall of Beatifications. They then repaired to the Sistine Chapel where they prostrated themselves and covered their heads with the cappa. The dean of the Sacred College recited the prayer *Super creatos Cardinales*.

After this ceremony the Pope met them in secret consistory, and closed their mouths in an impressive ceremony signifying the secrets which they would have to guard, the greatest of which would be those of the conclave. This secrecy would put no great burden on the taciturn Della Chiesa. In a second ritual gesture their mouths were again opened to signify the counsel that they would be asked to give the Pope in the government of the Church. Like the seventy elders whom God commanded Moses to appoint as advisers, the college of seventy was to be prepared to give counsel to the Holy Father. Finally he placed on the finger of each a sapphire ring and assigned the titular churches.

In choosing a church for Cardinal Della Chiesa, Pope Pius again showed his kindness. He gave him the Church of Santi Quattro Coronati. This ancient house of worship had been in the news just before the consistory, for in February its complete restoration had been completed under Antonio Munez.[14] The thoughtfulness of the Holy Father in assigning this particular church to the Archbishop of Bologna is manifested in the fact that he kept in mind Della Chiesa's love for things ancient.

Giacomo made a private visit to his church, confident that he knew it well from his many visits in the past. He was amazed, however, at the extent and thoroughness of the restoration. A convent of cloistered Augustinian nuns is adjacent to the church. He always made it a point to show himself especially amiable to nuns, and so he decided to pay them a visit. At the end of the visit, they asked as a favor to be permitted to leave their enclosure so as to attend the Pontifical High Mass at which he would take possession of his church. The answer of the otherwise so congenial prelate was abrupt and startling: "No, no, no! Stay inside, because by going out, one always runs the risk of losing."[15] The nuns were manifestly disappointed. Had Della Chiesa been one to court public applause, what a reputation for benignity he could have built up for himself by giving a mere nod of assent. But daily reader of the *Imitation of Christ* that he was, in Thomas à Kempis' powerful chapter, *Of the Love of Solitude and Silence* he had read: "In thy chamber thou shalt find what abroad thou shalt too often lose. . . . What canst thou see elsewhere which thou canst not see here?"[16] On June 4, he took solemn possession of Quattro Coronati. On June 10, he took leave of Saint Pius X in an audience which was to be his last.

The following day he began his journey back to Bologna. On the fourteenth of June there was a magnificent reception for him at home. The people had collected 26,000 lire for an automobile to replace that unpredictable vehicle which had been at the Archbishop's disposal previously. After the purchase of the car, there was a considerable amount left over. Della Chiesa ordered a festive meal to be prepared at the various convents of the city to which the poor were to be invited without discrimination.

After the festivities the Cardinal resumed his routine as though no change had taken place in his rank. He continued to get along on incredibly little sleep. Time and again, when the servant came in the morning to tidy his room, he found that the bed had not been slept in. A tall stack of envelopes neatly addressed, stamped, and ready to be posted told the tale. Della Chiesa seemed to enjoy writing letters and usually he did not relegate this task to secretaries.

Normally he rose at 5. Then he would say his morning prayers, the "Little Hours" of the Breviary, make his meditation, a preparation for Mass, celebrate Mass, and make a thanksgiving of twenty minutes. At 7 he would appear in the dining room for the standard continental breakfast of *Caffé-Latte,* a hard roll, and unsalted butter.

At his office he would spend the morning in correspondence and appointments. At 1:30 he would have a frugal dinner after which he would repair to a common sitting room and browse through the newspapers while he chatted with the priests who shared the house with him. Then he would ride by horse-drawn carriage or by auto to a church in Bologna where the Blessed Sacrament was exposed. The Bolognese churches at that time had the practice of rotating so that a different church would have public exposition every day. The Cardinal wanted this Holy Hour to be a private practice of his own, even though each church had a special prie-dieu prepared for his visit. In this daily devotion one can again detect the example of Rampolla. On his return to his residence his hand went out to his breviary for the recitation of Vespers and Compline. Then he would resume work in his office which meant correspondence on details of chancery, study for addresses and sermons, recitation of Matins and Lauds.

At 8:30 he recited the rosary with the members of his household. Immediately upon this followed the evening meal, after which a period of conversation over papers and periodicals in the community room ensued. Then he withdrew to his rooms for leisurely reading or letters to relatives and acquaintances.[17]

On June 28, 1914, about two weeks after his return to Bologna, Cardinal Della Chiesa read of the assassination of Francis Ferdinand, the nephew of Emperor Franz Josef of Austria, at Sarajevo. Knowing the feelings of the Austrian people as he did, he realized that this would ignite the tinder which had been waiting for a stray spark. On July 28 Austria declared war on Serbia. On August 1 Germany declared war on Russia, and on August 3 on France. On August 4 England declared war on Germany just as the German troops were crossing and violating neutral Belgium.

Saint Pius X took most grievously the thought that he had to live to see the beginnings of this carnage. His health declined so rapidly that in two weeks his rugged resistance was gone. The most authentic and, because it is so unembellished, the most impressive account of Saint Pius' death is found in the memoirs of Cardinal Merry del Val, his dearest son in Christ. He writes that he visited the Pope in his bedroom at about 10 o'clock on the last night that he had the gift of speech, and "The moment he saw me he clasped my hand firmly. 'Eminenza! . . . Eminenza! . . .' was all he said."[18] On the eve of the Pontiff's death, the Cardinal Secretary of State made a very late visit to the sickroom, thinking as everyone else did that the Pope was unconscious. But he said that the piercing look followed him as he tiptoed around the bed. He writes:

> . . . when I sat down quite near to him, he seized my hand and held it in his grasp with a vigour that astonished me. He then gazed intently at me and his eyes were riveted on mine. How I longed to read his thoughts at that moment and to hear his voice whilst we looked so steadfastly at each other! What was it he was endeavoring to convey in those eyes that seemed to speak?[19]

CHAPTER VIII

The Conclave

ON AUGUST 20, 1914, black-bordered newspapers carried the somber headline: *Pio X e morto!* Two days later Cardinal Della Chiesa left Bologna to assist at the funeral of Pius X and to participate in the conclave where a cardinal exercises his chief privilege, that of electing the new supreme pontiff. A priest from Cardinal Della Chiesa's native Genoa, who happened to be at the railroad station, reminded Giacomo that one of his predecessors in the see of Bologna, Prospero Lambertini, had departed for a conclave from which he emerged as Benedict XIV. By changing the punctuation in the often sung versicle, *Prospere procede, et regna* ("Proceed prosperously and reign!"), the priest called after Giacomo, *"Prospere, procede et regna!"* He had turned the adverb *prospere* into the Christian name of the famous archbishop of Bologna of some two centuries before. The versicle by allusion now said: "Prospero, go forth and reign!"[1]

"Very good, very good," replied Della Chiesa in appreciation of the word play, "but the trouble is, my name is Giacomo and not Prospero."[2]

A prelate from the diocese piously, if somewhat tritely, hoped that the Holy Spirit would alight upon the Cardinal of Bologna. To this the latter replied drily that he hoped the Spirit Dove would flutter on His way and allow him to return to Bologna as quickly as possible to continue the projects which he had begun.[3]

It is unfortunate that Giacomo Della Chiesa was of so reticent a nature. It would be interesting to know what his thoughts were on the journey from Bologna to Rome. That he felt some anxiety can be gathered from a stray sentence in a letter which he dashed off to his brother before departing. Among a few personal remarks concerning himself and the family, he injected this sentence: "A conclave is always a riddle."[4]

At the station in Rome an ecclesiastical functionary with whom he had once been associated made the foolish and sycophantic mistake of attempting to kiss Della Chiesa's toe. To this careful student of protocol and lover of the Church's ritual any parody of ceremonies was offensive. The habitually melancholy smile twisted and became wry. He withered the jester with a remark which stung all the more because it savored of pity for the man's patently bad taste.[5]

Until the opening of the conclave he again stayed at the Academy of Noble Ecclesiastics[6] where thirty-five years before he had made his beginnings as a lodger preparing for his comprehensive examinations preliminary to the doctorate in canon law. He was once more in the heart of Rome. As he emerged from the *Academia,* he saw in front of it that strange papal monument of the patient-looking elephant bearing an obelisk on its back. How silently and patiently had the Papacy borne its burden since 1870. Close by was the *Palazzo Brazza* where his beloved mother had lived. Around the corner was the Church of San Eustachio, at whose altar he had offered his daily Mass, from whose pulpit he had preached, and in whose choir stalls he had made many an inspiring and comforting meditation.

In the Chapel of the Blessed Sacrament in Saint Peter's, he paid his respects at the slanting bier of the deceased Pontiff, Saint Pius X, looking regal even in death as his white silky hair protruded from under his huge renaissance miter. He was present daily in the choir for the *Novemdiales,* liturgical services celebrated for nine days in succession. He was present for the *tumulatio* or final deposition of the deceased Pontiff in the three coffins. He saw the face of Merry del Val, Archpresbyter of Saint Peter's, distorted with grief. He heard his otherwise so sonorous voice choked by tears as he tried to chant: *Requiescat in Pace!* He saw him bend down quickly and impulsively to kiss the final resting place of his saintly friend.[7]

At this time the college of cardinals numbered sixty-five. Only fifty-seven were able to participate in the conclave. Two were absent because of illness. The others could not come because of age or distance.[8] Cardinals Gibbons, O'Connell, and Begin of the Western Hemisphere arrived at Naples just in time to be informed that the election had already taken place. It was on this occasion that Cardinal Gibbons, when told that Della Chiesa was the new pope, innocently asked the question which since has made history: "Who's he?"[9] Cardinal O'Connell was disappointed, but he was doomed to disappointment once more eight years later when again he arrived too late. The papal bull *Ubi Periculum* issued by Gregory X in 1274 fixed the opening of the conclave ten days after the demise of the Supreme Pontiff. It was Pius XI who was to arrange that the intervening time be lengthened. Cardinal O'Connell lived to be present at the conclave which elected Pius XII.

The word *conclave* is Italian *con clave* (with key) and it means a room or rather a body of men in a room locked with a key. Immediately after the death of a pope temporary partitions are erected throughout the halls and offices of the Vatican to house the cardinals, their secretaries and chamberlains, other officials and servants, all of whom are designated by the generic word "conclavists." Over two hundred rooms must be provided.

The rooms are assigned by lot. The apartment of Cardinal Della Chiesa was number 57, the *Ufficio delle opere di religione*, and he was to use the stairs of the *Cortile di San Damaso*. Number 57, incidentally, was the same cell occupied by Giuseppe Sarto in the conclave of 1903.[10] As his secretary he chose Monsignor Giuseppe Migone and as his chamberlain, Mariano Faggiani.

It would indeed be interesting to have some record of the thoughts of this silent man as he left the Kingdom of Italy and entered the portals of the Vatican for the last time, even though the finality of his crossing this threshold was certainly unknown to him. His many years of service to Cardinal Rampolla had made him acquainted with every inch of the patchwork of rooms and corridors which make the *Palazzo Vaticano* the venerable labyrinth that it is. Undoubtedly there were heartaches as ill-defined and fleeting memories impinged upon him from all sides. Anyone who has been promoted with dubious honor and transferred from a place without suitable explanation, has had that chill of sorrow mingled with the joy of recognition when he revisits those sites of his past activities.

On Monday morning, August 31, the holy Sacrifice of the Mass was offered by Cardinal Ferrata in the Pauline Chapel. Monsignor Aurelius Galli[11] of the secretariat of Latin letters delivered an address to the assembled princes of the Church in which he praised the late Pontiff and impressed upon the cardinals the gravity of the task before them. In this period of political upheaval, he said, the pope to be elected must be a man of superior intelligence, of *savoir-faire*, of holiness of life, but above all he must be one who excels in Christian charity great enough to embrace both Jesus Christ and the whole Church of Christ. If they should find a man with the first-mentioned qualities but not possessing the charity just described, they were to deem him not worthy of this high office.[12]

At 5:30 that evening, the cardinals assembled for their first session. Since Saint Pius X stringently enforced the previously enjoined but ill-kept silence on what occurs in the conclave,[13] the veracity of the anecdotes concerning the various ballotings in the conclave of 1914 cannot be guaranteed. In fact, they disagree on many points. For example, Schmidlin says that in the final vote, fifty-five ballots went to the Archbishop of Bologna.[14] Seldes writes: "Della Chiesa was elected on the final ballot with the formidable vote of fifty out of fifty-seven participants."[15] Count Sforza says that Benedict obtained "exactly two-thirds of the votes required for his election."[16] And Father Humphrey T. J. Johnson, writing in 1954, says, "Della Chiesa was elected on the morning of September 3rd, receiving thirty-nine votes, or one more than the two-thirds required for a valid election."[17] Therefore, it is futile to attempt a weighing of the data.

Except for one offhand, jocose remark made by Benedict on the day of his election, which will be recounted presently, he is said never to have spoken about the votes and discussions relative to the conclave of 1914.[18]

Count Sforza relates this anecdote, a verification of which seems useless to undertake: After the last ballot on Wednesday night Della Chiesa had received precisely two thirds of the vote, just enough to elect. Someone insolently objected that Della Chiesa must have voted for himself. Gregory XV had ruled that in order to preserve the dignity of the pontificate, no elector may ever vote for himself. If a cardinal should do so, the whole balloting must be regarded as invalid.

In the morning the balloting was resumed. Cardinal Della Chiesa was one of the tellers and it fell to his lot to read the names. His rather high-pitched voice read the name of each candidate and voter slowly, calmly, and distinctly as though it were his task to read a bulletin which had reference to some person who concerned him only very remotely. After the balloting was ended and the ballots had been pierced with the needle and red silk thread, Della Chiesa rose impassively, walked with dignity to his throne, and waited imperturbably for the homage of the Apostolic College. In other words, he had gone to bed the night before, thoroughly aware of the fact that he was the new pope, for he knew that he had not voted for himself.[19]

Perhaps the incident is only a legend. But it is the peculiar genius of legend to epitomize a trait of character and to impress it with uncanny vehemence. In this case the attribute is Della Chiesa's control over his emotions acquired by long practice in the best tradition of the school of diplomacy where men learn to control the tone of the voice and all facial expression so as not to betray any inner agitation.

On the other hand, in favor of the truth of Count Sforza's story is the remark made on the day of the election by Benedict to the delegation from Bologna. This delegation consisted of friends who spoke very freely to their former bishop even though he had become the supreme pontiff. They mentioned that while they were standing on Saint Peter's Square a report had leaked out of the Vatican that a pope had been elected.

Leaks of information of this kind are strictly forbidden. From time immemorial the Vatican has had its own way of announcing the election of a pope. In the sacristy of the Sistine Chapel a stove is set up which connects with a metal chimney temporarily erected which rises high above the roof of the Vatican so that its smoke can easily be seen from the square before the basilica. The ballots are burned after the scrutinies, and if no majority is reached, wet straw is added to create a heavy black smoke. If a majority is reached, the ballots are burned without the straw, and the result is a thin white smoke.

The people from Bologna mentioned that they had doubted the rumor rampant in Saint Peter's Square because for a long time there was no smoke forthcoming, though at long last the white smoke did appear over the Vatican.

"Oh you waited, did you?" asked Benedict briskly. "They had to open my ballot to see for whom I had cast my vote. As a matter of fact, I voted for Cardinal Serafini."[20]

Incidentally, in his apostolic constitution of December 8, 1945, *Vacantis Apostolicae Sedis*,[21] Pius XII rendered impossible the situation described in Count Sforza's rumor by requiring for election a two-thirds majority plus one vote.

In the past, where there was a bare two-thirds majority, the vote of the cardinal who received that number had to be checked. Hence each voting paper had to contain the name of the voter and a distinguishing number. The extra one vote will obviate the possibility of such an awkward situation.[22]

From Pius XII's wording it seems legitimate to conclude that he is not speaking of a merely hypothetical case.

Pius XII imposed even greater safeguards of secrecy than those proposed by Saint Pius X in his constitution, *Sede Vacante,* which was published to prevent a repetition of the scandal of the infamous veto against Rampolla which took place in the conclave of 1903.

> For greater security, after each double ballot not only the voting papers, but whatever notes the cardinals make about the voting, will be burned. It has happened in the past that such notes found among cardinals' papers after their deaths, have revealed details of the voting in a conclave.[23]

The circumstance which occasioned this latter part of the decree is well known. When Cardinal La Fontaine, patriarch of Venice, died, among his books and papers were found pieces of scratch paper bearing his jottings made during the fourteen ballotings of the conclave of 1922. The Cardinal's heirs sold these notations to the *Paris-Soir.*[24]

When Cardinal Della Chiesa was asked whether he would accept, he replied tersely that though he was aware of his unworthiness and lack of certain abilities, he felt it his duty to yield to the wishes of his colleagues.[25] The other cardinals lowered their baldachins which up to now had all been raised as a sign of equality. At last only one canopy remained horizontal — over the small huddled figure of Giacomo Della Chiesa. The next step in the ceremony was to ask what name he would choose. It has always been interesting to hear the reasons for the choice, and for the press this statement always has great human-interest value. For example, Saint Pius X had said: "Well, the popes who have suffered most for the Church in this age have had the name of Pius, and I too shall take that name."[26] Pius XI[27] and Pius XII[28] made long statements explaining their choice.

But to the question of the Cardinal Dean *"Quomodo vis vocari?"* ("How do you wish to be called?") Della Chiesa's answer was terse and clear: *"Benedictus Decimus Quintus!"*[29] Then his lips closed again without one syllable of elucidation. Everyone was amazed at the divergence from tradition in the selection of the name.[30] In view of his training and of his tendencies, it was expected that he would call himself after Leo XIII. Others saw something in him analogous to Gregory the Great.[31] It was the first time in 140 years that a pontiff had not selected the name of Leo, Gregory, or Pius.[32]

It had always been assumed that the newly elected Pope chose the name of Benedict in honor of Benedict XIV, that is, Prospero Lambertini, the last archbishop of Bologna to be elected pope.[33] However, information has come to light which attributes a different reason for the choice of the name. On September 20, 1914, Benedict XV received in audience Abbot Fidelis von Stotzingen, the primate of the Benedictines, who expressed the hope that the new Pope would reserve for himself the protectorate of the Benedictines as his predecessor, Saint Pius X, had done. The Holy Father replied that he would gladly do this because of the special devotion to Saint Benedict which he had entertained ever since childhood. He added that in fact he had chosen the name of Benedict in order to win "the new world for Christ through the intercession of Saint Benedict."[34]

The new Pontiff was next conducted to the sacristy where three white cassocks — large, medium, and small — were in readiness. For Benedict even the smallest was much too large. The sleeves were so long that his finger tips barely extended beyond the cuffs, and the small shoulder cape looked huge and ungainly on the very narrow and unevenly sloping shoulders.

Monsignor Migone, who in a sense had always looked upon himself as the protector of his somewhat pathetic and misunderstood patron, could not grasp the truth that this man had suddenly become supreme pontiff. When the realization struck him fully, he was so moved that he saw all the cardinals and bishops through a blur of tears. He was to help in pinning the superfluous cloth into place. Tears, however, so obscured his vision, that he dropped pins and fumbled and almost fainted.

"Come now, come," said Benedict through a smile of simulated petulance. "One would think you had been elected pope, and not I."[35] This remark was typical of the way in which he put the ministers of the Mass at ease during pontifical functions. He had the ready faculty of dissipating nervous tension through kind humor or smiling irony. Even though he had a fiery temper, like all men of moral greatness, he never exhibited bumptiousness when blunders were made by the timorous or nervous.

Assisting in the robing of the new Pope was the aged Vatican tailor. He had been there when Giacomo was a mere apprentice in the secretariat of state. The old gentleman was buzzing about with tape measure in his hands and pins in his mouth. The new Pope turned toward him and with a feigned look of disappointment asked, "My dear, had you forgotten me?"[36] The next day, however, when the tailor reappeared with a cassock made to fit Benedict's irregular form, he had recovered his aplomb. As he helped the Pontiff into the fine new cassock, he kept saying with overwhelming self-assurance: "O Holy Father, I never had any doubt about it. I knew all along that you would be the next pope."

Benedict, who was never very sympathetic with idle chatter, answered dryly, "Well, if you were so sure of that, you should have made a cassock to fit me."[37] This conclusion was indeed irrefutable because of its cold logic.

A chair was set before the Gospel side of the altar in the Sistine Chapel and Benedict XV sat there to receive the second mark of obeisance from the cardinals. In the ceremony, each cardinal approaches, kneels, kisses first a cross embroidered on the toe of the pope's slipper, then kisses his hand to express absolute submission, and finally receives the so-called *accolade* in which the cheeks of pope and cardinal meet. One can but wonder what thoughts crossed the minds of the intransigents, as their lips touched the slippered toe of him who to them had never seemed quite "integral." He is said to have remarked with a smile to one expression of congratulation, "And We assure you that the Holy Father is not a Modernist."[38] Eight years later when the cardinals were to listen to the eulogy which Pacifico Masella was to preach over the mitered Benedict, wan in death, the startling text was from Isaias: "See how the men that once despised thee worship the steps of thy feet."[39]

There are unpleasant anecdotes concerning the first meeting of Benedict XV and Cardinal Merry del Val[40] — not one of them traceable to an eyewitness! On the contrary, one fact at least indicates that only the most cordial relations existed between Benedict and the former Secretary of State. When the turn came for Merry del Val to make his obeisance to the new Pontiff, he asked for two favors: first, would His Holiness be so kind as to make the nephew of the deceased pope, Monsignor Giovanni Battista Parolin, a canon in the chapter of Saint Peter's? Merry del Val explained that he

had asked Saint Pius X repeatedly to give his nephew this honor
but the Pope had always refused for fear of being accused of
partiality or nepotism. Second, would His Holiness continue the
small pension which the former Pontiff had granted to his sisters?
The Cardinal explained that this was simple justice because of the
many years of sacrifice that these sisters had borne for their
brother who all the days of his life had spent himself and his substance for the Church. Benedict XV not only granted the request
but quintupled the amount of the pension. That night *L'Osservatore
Romano* carried but two announcements. The first was the factual
statement that Giacomo Della Chiesa had been elected supreme pontiff and had taken the name of Benedict. The second item stated that
His Holiness had graciously appointed Monsignor Parolin to the
office of canon in the Basilica of Saint Peter.[41] The humility of the
request and the promptness and graciousness of the response surely
do not allow one to infer any breach of Christian charity. Giuseppe
Dalla Torre, who knew Benedict intimately, characterized him in
two vigorous Italian phrases: *"Incapace di rancore, dimentico di
ogni offesa"* ("Incapable of rancor, forgetful of every offense").[42]

By now the populace had seen the puff of white smoke coming
from a little pipe protruding from the roof of the Vatican. A tapestry
had been lowered over the balcony on the façade of Saint Peter's
Basilica. Della Volpe, preceded by the processional cross and accompanied by other dignitaries, appeared and announced the result
of the election. No one can appreciate the excitement of this scene
if he has not been in the square for the election of a pope. Unlike most ceremonies which act out an ancient drama the plot
of which we have known from our infancy, this ceremony, despite
all its punctilious compliance with tradition, always possesses the
element of sovereign surprise. *"Annuntio vobis gaudium magnum"*
("I announce a great joy to you"), said the voice of Della Volpe
loudly, slowly, and distinctly, *"Habemus Papam Eminentissimum
et Reverendissimum Cardinalem Dominum Iacobum Della Chiesa
qui sibi nomen imposuit Benedictum XV"* ("We have as pope the
Most Eminent and Most Reverend Lord Cardinal Giacomo Della
Chiesa who has selected the name Benedict XV").

Instantly the happy, ebullient Italian temperament broke loose
amid the thousands in the square. *"Eviva il Papa, eviva Benedetto!"*
were the hoarse cries which could be sifted out of the general
jubilation. During a momentary lull, someone cried out: "He is the

one Rampolla obtained for us by his intercession with God!"[43] To restore order, a motion for silence was given, and from the balcony was intoned: *"Te Deum laudamus!"* From thousands of throats in those musical vowels which only the Italians can graft on to the ancient Latin, the hymn was taken up: *Te Dominum confitemur....*

The Cardinal *Camerlengo* had slipped the Fisherman's ring on Benedict's finger, the most distinctive sign of his authority until death. At that time it would be removed from his stilled hand and ceremoniously broken between anvil and mallet. Benedict did not deem the time ripe as yet for the imparting of his first apostolic benediction *Urbi et orbi* from the balcony which really protruded over territory considered outside the Vatican. Achille Ratti was to be the first to resume that step in 1922. When the *Te Deum* reached its culmination in that tremendous *finale,* "In Thee, Lord, have I hoped, let me not be confounded forever," the faithful streamed through the portals of the Basilica to receive Benedict's first blessing.

And now the bells in every campanile began to ring. First the tremendous bell on Saint Peter's boomed forth its message. It was contagious. The bells in the *Trastevere* section took it up; San Luigi dei Francesi tried to imitate it with its smaller bells; San Eustachio — Benedict's favorite church — did its part; the Church of San Andrea, of Santa Maria in Aquiro, of San Ignazio, of the other three major basilicas, and the countless others began to make their din. They all attempted to talk at once, breaking in on one another. The bells surged one into the other like stormy winds into the sea. At last Benedict's composure began to melt. As he stood vested in crimson mozzetta and red stole, the tears were streaming down his cheeks.[44]

He proceeded to the *Sala della Benedizione,* a long hall above the vestibule of Saint Peter's. To the right is the door which leads to an inner balcony of the Basilica. After the people were in the enormous church, they saw on the balcony Benedict XV, now Vicar of Jesus Christ, Bishop of Rome, Successor of Saint Peter, Supreme Pontiff of the Universal Church, Patriarch of the West, Primate of Italy, Archbishop and Metropolitan of the Province of Rome, Supreme Steward of the Temporal Possessions of the Holy Roman Church.

"Sit nomen Domini benedictum!" rang out strongly and clearly. *"Ex hoc nunc et usque in saeculum!"* responded the mighty

throng. Finally the hands spread as though to gather up as many of God's gifts as possible and he began to chant — perhaps not according to the traditional notation since he sang so badly — *"Benedictio Dei omnipotentis Patris et Filii et Spiritus Sancti, descendat super vos et maneat semper!"*

The mighty *Amen* from the multitude was an unmistakable symbol of the joyous acclaim which came to Benedict from all Christians, now his children in a unique way.

Unlike the end of the conclave which elected Pius X there are no homely stories about Benedict XV sitting in his cell that night, reading his breviary like a weary pastor after a hard day's work, yet anxious to have a chat with a visitor. There is no denying the fact that with the accession of Benedict XV something romantically simple and homespun had left the Vatican. Within two hours after the election, with his brisk, limping gait, Benedict XV had combed all the offices of his immediate domain. Vercesi says that the new Pope wandered about the halls of the Vatican within the very first hour, *"come se fosse stato Papa da anni"* ("as if he had been pope for years").[45]

CHAPTER IX

Coronation and First Acts

BENEDICT's blessing ended the ceremonies of the conclave. The new Pope wished to get the pressing work of his pontificate under way and he began work at once. As the veteran Vatican reporter, Camille Cianfarra, remarked, "Benedict walked about as though he were in his family home ten minutes after his election."[1] He interrupted the chain of details calling for his attention only when he heard that a group of people from Bologna were waiting to see him. Even though he was thrilled because of his sudden unexpected elevation which was the vindication *par excellence* of his rejection seven years before, he was struck with the full realization that the consoling contact with the good people of Bologna was forever a thing of the past.

To prevent an emotional breadown, he tried unsuccessfully to enliven the occasion with a witticism. In the front line of the delegation he saw a lawyer from Bologna who had been his legal counselor in every weighty decision he had to make. "You see, my friend," he said with an attempt at gaiety, "they decided to make me pope, and for once I did something without seeking your advice. I accepted."[2] During the course of the audience, as he made his farewell to individuals, the tears welled up in his eyes, and he could not speak.

So many things claimed the new Pontiff's attention that he had no time to think of food on that first day. Suddenly, late in the evening — Romans eat their dinner around nine o'clock — he thought of his secretary. He called an attendant and said, "See that Monsignor Migone will be served a good dinner . . ."; then he paused as his face became meditative and somewhat sad — "because the pope eats alone," he concluded. It had come to him suddenly that from now on he would have to be governed by protocol, and the camaraderie at the table, which he had enjoyed so much, would cease. No dinner would be *good,* as it had been in the past with cheerful friends about him.[3]

When he finally reached his apartment, which was the room he had occupied during the conclave, he wrote in his own hand the messages to the various heads of government so that in the morning the secretaries had only to transcribe them on the official stationery.[4]

The coronation was to take place on the following Sunday. Benedict did not choose to have the ceremony in Saint Peter's as Saint Pius X had done. He wished to be crowned where Leo XIII had received the tiara, in the Sistine Chapel. Benedict felt that a magnificent ceremony in the mighty basilica would seem out of tune with the miseries of war.

Sunday morning, September 6, was warm and clear. Although the ceremony was not to begin until 9:30, priests, seminarians, brothers, nuns, and lay people thronged toward the "Bronze Door" as early as 6 o'clock. The Swiss Guards and the Vatican police pushed the people back; but like water rushing through a breaking dam, they walked around the police, bracing themselves against the portals. No one without a ticket, the so-called *Biglietto Personale,* was to be admitted. These tickets are gay-colored sheets of paper, measuring about six by eight inches. Very few of the rank and file possessed these, but they were interested only in standing room along one of the many halls. All they wanted was a glimpse of the new *Santo Padre.* They wanted to see the man whom seven years before they had seen hurrying back and forth between the Church of San Eustachio to the Vatican. How would he, whom they remembered as the thin little priest with the slight limp, officiate as pope?

Those who were able to find standing room in the *Sala Ducale* (Ducal Hall) could see the beginning of the procession. At one end of this hall there are four steps, at the base of which rested the *sedia gestatoria,* a large platform on which is fastened a chair upholstered in red plush.

At 8:30 the first part of the procession emerged. First marched the Swiss Guards, then the heads of the various religious orders, then the confessors of Saint Peter's with their penitential rods protruding from bouquets of flowers. After them came the priests, canons, monsignori, and the papal cross surrounded by seven prelates carrying lighted candles. Next walked two deacons and two subdeacons, one of each rank clad in Greek vestments because, after the Epistle and the Gospel are chanted in Latin by a sacred minister of the Latin rite, they are repeated in Greek by an ecclesias-

Benedict XV
in winter mozzetta
and camauro.

— Felici

Benedict XV in
mozzetta and
pontifical stole.

— Felici

Benedict XV in Vatican Gardens with his brother, Admiral Giovanni Della Chiesa, victim of a stroke, 1918.

Cardinal Merry del Val,
Secretary of State to Pius X.

— FELICI

Monseigneur

Parmi les lettres de condoléances que j'ai reçues à l'occasion de la mort du regretté Cardinal Rampolla, celle que Votre Grandeur a bien voulu m'adresser le 23 Décembre a eu pour moi un cachet tout particulier. Ce n'est pas parce qu'elle venait de si loin; c'est parce qu'elle réveillait dans mon âme le souvenir de ce que tant de fois j'avais entendu de la de A. La Grandeur
Mgr. Ireland archevêque de
Saint Paul

First page of a letter written by Archbishop Della Chiesa, acknowledging a letter of sympathy sent by Archbishop John Ireland of St. Paul.

Bronze effigy of Benedict lying in state on his tomb in the Vatican grottoes, gift of the people of Bologna. It is the work of Giulio Barbarieri.

— FELICI

Monument in St. Peter's by Pietro Canonica. In the background the various types of warfare are depicted.

tic of Oriental rite. After them marched the patriarchs, archbishops, bishops, and abbots, altogether about sixty, all wearing linen miters. The cardinals followed, their rich red cassocks standing in vivid contrast to their white jeweled copes.

An American reporter, Robert Garland, a Protestant, makes special mention of Cardinal Gibbons, calling attention to "his sweet kindly face in profound repose, his eyes gazing straight ahead to where the candles in the Sistine Chapel flickered beyond a screen of gold."[5] Finally Pope Benedict arrived, and with majestic gravity seated himself upon the chair. "As the *Sedia Gestatoria* was lifted shoulder high," writes Garland, "a shout such as we had never heard before arose, a mighty roar, piling sound upon sound, the high-pitched voices of women mingling with the deeper ones of the men, forming one huge crashing chord of human tones."[6] Sixteen men carried the Pope. Over him was a canopy undulating gently at each step of its bearers. On each side of the chair were the *flabelli*, two great fans of ostrich feathers like those which are borne by the slaves of Oriental monarchs in order to keep flies and gnats away from the countenances of their august masters. Of all this grandeur H. V. Morton, who was present, wrote: "There was not one meaningless thing in all this rich display. There was not one piece of embroidery that had not been pinned in position by Time."[7]

By standing on tiptoe, the faithful could see Benedict. He looked very small in the large red chair. The thin face moved slowly from side to side, and the two extended fingers and the folded thumb traced the sign of salvation slowly, solemnly, and impressively. Benedict's blue-veined face had something otherworldly about it. He saw all; yet his eyes seemed to focus on nothing here before him. He represented Christ, and this was his Palm Sunday; beyond it, he looked ahead to his Calvary. Like St. Peter he was making a symbolic entry into Rome, where he too would die on Vatican Hill, misunderstood by his own generation. The large Renaissance miter, almost onerously studded with jewels, was too large for the small, thin face beneath it, and he interrupted his blessings repeatedly in order to adjust it.[8]

The procession passed into the *Sala Regia* (Royal Hall), and from there into the Pauline Chapel. Here the platform was set down, and Benedict entered to make a visit to his Saviour in the Holy Eucharist, for many years his Life and his Consolation. The canonical hour of None was recited on the throne prepared. As the procession resumed its course, a plate was set before the eyes of the Pope. On it some flax soaked in oil was ignited. There was a sudden flare of light, then a moment later only a string of greasy smoke was left to remind the bystanders that they had seen a bright light. A prelate now approached Benedict and chanted as if in taunt, *"Pater Sancte, sic transit gloria mundi!"* ("Holy Father, thus the glory of this world passes!") For his short reign and the inexplicable oblivion into which he fell the symbol was cruelly apt.

In front of Michelangelo's awesome "Last Judgment," the papal Mass followed. In this Mass the liturgist sees traces of the pristine Roman rite before it was colored by so-called Gallican influence. Before the Communion, after having given the kiss of peace, the pope leaves the altar and goes to the throne. He kneels at a prie-dieu while the subdeacon brings him the Sacred Host, and the deacon hands him the chalice with the Precious Blood, which he consumes through a golden tube.

The Mass of Coronation with all its special ceremonies constitutes perhaps the most complicated function in the Roman rite. Yet, the new Pontiff needed no direction from Monsignor D'Amico, the pontifical master of ceremonies. With downcast eyes he stood, knelt, and sat. He knew just what to do, though with his usual delicacy he waited courteously for the nod from the master of ceremonies. Many expressed amazement, asking when he had found time to study these details.[9]

After the Mass, the Cardinal Deacon placed the tiara upon the head of Benedict and said:

> Receive this tiara adorned with three crowns, and know thyself to be the Ruler of the World, the Father of Princes and Kings, the earthly Vicar of Jesus Christ our Savior.

After the ceremony, in the *Aula Paramentorum* (Hall of the Vestments), before the sacred ministers took their leave, Cardinal Agliardi, subdean of the Sacred College, stepped forward and wished Benedict the wisdom of Leo the Great, the fortitude of Gregory VII, the nobility, sagacity, and prudence of Leo XIII, and the magnanimous and paternal heart of Saint Pius X. The Cardinal reminded the Pope that one of his greatest predecessors, Benedict XIV, whose name he had chosen, had contributed greatly to the development of canon law. The representative of the Apostolic

College therefore expressed the wish that Benedict XV would soon publish the new code of canon law begun by his predecessor. He ended his address with the solemn sentence, *"Da nobis codicem!"* ("Give us the Code!")[10]

When the ceremonies were over, work began in earnest. On September 8, two days after the coronation, Benedict released his first message to the Church. It began with these words: "When first we were called to the Chair of Saint Peter, knowing very well how unequal We are to so great a task, We bowed most respectfully to the secret design of an all-seeing God Who had raised the lowliness of Our person to such sublimity of dignity." From his lofty vantage point, he went on to say, he saw Europe torn by war and blushing with the freshly shed blood of Christians. Before he would address his bishops in an encyclical, as is the custom of the Roman pontiffs at the beginning of their pontificate, Benedict preferred to recapture the last words of his "very holy predecessor, worthy of immortal memory, Pius X." The last utterance of the dying Pontiff heard during this war's first clash of arms, Benedict pointed out, wonderfully expressed his predecessor's apostolic solicitude and love for the human race. Benedict did not quote this last message verbatim. He took for granted that it would be vividly alive in the memory of all. The papers of that era had described the impressive occasion when the brokenhearted, white-haired figure had stood before an assembly of Austrian soldiers, pleading in a voice quavering with emotion for prayers that God would guide the heads of government to "think thoughts of peace and not of affliction."[11]

The Latinity and delicacy of expression in Benedict's first exhortation, entitled *Ubi Primum*,[12] are superb. Its words throb with a disciple's reverence for a saintly master. Despite the gentle wording of the new Pontiff's first message, it is no mere composite of laudatory phrases. Someone has pointed out that even this short statement carries the language of a strong-willed man and a trace of that light satire so characteristic of him, when, for example, he asked "the rulers of the peoples *to be satisfied with the ruin already wrought.*"[13]

It is said that on the very day of his election Benedict had already determined on the changes or "shake-up" in Vatican personnel.[14] As is customary, Merry del Val, secretary of state under Saint Pius X, tendered his resignation.[15] To succeed him Benedict chose Domenico Cardinal Ferrata, whom the Pontiff had known for many years, and with whom he looked forward to a happy association and friendship. Born at Gradoli in Umbria in 1847, Ferrata had held important diplomatic positions under Leo XIII and Pius X. He had been nuncio to Brussels and to Paris. Leo XIII had created him cardinal in 1896. Pius X sent him as his legate to the Eucharistic Congress in Malta and made him secretary of the Holy Office to succeed Cardinal Rampolla. As rector of the Academy of Noble Ecclesiastics, Ferrata had learned to know Giacomo Della Chiesa more intimately; and the two, for a short time, had that pleasant camaraderie enjoyed by faculty members of the same institution which renders institutional life more agreeable in the absence of certain consolations connected with parochial life.

However, Divine Providence "in its secret designs," as Benedict was wont to say, did not will that he should be associated with his friend for any length of time. The Cardinal had just time to resolve unfinished business in the Holy Office when he was stricken with a severe illness that was diagnosed as appendicitis. The physicians thought it unwise to perform surgery. Peritonitis set in, and on October 10, 1914, he died. So short was his term of office in the secretariat of state that in the *Acta Apostolicae Sedis* not a single document emanating from the secretariat bears his signature.

Within three days after Ferrata's death Benedict had already named a new secretary of state. This time it was Pietro Gasparri, who had been placed in charge of the codification of canon law by Saint Pius X. When, on October 13, 1914, the announcement of Gasparri's appointment was made public and the fact of his close collaboration with Rampolla was recalled, wags began to chant *"Rampolli di Rampolla"* ("Rampollas from Rampolla").[16] It was an illusion to words in the Nicene Creed, *Deum de Deo, lumen de lumine* (God of God, light of light). The remark, not meant to be irreverent, reflects a certain mentality. There were those who had convinced themselves that under Benedict there would be a complete return to the policies of Cardinal Rampolla and Leo XIII. And at first sight it did seem as though they might be right. But in one respect, at least, Benedict broke a long tradition in this appointment because Gasparri, unlike his predecessors, had never attended the Academy of Noble Ecclesiastics. Even though a man could become pope without having attended the academy, it was unthinkable that one should rise to the highest office in the specialized field of Vatican diplomacy without the training of that school.

The death of Ferrata was a severe blow to Benedict. It is undoubtedly true that the Church's role in World War I would have been different had Ferrata been secretary of state throughout the whole of Benedict's pontificate. The Pope himself might never have taken over the reins so completely as he did with Gasparri. Several considerations point to this judgment. For one thing, Ferrata was seven years older than Benedict, and had the secretary lived, Benedict would undoubtedly have shown deference to him because of his age and experience. Then too, the diplomatic posts, such as that of nuncio to Paris, which Ferrata had held, had been frought with delicate implications and had entailed great responsibilities. This experience would have caused Benedict to concede in matters in which his own opinions differed from those of Ferrata. That Ferrata was aggressive and ambitious seems to have been no secret at that time. Pius X with a twinkle in his eye had once told Ludwig Pastor that he was aware that Cardinal Ferrata would not be adverse to succeeding him in the apostolic chair.[17] In retrospect today one can see the hand of Providence. God did not want a pope in that era who would enter the verbal battlefield but He wanted the vicar of His Son to speak the language of His Son and cry without ceasing, "Peace, peace, peace!"[18]

Cardinal Gasparri, Ferrata's successor, in appearance at least, did not agree with the conventional picture of the polished diplomat. Ferrata had had a certain ascetical cast to his person — a faraway look, a calmness of demeanor, a chin tilted slightly upward — indicative of a man spending himself for those whom he serves and being a living observation tower ever on the lookout for his master. The new Secretary of State, on the other hand, though of medium height, was so rotund that he gave the impression of being very short. His obesity was accompanied by a certain joviality and *bon-vivant* manner.

Pietro Gasparri, the son of a sheep raiser, was born in 1852, in the Umbrian hills, on what in the United States would be called a sheep ranch. He had a remarkably keen intellect and a great capacity for work. Successively he obtained a professor's chair in sacramental theology at the Apollinaris, in canon law at the Propaganda, and later at the famed *Institut Catholique* in Paris. In 1898 Leo XIII called him from his beloved books, bade Cardinal Rampolla consecrate him titular bishop of Caesarea, and then sent him as apostolic delegate to Peru. On his return from this mission, he was appointed secretary of the Congregation of Extraordinary Affairs. Saint Pius X at the beginning of his pontificate had wisely placed him in charge of the codification of canon law.

A clique of noble-born and aristocratic functionaries, disdainful of his humble origin and unpretentious manner, secretly dubbed him *Il Pecoraro* (sheep tender).[19] He knew of this but did not allow it to disturb his equanimity; for what Gasparri lacked in *finesse* he made up in genuineness of character. His methods of maintaining a secretariat of state were most unsystematic. His acuteness of mind and faculty for arriving at the heart of a problem almost instantaneously eliminated intermediary eyes and hands. The accouterments of a modern office with perforated cards, intercommunication systems, and other gadgets would only have confused Gasparri. His offices as well as his living quarters had a homelike, "lived-in" appearance. About half a dozen parrots which he had learned to cherish in his years in South America played no small part in his daily routine. Their shrieks, echoing his preoccupied mutterings, at times gave a clue to what he was planning. When the persecution of the Church was raging in Mexico, a visitor heard the parrots shouting, *"Non praevalebunt, non praevalebunt!"* ("They shall not prevail, they shall not prevail!")[20]

Unlike Rampolla, who, as has been pointed out, tried at times to force the hand of Leo XIII, Gasparri did not tell Benedict what course to follow. His title was secretary of state and that was what he preferred to remain, a subordinate who carried out policies, not one who dictated them.[21] He was first mate in the boat of Peter. The Pope alone was the captain who was ultimately responsible. If Gasparri wrote letters to the press or to officials of other countries and made definite statements, calling them expressions of the Holy Father's thought, that was precisely what they were. Protocol at times demanded that a letter should come from the secretariat, not from the desk of His Holiness himself. In such cases, if the letter was likely to contain something which would have far-reaching repercussions, a draft was first sketched by Benedict and then handed to Gasparri with instructions that it was to appear above the latter's signature.

Cardinal Merry del Val, the former secretary of state, was appointed secretary of the Holy Office, the very position which Pius

X had assigned to his own predecessor's secretary of state, Rampolla.

Monsignor Nicola Canali, the intimate friend of Merry del Val, who had succeeded Giacomo Della Chiesa as *Sostituto* in the secretariat of state, was appointed secretary of the Congregation of Ceremonies.

Monsignor Federico Tedeschini became *Sostituto* in place of Canali.

Sanz de Samper was transferred from the position of secretary of the Congregation of Ceremonies to that of *Maestro di Camera* (master of the chamber) of His Holiness.

Monsignor Vittorio Amedeo Ranuzzi de'Bianchi continued as *Maggiordomo* of His Holiness.

Luigi Misciatelli continued as prefect of the apostolic palace.

Monsignor Camillo Caccia-Dominioni, Monsignor Alberto Arborio Mella di Sant' Elia, Monsignor Rudolf Gerlach, and Monsignor Giuseppi Migone were appointed *Camerieri Segreti Partecipanti*, that is, papal chamberlains on active duty.

There were other transfers but the names mentioned here are of special interest because their bearers played important roles in the history of the Vatican in that era. Some, like Ranuzzi de'Bianchi, were created cardinals by Benedict; others like Tedeschini, Canali, and Caccia-Dominioni were admitted to the apostolic college by his successor, Pius XI.

There is an unconfirmed rumor that the deceased Saint Pius X appeared to Benedict several times within the first two weeks after his election. According to the rumor — and it should be emphasized that it is only hearsay — the white figure of Saint Pius X did not speak or concern himself with the presence of his successor, but walked with calm dignity as though going from one routine task to another. If for a moment we assume the story to be true, we may ask what the message was. We know that one of the two public occasions when Benedict's voice was choked with tears was that in which he spoke of his saintly predecessor.[22] There is no doubt that Benedict prayed to him for guidance. Was the answer to his prayer a wordless message like the unspoken revelations only symbolically enacted in the visions of the prophets? If Saint Pius X meant that his *Filius devictissimus* (most obedient son), as he was wont to call him in his letters, would best spend the days of his pontificate by an unostentatious performance of his daily routine, the celestial advice was fulfilled to the letter.

CHAPTER X

The Human Benedict

DURING the pontificate of Saint Pius X, the title, "Holy Father," had created in men's imaginations the well-defined picture of a fatherly man with a moderately corpulent frame and a heavy head of snow-white hair. The personal appearance of the new Pope would also be of great interest to visitors. Descriptions of him in his pre-cardinal days had not been very complimentary; most of them spoke of his emaciation, the raised shoulder, and the crooked face. Now that he was pope, his white cassock seemed to have conferred on him something almost charismatic. His crisp cleanliness and neatness soon became the subject of comment by all who saw him. Spotless French cuffs extend neatly from the cassock sleeves on every picture that shows his hand raised in blessing. His cassock never showed a stain; his sash, his chain and pectoral cross — everything about him — possessed almost military symmetry and correctness.[1]

Cardinal Baudrillart, rector of the *Institut Catholique* in Paris, gives us the following reminiscence concerning Pope Benedict:

> The first time I saw him, I was struck by a certain inborn distinction which characterized him, by his elegant manners, by the vivacity of his intelligence. Small, very alert and hard working — six hours of sleep were enough for him — he was endowed with a prodigious memory so that he invariably recognized people even if he had met them but once. I can still see the glint of his scrutinizing glance from behind the golden rims of his glasses and the glossy blackness of his hair which made him look very young.[2]

Benedict's neatness of dress was but one indication of the precision which characterized his whole life. Once when the well-known sculptor, Raffaele Romanelli, was commissioned to execute two busts of Benedict, Monsignor Misciatelli, prefect of the apostolic palace, following the precedent of previous popes, allowed the artist a place in the papal study while the Pontiff was working at his desk. However, when Benedict arrived in his study, he turned to

94

the sculptor and said with a gracious smile, "I am at your service, but only on the condition that you leave at ten minutes to four."

Romanelli, who had considerable experience in reading human features, has left us a verbal impression of what he saw while he worked:

> The pope has a very interesting head, somewhat reminiscent of the head of Niccolo da Uzanno sculptored by Donatelli or the head of Fra Girolamo Savonarola. The Pontiff's head radiates lively intelligence. The forehead is spacious but somewhat compressed at the temples. The skull is round with plenty of room for the brain. These are characteristics of a serene and well-balanced mind. The nose is aquiline, the eyebrows deep and well designed, bringing out the splendor of the eyes which are not large but very bright and very piercing. They are somewhat shortsighted and are usually hidden behind thick glasses, but the glances which at times are seen to come darting over the lenses reveal an intelligence which is clear and quick. The mouth is large but well chiseled in sure and vigorous lines, indicating chiefly a firmness of resolve. The chin is prominent as is seen in the classic types of Caesar or Napoleon. These linear characteristics undergo strange changes under various physiognomical combinations which are sudden and frequent because of the nervous, almost restless temperament of the Pontiff.[3]

Benedict's candor in advising the distinguished artist of the precise moment he was expected to withdraw from the papal presence is an indication of the new order in the Vatican.

One day, as Benedict was about to perform some official act, one of his advisers expressed doubt as to whether there was a precedent for the course he was intending to take. The Pope insisted there was, and asked whether his monitor had searched the archives thoroughly. The Pontiff sent the ecclesiastic to the secretariat of state, told him which cabinet drawer to open, and instructed him under what category he would find the schedule filed. Benedict added sharply, "It must be there." A few minutes later the amazed priest returned with the schedule showing that a previous pope had done the very thing which Benedict was contemplating. It must be noted that it was at least a decade since Benedict had been employed in the secretariat, and he had had no opportunity since that time to see the files where this documents was kept.[4]

The easy going family spirit which had colored life in the Vatican under Saint Pius X had disappeared. Never having been a pastor,

Benedict had never enjoyed the consolations of a parish priest. Since the death of his mother, he had led a very lonely life. Excellently versed in the strictest traditions of Vatican protocol, he realized that solitude would now be an integral part of his new life.

As the loneliness of the position impressed itself on Benedict with ever increasing acuteness, he withdrew farther and farther from the members of the Apostolic College. With Cardinal Gasparri alone did he maintain an intimacy of friendship. Concerning the close association of these two men who complemented each other so remarkably, several charming anecdotes are related. It is said that even though Gasparri's consistent good humor amused Benedict, certain manifestations of the Cardinal's want of finesse did annoy him.

Until the doctor ordered Gasparri to abstain from tobacco completely, he was an inveterate smoker. With a quick, nervous relish he used to smoke very choice cigars, gifts from his many admiring guests. Benedict, himself a nonsmoker, would wince painfully when Gasparri would come into his presence with his cardinal's robes reeking of these strong cigars. And, it would all but ruin the Pope's day when Gasparri would enter the papal study early in the morning, puffing nonchalantly on an odoriferous pipe. One day, however, Benedict prepared a stratagem. Just as the Cardinal had finished stuffing the capacious bowl of his pipe and was searching his pockets for a match, Benedict handed him a freshly opened box of mints.

"Here, I think these will do just as well!" he said.

Benedict could not tell whether the good-natured Cardinal saw through his strategy, but His Eminence did begin to eat the candy with a vengeance. At the end of the interview, the Pope was amazed to see that the box was empty. From that day on there was always a box of candy on the Pope's desk when he expected Gasparri.[5] One cannot but wonder how the Cardinal's stomach stood up under the sudden change. This nervous habit of eating everything offered to him would go a long way in explaining his obesity.

Another person who enjoyed the intimacy of Benedict's friendship was Mariano Faggiani, a servant who lived with his family in the Vatican not far from Benedict's quarters. When life became especially irksome to Benedict, he would find respite from his anxieties by sitting in the Faggianis' kitchen and eating the humble cooking of his servant's wife. Vatican protocol demands that when the pope is served his regular meals, he is to eat alone. Benedict, however, considered his walks in the Vatican gardens, which he took all too rarely, outside the sphere of his official life. His reason for eating in this kitchen was that he loved to chat with the uninhibited children who sat around the table. The chronicler who describes the scene aptly closes the incident with the exclamation, "What a subject for a painting! A pope of aristocratic blood seated in a kitchen surrounded by his servant's children!"[6]

Benedict made no provision for his beloved sister Julia or any other member of his family to have regular audiences with him on specified days as did Saint Pius X, whose sisters visited him once or twice a week. However, in 1918, Benedict made an exception to his rule. His brother, Admiral Giovanni Della Chiesa, suffered a double misfortune within twenty-four hours. First, he lost his wife and the next day he was stricken with a cerebral hemorrhage which left him partially paralyzed. The Pope thought that the cool breezes in the meticulously cultivated Vatican Gardens would lend welcome diversion to his brother's cheerless life. Three times a week a carriage brought Admiral Della Chiesa to the Vatican, and Benedict would meet him at the same time and in the same place. It was at the shrine of the Madonna della Guardia, a gift to Benedict from the people of Genoa.

"Well now, see, I have made you happy at last. I have gone into the Vatican Gardens," he would say with mischievous irony to those who had annoyed him by their well-meant exhortation that he should take some physical exercise.

Because Benedict appeared in public so rarely, visitors would line up at certain places along the path which the Pope was known to take when he went to join his brother. Benedict did not wish his brother to be made to feel even more self-conscious about his paralysis by having their meeting subjected to the scrutiny of gaping spectators. Hence, he looked for a way of slipping out of the building in another part of the Vatican so that he would not always have to make his formal exit through the same door. It occurred to him that there was a way of entering the Vatican Gardens through a side door of the Vatican Museum. However, when he tried this for the first time he found that the turnstile did not move unless a coin was dropped into the slot. He vaguely remembered from his days in the secretariat of state when he had had to pass through this entrance on an occasional errand that there was a hidden lever or button which the guard manipulated so as to allow Vatican personnel to pass without paying. Benedict had purposely chosen a time outside the regular hours for visiting the museum, and the lone guard naturally became alarmed when he heard someone tampering with the turnstile. When he ran to the scene he was surprised to find that it was the Holy Father himself. In trying to help him he became flustered and was of no assistance in the attempt at making the metal barrier move without a coin. Benedict carried no small change because the appeals made to him as supreme pontiff were aimed at much larger donations. Bank notes of substantial size he carried with him always. He gave one of these to the guard who dashed off to have it changed. When he returned, the proper coin was inserted, and the turnstile clicked. Benedict passed through, and the attendant was delighted when Benedict called back over his shoulder, "Keep the change."[7] From what we know about the woefully small wages Italians received at that time, we can surmise that the "change" in the hand of the surprised guard represented many days' work.

On these more furtive expeditions into the Vatican Gardens, Benedict would take a box of biscuits with him to feed the birds,[8] which, in the course of time, began to recognize their modern version of Saint Francis.[9] The Pope's enjoyment was undisguised when he observed that clergy in red or purple or black went unnoticed by the birds but that his own white-clad, limping figure brought chirps of wild delight from all directions.

The spirit of Saint Francis in Pope Benedict is further shown in another incident. One day a young priest from Bologna, whose vocation to the priesthood Benedict had fostered while he was archbishop of that see, visited the Pope and brought him a gift. It was an eaglet which the priest himself had caught at the risk of life and limb. With typical Italian vivacity he related how he had clambered to a precarious position on the peak of a jagged cliff, and how he had warded off the vicious attacks of the mother eagle.

Benedict looked at the young priest with great disappointment and said, "I would not boast about this horrible exploit. Believe me, I appreciate the fact that you meant well and I do not want to have you think me ungrateful. However, I find it impossible to conceal my displeasure at the cruelty of the whole incident."

The Pope kept the eaglet until it could shift for itself. One day, with his own hands he opened the cage and allowed it to have its freedom in the open sky.[10]

Rigorous routine governed the life of the Pontiff. Summer and winter he rose promptly at 5:00 a.m. He took his noon meal at 1:30. He recited the rosary with the members of his household at 9:30 p.m. He ate supper at 10:00, and retired at 11:00 unless pressing affairs caused him to work throughout the night without retiring.[11]

Benedict followed the precedent set by Pius X, that "everyone has the right to see the pope."[12] Therefore he granted semipublic audiences twice a week. His keen observation enabled him instantly to judge the nationality of individuals, no matter how the visitors from all over the world intermingled. He would then address a question in Italian, French, Spanish, or German. These languages he spoke fluently. In other languages he would bid the time of day, inquire about the health of the visitor, or make some memorized remark. He prided himself on never failing to identify the proper nationality. His keen observation and infallible memory had noted and filed away the national traits of the myriads of people whom he had met.[13]

Benedict expected from others the precision and prudence which he had cultivated within himself. On one occasion a distinguished visitor came to the Vatican. Benedict realized that if the visit became public knowledge many quarters would attach political significance to it. So he ordered that no account should appear in *L'Osservatore Romano's* column, *"Nostre Informazioni."* Nevertheless, the audience became a matter of public knowledge. The Pope left no stone unturned until he uncovered the leak. A talkative private chamberlain of high rank was guilty. Benedict called him and said to him, "A *secret* chamberlain who cannot keep a secret dwindles to nothing but a *simple* chamberlain."[14] By this trenchant statement the man was removed from active service.

Punctuality was the watchword of Pope Benedict's life. Once he allowed a cardinal to wait while he deliberately bade his barber to come in first. His explanation was that the cardinal had not been present at the precise minute for which his audience had been scheduled.[15] For every liturgical function, for every public audience, Benedict XV could be relied upon to be standing at the door, waiting for those who were to meet or accompany him.

With the love of punctuality Benedict had a passion for watches. He was often seen with his watch in his left hand. This idiosyncrasy obviously did not help to lessen the nervousness of his visitors. If one of his servants was late, and Benedict found that the man did

not possess a watch, he gave him one.[16] On one occasion the manager
of the Vatican printing press prevented Benedict from giving an
audience to a man who would have embarrassed the Pope publicly.
When Benedict learned of this act of prudence, he repaid it by
presenting the man's favorite nephew with a watch on the occasion
of his First Holy Communion.[17] The prizes which he awarded to
students in the Roman Seminary were always watches.[18] On all
these gifts the inscription was the same: "A Father's love for the
fidelity of his sons — in loving remembrance."[19]

In Pope Benedict XV the editor of *L'Osservatore Romano* had
a most exacting master and meticulous censor. The poor editor
sighed with relief when he could leave his office at night without
having found on his desk a large envelope addressed to him in the
unmistakable, long strokes of Benedict's hand. Almost invariably
the envelope contained *L'Osservatore* of the previous day with
passages underlined and the margin filled with arrows and annota-
tions in heavy red crayon.

One example will suffice to show how difficult it was to sense the
fine distinctions in Benedict's mind. The editor had received notice
that a patrician relative of the pope had died in Genoa. Once before
when a relative of Benedict had died, the editor had added an editorial to the news item. He went to some lengths to divine how
great the sorrow of the Pope must be and assured him of the
sympathy of the world. On that occasion Benedict had returned
the paper with a comment to the effect that the world was at war
and valuable news was crowded out because space was dedicated
to personal ruminations of this nature. The editor decided that he
was not going to be reprimanded again for this mistake. Hence
he reported the second death very concisely and gave an arresting
caption to the bulletinlike notice. The next day, however, the awe-
inspiring envelope was found again on the editor's desk, and
L'Osservatore's margin carried the note: "A relative of the pope dies,
and his own paper does not have so much as a word of sympathy!"[20]
Benedict, it is true, was hard to please but he drew a sharp distinction between empty phrases and genuine courtesy.

On still another occasion the editor opened the envelope with
his usual fear and trepidation. But when he saw that the wrapper
did not contain *L'Osservatore Romano* but a Bolognese paper, *Il
Resto del Carlino,* he heaved a sigh of relief. An article in this
paper was encircled with red crayon, and written in the margin

was a morsel of cynicism, typical of the Della Chiesa of old: "Were I the editor of *L'Osservatore Romano* — and I realize I'm not worthy of this honor — I should not have allowed this article to pass without a refutation!"[21] The editor had granted himself the sigh of relief too early.

No detail was too small to be of interest to Benedict. Once when a meal was to be served for distinguished guests, Benedict hurried to the banquet hall in person before any of them arrived and surveyed the whole display to see whether the silverware had been laid out correctly and whether the flowers and other dinner arrangements were in order.[22]

Benedict's conscientious preoccupation with these minutiae reflected a similar state of affairs in his spiritual life. It denoted a preparedness for any eventuality. No detail was left undone. He maintained this state of readiness throughout his entire life. When an earthquake rocked Rome most unexpectedly in January, 1915, he was on a prie-diu making his thanksgiving. Monsignor Migone was saying Mass in the Pope's presence. Suddenly the Vatican trembled and plaster began to fall. Candelabra and sacred vessels rang with vibrations. Neither the Pope nor Migone had ever experienced an earthquake, and undoubtedly they had no concept of what was happening. Since the world was at war and since newspapers had been conjecturing about the possibility of an air attack on the city, they may have thought that explosives were falling on the Vatican.

Monsignor Migone, becoming deathly pale, turned as if to flee from the altar. His eyes were wide with terror. His dry lips were murmuring incomprehensible supplications to God, and he looked at Benedict as though he expected his beloved patron to stop this cataclysm. The Pope rose calmly, then took a step forward. He smiled and laid a paternal hand on Migone's arm before gently turning him back to the altar. With warmest affection, yet with just a trace of kindly reproof he said only the word, *"Bambino!"*[23] The incident is reminiscent of the scene on the tossing sea when the disciples in their terror invoked the divine Master. Benedict seems at all times to have possessed the charismatic gift of restoring courage to others, the gift promised to the first pope when Christ said to Peter, "Later on, therefore . . . it is for you to strengthen your brethren."[24]

CHAPTER XI

The First Encyclical, Ad Beatissimi

THE world was anxiously awaiting the publication of Pope Benedict's first encyclical, but when the letter was released in November of 1914, it caused keen disappointment. In the estimation of a vindictive world the document was too gentle[1] and weak.[2] It was termed disorganized and lacking in unity. On the other hand, because the encyclical was so different from those of former supreme pontiffs, in certain quarters it was hailed as a divinely inspired document.[3] Actually, all these divergent views were wrong because their advocates did not understand what Benedict had meant the encyclical to be.

L. J. S. Wood, M.P., who wrote the obituary for Benedict XV in the *Dublin Review,* pointed out that *Ad Beatissimi* was an uncannily precise document intended as a blueprint for the whole pontificate, that it was meant to be a chart and guide to the Pope himself, and that it would have provided direction to the faithful had they but analyzed its content and taken it to heart.

There exists a practically complete guide to the pontificate of Benedict XV, issued less than four months after his elevation to the Chair of Peter, written by himself, the encyclical *Ad Beatissimi* of November first, 1914. Written before the events of the subsequent seven years of his pontificate, it cannot be a history; it is, nevertheless, a guide; and those who, looking back now on those events, seek light by which to form judgment, find it wonderfully illustrative. In 1914, real students here of times past, long past, and immediately past, recognized in it a really great pronouncement, a programme founded on one supreme conception, a "rock" conception: and just as the Rock of Peter can support the whole edifice of the Church of Christ, so on that base conception could rest every phase and aspect of that Church's inner and outer life in the pontificate to come. Nor have such students been disappointed; rather, looking back now on the story of the seven years, they see how coherent all Benedict's pronouncements, all his actions, were with the encyclical message of his first days: "Love one another, Peace!"[4]

The encyclical is dated November 1, 1914. Benedict chose the feast of All Saints designedly for the publication because he wanted to call attention to the incongruity of war in the Communion of Saints.[5] Furthermore, the feast of All Saints in those days still had the impressive first Vespers of the Commemoration of All Souls. Benedict was very devoted to the souls in purgatory and especially to those who died on the battlefield. In 1917, he was to decree that one of the three Masses on All Souls' Day was to be said for the soldiers who fell in combat.

A translation of *Ad Beatissimi* was published in England with convenient captions for the various topics on which the Pope wished to touch. These headings have been retained in this summary.[6]

FEED MY SHEEP

The encyclical begins with the usual salutation to the patriarchs, primates, archbishops, bishops, and other local ordinaries having peace and communion with the Apostolic See, to whom Benedict XV wishes health and apostolic blessing. The tone of divine charity is struck in the first paragraph.

> When by the unsearchable counsel of God's providence, and without any merit of Our own, We were called to the Chair of the most blessed Prince of the Apostles — for the same voice of Christ Our Lord which came to Peter, came also to Us, "feed my lambs, feed my sheep" — immediately We began to regard with unspeakable affection the flock committed to Our care: a flock truly immense, for in one way or another it embraces all mankind.

NATION SHALL RISE AGAINST NATION

With a charming note of informality not usually found in encyclicals, Benedict writes that he will not keep it a secret that the first movement of his will was a zealous resolution to save all mankind. His very first prayer had been the prayer of Christ, "Holy Father, keep them in thy name whom thou has given me" (Jn. 17:11). He remarks how disappointing was the sharp disparity between his kindly thoughts and the world carnage at a time when the lot to preside over the flock fell to him. "Who could realize that they are brethren, children of the same Father in Heaven?" he asks in consternation.

PEACE ON EARTH

The Pope asks all to call to mind the last public utterance of his predecessor, "a pontiff of illustrious and so holy memory," the theme of whose last discourse was "Peace on earth to men of good will." He implores all "those who hold in their hands the destinies of the people to give heed to that voice."

THE EVIL AND ITS FOUR CHIEF CAUSES

In his evaluation of the situation, the "murderous struggle," as he brands the war, came about because of four prominent disorders: (1) the lack of mutual love among men; (2) disregard for authority; (3) unjust quarrels between the various classes; (4) unbridled cupidity for perishable things, as though there were no better goals for human effort. These four causes he then develops in detail.

1. *The Lack of Mutual Love Among Men*

By means of twelve quotations from the lips of our Lord, the Pope shows how eminently necessary mutual love is. He gives a rapid word picture of the crucifixion. "When hanging on the cross, He poured out His blood upon us all, so that, as if compacted and joined together in one body, mutual love should be found among us, just as mutual sympathy is found among the members of the same body." "Paradoxically," remarks Benedict, "human brotherhood has never been preached more than it is preached today." He points out, however, that this type of preaching is vain because it is divorced from the Gospel. The secularistic, humanitarian approach is bound to end in failure. Already in 1914, he sees the rise of racism which was to become so serious a problem for his successors, Pius XI and Pius XII. "Race hatreds are becoming almost a frenzy," he exclaims. He ends the discussion of the first cause of evil by announcing the motive for all his future actions: "To bring back among men the power of the Charity of Christ. This shall be Our constant endeavor, the chosen task of Our pontificate."

2. *Disregard for Authority*

Benedict sees man's emancipation of himself from God, the Master of the Universe, as the ultimate root of this disregard of authority. He indicts "the unbridled spirit of independence joined with pride" which has "permeated everywhere, not sparing the family or even the sanctuary." He restates the Catholic doctrine of government: "All power, whether of the sovereign or of subordinate authorities, comes from God."

A WARNING TO RULERS

Benedict, in an apostrophe, addresses himself to rulers and points out the serious flaw in divorcing government from religion.

> Let princes and rulers of the peoples bear this in mind and bethink themselves whether it be wise and salutary that public authority should divorce itself from the holy religion of Jesus Christ, in which it may find so powerful a support. Let them seriously consider whether it be politically wise to banish from public instruction the teachings of the Gospel of the Church. Experience teaches only too well that where religion is absent, public authority falls.

He closes his discussion of violated authority with the remark, "Certainly there remains the usual expedient of suppressing rebellion by violence; but where is the gain? Violence may subdue the body, it cannot conquer the will."

3. *Strife of the Classes*

The Pope points out that all men enjoy an equality of nature, but from this principle men are not to conclude that they have an equality of rank in social life.

> When, therefore, the poor assail the rich as though those had appropriated to themselves what belongs to others, they are acting not only against justice and charity, but even against reason, particularly because they themselves might better their own position by force of honorable labor.

As a concomitant to this class strife, Benedict makes explicit mention of strikes. During his pontificate he was to make no new pronouncements on labor. The encyclicals of Leo XIII, especially *Rerum Novarum*, were to be the guide. On several occasions, when Benedict wrote to bishops who had labor troubles in their sees, he confined his advice to the thoughts and words found in Leo's writings.[7] In *Ad Beatissimi*, however, he makes a statement which at that time was ridiculed, but which today is taken for granted in our legislation.

> It would be superfluous to point out the consequences, disastrous alike to individuals and to the community, that flow from this class hatred. We all know and deplore those frequent *strikes by which the whole of public life even its most necessary activities, is suddenly checked;* and then the riotous outbreaks, in which recourse is frequently had to arms, and this followed by bloodshed.

Robert Dell, noted foreign correspondent for several British newspapers, excoriated Benedict for those words in the encyclical. He wrote sarcastically, "Those dreadful workingmen get out of hand and actually begin to think themselves as good as their betters and to claim their share of the national wealth. The pope is quite pathetic on this point. I hope that some society will circulate this encyclical broadcast among the working classes, especially in the United States, where its precepts would be particularly appreciated by the intelligent artisan."[8]

Thirty-three years after the publication of the encyclical, however, the Taft-Hartley Act of 1947 was to allow for national emergency provisions whenever a strike would cripple the "national health and safety."

To avoid a recurrence of socialism and other errors, Benedict advises study of the encyclicals of Leo XIII. He asks all bishops to exert their influence through "Catholic associations and congresses, sermons, and the Catholic press."

4. The Root of All Evil

Pecuniary greed is the ultimate cause of all the troubles the Pope has enumerated. In substantiation of his statement, he quotes Saint Paul, "The desire of money is the root of all evils" (1 Tim. 6:10).

When godless schools, moulding as wax the tender hearts of the young, when an unscrupulous press, continually playing upon the inexperienced minds of the multitude, when those other agencies that form public opinion, have succeeded in propagating the deadly error that man ought not to look for a happy eternity; that it is only here that happiness is to be found, in the riches, the honors, the pleasures of this life, it is not surprising that men, with their inextinguishable desire of happiness, should attack what stands in the way of that happiness with all the impelling force of their desire.

MAN'S TRUE BEATITUDES

Benedict points out that Christ foresaw all these difficulties and therefore in the Sermon on the Mount "laid the foundations of Christian philosophy."

Now the deep and underlying thought of this divine philosophy is, that the good things of this life have only the appearance without the reality of good, and so cannot bestow true happiness. . . . We urge therefore all who are suffering under any kind of hardship, not to keep their eyes fixed on earth, which is but a place of exile, but to lift them up to heaven, whither we are tending; for "we have not here a lasting city, but we seek one that is to come."

The more faith grows amongst men, the more will the feverish pursuit of earthly vanities cease, and as charity grows strong, social conflicts and tumults will gradually die away.

THE ADMIRABLE FRUITS OF THE LAST PONTIFICATE

It cannot be denied that *Ad Beatissimi* lacks the unity one finds in the encyclicals of Leo XIII. Yet it must be remembered that this encyclical was to be a blueprint for the whole pontificate which was to concern itself with matters in a variety of fields. The Pope treats political and social subjects first because the war and the havoc accompanying it were uppermost in men's minds. He closes his delineation of the ills of the times with this sentence, "And now leaving this subject, and turning to what more immediately concerns the state of the Church, Our spirit, saddened by the present calamities of the world, finds some relief." His source of consolation lies in the fruits of the pontificate of his predecessor, Pius X, "who during that pontificate adorned the Apostolic See with the example of a life in every way saintly." The following are the fruits which Benedict mentions expressly: (1) the universal intensification of the religious spirit of the clergy; (2) the general increase of piety among the laity; (3) a promotion of disciplined activity in Catholic associations; (4) the consolidation and extension of the sacred hierarchy; (5) a tightening of the reins in the education of aspirants to the priesthood; (6) the condemnation of Modernism; (7) an elevation of the role of music in the solemn service of God; (8) an enhancement of the dignity of the liturgy; (9) a wider dissemination of the knowledge of Christianity "by fresh contingents of ministers of the Gospel." Benedict is conscious of his singular good fortune in falling heir to the papal throne at a time when the Church can hand on so rich a heritage. As the beneficiary of all these blessings, Benedict can only say, "We shall labor incessantly to the best of Our power in opposing what is evil, in promoting what is good, until it shall please the Prince of Pastors to demand an account of Our stewardship."

108 THE LIFE OF BENEDICT XV

THE NEED OF CONCORD

Benedict now turns to more specific points of policy within the Church. "The first element on which the success of any society of men depends is the concord of its members." The enemies of the Church, he says, see opportunities for victory in our internal dissensions. Benedict states a number of rules which he expects to be obeyed.

1. No private person is allowed, by the medium of books or of newspapers or of public speeches, to put himself forward as teacher in the Church. All know to whom God has given the teaching authority of the Church. To him it belongs to decide when and how he shall speak.

2. In matters about which the Holy See has not given a decision, and in which, without injury to faith and ecclesiastical discipline, there may be differences of opinion, each may lawfully defend his own. In such disputes there must be no offensive language, for this may lead to grave breaches of charity.

3. If others do not accept a writer's view, he must not cast suspicion on their faith or spirit of discipline.

4. We desire that that practice, lately come into use, of using distinctive names by which Catholics are marked off from Catholics should cease. Such names must be avoided not only as "profane novelties of words," that are neither true nor just, but also because they lead to grave disturbances and confusion of the Catholic body. It is of the nature of the Catholic faith that nothing can be added to it, nothing taken away; it is either accepted in full or rejected in full. "This is the Catholic faith, which unless a man believe faithfully and steadfastly, he cannot be saved." There is no need to qualify by fresh epithets the profession of this faith; let it be enough for a man to say: "Christian is my name, Catholic is my surname." Only let him take heed to be in truth what he calls himself.

5. As for those who devote themselves to the good of the Catholic cause, the Church now asks of them not to be over eager about useless questions, but following the leadership of him whom Christ has appointed guardian and interpreter of the truth, to use all their power to preserve the faith in fullness and freedom from error.

The whole section just quoted refers, of course, to the integralists or "integral Catholics." Benedict does not call them by name, but his reference to an adjective which was recently applied to the word *Catholic* is unequivocal.

MODERNISM AND THE MODERNISTIC SPIRIT

Writers who have tried to define Modernism have found it impossible to do so in a single sentence because of Modernism's many facets.[9] Benedict attempted a descriptive definition which is clear and sufficiently comprehensive. He wrote:

> Some there are who, puffed up and emboldened in mind by the wonderful advance of natural science — an advance due to the gift of God — have gone so far in their rashness, that, exalting their own judgment over the authority of the Church, they have not hesitated to reduce the deep things of God, and the whole revelation of God to the measure of their own understanding, and to accommodate them to the modern spirit. Hence have arisen the monstrous errors of Modernism, which Our predecessor justly declared to be "a synthesis of all heresies," and which he solemnly condemned. That condemnation, venerable brethren, We now renew to the full.

CATHOLIC ASSOCIATIONS

Benedict suggests that more Catholic associations be formed, for "men are greatly helped by mutual encouragement and example." He looks forward not only to an increase in number but to an enhancement of their quality and productivity.[10] He reminds them, however, that they will flourish only to the extent that they are obedient to the Church. "For unless they are obedient to God by following the guidance of the Church, they must not expect the help of God, and will labor in vain."

THE CLERGY

The Supreme Pontiff implores the bishops to inculcate not only holiness but also zeal in their aspirants to the priesthood. He reminds the readers that his immediate predecessors, Leo XIII and Pius X, had done much toward this end, and hence he will make no further recommendations on this subject.[11] He suggests, however, that a close study of Pius X's *Exhortatio ad clerum* be made and he pleads that its prescriptions be "most scrupulously observed."

UNION WITH THE BISHOP

Benedict reminds priests that obedience to their bishops is absolutely necessary for the salvation of their own souls and for the fruitfulness of their ministry. In corroboration he quotes Saint Ignatius, Martyr:

110

Since charity does not suffer me to be silent in your regard, therefore have I been forward to admonish you, that you be in agreement with the mind of God. For Jesus Christ, our inseparable life, is in the mind of the Father as the bishops also, set throughout the earth, are in the mind of Jesus Christ. Wherefore it is fitting that you run in agreement with the mind of the bishop.

The work of a conscientious bishop, says Benedict, is already sufficiently heavy. "Is it not cruel that anyone, by refusing proper obedience, should increase the weight and anxieties of their office?"

THE FREEDOM OF THE CHURCH AND OF ITS HEAD

Finally the Pope touches on the Roman Question, the so-called imprisonment of the Pope in the Vatican. The world had wondered what the "diplomatic Pope" would do about it.

Too long has the Church been curtailed of its necessary freedom of action, ever since the head of the Church, the supreme pontiff, began to lack that defense of his freedom which the providence of God had raised up during the course of centuries. The loss of that protection has inevitably caused no light anxiety in the Catholic body; for all the children of the Roman pontiff, whether near or living afar, have a right not to be left in doubt concerning the possession by their common father of true and undeniable freedom in the exercise of his apostolic ministry.

While We pray for the speedy return of peace to the world, We also pray that an end be put to the abnormal state in which the head of the Church is placed — a state which in many ways is an impediment to the common tranquillity. Our predecessors have protested, not from self-interest, but from a sense of sacred duty, against this state of things; those protests We renew, and for the same reason — to protect the rights and dignity of the Apostolic See.

PEACE

The document closes with a call for prayer to Christ, the giver of peace, and to His Mother, "who bore the Prince of Peace."

L'Osservatore Romano commented on the encyclical in these words, "Benedict XV has spoken with the wisdom of a pontiff, with the illumined and generous love of a father, with the authority of a pastor of souls, with the fervor of an apostolate ready to stand erect before adverse authority, just as it was never a stranger to the greater works of apostolic charity toward the obstinately wayward."[12]

CHAPTER XII

The Incessant Cry for Peace

WHEN the name Benedict was chosen by Giacomo Della Chiesa in 1914, a Frenchman who dabbled in the literature of the occult suddenly remembered a prophecy about a Pope Benedictus whose Pontificate was to occur during an especially violent war. A search of his library produced a volume by a seventeenth-century seer, Joannes of Strassburg. The particular passage in the prophecy was published in the French press:

> Pope Benedictus, having cursed the antichrist, will proclaim that those who combat him will be in the state of grace, and, if killed, will go right to heaven like martyrs. The bull that will proclaim these things will reverberate far and wide; it will revive courage and it will cause the death of the ally of the antichrist. One will know the antichrist by various signs. He will bear in his arms an eagle, and an eagle will be found in those of his acolyte, the other bad monarch. The latter, however, is a Christian and will die in consequence of the malediction of Pope Benedictus who will be elected at the close of the reign of the antichrist.[1]

In France, fighting for her life, this prophecy built up morale inestimably. A consoling interpretation sprang spontaneously from the text which spoke of war and a pope named Benedict. In French eyes, of course, Kaiser William of Germany was the antichrist. Every country in time of war tries to identify the enemy with the beast of the Apocalypse, and it was of immense relief to know that according to this prophecy the Kaiser would not live long. After all, according to Joannes of Strassburg, Pope Benedictus would be "elected at the close of the reign of the antichrist." Further verification was found in the fact that both the German and the Austrian imperial coats of arms bore an eagle. The prophecy spoke of a Christian and of a non-Christian emperor. Francis Joseph was a Catholic; William II was a Protestant. To France, a country nominally Catholic, "Christian" could easily act as a synonym for "Catholic." Because of all the atrocities attributed to the very person of the Kaiser, the French simply did not consider him a Christian.

The first disillusionment came when, two days after his coronation, "Pope Benedictus" delivered his first consistorial address, that is, an allocution to the cardinals assembled in the consistorial hall. In it he simply underscored the last public utterance of Saint Pius X, in which that Pontiff had urged peace. However, all was not lost. The prophecy had spoken of a document. Since no encyclical had yet been issued, there was no need for total discouragement.

On All Saints' Day, November 1, came the long-awaited document which would "cause the death of the ally of the antichrist." As was seen in the chapter which outlined the encyclical, *Ad Beatissimi*, its tone was anything but harsh. It was the call of a very gentle and loving father to his children to stop their fighting. The bitter disappointment of the French and English press can be seen from the following comment: "It is really difficult to believe that this was actually written in the year 1914; it sounds like the utterance of an elderly gentlewoman of about the year 1830."[2]

If some felt that the encyclical, despite its calm and gracious tone, might conceal some subtle malediction which would bring immediate harm to the Austrian Emperor, they too were doomed to disappointment. Francis Joseph continued to live for two full years more. He died November 21, 1916, of extreme old age. Even the prophecy's most ardent believers found it difficult to claim a bond of cause and effect in so lengthy an interval.

The bitterness occasioned by Benedict's pacific encyclical knew no bounds. No matter how charitably his words were phrased, ways were found of twisting them and reading into them a malevolent meaning. For example, in *Ad Beatissimi* he had said,

> Never perhaps was human b r o t h e r h o o d more preached than now; nay it is pretended that, without any help from the teaching of the Gospel, or from the work of Christ and the Church, the spirit of b r o t h e r h o o d has been one of the highest creations of modern civilization. Yet the truth is, that men never acted towards each other in less b r o t h e r l y fashion than now.[3]

This paragraph, quoted from the encyclical, was seized upon as an instance in which Benedict, instead of practicing the impartiality which he preached, actually cast a pointed reflection on France. A tortuous train of reasoning started with the word *brotherhood*, which, the critics charged, had a most sinister ring to papal ears. The watchword of the French Republic was, "Liberty, Equality, Fraternity." Fraternity means brotherhood. Therefore, when the Pope complains that brotherhood is being preached intensively but apparently to no avail, he is craftily castigating France.[4]

Benedict XV was aware of these criticisms. With apparent impassivity he read the editorial comments which branded him as being completely in sympathy with Germany and Austria. He must have felt the injustice of his critics sharply, but he accepted the abuse as part of his office as pope. It was his lot to endure what his Master had prophesied, "Blessed are you, when men revile you, and persecute you, and speak all manner of evil against you falsely, because of me. Be glad and lighthearted, for a rich reward awaits you in heaven; so they persecuted the prophets who went before you."[5]

Once, in an audience, Benedict chanced to make the paradoxical remark that this nearly universal vilification of himself proved to his own conscience that he was actually impartial. He alluded to the fact that whereas the French were denouncing him, through Georges Clemenceau, as *le pape boche,* the Germans, through the mouth of von Ludendorf, spoke of him disparagingly as *der französische Papst.*[6]

Benedict was very precise in the use of words. He wished his policy to be considered one of *impartiality,* not of *neutrality.* "The Holy See," he said, "has not been, nor wishes to be *neutral* in the European War. It has, in turn, the right and the duty to be *impartial.*"[7] As the father of Christendom, the Pope could not be *indifferent* which was the shade of meaning that Benedict saw in the word *neutral.* The spiritual father of all nations, he reasoned, had the duty of loving them all and could not take the part of one against the other. Benedict felt the word *impartial* expressed this second attitude.

Men in the secretariat of state, who had rather frequent access to Benedict's private study, at times had the opportunity of hearing him muse articulately as he perused the newspapers and periodicals laid before him. "My appeals not only have gone unheeded, but have been scandalously misinterpreted," he was heard to murmur one day.[8] Once, when the prefect of the Vatican Library, Achille Ratti, who was to succeed Benedict as Pope Pius XI, came to deliver his answer on some point of research requested by the

Pope, Benedict expressed himself more definitely. He said that it was his conviction that these criticisms were part of a vast conspiracy to stifle all further papal utterances. "They want to silence me," he said, "but they shall not succeed in sealing my lips; nobody shall prevent me from calling to my own children, peace peace, peace."[9]

It would be interesting to know whether Benedict's remark to Achille Ratti had been prompted merely by certain deductions in his own mind trained in statesmanship or whether he had factual information about the insidious clause in the Treaty of London signed on April 26, 1915. On this day, Sidney Sonnino, the Italian foreign minister, met in London with representatives of the British and French governments. Clause 15 of the resulting treaty stipulated that the Entente should support Italy in barring the Pope from any participation in the final treaty of peace. Even though there was whispered gossip concerning this pact as early as January, 1916, the text of the agreement became known only at the end of the year 1917, when the new Bolshevik government of Russia published it.[10] The fifteenth article was included solely on Sonnino's initiative and was prompted by his undisguised hatred of Catholicism. According to Ludwig Pastor no member of the Italian government did greater harm to the cause of the Holy See.[11] Britain, it was learned, agreed most reluctantly to Sonnino's proposal, but she and France were so anxious to have Italy enter the war on their side that they could not afford to haggle.[12]

The most notorious distortion of Benedict's utterances was the interview which Louis Latapié, a French reporter, published in *La Liberté,* June 22, 1915. At the beginning of his pontificate Benedict had instituted the practice of granting press interviews. In due time Latapié applied for an audience which was granted. He asked the Pope a number of questions concerning the war and the relationship of the Holy See with the kingdom of Italy. When it was published, however, the interview consisted of a series of statements, some of which had actually been made by Benedict, but which in print were wrenched from their proper context. Others were crass misquotations, and there were still other statements which the Pope had never made.

The article opened with a description of Benedict.

At first sight Benedict appeared to me entirely free of hauteur, yet at the same time he was formidable, simple, and subtle. This man, I thought, ought to be a fencer of the first rank. His face at one and the same time expressed tenacity and finesse. The gold glasses stamp the good nature of a man of study on his nose which is typical of an authoritarian prince; and, incidentally, that nose is not very straight. Everything in his face is mobile and each trait leaves its impression of sweetness or energy at the command of an aristocratic hand which is in perpetual motion.

Catholics resented the preponderance of loaded words and expressions, such as "formidable," "subtle," "fencer of first rank," "authoritarian prince," "nose . . . not very straight," "aristocratic hand in perpetual motion." It gave the impression of a Renaissance pope, a disciple of Machiavelli. As one Catholic writer expressed it, the emphasis on the nose which was not very straight contained the innuendo that the Pope's spirit and heart were likewise not very straight and was indicative of a man practicing a crooked line of politics amid the belligerents.[13]

Among the blatant lies and misrepresentations is the answer which Latapié attributed to Benedict when he was asked about the Holy See's silence on the violation of Belgium's neutrality. Benedict was represented as having sloughed the question off easily with the remark, "Oh that, that was in the pontificate of Pius X." Readers hostile to Benedict interpreted the remark as a disparagement of the memory of Pius X and as a convenient device on Benedict's part for covering up his failure to condemn Germany. Asked about the Holy See's relationship with Italy, Benedict was reported as having complained that Italian censorship was tampering with mail clearly addressed to him. This published criticism of Italy jeopardized the success of the Pope's efforts to solve the Roman Question. The Italian government published a sharp protest.[14] *L'Osservatore Romano* published an explanation which Cardinal Gasquet branded as "ridiculous." In his opinion the article lost all vigor, and could not be considered a rebuttal because its author devoted most of it to a distinction between the words of a pope spoken in private and his public utterances.[15]

Finally, Cardinal Gasparri, who was vacationing at Camaldoli near Frascati, read the accounts in the daily press. He took the next train back to Rome and summoned the representatives of the Italian papers for a press conference. Before he permitted any questions, he excoriated Latapié's misrepresentations. "This happens often," he said, "in cases where the interviewer, like Mr.

Latapié, has to speak of things about which he does not know very much!" Then he invited the reporters to ask questions on all points needing clarification. He showed how Benedict's answers had been quoted out of context or how he had been maliciously misquoted.

The Cardinal was interrupted by a messenger who said that two cardinals had an urgent communication for him. He announced that he would have to end the conference, but as he rose to go, he snapped:

> There is plenty more that I could say and much of it very important. However, this I shall say, Mr. Latapié has not reproduced exactly the thought of the Holy Father in any one single point and in many he has utterly and shamefully misrepresented him.
>
> To spare the Holy See similar deplorable indiscretions — to call them by no worse name — Mr. Latapié will have the honor of being the last journalist received by the Holy Father during the war.[16]

The fact that Cardinal Gasparri had to interrupt his well-earned holiday to restore order after the pandemonium[17] created by the article in *La Liberté* might seem to indicate that Benedict conducted himself poorly and rather helplessly in an interview. In reality, exactly the contrary was true. An example of the suave and masterful manner in which he conducted press conferences is recounted by Vercesi, an Italian journalist.[18] Vercesi relates that in one interview the Pope quoted a German as having told him that even Belgian priests lost their dignity to the extent of throwing missiles at Germans whom they chanced to meet on the street. Vercesi cut into the Pope's narration sharply by saying, "But, Holy Father, you cannot believe everything you hear."

Benedict's eyes lit up with a twinkle as he said that this was precisely the point he had been trying to make to the world at large. The world had been criticizing him for not condemning the alleged German atrocities. The atrocities were reported to the Pope from only French and English sources. How was he to know that only the horrors alleged by the Entente were true?

This question he had always in mind when evaluating any report that came to him. When blanket allegations were brought to him, he may have listened in silence, but he reserved judgment until he was able himself to conduct some kind of probe. For example, once after Germans had insisted that guns had been implanted amid the beautiful ornaments of the spires of Rheim's famed cathedral, he caught some pilgrims off guard when he suddenly interrupted their carefully worded protestations of homage to ask what guns they had actually seen in the cathedral.[19]

The *New York Times* correspondent, Anne O'Hare McCormick,* describes her interview with Benedict:

Benedict encouraged his visitors to the expression of views on all subjects, controversial or otherwise. And it is proof of his simplicity — or yours! — that you found yourself telling him quite freely what you thought. . . . He always interviewed his interviewers. He darted from point to point, probing the mind of his visitor. . . . The desire to savor for himself all sorts of divergent and uncensored views and all varieties of information was typical of his conversation.

As I look back upon that audience and recall the number of unrelated subjects he was able to touch upon in less than half an hour, how frankly he talked and questioned, how open and fluid was his mind and how eager his intellectual curiosity, I regain the impression so strong at the time — that Benedict was astonishingly unknown to the outside world.[20]

During this period, Benedict spoke to the world again and again through papal documents and consistorial allocutions. The message was always the same: the great crime was the war itself. Francis Pichon suggests an interesting project, that is the listing of the synonyms and epithets with which Benedict referred to war. World War I is "an unparalleled scourge," "a carnage which is without example," "this monstrous spectacle," "a horrible plague."[21]

One utterance in particular showed the depths of soul whence came the Pope's cry for peace. It was his first Christmas Eve allocution which has come to be called the *"Clama ne cesses* allocution."* At this meeting, Benedict reinstated a custom which had fallen into disuse under Pius X who had conducted this session in an informal manner. Under Saint Pius X each cardinal expressed a Christmas wish in his own way, and the Pope moved about, replying to each member of the Apostolic College individually. In 1914 the cardinals were informed that Benedict desired the audience to be formal and to be held in the throne room with their eminences seated around the throne. In addition to the cardinals he requested all high ecclesiastics of Rome, archbishops and bishops,

* In *Vatican Journal 1921–1954,* edited by Marion Turner Sheehan, copyright 1957 by Farrar, Straus and Cudahy, Inc. Used by permission of the publishers, Farrar, Straus and Cudahy, Inc.

prelates, judges of the Rota, members of the congregations, and the like to be present.

Promptly at 11 o'clock in the morning, Benedict appeared in the consistorial hall.[22] Punctilious in his fidelity to tradition and protocol, he wore the camauro, that strange ermine-trimmed cap of dark red velvet which covers the ears of the wearer, and which symbolizes that the pontiff is "at home" for a more chatty visit with his co-workers than in the formal audiences conducted throughout the rest of the year.

With grave dignity Benedict took his place on the throne. The greetings from the college of cardinals were tendered in a formal address which, because of his failing eyesight, Serafino Cardinal Vannutelli, dean of the Sacred College, had requested to be read by his younger brother, Vincenzo Cardinal Vannutelli. Even though the address was in Italian, the key sentence, with which the Christmas message ended, was in Latin. Everyone present was familiar with it because it occurs frequently in the breviary, verse 15 of Psalm 33, *"Inquire pacem et persequere eam!"* ("Seek after peace and pursue it!") The Cardinal, looking over his manuscript at Benedict, read it with personal feeling. Vincenzo Vannutelli then added something not in the manuscript, "Seek, demand, obtain this peace for trembling humanity which trusts in you." He ended by asking the Pope to give the Apostolic Benediction to those assembled.

It was Benedict's turn to reply. When at ease in a small group, he spoke in a very pleasant voice. Under strain, on the contrary, his voice would ring in a shrill and somewhat unpleasant tone. This off-key quality was undoubtedly due to his defect in hearing. Now, after the first few sentences he was perfectly at ease and his voice had music in it. Literature was his avocation, he wielded a beautiful Tuscan style, and the magic of his words compensated amply for any defect of elocution. "Apparently," he began almost casually, "it does not please Divine Providence that Our pontificate should close its first year under joyous auspices." This year of 1914, he said, had brought a twofold calamity: first, the death of Pius X, ". . . so holy a pontiff with his never ceasing care to hide the singular virtues which adorned his saintly soul"; second, the horrible presence of war.

The Pope said that he had looked forward to greeting the cardinals in a voice filled with joy. Instead, the new father of the world's

Christian family must receive his Christmas greetings in the form
of cannon's thunder and the clash of arms. How he had hoped in
his capacity of universal father to console grief-stricken mothers
with the assurance that at least in the next few hours consecrated
to the memory of Christ's birth, their sons would not be exposed
to enemy shrapnel! He had hoped that the belligerents would accept
his suggestion to adopt the time-sanctioned Christmas truce. "It
was indeed with this hope that there came to Our mind the proposal
to pierce this darkness of warring death with at least a ray, one
single ray of the divine sun of peace." Alluding to Horace, he
terms his proposal but "a dear hope and a dear illusion."

It seemed to him, he continued, that the Holy Spirit was now
speaking within him as He had once spoken through the prophet
Isaias: *"Clama ne cesses!"* ("Cry, cease not!") Just as Cardinal
Vannutelli had made his address in Italian but had drawn his key
sentence from the Latin Psalter, Benedict seized upon Isaias 58:1,
which he also kept in Latin. This sentence now became the text
and refrain, like an antiphon in the breviary, a sentence occurring
at the beginning and at the end of a plaintive psalm, so that
the thought cannot be lost sight of. "Cry, cease not" had been his
plea for an exchange of prisoners unfit for military service. "Cry,
cease not," had been his hope that the poor prisoners be given priests
who could bring them comfort in their own language. "Cry, cease not
to do sweet violence to the Most Sacred Heart of Jesus. . . ."

Few of the cardinals had ever had the opportunity of hearing
Della Chiesa deliver an address. Now as they listened to his carefully chosen words, his impassioned appeal, and his inspiring
thoughts, they sat as if electrified. Benedict continued, "Ah, may
the fratricidal weapons fall to the ground! Already they are too
bloodstained; let them at last fall! And may the hands of those
who have had to wield them return to the labors of industry and
commerce, to the works of civilization and peace."

Some of those present, though they had known him for many
years, had thought of him as an unimaginative, plodding worker
at a desk. They had never divined his oratorical ability. This man,
so small of stature, clad in a garb of long ago, seemed like a reincarnation of the prophet of old whom he quoted so dramatically.
Then he paused, and humbly begged his audience for prayers. The
spell was broken. They knelt and he imparted the requested blessing. Each cardinal kissed his ring and received from the Pope a

kind word and a personal greeting. Then he turned, and with his dignified but slightly limping gait, walked through the chilly halls to his noonday meal, traditionally eaten in ceremonious solitude.

Benedict himself gave the good example in crying without ceasing. As the year 1915 dawned, the press was almost unanimous in denouncing the Pope's refusal to indict the Central Powers as sole war criminals. By way of response, he delivered a consistorial allocution on January 22, 1915, in which he vindicated his impartiality. He said:

> Certainly anybody who judges carefully cannot fail to see that in this enormous struggle the Apostolic See, though filled with the greatest anxiety, must remain perfectly impartial. The Roman Pontiff, as Vicar of Jesus Christ, Who died for men, one and all, *must embrace all the combatants in one sentiment of charity;* and as the Father of all Catholics he has among the belligerents a great number of children, for whose salvation he must be equally and without distinction solicitous. . . . We note more vividly in our children their reverent affection for the Father of the faithful; and of this, as far, for example, as concerns the beloved Belgian people, one proof is to be found in the letter which we addressed recently to the Cardinal Archbishop of Malines.[23]

The letter to which the Pope referred was one written to Cardinal Mercier on the feast of the Immaculate Conception in 1914.[24] Throughout the war it was to be Benedict's unswerving policy to commend a nation, no matter which side it was on, whenever it showed signs of good will. Accordingly he expressed to Cardinal Mercier his profound emotion upon hearing that the Belgians, despite their war-ravaged condition, had taken up the Peter's Pence collection as usual. In return, Benedict had asked the Cardinal to keep it and to spend it for the alleviation of poverty in Belgium. However, in this letter, Benedict carried his impartiality to the extent of reminding the sensitive Belgians that thanks were due to Cardinal Hartmann, Archbishop of Cologne. The German prelate had wrested from his government the concession that French and Belgian priests held as prisoners of war should be treated as though they were officers. This kindness on the part of a German, even though he was a cardinal, must have tried the Belgians sorely in view of the fanatical propaganda which depicted every German as lacking both virtue and decency.

In his consistorial allocution of January, 1915, Benedict said that it is his right as Roman Pontiff, the divinely appointed and supreme interpreter of the eternal law, to proclaim that no one has the right to offend justice, no matter what the plea may be. He concluded by saying:

> And We do proclaim it without modification, condemning openly every injustice by whatever side it may have been committed.[25]

The press shrieked its anger at Benedict because he had not condemned Germany. VATICAN ATMOSPHERE MADE IN GERMANY was the headline of one newspaper.[26] Obviously, in the opinion of the Belgians also, Benedict had spoken with insufficient vehemence. A few days after the allocution Cardinal Gasparri delivered an explanatory note to Mr. Van den Heuvel, Belgian minister at the Vatican. In the note, the papal Secretary of State declared that the Pope could not utter condemnations and denunciations which under the circumstances would be based solely on the slanted accusations made by the belligerents. However, Cardinal Gasparri continued, the Pontiff would condemn unequivocally whenever he had incontrovertible facts. "The violation of the neutrality of Belgium, carried out by Germany on the admission of her own chancellor, contrary to international law, was certainly one of 'those injustices' which the Holy Father in his consistorial allocution of January 22 'strongly reprobates.' "[27]

It was now Germany's turn to attack Benedict. THE ONE BELLIGERENT POWER AGAINST WHICH THE VATICAN HAS OFFICIALLY SPOKEN IS GERMANY headlined the *Hamburger Fremdenblatt*.[28] In the estimation of the Entente, on the other hand, this implied denunciation of Germany was much too mild and timid.

On May 24, 1915, Italy entered the war, and, as a consequence, the representatives of the Central Powers left the Vatican. Since England and France had no ambassadors at the papal court, the Pope was now bereft of all firsthand information.

On May 25, Benedict wrote to Serafino Vannutelli, dean of the college of cardinals, advising him of his desire to convoke the cardinals as soon as possible, since there were many matters of grave importance on which the Pontiff stood in need of counsel. He adverted to the fact that the gigantic scourge of war made his task all the more difficult at that very moment when it had even extended to his "beloved Italy" (*si è estesso anche alla Nostra diletta Italia*).[29] The adjective *diletta* (beloved) was music to the ears of a people for many years nervous because of the strained relations.

In his letter to Cardinal Vannutelli, Benedict reiterated his appeal for peaceful settlement of differences. He quoted verbatim from *Ad Beatissimi*, the blueprint for his pontificate, his first encyclical. To the quotation he added, "However, the voice of their friend and their father went unheeded. The war continues to bathe Europe in blood; they have recourse on land and on sea to means of warfare which are contrary to law and humanity."

On July 28, 1915, the first anniversary of World War I, the Holy Father was heard once more, in an "Apostolic Exhortation to the Peoples now at War and to their Rulers." It was issued not in Latin but in Italian, and began with the words *"Allorchè fummo chiamati."*[30] In it, Benedict stressed the following points: (1) His plea for peace should be considered as a piercing cry heard above the "dreadful clash of arms." (2) He desires his hearers to be reminded of an old principle, that a yoke received unwillingly under force will leave chafing bruises for the next generation which will throw off the yoke and fetters in bitter revenge.[31]

Not many years passed before events proved that Benedict had indeed been a prophet. Hitler, as if echoing Benedict's words, denounced those who dictated the policies of World War I, "Peace treaties whose demands are a scourge to a people not infrequently beat the first drum roll for a coming rebellion."[32]

The consistory for which the Pope had asked the co-operation of the Cardinal Dean finally took place on December 6, 1915. In his allocution Benedict pointed out that the war was in its sixteenth month. His exhortation of July 28, he said, had been reverently enough received, but to his knowledge it had borne no fruit. He said that it was absolutely necessary that the belligerents make renunciations, concessions, and sacrifices of pride. Should the leaders refuse to do this, then they alone would "bear before God and men the enormous responsibility for the continuation of a carnage which is without example."

It is said that William II was deeply affected by these words of the Pope, and that for a moment he had in mind to make a public statement protesting that he was not the chief offender among those to whom the Pontiff imputed the responsibility for the carnage.[33]

On January 10, 1915, Cardinal Gasparri published the details of a day of prayer which the Holy Father wished the whole world to observe. Benedict himself had outlined the order of the versicles, orations, and litanies to be used. He also composed the following prayer which was to be said on the day appointed and for the duration of the war.

> Dismayed by the horrors of a war which is bringing ruin to peoples and nations, we turn, O Jesus, to Thy most loving Heart as to our last hope. O God of Mercy, with tears we invoke Thee to end this fearful scourge; O King of Peace, we humbly implore the peace for which we long. From Thy sacred Heart Thou didst shed forth over the world divine Charity, so that discord might end and love alone might reign among men. During Thy life on earth Thy Heart beat with tender compassion for the sorrows of men; in this hour made terrible with burning hate, with bloodshed and with slaughter, once more may Thy divine Heart be moved to pity. Pity the countless mothers in anguish for the fate of their sons; pity the numberless families now bereaved of their fathers; pity Europe over which broods such havoc and disaster. Do Thou inspire rulers and peoples with counsels of meekness, do Thou heal the discords that tear the nations asunder; Thou Who didst shed Thy Precious Blood that they might live as brothers, bring men together once more in loving harmony. And as once before to the cry of the Apostle Peter: *Save us, Lord, we perish,* Thou didst answer with words of mercy and didst still the raging waves, so now deign to hear our trustful prayer, and give back to the world peace and tranquillity.
>
> And do thou, O most holy Virgin, as in other times of sore distress, be now our help, our protection and our safeguard. Amen.[34]

It was translated into the languages of the various belligerents and printed on prayer cards. February 7, 1915 (Sexagesima Sunday), was the day set for Europe. Since transportation by sea was slow and uncertain because of the war, the crusade of prayer was to open six weeks later in non-European countries — on March 21 (Passion Sunday).

When the copies arrived in the various countries, reaction to the wording of the prayer was generally unfavorable. In Italy it received severe criticism from one from whom in later years the world was to hear much more, Benito Mussolini. He complained of what he called "Benedict XV's encyclicals, his discourses, his laments." But what was worse in his estimation was the fact that the Pope circulated "ridiculous prayers for peace even among the fighting soldiers."[35]

French disapproval was not limited to words. One bishop tampered with the printed text which had been released from the Vatican in an official translation. The sentence, "O King of Peace, we humbly implore the peace for which we long," was altered to read, "O King of Peace, we humbly implore peace *on conditions honorable for our fatherland.*" The prayer was now no longer a humble petition for peace but a demand with conditions.[36]

On the Sunday preceding the opening of the crusade of prayer, the French police, acting under secret orders, suddenly seized all papers which had published Benedict's prayer as well as packets of the Pontiff's picture which had the prayer printed on the reverse side. The next day, however, the prayers and pictures reappeared equally mysteriously. On the following Sunday, Cardinal Amette of Paris mounted the pulpit of Sacré Coeur at Montmartre and also that of the basilica of Notre Dame, and interpreted the prayer in the light of what the Holy Father had "really meant to say." The "interpretation" was really a statement of what the Cardinal wished that Benedict had said. Cardinal Amette explained that the Holy Father had "a victorious peace" in mind for France.[37]

All this nervousness on the part of the French is explained by the fact that at the very time the printed copies of the prayer were being delivered, the situation did not appear at all propitious for the Entente. Francis Pichon's sardonic comment on the dilemma in which French leaders found themselves is, "They were unable to give the people victory but they did not have the courage to give them peace. The prime obligation seemed to consist in saving the prestige of those who had plunged them into war."[38]

Perhaps the hostility of churchmen of high rank and apparently of education was best explained by Don Luigi Sturzo, an Italian priest, who undoubtedly understands the tenor of Italy's political life better than any man alive today. Reminiscing in 1938, Don Sturzo wrote of the misunderstandings which Benedict's philosophy of war and peace had occasioned.

> Benedict XV wanted to make of the Vatican not a judge of the morality of the war, but the Good Samaritan binding up the wounds, and reserving for itself, if opportunity arose, the role of peacemaker. We believe that Benedict's act was a prudent one, the only one possible for a pope in the conditions in which he found himself.

The problem of the justice of the war, rising from the depths of the human conscience, showed the ripening of an unprecedented moral crisis with insufficient means for resolving it. . . .

The religious authorities were asked not to resolve a doubt, but to confirm the justice of the cause. The answer came, alike for all, all were fighting for justice. Such was the moral crisis of Europe in 1914. Could it have been otherwise? Could Catholic and Protestant bishops, once war had broken out, tell their faithful that theirs was an unjust war? If they had thought so and wished to say so, what government would have allowed it? Thus churchmen, at the moment of having to give a moral and religious answer, found themselves bound up with the powers that had prepared and launched the war, or had not known how to avert it. Their sacerdotal word could no longer be freely uttered. One of the reasons for this crisis came from the fact that the theologians and canonists of the nineteenth century *had not brought the theory of the right of war up to date.* They still considered war as the business of the monarch who, in his conscience and after hearing the advice of jurists and moralists, must judge of the justice of war.[39]

Only the Bishop of Rome dared to speak of peace without victory. His denunciation was more fundamental than any condemnation of acts perpetrated by this or that nation. He denounced the "burning hate" which fed the monster, war. War was the monstrous criminal to be slain. In his place was the reign of the Prince of Peace.

CHAPTER XIII

Treason

ON AUGUST 2, 1916, the harbor of Taranto was as peaceful as at any time in its history. Fishermen were busy with their nets. Sailors and deckhands went about their chores. Children scampered back and forth, playing their noisy games. Old men, their wrinkled hands holding the huge bowls of their pipes, sat on benches as they gazed idly over the blue expanse of sea. With their hats pulled far over their eyes, sometimes they conversed, sometimes they dozed. The warship, *Leonardo da Vinci*, with its gently quivering stacks, was the only object in sight that could remind the onlookers that the country was not at peace.

Suddenly the whole harbor was rocked by a mighty explosion. Billows of greasy smoke and the hissing sound of hot metal hitting water suddenly came from the *Leonardo da Vinci*. Like a wounded beast, the dreadnaught fell over on her side, catapulting three hundred of its five hundred crew members into the sea.[1] Two hundred and forty-eight of them died with their ship.

After rescue operations had ended and the initial shock had passed, investigators began to discover several additional mysteries. For instance, a roll call disclosed that the ship's key officers and stokers had not been on board at the time of the explosion. The absence of those who should have been supervising the final preparations for embarkation brought to mind another mysterious explosion at Brindisi in September of the preceding year. The *Benedetto Brin*, also lying at anchor, had likewise suddenly exploded and gone down. Its officers and stokers too, by a remarkable coincidence, had been absent on a variety of legitimate errands at the moment of the blast.[2]

Beginning with the sinking of the *Leonardo da Vinci*, Benedict XV went through excruciating torments of mind and endured eight months of shameless calumniation. In the minds of many, the Holy Father was ultimately responsible for these maritime disasters. An amazing chain of events was to lead Italian naval investigators to the very door of the Vatican before the case could reach its bizarre conclusion. At this time, hatred and prejudice had help from a peculiar set of circumstances in placing Benedict in an ambiguous position before the world.

From the very beginning, the investigation of the *Leonardo da Vinci* explosion brought to light a series of names which were connected with the Vatican. For instance, a Monsignor Rudolf Gerlach, first chamberlain of Benedict XV, *Guardaroba* (keeper of the wardrobe) of the Holy Father, and one of his most intimate friends, had remarked to an acquaintance, "Well, a few hours ago, Italy paid the price of her treachery to Germany."[3] Normally in time of war, one might expect this from any patriotic German, even an ecclesiastic. What made Gerlach's remark astounding, however, was the fact that it was uttered several hours *before* news of the explosion reached Rome from Taranto!

That the Vatican should be involved in espionage and treason was all that Benedict's enemies needed. The seriousness of the situation was the more aggravated because the "Roman Question" was still unsolved. Benedict, "the diplomatic Pope," was the political messiah who would restore friendship with unified Italy. Therefore, it was necessary for the Vatican to employ more than ordinary caution in anything which might affect even remotely the Italian government. To evaluate the unfortunate event, it will be necessary to review the facts of Benedict's acquaintance with Rudolf Gerlach.

During World War I reams of published misinformation gave rise to what might be called a "Gerlach Legend." Before getting at the facts of his life it may be well to examine the wartime fiction.

Rudolf Gerlach is often mistakenly called the "Austrian prelate."[4] It has also been alleged that the friendship between Benedict and Gerlach dated from Benedict's student days in the Academy of Noble Ecclesiastics. It will be remembered that Giacomo lived there from 1879 to 1882 when he accompanied Rampolla to Spain. In 1887 he resumed residence at the Academy until 1892, when he took up lodgings with his mother in *Palazzo Brazza*.

Much of the misinformation about Gerlach seems to stem from an article written by Dr. E. J. Dillon,* which appeared in the

---

*Dillon, a famous Irish journalist and foreign correspondent, sometimes called the "knight of the poisoned pen,"[6] had once been a Catholic seminarian but later, after making contact with Renan and other rationalists, apostatized from the Faith. There is no denying the fact that he was a man of extraordinary erudition which he used to great advantage in his coverage of the news. He maintained secretaries and correspondents in almost every European capital.

Fortnightly Review in 1915, a full two years before the German priest's name became one of infamy.[5] Though in his article treating of Benedict and Gerlach, Dillon shows himself to be misinformed on the past history of the German ecclesiastic, he makes a very perspicacious statement about Gerlach's character. He wrote, "This ecclesiastic is one of the most compromising associates and dangerous mentors that any sovereign ever admitted to his privacy." It must be borne in mind that when Dillon published these words Monsignor Gerlach appeared at the Pope's side as his chaplain at almost every public function. So that the disparity between Dr. Dillon's narration of the facts and his judgment of Gerlach's character can be better appreciated, the article from the *Fortnightly Review* is quoted at length.

. . . Personally Benedict XV has been careful to keep aloof from Bülow and his band, and has neither said nor done anything blameworthy with the sole exception of the interview and message which he gave to an American-German champion of militarism at the instigation of his intimate counsellor, Monsignor Gerlach. This ecclesiastic is one of the most compromising associates and dangerous mentors that any sovereign ever admitted to his privacy. He is described as a man of Austrian nationality, German Christianity, who when in Vienna consorted with ecclesiastics of the type depicted by Poggio and incarnated by French Abbés of the free and easy days of the Regency. . . .

Years ago, the story runs, Gerlach made the acquaintance of a worldly-minded papal Nuntius in the fashionable *salons* of gay Vienna, and being men of similar tastes and proclivities, the two enjoyed life together, eking out the wherewithal for their costly amusements in speculations on the Exchange. When the Nuntius returned to Rome, donned the Cardinal's hat, and was appointed to the See of Albano as Cardinal Agliardi, he bestowed a canonry on the boon companion who had followed him to the eternal city. The friendship continued unabated, and was further cemented by the identity of their political opinions, which favored the Triple Alliance. Gerlach became Agliardi's tout and electioneering agent when the Cardinal set up as candidate for the papacy on the death of Leo XIII. But as his chances of election were slender, the pair worked together to defeat Rampolla, who was hated and feared by Germany and Austria. . . .

Some years ago Gerlach's name emerged above the surface of private life in Rome in connection with what the French term *un drame passionel,* which led to violent scenes in public and to a number of duels later on.[7]

In order to get a true picture of the history of the Gerlach-Benedict association it might be well first to point out two of the over-all biographical errors in Dillon's article. First of all, Gerlach was a Bavarian and his home was in Baden, hence, manifestly, he was not an Austrian.

Gerlach was born July 7, 1886, and Benedict in 1854. Benedict was thirty-two years older than Gerlach — therefore they would hardly have been schoolmates. When Della Chiesa began his second sojourn in the Academy of Noble Ecclesiastics in 1887, Rudolf Gerlach would have been only one year old.

Gerlach's alleged association with Agliardi furnishes further opportunity for checking on the accuracy of Benedict's confident critics. Archbishop Antonio Agliardi served as nuncio to Austria from 1893 to 1896. Monsignor Gerlach must indeed have been a child prodigy to have been able, at the age of seven to act as host and guide in Vienna to the newly arrived Archbishop, and to play the stock market with him. In 1903, when Cardinal Agliardi is said to have "set up as candidate for the papacy," Gerlach, his purported vote-getter among the other members of the Apostolic College, would have been only eighteen years of age.

Another inconsistency becomes obvious at this point. In the eyes of some, Benedict XV was almost fanatically loyal to the memory of Cardinal Rampolla. But to make the past of Gerlach appear more sensational, he is depicted as the enemy of Cardinal Rampolla. Would Benedict XV have appointed a man of such background as his "chamberlain in active attendance" and "keeper of the Holy Father's wardrobe"?

Again, Father Gerlach is depicted as the well-known participant in *un drame passionel* and as a duelist of distinction. From time immemorial, participation in a duel brings about automatic excommunication, absolution from which is reserved to the Holy See.[8] In the days of Saint Pius X and the rigoristic Merry del Val, there was an unbroken exodus of ecclesiastics and Vatican functionaries upon whom only the slightest breath of suspicion had blown. Yet, under that regime, Rudolph Gerlach was a priest-student, residing from November 13, 1910, in the Pontifical Academy of Noble Ecclesiastics, whose residents are hand-picked by the Holy See. Not only that, but after finishing his studies in the spring of 1914, he was chosen as an auditor on the sacred tribunal of the Roman Rota. This tribunal of the Holy See was restored to its former prestige by a special decree of Saint Pius X, and its staff was chosen with great care.

There is a further detail that every version of the Gerlach legend should have to make it complete, and that is to insist that he had once been a renowned cavalry officer in the Prussian army.[9] Gerlach did indeed attend a military academy in Kassel, and it is true that after his graduation from that school he became a cavalry officer in Saarbrück. His military career must have been very brief, however, because he was a seminarian at the *Capranica* prior to his ordination in 1910. He was twenty-four years old at the time of his ordination, which means he was ordained at a somewhat earlier age than is usual. Therefore, Gerlach could not have had much opportunity to achieve great fame as a cavalry officer, and he could not have been in the army more than a year. It was undoubtedly the year of compulsory military training in the German Empire. His fine posture and erect carriage were probably responsible for the stories about his former military rank.

When was Giacomo Della Chiesa first introduced to Rudolf Gerlach? Many sources claim that the new Pope "became acquainted with Gerlach when he was a cardinal."[10] This makes the friendship very brief indeed, since Della Chiesa was a cardinal for only a few days over three months, from May 25, 1914, to September 3, 1914. Older authors insist their friendship went back to a sojourn in the Academy of Noble Ecclesiastics. These two versions can be reconciled if it is recalled that Cardinal-designate Della Chiesa lodged at the Academy for a few days before the consistory which conferred upon him the red hat. His stay in Rome on that occasion was less than a week. We can well imagine the debonaire and ambitious young German doing all in his power to make the shy Archbishop feel at home. He would see to it that the distinguished visitor lacked nothing.

In the plans of Divine Providence the new Cardinal was to return in less that three months. Late in the evening of August 22, 1914, he again arrived at the Rome railroad station.[11]

It is a Roman custom to turn out at the railway station when cardinals from all over the world arrive for the conclave. Italian railroad platforms are always crowded, but on these occasions the situation is worse than ever.[12] When a cardinal appears in the doorway of his railroad coach, those delegated to receive him are sometimes unable to get through the throngs to his point of exit. One can sympathize with a visiting prelate who may be confused by the lights and lanterns, the noise of the trains (especially in the days of 1914 when the pounding, hissing, steam-driven locomotives stood in sharp contrast to our silent Diesel-driven trains). The shouting of the porters, cab drivers, and excited onlookers in general will not add to the serenity of any tired traveler.

The houses where prelates are to stay send representatives to meet their distinguished guests. Even though the name and picture of Rudolf Gerlach has been expunged from most records, the annals of the Academy of Noble Ecclesiastics record that he was the house prefect. In ecclesiastical institutions of this kind, especially when the students are priests of the diocesan clergy, the student prefect finds himself called upon to perform various tasks. The arrangements for meeting a cardinal who had chosen to honor the school with his presence would naturally fall to the prefect. One can well imagine how Father Gerlach performed this labor of love, fond as he was of doing everything with a touch of the dramatic.

Giacomo was never so lonely and out of place as when he was in a crowd. His conduct in a large gathering has already been depicted. When, early in his service in the secretariat of state, he was sent by Cardinal Merry del Val to represent him at a program given by the College of the Propaganda, the vice-rector left us a description of that occasion. He remarked on the nervous, "almost childlike manner" in which the visitor clutched the vice-rector's wrist until he had been safely installed in his chair of honor.

In the same way, on August 22, 1914, Father Gerlach seems to have inspired a sense of security in this timid man. As the carriage rattled over Rome's narrow cobblestoned streets, one can picture Gerlach, riding backward in the carriage, his handsome face bending forward to the Cardinal and the rector of the academy sitting opposite him, giving him a reassuring nod as his well-manicured fingers adjusted the robes of the future pope.

On August 31, the conclave began. Monsignor Migone accompanied Cardinal Della Chiesa to the Vatican as his secretary. On September 3 came the surprising election. That night, after all the felicitations had been given and the new Pope had performed the necessary formalities, he retired to his cell and made over eighty changes in the staff of the Curia and papal household. Among those was one which caused amazement.[13] "Monsignor Rudolf Gerlach was named Secret Chamberlain on active duty to His Holiness" as the next issue of *Acta Apostolicae Sedis*[14] noted. Three others were appointed with Gerlach. Papal chamberlains on active duty serve in pairs, always flanking the Holy Father when he makes a public appearance. They also act as personal servants during the pope's private audiences and daily working hours.

At the coronation, on September 6, it was Monsignor Gerlach and Monsignor Migone who accompanied the Holy Father from his private apartments to the *sedia gestatoria*.[15] On September 8, when Benedict addressed the assembled cardinals for the first time, Rudolph Gerlach and Camillo Caccia-Dominioni flanked the Holy Father at the throne.[16] It did not go unnoticed that Benedict seemed to have a special affection for the young German prelate.

In the spring of 1915, when Italy entered the war on the side of the Entente, all Germans and Austrians were ordered to leave Italy.[17] Monsignor Gerlach asked the Pope to arrange that he might stay. Benedict complied gladly for two reasons. First, he was much attached to Gerlach, who, endowed with ready wit, was able to wrest a spontaneous laugh from the overburdened Pontiff. Second, Benedict wished to clarify a principle. The Law of Guarantees of 1871 had promised absolute noninterference with the personnel of the papal household. If the Law meant what it said, there was no reason why Monsignor Gerlach should leave.

However, in his desire to prevent any situation which might prove embarrassing, the Holy Father asked Monsignor Gerlach to submit to voluntary imprisonment in the Vatican for the duration of the war, not unlike that observed by the Pope himself. Gerlach promised eagerly enough, but he had no scruples about breaking his promise.[18] Soon he was seen openly on the streets of Rome, and he freely visited homes and apartments. More serious than this, his association with people of questionable political activities was brought to Benedict's attention. Because of his strong loyalty to his friends, however, the Pope refused to listen to any accusations.[19]

Members of the papal household became more suspicious of Gerlach when he decorated and furnished his rooms in renaissance splendor at an incredibly high cost. He also bought a Lancia, one of the luxury automobiles of the day for which he was said to have paid about $4,000.[20] In view of the fact that the Monsignor was not to leave the Vatican, one might question the practicality of an automobile for the four or five miles of road in Vatican grounds.

The expenditures for furnishing his apartments and for the Lancia perhaps indicate a fundamental lack of practical judgment not infrequently found in men otherwise highly gifted. It was known that while he was living in the Academy of Noble Ecclesiastics he was relatively "impecunious" as the staid journalism of the London *Times* reported.[21] In modern times because of the Holy See's limited resources, ecclesiastics working in the Vatican have been woefully underpaid.[22] Knowing with what suspicion he, as an "enemy alien," was being regarded, Gerlach should have realized that questions would ultimately be raised concerning his sources of revenue. Vanity, no doubt, and a desire to be noticed overrode prudence and dictated the lavish display that he tried to make. The particle *von* began to appear before his name, the sign of nobility to which he had no right.[23] All these signs of exhibitionism began to etch the character of the man.

Not long after the sinking of the *Leonardo da Vinci*, Gerlach's name was linked with the case. The rumors became louder, and early in 1917 Benedict was presented with proof of Gerlach's complicity in a plan to destroy the entire Italian navy. Benedict now had the sorrowful task of confronting his "Guardian of the Papal Robes" with the charges. The encounter was secret. The wording of the most reliable accounts bears the mark of the Vatican's cool prudence: "He did not respond as he should have done."[24]

Fantastic stories began to circulate. One story is that Gerlach's failure "to respond as he should have done" took the form not of shamed confusion but of defiant arrogance.[25]

When the Italian government presented its case, the Pope was naturally placed in an embarrassing position.[26] For many months he had defended his private chamberlain[27] who had collaborated in the treasonable acts of certain Italian citizens. Gerlach had certainly received money from the Central Powers and he had used it to subsidize various pro-German newspapers. He had furnished information to the enemy. Lastly he was found to have been involved in "attempts against the realm of Italy."

Benedict had no choice, now that he was in possession of the facts. He ordered Monsignor Gerlach to be turned over to the Italian authorities, who in strict compliance with the "Law of Guarantees" came only as far as the "Bronze Gates." As a whole, an Italian regime may be anticlerical in the resolutions which it commits to writing, but the individual Italian instinctively respects a priest. With all courtesy these Italian officials quietly conducted the Monsignor to the Italian-Swiss border at Lugano. Gerlach then crossed the frontier into Switzerland. In this way a very awkward situation for both the Holy See and the Italian government was avoided.[28]

As the Vatican gendarmes escorted the private chamberlain from the Holy Father's presence, Benedict was seen to tilt his head, a pose characteristic of him when he became meditative and introspective, and was heard to murmur, "He was always so jolly and seemed so frank and loyal."[29] Evidently the Pope, personally fond of Gerlach, had rationalized himself into believing that the German priest's joviality was a manifestation of the supernatural joy which Saint Paul enumerates among the fruits of the Holy Spirit.[30]

How did Gerlach's name come to be linked with the sinking of the *Leonardo da Vinci*? First of all there was his unguarded remark hours before strict censorship released any news about the catastrophe. He had said, "A few hours ago Italy paid the price of her treachery to Germany." This had been overheard. Second, Italy's secret service shadowed the engineers and machinists who at the time of the explosion had all been so conveniently absent from the ship. Many of the people whom they visited had also received calls from Monsignor Gerlach.

Two of the ship's crew visited Archita Valente, editor of *La Vittoria,* an allegedly Catholic newspaper which previous to Italy's entry into the war had taken a pro-Austrian stand. Valente had had a chequered career, having once been a well-known actor. The police had therefore made doubly sure to put him under surveillance because they suspected that he might be using his knowledge of stagecraft to make his editor's office serve as a screen for more sinister activities.

The business manager of this paper was Giuseppe Ambrogetti who was also a so-called "ecclesiastical provider," i.e., he acted as an agent for the clergy in such business matters as required an intermediary. In the days when the hostile spirit of the *risorgimento* was still active there were certain places of business which a priest could not easily frequent without risking embarrassment. Dapper Giuseppe Ambrogetti would be engaged, and the priest could rest assured that all would be taken care of. For example, when Cardinal Früwirth was invited by Benedict to take up his residence in Rome, it was Ambrogetti who selected an apartment for him, furnished it, provided servants and other details so that when the Dominican Cardinal arrived in Rome he could take up his duties at once.[31] The very fact that Ambrogetti had expended so much energy in the service of an Austrian, an "enemy alien," even though he was a cardinal, in those days of war was enough to put him under suspicion. Ambrogetti, as the court was to prove later, was a man of good intentions but likely to act imprudently in his enthusiasm. He was one of those resourceful characters who welcome the challenge of obtaining for a client articles which others insist cannot be procured. The court could find little more than that "he managed the financial affairs of Monsignor Gerlach."[32]

Another paper with which personnel of the *Leonardo da Vinci* were found to have had communications was *Il Bastone*. This paper, which termed itself "Catholic," had been reprimanded sharply by Benedict in 1914. However, the journal had not paid the slightest attention to the reprimand.[33] Its editor was Vitaliano Garcea. He and two other publishers, Mario Pomarici and Francesco Nicolosi-Raspagliesi, were also arrested. Gerlach had also consorted with these men. Despite his promise to the Pope to become a voluntary prisoner like the Supreme Pontiff, Gerlach had provided himself with a police permit allowing him to go about freely throughout Rome.[34]

In addition to this circumstantial evidence the Italian police received a copy of an interesting document from the British secret service which had made a raid on the Austro-Hungarian consulate in Zürich where they had found a written list of "friends" residing in Italy. Gerlach's name was on that list.[35]

The trial was a military one which opened April 12, 1917, and ended on Saturday, June 23, of the same year. It was conducted behind closed doors, and at the time, Italian censorship forbade publication of anything except the bare essentials of the final verdict. Mario Pomarici was found to have been the head of an espionage organization operating out of Switzerland, and was sentenced to be shot in the back as a traitor. Since he refused to appear for his trial, he was judged contumacious and was granted no extenuating circumstances by the court. Archita Valente escaped the death sentence because he appeared for trial and availed himself of the right of a defending attorney. He was sentenced to life imprisonment at hard labor.

Rudolf Gerlach, who had already escaped, was tried in absentia and sentenced to life imprisonment at hard labor. This meant that should he ever again set foot on Italian soil and be recognized, he would be taken into custody to begin serving his sentence at once. The court explained that an extenuating circumstance had been found which prevented his receiving the same fate as Pomarici, but there was no statement as to what the extenuating circumstance was. Pomarici, Valente, and Gerlach were proved to have had the "intention of doing harm" and were proved "actually to have done harm."[36]

The "ecclesiastical provider," Giuseppe Ambrogetti, was sentenced to three years, and Vitaliano Garcea, editor of *Il Bastone,* received the same sentence. The court ruled that the latter two, while they had done harm, were innocent of the charge of having *intended* harm.[37]

L'Osservatore Romano, which, it will be remembered, Benedict supervised very strictly, instantly published an acknowledgment of the "praiseworthy rectitude and impartiality of the military judges."[38]

In the wording of the court, the sentence regarding Gerlach reads:

> The evidence given has shown most clearly how Gerlach, successively evading by means of artful expedients the strict orders of the ecclesiastical authorities, and betraying their confidence, used his own means for the dispatch of secret correspondence and for his other unlawful acts, and these means were not connected in any way with the arrangements of the Vatican mailbag. Nor is it shown in any way that his guilty acts were carried out in the precincts of the Vatican, much less that they were rendered possible by the fact that they took place in the territory of the Holy See, which is not connected in the slightest way with the events which form the object of the present judgment. Furthermore, it is established that there is no connection at all between the acts alleged against Gerlach and the ecclesiastical duties, whatever these might be, with which he was charged.[39]

To summarize, the court found:

1. Gerlach had been disobedient to the Holy Father.
2. Gerlach had betrayed the Pope's confidence.
3. Gerlach had not used Vatican facilities such as the mail pouch or diplomatic valise for sending or receiving information and funds.
4. His guilty acts were not executed on Vatican territory.
5. His treasonable acts had not the slightest connection with his ecclesiastical duties as private chamberlain or guardian of the robes.

Fair-minded people, even those not known for their love of the Vatican, were satisfied with the sentence which exonerated the Vatican of any complicity. In fact, the incident evoked sympathy for the Holy Father.

About two months after the furor had died down, the *Times* of

London conducted an investigation of its own. The purpose was not
to vindicate Gerlach but to disentangle certain threads. Their conclusions were that:

1. Gerlach's work of espionage was of very little importance.

2. He was greatly overpaid for the information which he
delivered.

3. He had done no planning in the sabotage but had been the
paymaster to the Italian traitors.

4. The information which he had transmitted was of very little
moment.

5. Gerlach was a man of insufficient intelligence to have perpetrated some of the things popularly credited to him.[40]

There are those who saw in this incident evidence for the charge
that Benedict was a poor judge of character, that the "science of
the saints" was wanting in him. The refutation lies in an expression
of hyperbole which an aged and respected priest in Rome made to
the editor of the *Tablet* in the early stages of the trial: "Monsignor
Gerlach's deed was the worst betrayal since Judas."[41] In that stray
remark the answer is implicitly contained. The mysterious and inscrutable ways of God allowed a traitor to be chosen as part of the
very entourage of the Vicar of the Son of God.

The London *Tablet* reported that the Italian papers printed a
story to the effect that the Holy Office would convene in a special
session to deal with Gerlach because he had "violated the confidence
of the Vatican."[42] This could mean one of two things; either that
Gerlach did not show himself worthy of the privileges the Holy
Father had granted him, or that he had violated a confidence, that
is, broken the strict seal of secrecy which his position in the Vatican
demanded. Vatican spokesmen immediately denied and suppressed
the rumor. The Pope himself is the prefect of the Holy Office, and
its acts constitute the world's most tightly guarded secret. Any
revelation, even an indirection, brings about automatic excommunication. Absolution from that ecclesiastical censure can be imparted
only by the pope himself. It is sometimes said, humorously but with
a grain of truth, that the members of the Holy Office are so afraid
of violating their oath of secrecy that they are slow to admit that
there even is a Holy Office.[43] The *Tablet* concluded its coverage of
the story with this sentence:

Regarding the action of the Holy See, I am advised that while one
may be quite sure that the next issue of the *Annuario Pontificio* will

THE LIFE OF BENEDICT XV

138

not contain the name of Gerlach, there are no safe grounds for presuming that the case calls for anything more actual than that happening.[44]

With this rumor and its inconclusive refutation the story seemed to end. Gerlach's name was removed from the records and because of the harm he did to Italy, Roman photographers destroyed their file of negatives of his photograph. Of him the words of the psalmist seemed to be especially true, "In the next generation may his name be blotted out."[45] However, his name has been resurrected in recent years and in most unexpected sources, in the biographical accounts of a saintly young nun, Sister Gertrudis, the onetime Maria Erzberger.[46]

Mathias Erzberger, her father, was the leader of the German Center Party in the years immediately preceding World War I. Before Italy's entry into the war Erzberger spent considerable time in Rome with Pope Benedict in order to see whether the spread of the war could not be halted and peace restored. Here Erzberger met Monsignor Gerlach frequently and invited him to visit his family, should the prelate have occasion to come to Germany. Gerlach accepted the invitation and made a very favorable impression on the members of the Erzberger family and especially on Maria, the thirteen-year-old daughter, the favorite of her father. Because of Mr. Erzberger's varied activities the family traveled extensively, sojourning in places like the picturesque and historic Einsiedeln in Switzerland. The handsome and personable Gerlach would join the family on holidays of this kind. His wide knowledge of persons and places, his sparkling conversation, his ready wit, and his fine manners made him a welcome guest and companion. In little Maria's eyes he became the epitome of what the word "priest" should connote.

In 1917 or early in 1918, at least after Gerlach's defection, when Maria was about fifteen years of age, the Erzbergers were entertaining guests. The visitors, paying no attention to the children in the room, began to talk about Monsignor Gerlach, mentioning that he had left the Vatican, that he had given up living as a priest, that he had attempted marriage with a wealthy Protestant woman from Holland. The tender and hitherto sheltered ears of Maria overheard this. Shocked she left the company and ran to her own room where she fell on her knees before a picture of the Sacred Heart.

"Heart of Jesus pierced with a lance," she kept saying in her turbulent efforts to quiet her own violently beating heart. She did not return to the living room to rejoin the guests that night. Instead, she remained on her knees, shaken at the thought that her erstwhile revered friend had valued his eternal salvation so lightly.[47]

Maria made a momentous decision. She resolved upon the heroic step of offering her life for the salvation of Rudolf Gerlach's soul. She entered the Carmelite convent at Echt in Holland. For a girl who came from a family in the higher social brackets, life in a convent with bare, unheated cells was physically very difficult. She suffered from prolonged sieges of illness and from severe spiritual trials. Her love for her father made the separation from home all the more difficult. In 1921 she had the added grief of hearing that he had been murdered in cold blood on his way to Mass. At the time of her final vows she had a paper concealed under her scapular on which she had written the names of those for whom she was bringing this sacrifice. When she died at the age of thirty-five the paper was found. It bore the names of her father and of Rudolf Gerlach.[48] Her death was all the more pathetic because her life of voluntary hardship seemed to have been lived in vain. There was no encouraging word about the erstwhile Monsignor Gerlach.

On November 14, 1946, Rudolf Gerlach died in England, after a painful and lingering illness. As death drew closer to him, he called for a priest. The faith of his childhood gave him the courage to seek reconciliation with his Church and his God. He had assumed another name and his neighbors did not know that in their midst lived the man who had once been the hateful object of the British press. The bishop of the diocese in which Gerlach died informed all those whom the dying man requested to be notified — the rector of the Academy of Noble Ecclesiastics among them.[49] Evidently, the dying priest yearned for forgiveness of all those on whom his association with them had cast a shadow.

It is not considered good taste to attempt to lift the veil beyond the grave. But since Benedict XV in his documents and allocutions never seemed to have lost the thrill at the thought that he was called to lead shepherds as well as sheep to God, one is tempted to imagine Benedict's radiant presence with that of Maria Erzberger when Rudolf Gerlach's soul came before the eternal Judge to render his account. "Where the offence has abounded, grace had abounded yet more."[50] Maria Erzberger's life as a Carmelite had not been lived in vain.

CHAPTER XIV

The Papal Peace Note of 1917

A NOTE FROM THE CENTRAL POWERS

ON DECEMBER 12, 1916, the Central Powers, Germany, Austria, Bulgaria, and Turkey, dispatched a note to the heads of governments with whom they maintained diplomatic relations. The Kaiser believed sincerely that everyone secretly desired peace but that each was reluctant to be the first to admit it openly.[1] The note may have been well enough meant but unfortunately it had a smug and arrogant tone. It deplored the fact that this war of unprecedented fury was threatening to destroy the spiritual and material progress of which the twentieth century could justly be proud. The Central Powers, the note said, had amply demonstrated their might. Their lines had held, and, should the war continue, there was every indication that they would have further victories. These four allies had been forced to arms in defense of their very existence and freedom of development. Confident of their military and economic strength, and prepared, if need be, to fight to the uttermost extreme, they were nonetheless desirous of putting an end to bloodshed. Therefore, the note stated, the Central Powers were suggesting to the Entente[2] — Great Britain, France, Russia, and Italy — that peace negotiations be entered upon as soon as possible. If this advice were followed, the Central Powers would guarantee existence, honor, and freedom of development, and would do everything possible to restore a lasting peace. However, should the war rage on despite this offer of peace and reconciliation, then the Central Powers could do nothing else than disclaim all responsibility in the face of humanity and history.[3]

No answer was received from the Vatican. This apparent indifference occasioned surprise and cast doubts in certain circles on the sincerity of Benedict's incessant plea for peaceable settlement. In a letter to the cardinal archbishop of Cologne, dated March 7, 1917,

Gasparri explained that a note had also been received from England which said that any intervention on the part of the Pope at that precise moment would be ill-received by France and England. Benedict realized that if he offended the Entente now, any future efforts would be met with antagonism.[4]

In the light of his program of absolute impartiality, Benedict could do little but be silent. The governments of the Entente, angered by the tone of the Kaiser's note, refused any attempt at understanding the spirit which had prompted the note, and, instead, preferred to look upon it as an ultimatum. Briand curtly rejected the offer as a "trap." Lloyd George of England pledged himself to a program of total victory.[5] For the moment, Benedict could say absolutely nothing.

Although Benedict XV did not publicly voice his opinion of the peace offer, he was not idle. He acted on the peace feeler of the Central Powers in another way. His memory carried him back to an apprentice whom he had trained in the secretariat of state, from whom he had always received most conscientious co-operation. This was the peace-minded Eugenio Pacelli, whose very name connoted peace. It was he whom Benedict decided to appoint as nuncio to Bavaria. This appointment meant two things. First, at Munich, capital of Bavaria, Archbishop Pacelli would be the Pope's official delegate. Second, although he would have no official connection with the rest of Germany, his position at the court in Munich would give him frequent opportunities to act and speak for Benedict at the court of Kaiser William II.

To lend prestige to the young Nuncio, Pope Benedict nominated him to archiepiscopal dignity. So anxious was the Pontiff that work should begin at once in Germany that Bishop-elect Pacelli was not given much time to prepare himself. The nomination was made on April 23, 1917, and the consecration took place in the Sistine Chapel on May 13.

As Pius X had consecrated his successor in the Sistine Chapel ten years earlier, Benedict XV in that same chapel consecrated one who would succeed him twenty-one years later.[6] On May 26, Archbishop Pacelli presented his credentials to Ludwig III, king of Bavaria. Exactly a month later, he visited the distinguished chancellor of the German Empire, Dr. Theobald von Bethmann-Hollweg. In their conversation oral agreement was reached on the following four points:

1. General limitation of armaments.
2. Establishment of international courts.
3. Restoration of the independence of Belgium.
4. Alsace-Lorraine and other such territorial questions were to be settled by agreements between the countries concerned.[7]

Harmony on these points of view raised the hopes of the Papal Nuncio who faithfully reported them to the Pope. There are historians who think that Archbishop Pacelli and the Pope allowed themselves to be lured into a foolhardy optimism by the silken tactics of a veteran diplomat accustomed to the making of vain promises.[8] Bethmann-Hollweg, however, was definitely not the Machiavellian type. His severest critics admitted that he was thoroughly honest and because of this straightforwardness lacked the scintillating note of the perfect diplomat which characterized his predecessor, von Bülow. Therefore, when Dr. Bethmann-Hollweg gave his word that he agreed to four clearly defined points, it seems safe to believe that he himself had confidence in their worth and that, had he remained chancellor, he would have seen to it that every letter of the agreement was carried out. Archbishop Pacelli realized that he was dealing with a man of sincerity, but what he did not know was that insidious forces were spelling the doom of Bethmann-Hollweg's chancellorship.

Although the Chancellor was generally characterized as hostile to Catholicism,[9] he was very courteous to the Nuncio and graciously promised to arrange a meeting between the Emperor and Archbishop Pacelli. On June 29, 1917, three days later, the Kaiser received the Papal Nuncio at Kreuznach. Unfortunately, historians have not treated this interview with objectivity. The press of the Entente could find no words sufficiently derisive to belittle the Kaiser. Present-day biographers of Pius XII, in their desire to bring into focus the coolness and calmness of the Nuncio, have tailored the personality of the shrieking Adolf Hitler to fit the German ruler of World War I. A comparison of this kind is unfair; William II was a man of culture and of the poise characteristic of the German nobility.

The young Archbishop presented the Emperor with a letter in Benedict's own hand which pleaded that William should redouble his efforts to hasten the advent of peace even though it should be at the expense of some of the German objectives. As William read this his brow began to contract in irritation. He spoke plainly, saying that he would not conceal his annoyance that his own peace efforts of December 12, 1916, had been "snubbed by Benedict XV in so unheard of a manner as not to have merited the courtesy of some reply." The Nuncio in turn pointed out that certain actions of Germany had not given the Pope reason to attach much confidence to the peace overtures. As an example he pointed out Germany's ruthless deportation of Belgium workers.

Strange to say, the Emperor seems to have taken this argument in good part. He admitted that although the action looked bad at first sight, it had not been against international law. He could not be forced to run the security risk of allowing civilians to remain behind the German front. The rest of the meeting consisted of a fiery lecture by the Kaiser in which he voiced his regret that the Pope had not used his prerogative of papal infallibility for a denunciation of the atrocities committed by the Entente. He freely offered advice on how the Vatican might fortify itself against attack. He ended his discourse with a verbal picture of the edification which the Pope could give the world were he to die a martyr's death in the interests of peace.[10]

Archbishop Pacelli's visits to Bethmann-Hollweg and to the Emperor had gone far to smooth the path for a papal peace plan. Had conditions of communication enabled Benedict to release his plan immediately after this interview, it is quite probable that Germany would have accepted it, and World War I might have been shortened.

For some time impatience had been voiced in Germany because of the conservative views and methods of the chief of staff, General Falkenhayn. In August, 1916, the Kaiser reluctantly ceded to popular pressure by appointing Paul von Hindenburg field marshal and Erich von Ludendorff quartermaster general. With the elevation of these two men a veering in the direction of military autonomy became perceptible. Bethmann-Hollweg sensed the danger of a military dictatorship and voiced his fears, whereupon von Hindenburg and Ludendorff clamored for his removal. The Emperor was most reluctant to comply with their request. On July 12, about two weeks after William's conversation with the Apostolic Nuncio, the Emperor arranged a dinner meeting at which the Chancellor was to present the final draft of the peace resolution before it was to go to the Reichstag. The Kaiser was pleased with the resolution. It was flattering to him because it was an expansion of his so-called

Address from the Throne of August 4, 1914. The first point of that address had been, "We are not animated by any desire for conquest." It repeated the statement that Germany had taken up arms only to preserve her independence and to keep intact her possessions. She sought only a peace of mutual understanding and a lasting reconciliation of the nations involved. As long as the other nations and their allies would not see the reasonableness of a peace of this kind, the Germans would continue to fight in perfect unity until their right to life and development was assured.[11]

The text of the resolution was telephoned to von Hindenburg. The Emperor and his guests had hardly withdrawn to the dining room when a messenger announced that von Hindenburg and von Ludendorff had just telephoned their resignations, indicating the impossibility of further co-operation with so conciliatory a chancellor. Von Hindenburg, *der alte Kerl,* as the rank and file called him with affection, was the idol of Germany. The Chancellor knew that he could not compete in this popularity contest. That night he returned quietly to his office and in unruffled dignity wrote a letter of resignation which completely ignored the querulous threats of the army personnel.

Two days later, July 14, Germany had a new chancellor, Dr. Georg Michaelis, the choice of the general staff. On the very day of his appointment, the new Chancellor laid before the Emperor a revised draft of the peace resolution and a sketch of a reply to be sent to the Pope's letter. The reply was dated July 13. When William saw this, he frowned and wrote in the margin, *"Vier Wochen, das ist unhöflich gegen den alten Pontifex!"* ("Four weeks, that is discourteous toward the aged Pontiff!")

Whenever this scribbled comment is mentioned in the literature which seeks the causes of the failure of the papal peace note, it is always quoted as an example of the Emperor's cynical and antipapal sentiments.[12] The impression is given that because of William's mental attitude, the peace plan was doomed to failure from the very start. In all fairness to the Kaiser it must be said that he habitually studied with pencil in hand and that his thinking was always recorded in the margins of whatever he happened to be reading. That he called the Pontiff aged can be accounted for by his mental image of a pope. The only pope he had visited was Leo XIII who at William's last visit was over ninety. One of the most charming passages in his memoirs is the description of the smiling Leo tottering forward with trembling hands outstretched to greet William II.[13]

On July 19, the new Chancellor met the Reichstag for the first time. Michaelis was no bearer of titles of nobility, nor did he have the distinguished appearance of Bethmann-Hollweg, but he was not devoid of psychological technique. When the peace resolution was read, he arose and assured the members with these words, "Within the limits of your resolution, as I understand it, all these aims can be realized."[14] The hall rang with a tumultuous ovation. Everyone agreed that here was a man of action, willing to assume responsibility.

Within a week, however, he wrote to the Crown Prince whose sympathies were on the side of the army, "The infamous resolution was adopted. *But by my interpretation* I have rid it of its most dangerous feature. With that resolution we can conclude any sort of peace we want."[15]

The reports of these pacific developments raised the hopes of everyone. More elated than anyone else was the Nuncio. He spent two days (July 24–26) in conference with Michaelis and returned to Munich with the understanding that the German government was now ready to accept papal peace proposals. All that remained, said Michaelis, was to inform Austria. In Munich, Archbishop Pacelli waited until August 4, when he sent a telegram of inquiry. Michaelis responded at once and expressed his amazement that the Nuncio should be in a state of anxiety. The Chancellor felt that at the last meeting he had made it sufficiently clear that "no controversial points remain." Archbishop Pacelli now communicated this welcome response to Benedict.

The Pope summoned Count de Salis, British minister to the Holy See, and gave him several sealed envelopes. Each contained a copy of the peace note. The British government was asked to forward the note to France, Italy, and the United States whose governments were not officially represented at the Vatican.

The note was dated August 1, 1917. In his introductory paragraph Benedict stated that at the time of his election he had made a threefold resolution: (1) to maintain an absolute impartiality toward all belligerents; (2) "to endeavor continually to do the utmost good to all without distinction of persons, nationality, or religion"; (3) to omit no action which could expedite or hasten the end of the war. He stated that in his own conscience he felt that he had been most faithful to his resolutions.

The Pope enumerated the appeals he had previously made in *general* terms. He said that the time had come when he ought to propose *concrete* and *practical* propositions which could form the bases of "a just and lasting peace." The task of adjusting and completing them he would leave to the nations themselves.[16] The following are the seven points of Benedict's plan:

1. SUBSTITUTION OF "THE MORAL FORCE OF RIGHT" FOR THE LAW OF MATERIAL FORCE.

   First of all, the fundamental point must be that the moral force of right shall be substituted for the material force of arms.

2. A SIMULTANEOUS AND RECIPROCAL DECREASE OF ARMAMENTS.

   Thence must follow a just agreement of all for the simultaneous and reciprocal diminution of armaments, in accordance with rules and guarantees to be established hereafter, in a measure sufficient and necessary for the maintenance of public order in each State.

3. INTERNATIONAL ARBITRATION.

   Next, as a substitute for armies, the institution of arbitration, with its high peace-making function, subject to regulations to be agreed on and sanctions to be determined against the State which should refuse either to submit international questions to arbitration or to accept its decision.

4. TRUE FREEDOM AND COMMUNITY OF THE SEAS.

   Once the supremacy of right is thus established, let all obstacles to the free intercourse of people be swept aside, in assuring, by means of rules, to be fixed in the same way, the true liberty and common rights over the sea, which on the one hand would eliminate numerous causes of conflict, and, on the other, would open to all new sources of prosperity and progress.

5. RECIPROCAL RENUNCIATION OF WAR INDEMNITIES.

   As to the damage to be made good and the cost of the war, We see no other way of solving the question but to lay down, as a general principle, an entire and reciprocal condonation, justified, moreover, by the immense benefits which will accrue from disarmament — the more so as the continuation of such carnage solely for economic reasons would be inconceivable. If in certain cases there are, on the other hand, particular reasons, let them be weighed justly and equitably.

6. EVACUATION AND RESTORATION OF ALL OCCUPIED
TERRITORIES.

But these peaceful agreements, with the immense advantages
which flow from them, are not possible without the reciprocal restitution of territories at the moment occupied — consequently, on the
part of Germany, a total evacuation of Belgium, with a guarantee
of her complete political, military, and economic independence, as
against any other power whatever; similar evacuation of French
territory; on the part of other belligerent powers a similar restitution of the German colonies.

7. AN EXAMINATION "IN A CONCILIATORY SPIRIT" OF
RIVAL TERRITORIAL CLAIMS.

As regards territorial questions — as, for instance those pending
between Italy and Austria, and between Germany and France —
there is ground for hope that in view of the immense advantages
of a permanent peace with disarmament, the disputants would feel
disposed to examine them in a conciliatory spirit, giving due weight,
within the limits of justice and feasibility, as We have said previously, to the aspirations of the populations, and, on occasion,
bringing their particular interests into harmony with the general
welfare of the great community of mankind.

The same spirit of equity and justice must direct the examination of the remaining territorial and political questions, and particularly those which concern Armenia, the Balkan states, and the
territories which form part of the former kingdom of Poland, which
in particular, by reason of her noble historical traditions and the
sufferings endured especially during the present war, has a just claim
on the sympathies of all nations.

In conclusion Benedict wrote:

Such are the principal foundations on which We believe that the
future reorganization of the peoples must be built. They are of a
nature to make impossible the return of similar conflicts, and to prepare
the solution of the economic question, which is so important for material well-being of all the belligerent states.

The first answer to the note came from Britain. On August 21,
Arthur James Balfour, minister of foreign affairs, telegraphed an
instruction to Count de Salis, British minister to the Holy See.

His Majesty's Government, not having as yet been able to take the
opinion of their Allies, cannot say whether it would serve any useful
purpose to offer a reply, or, if so, what form such a reply should take.

Although the Central Powers have admitted their guilt in regard to Belgium, they have never definitely intimated that they intend either to restore her to her former state of entire independence or to make good the damage she has suffered at their hands. Till they and their Allies state officially how far they are willing to go in the matter of reparation and restoration, have announced their war aims and put forward suggestions as to the measures which may offer an effective guarantee that the world will not again be plunged into the horrors by which it is at present devastated, His Majesty's Government considers it unlikely that any progress towards peace can be made.[17]

On August 23, de Salis relayed the message to Cardinal Gasparri. The Papal Secretary of State insisted that Germany had already announced her intention of restoring Belgium's independence. Not only had Bethmann-Hollweg stated this but a resolution in favor of peace without annexation had been voted by the Reichstag. Count de Salis pointed out, however, first that the Reichstag did not govern Germany and, second, that the British government possessed no authentic text whatsoever of the aforesaid resolution.[18]

Before Balfour had telegraphed his advice to de Salis, France had expressed a desire to be associated in whatever step England would take on the matter of papal suggestions. Balfour had, therefore, proceeded without consulting France further. But when it became known that Count de Salis had actually delivered a written note to Cardinal Gasparri, the French president, Alexander Ribot on August 26 sent a sharply worded complaint to the British government, saying that the French government in leaving England free to communicate with the Vatican had had in mind oral communications but not formal messages which might be construed as commitments rendered permanent and irrevocable by the fact that they were presented in written form by an accredited minister.

France had no desire, the note continued, to be involved in a discussion of Belgium's independence. "Monsieur Ribot hoped that the British government would share this sentiment and would give Count de Salis instructions to discourage any further attempt on the part of the Papal Secretary of State in the direction of an official intervention between the belligerents."[19]

While the British wondered how best to get themselves out of this awkward situation, their problem was unexpectedly solved by Woodrow Wilson, the president of the United States. When he received the papal peace note, he is said to have remarked testily,

"What does he want to butt in for?"[20] However, he composed a note which he instructed his secretary of state to send to the Pope. The tone is polite in the first sentence but thereafter the president begins to lecture Benedict in a manner that approaches condescension.

The White House

August 27, 1917

To His Holiness Benedictus XV, Pope:

In acknowledgment of the communications of Your Holiness to the belligerent peoples, dated August 1, 1917, the President of the United States requests me to transmit the following reply:

Every heart that has not been blinded and hardened by this terrible war must be touched by this moving appeal of His Holiness the Pope, must feel the dignity and force of the humane and generous motives which prompted it, and must fervently wish that we might take the path of peace he so persuasively points out. But it would be folly to take it if it does not in fact lead to the goal he proposes. Our response must be based upon the stern facts and upon nothing else. It is not a mere cessation of arms he desires: it is a stable and enduring peace. This agony must not be gone through with again, and it must be a matter of very sober judgment that will insure us against it.

His Holiness in substance proposes that we return to the *status quo ante bellum,* and that then there be a general condonation, disarmament, and a concert of nations based upon an acceptance of the principle of arbitration; that by a similar concert freedom of the seas be established; and that the territorial claims of France and Italy, the perplexing problems of the Balkan States, and the restitution of Poland be left to such conciliatory adjustments as may be possible in the new temper of such a peace, due regard being paid to the aspirations of the peoples whose political fortunes and affiliations will be involved.

It is manifest that no part of this programme can be carried out successfully unless the restitution of the *status quo ante* furnishes a firm and satisfactory basis for it. The object of this war is to deliver the free peoples of the world from the menace and the actual power of a vast military establishment controlled by an irresponsible government which, having secretly planned to dominate the world, proceeded to carry the plan out without regard either to the sacred obligations of treaty or the long-established practices and long-cherished principles of international action and honour; which chose its own time for the war; delivered its blow fiercely and suddenly; stopped at no barrier either of law or mercy; swept a whole continent within the tide of blood — not the blood of soldiers only, but the blood of innocent women and children also and of the helpless poor; and now stands balked but not defeated, the enemy of four fifths of the world. This power is not the German people. It is the ruthless master of the German people. It is no business of ours how that great people came under its control or submitted with temporary zest to the domination of its purpose; but it is our business to see to it that the history of the rest of the world is no longer left to its handling.

To deal with such a power by way of peace upon the plan proposed by His Holiness the Pope would, so far as we can see, involve a re- cuperation of its strength and a renewal of its policy; would make it necessary to create a permanent hostile combination of nations against the German people who are its instruments; and would result in abandoning the newborn Russia to intrigue, the manifold subtle inter- ference and the certain counter-revolution which would be attempted by all the malign influences to which the German Government has of late accustomed the world. Can peace be based upon a restitution of its power or upon any word of honor it could pledge in a treaty of settlement and accommodation?

Responsible statesmen must now everywhere see, if they never saw before, that no peace can rest securely upon political or economic restrictions meant to benefit some nations and cripple or embarrass others, upon vindictive action of any sort, or any kind of revenge or deliberate injury. The American people have suffered intolerable wrongs at the hands of the Imperial German Government, but they desire no reprisal upon the German people who have themselves suffered all things in this war which they did not choose. They believe that peace should rest upon the rights of the people, not the rights of govern- ments — the rights of peoples great or small, weak or powerful — their equal right to freedom and security and self-government and to a participation upon fair terms in the economic opportunities of the world, the German people of course included if they will accept equality and not seek domination.

The test, therefore, of every plan of peace is this: Is it based upon the faith of all the peoples involved or merely upon the word of an ambitious and intriguing government on the one hand and of a group of free peoples on the other? This is a test which goes to the root of the matter; and it is the test which must be applied.

The purposes of the United States in this war are known to the whole world, to every people to whom the truth has been permitted to come. They do not need to be stated again. We seek no material ad- vantage of any kind. We believe that the intolerable wrongs done in this war by the furious and brutal power of the Imperial German Gov- ernment ought to be repaired, but not at the expense of the sovereignty of any people — rather a vindication of the sovereignty both of those that are weak and those that are strong. Punitive damages, the dismemberment of empires, the establishment of selfish and exclusive economic leagues, we deem inexpedient and in the end worse than futile, no proper basis for a peace of any kind, least of all for an enduring peace. That must be based upon justice and fairness and the common rights of mankind.

We cannot take the word of the present rulers of Germany as a guaranty of anything that is to endure, unless explicitly supported by such conclusive evidence of the will and purpose of the German people themselves as the other peoples of the world would be justified in accepting. Without such guaranties treaties of settlement, agreements for disarmament, covenants to set up arbitration in the place of force, territorial adjustments, reconstitutions of small nations, if made with the German Government, no man, no nation could now depend on. We must await some new evidence of the purposes of the great peoples of the Central Powers. God grant it may be given soon and in a way to restore the confidence of all peoples everywhere in the faith of nations and the possibility of a covenanted peace.

Robert Lansing
Secretary of State
of the United States[21]

Wilson could not endorse Benedict's plan because the prime premises of the two men differed so radically. For Benedict peace rested on a willingness to forgive. Wilson, despite his disclaimers, was motivated by an urge to punish. In the President's opinion it was absolutely necessary that the ruling dynasties of Germany and Austria be forced to abdicate.

Since the United States in the capacity of "Associated Power" now furnished men, arms, and money, the Entente allowed Wilson's note to speak for them. France and England were also relieved that the original British note could at last be safely forgotten. Benedict's peace plan was now a dead issue with the Allies.

To understand what occurred in the political camp of the Central Powers, it is necessary to go back to August 20, 1917, the day on which the committee for external affairs of the imperial German government met. At this session the main item of business was the papal peace note. Chancellor Michaelis, of course, was the chief speaker. The Chancellor first explained that neither his predecessor in office nor anyone else in Germany had solicited the note from the Vatican. It had come spontaneously from Benedict. Since the minutes of the meeting have been published only recently, Michaelis' denial of responsibility for the peace note is of special interest. Commentaries had stated that the peace note was a tangible proof for Benedict's partiality; that the note had been prepared in Germany and had been issued from the Vatican to lend prestige. Therefore, when Michaelis insisted that the note had come entirely unsolicited, he was telling the truth and was not wooing the masses. This speech was made in a closed session, and by his prefatory remark he wished to remove any doubts that propaganda from the outside might have engendered in the very minds of the committee.

The Chancellor continued by saying that although he found the proposals of the Pope "very fine," he experienced great difficulties in coping with the details. He did not think it necessary to "harp on the minutiae" which the note might include. He said that he would advise the Reichstag against "unfurling the whole question of Germany's war aims a second time." He believed, furthermore, that the Pope did not expect that Germany's response would treat the details. The Pope would expect only a general expression of approval.

The minutes of the meeting give the impression that the members, unaccustomed to dealing with communications from the Vatican, were so surprised by Benedict's aggressive and pointed suggestions that they were at a loss how to act on them. One member voiced the opinion that the note was too favorable to the interests of the Entente. Another said laconically that he was in full accord with His Holiness that "this murdering should stop," but he was skeptical as to whether the adoption of the Pope's plan just now was to Germany's best interests.

The meeting closed with Michaelis' endorsement of a motion made by Count von Hertling of Bavaria, that the details could be treated fairly only if one were in communication with the opponents interested in specific details.[22]

Meanwhile, on August 30, Archbishop Pacelli sent Michaelis Balfour's instruction to Count de Salis, to which France had objected so vehemently. Unfortunately, Michaelis was absent on a visit to the front in Belgium, and so more time elapsed, which caused Benedict and his Nuncio excruciating anxiety. However, as soon as Michaelis was able to do so after his return to his office, he discussed the communication with Richard von Kühlmann, secretary of state for external affairs. Von Kühlmann proposed that

Germany ask a neutral country to make contact with Great Britain to learn precisely what the latter's peace intentions were.

On September 9, the Emperor was returning from an inspection of the Eastern front.[23] Michaelis went to greet him at the Friedrichsstrasse railway station in Berlin. William II invited Michaelis to enter his private car. On the way to Potsdam Michaelis informed the Emperor of the arrival of the Nuncio's letter with the copy of Balfour's instructions to de Salis.

The Emperor was visibly elated at the thought of England's having sent out a peace feeler, but he agreed with Michaelis that he ought to proceed cautiously and prudently. On one point, however, William was eloquent, namely, that the possible advantages to be derived from Germany's possession of the coast of Flanders or other parts of Belgium should in nowise be allowed to stand in the way of an honorable peace. He endorsed Michaelis' proposals that the whole Belgian question be discussed in a crown council, that is, a meeting of the heads of the various governmental departments in the presence of the Emperor.

The following night, toward midnight, Michaelis was rudely roused from slumber by an insistent pounding on his door. It was a special courier from the Kaiser, who delivered eleven pages from a telegram pad. In his message the Emperor apologized for the formlessness of this communication. Since talking to the Chancellor he had discussed the situation with naval officers who had tried to convince him of the necessity of retaining the coast of Flanders. William admitted that he was impressed by their arguments and was forced to the conclusion that if Germany did not retain the Belgian coast, then other points of defense would have to be built. Michaelis judged correctly that these memoranda were not to be construed as a reversal of the Emperor's decisions but merely a way of clarifying his own ideas. In fact, on the last of these scribbled sheets, the Emperor had written in a personal note to his Chancellor:

I have chosen this method, since the conversation of Your Excellency yesterday surprised me so completely that I was not able to see all its implications. By this time I have allowed these things to pass through my head and I have achieved a clear picture which I now wish to share with you so that any opinions of mine will not surprise you at the meeting tomorrow.[24]

Michaelis penned this account after his dismissal from office, yet he could not write in other but touching terms of his master's delicacy and sense of consideration toward him, his subordinate.

On September 11, the morning of the meeting of the crown council, the Chancellor begged the Emperor to give him a few minutes of his time immediately before the meeting scheduled for ten o'clock.[25] William was most gracious and in the conversation he promised to give Michaelis a free hand in conducting the discussion before the council.

The crown council decided that if an enemy stretched out a hand of reconciliation, Germany should not reject it. References were made to von Kühlmann's plan to delegate a trusted man to sound out England's intentions. William did not ask the identity of the man or of the "neutral nation," evidently feeling that such a demand would show lack of confidence now that he had promised Michaelis "a free hand." He congratulated von Kühlmann on his plan and told him to use his own ingenuity. He stressed that his only wish was to have peace by Christmas. Perhaps he recalled with some wistfulness Benedict's earnest pleas for a Christmas truce in the first year of the war. When the Emperor shook hands with Michaelis before his departure, he lingered in his handclasp long enough to look him in the eye and to repeat what he had said to von Kühlmann, "Now you have a free hand. Just see to it that the German people have peace by Christmas."[26]

Von Kühlmann now entered into communication with the Marquis de Villalobar, Spanish ambassador to Belgium, who resided in Brussels. Villalobar was to inform England that Germany would restore the integrity and sovereignty of Belgium provided that (1) Germany's boundaries remain intact; (2) her colonies be returned; (3) there be no war indemnities; (4) no economic war follow. The Ambassador, however, refused to be an independent and unsponsored go-between in such a delicate matter involving the world's mightiest powers. Therefore, he first communicated von Kühlmann's request to the Spanish government. Spain, suspicious as to whether she was being told all the facts, felt uncomfortable at the thought of possibly becoming involved in the war. Therefore all that the Spanish government did was to hand the English ambassador in Madrid a succinctly worded note that Germany had expressed a desire for peace parleys. In this communiqué no circumstances or conditions were stated.[27]

The next day, September 12, Michaelis wrote to Field Marshal von Hindenburg, asking his opinion on several points. One question was: "Should Liège and a stretch of land adjoining it be kept for the protection of Germany's western industries?" Michaelis added at once, "We would, therefore, demand Liège only as a security and only for some time. . . ."[28] To this von Hindenburg answered, "I am unable to think that within any appreciable time, such as can be fixed by agreement, we can let go of Liège."

On September 13, Michaelis laid before the Emperor a draft of his reply to Pope Benedict's peace note. The Emperor read it and signed it. The letter is addressed to Cardinal Gasparri and is a masterpiece of precise wording. In the introduction Michaelis makes it clear that this is an official answer to a communication "in which His Holiness, filled with grief because of the devastation of the World War, directs a stirring appeal for peace to the chiefs of state of the belligerent countries." The letter is too long to quote in full. Therefore, it will be given in condensed form.

> For a long time, His Majesty with profound respect and sincere gratitude has followed the efforts of His Holiness to assuage the sufferings of the war . . . and to hasten the end of hostilities.
>
> The emperor sees in this most recent step of His Holiness a new proof of noble and humanitarian sentiments, and he entertains the lively hope that . . . success may come to the papal appeal.

Here follows a résumé of William II's peace efforts since his coronation address, June 25, 1888. These efforts, says Michaelis, have culminated in the Pope's invitation to share in his peace efforts.

> Fully appreciating the significance of His Holiness' manifestation the imperial government has not failed to subject the suggestions it conveyed to a serious and conscientious examination. The several measures taken in closest touch with the representatives of the German people for the discussion and settlement of the questions under consideration show clearly, how much it has at heart . . . to find suitable foundations for a just and enduring peace.
>
> With particular sympathy does the imperial government welcome the leading thought in this appeal for peace in which His Holiness clearly states his conviction that in the future the moral force of right must take the place of material might of arms. . . .
>
> From the above principle, according to His Holiness, there would result simultaneously a reduction of armaments of all nations.

From the replacement of material force by the moral force of right there would result also a provision for competent treatment of international disputes.

We share the thought of His Holiness that stipulated rules and certain guarantees for simultaneous and mutual limitation of armaments on land, on sea, and in the air, as well as true freedom and community of the high seas would provide those conditions in virtue of which the new spirit, which henceforth is to hold sway in the conduct of nations toward one another would find its first promising expression. Next there arises the problem of settling international differences of opinion not through an increase of armaments but by peaceful means such as a court of arbitration.

The Chancellor gave his assurance in this letter that his government would support every effort of His Holiness which could be reconciled with the interests of the German people. He pointed out that Germany's geographical location and commercial aspirations demand peaceful communications with her neighbors and with more distantly located lands. No nation, therefore, had greater reason to desire that in place of common hate and strife a forgiving and brotherly spirit would come to life between countries.

Michaelis closed his letter by saying,

Our own earnest and sincere conviction gives us the courage to hope that also our opponents may see in the thoughts outlined by His Holiness a common basis; that in a spirit of equity they may meet the demands of the European situation, that they may approach true predispositions for a future peace.[29]

With the sole exception of Wilson's cold and unsympathetic letter, the Central Powers were the only ones to send a reply in the strict sense of the term. Balfour's telegram to Count de Salis was merely the British government's instruction to its ambassador to make an oral acknowledgment and to say that Germany had not expressed herself with sufficient clarity. France had petulantly advised England to inform Cardinal Gasparri that he should refrain from involving her in any further peace efforts. Italy had sent no written reply. Baron Sonnino took advantage of a foreign policy debate to reply on Italy's behalf in very derogatory terms,[30] claiming that the note was nothing but the work of Germany, and that the proposals were utterly impracticable. In a later meeting of the Italian Parliament, Enrico Ferri, always regarded as anticlerical, surprised his colleagues in the chamber by stating his opinion that the failure of the Entente to reply was a serious error in diplomacy, and, to say the least, not a mark of good breeding.[31]

Emperor Charles of Austria-Hungary, in a letter dated September 20, gave enthusiastic endorsement to the papal proposals. Ferdinand of Bulgaria replied on September 26 in terms of reverence and loyalty. He hoped, he said, that the Pope's note would achieve a brilliant triumph because the thoughts expressed by His Holiness coincided strikingly with his own. Even Mohammed V, the Moslem Sultan of Turkey, in an autographed letter of September 30, expressed himself as "deeply touched by the lofty thoughts of His Holiness."[32]

Michaelis had sent his draft of the note, which already had the Emperor's signature, to Archbishop Pacelli ostensibly for the purpose of learning the Nuncio's reaction and to arrive at a text agreeable to both parties.[33] The Nuncio at once communicated it in cipher to Cardinal Gasparri. The fact that Belgium was not mentioned was a great disappointment. Therefore, the Nuncio wired Michaelis, begging him to amend the note with a more definite statement concerning the crucial point of Benedict's proposal, namely the restoration of Belgium and payment of indemnities. To this telegram Archbishop Pacelli received no answer. On September 19, the draft without change was officially dispatched as Germany's direct reply to the papal proposals. On September 21, the Nuncio sent the following wire to Michaelis:

> In the interests of peace the Holy See will not publish the answer of the imperial government until Berlin has spoken its last word concerning the papal suggestions.[34]

A monitored telephone conversation of September 22, made to Michaelis by von Treutler, the Prussian ambassador at the Bavarian court, yields this information:

> I told the papal nuncio that now nothing could be changed any more. . . . He repeated what today's telegram to him from the cardinal secretary of state contained, namely, that if this were the case, then the whole peace action of His Holiness may definitely be regarded as defeated.[35]

The German Chancellor, however, did not ignore the Nuncio's telegram. On September 24, Michaelis wired a letter to Archbishop Pacelli in which he assured the Nuncio that should the Cardinal Secretary of State want to continue his peace efforts, he would always find the German government perfectly in accord. As to the British note, Dr. Michaelis maintained that war aims should be precisely stated and in a definite order. Belgium and the questions connected with her should come first.

All these efforts, however, Michaelis said would be fruitless and doomed to failure if there is no "spirit of objectivity and respect."

In this His Holiness during the entire duration of this terrible war has given so shining an example. Among our opponents in general, however, a tendency has come to the fore of heaping the blame for the war only upon the central powers and of speaking of them as if a criminal had to appear before the bench of a strict judge. Only a spirit of calm judgment and reconciliation can create a favorable atmosphere for successful exchange of ideas. . . . It would not be consonant with the justifiable pride of the German people to meet with their opponents for a discussion of the possibilities and conditions of peace in any other atmosphere. The door is not closed.

I can already give expression to our animating hope that the great undertaking of His Holiness, the Pope, to restore the blessings of peace to the nations after so many terrors of this unprecedented war be crowned with complete success.

With special tokens of reverence I have the honor of remaining Your Excellency's most respectful

Michaelis.[36]

In assessing blame for Germany's inconclusive answer on the Belgian question, most historians have followed the judgment of Friedrich Ritter von Lama, a German writer, who seemed to have exhausted the documentary evidence on the frustration of Benedict's peace plan.[37] In three large volumes he attempts to maintain the thesis that: (1) Benedict's plan was wrecked by Germany; (2) the Kaiser can be exonerated from any co-operation in this; (3) Dr. Georg Michaelis alone is to blame; (4) Michaelis acted out of crass bigotry, having allowed himself to be made the tool of German Protestantism.

Because of his amazing work of precise documentation von Lama was considered the unimpeachable authority on the rejection of the papal peace note. In recent years, however, another German scholar, Ernst Deuerlein,[38] gained access to archives opened after World War II and found that von Lama did not have all the facts. Deuerlein's research shows that the guilty party was Richard von

Kühlmann, secretary of state for external affairs, and not Chancellor
Michaelis.

The first evidence which Deuerlein cites is a passage from von
Kühlmann's *Reminiscences*. He describes the enormous pile of
agenda laid before him as he entered upon his duties of secretary
of state.

> I found as my first and most important task the preparation of a
> reply to the papal note. No matter how permeated I was with the
> conviction that the Central Powers should attain peace as soon as pos-
> sible, I was just as prejudiced against obtaining peace through the
> mediation of a third party.[39]

Von Kühlmann adds that when he heard of Ribot's rejection of
the Pope's offer, he resolved all the more against admitting a third
party.

The next piece of evidence which Deuerlein adduces is drawn
from an interchange of letters between Georg von Hertling, eventually to succeed Michaelis as chancellor, and Hugo von Lerchenfeld,
Bavarian ambassador to Prussia. In a letter dated September 14,
1917, von Lerchenfeld wrote that he had just returned from a
visit with von Kühlmann who had told him the Pope would not
be informed of Germany's war aims nor of what was going to
happen in Belgium.[40] He adds that he has the feeling that something is wrong. He complains that what von Kühlmann quoted himself as having said in the committee meeting about what was to
be told Pope Benedict was somewhat at variance with von Lerchenfeld's own distinct recollection of what had been said at the meeting, at which he had been present.

So uneasy was von Lerchenfeld about the way the new Secretary
of State was handling the papal peace note that, without waiting
for a reply from von Hertling, he wrote a second letter. In it he
reported a conversation he had had with Michaelis. The Chancellor
told him that his recent journey to the front had convinced him
personally that the annexation of Belgium would bring no good
fortune to Germany. Michaelis had also paid a visit to Cardinal
Hartmann, archbishop of Cologne, who, though he was a stanch
German patriot, also advised against any seizure of Belgian territory. Michaelis derived special satisfaction from the fact that both
von Hindenburg and von Ludendorff had told him that if a speedy

peace could be won that autumn through a renunciation of Belgium, they would not advise the continuation of the war because of possible territorial gains in that country.[41]

Lastly, Deuerlein quotes a letter dated December 18, 1917, written by Richard von Kühlmann to Archbishop Pacelli. This unsolicited letter seems to be an attempt on von Kühlmann's part to clear his conscience before the Pope.

As you know, we welcomed the peace effort of His Holiness with lively satisfaction and sincere sympathy. In accord with these sentiments, our answer associated itself with the basic principles outlined by His Holiness which were to serve as the foundation for further action. If the Entente had answered with a similar attitude, the papal efforts toward peace would have been enhanced considerably. Instead, the Entente found it fitting not even to answer the note. If this attitude did not effect the collapse of the peace action, it at least brought it to a standstill.

From a secret source which is entirely reliable we learned that the Entente had made a pact in which, out of consideration for Italy, the Holy See was to be kept out of all peace negotiations. It is for this reason that we wished to see whether the telegram from Great Britain might not be merely a camouflage. First we wanted to get a clear picture of these antecedents. Only thereafter could we advise the Nuncio about the intentions and demands of the imperial government especially on the question of Belgium. In order to find out about Britain, the secretary of state for external affairs decided on a way convenient at that time. He entrusted the mission of finding out England's intentions to an experienced, skillful, and reliable man acquainted with conditions and officials in England, who declared himself willing to perform this task. The Spanish government was not approached either directly or indirectly for the execution of this mission. Entirely against the will of the secretary of state as well as against that of the man entrusted with the task, the entire matter was construed in a manner which was at variance with the views here. The secretary of state deems it an honor to tell the apostolic nuncio confidentially that the man is a Spaniard. However, for reasons of discretion and loyalty, he must withhold his name.

Herr von Kühlmann would be grateful if the nuncio would communicate the above message confidentially to Rome and note especially that he as ever stands steadfastly by the sentiments expressed in the communication of September 24. Unfortunately, he must depart for the military headquarters and subsequently to Brest-Litowsk in order to inaugurate peace negotiations there. If more time were at his disposal, he would allow no one to prevent his making a personal appearance at Munich so that he might say orally what he is now communicating in this telegram.[42]

Deuerlein's conclusions are the following: von Kühlmann's explanation, his note to the Nuncio, the allegations of von Lerchenfeld leave no doubt that the treatment and answering of the papal peace note were left to him. It was he who charted the course of the deliberations in Germany. It was from him that the objections against a binding statement concerning Belgium emanated. It is evident that he preferred his own idea of peace negotiations to the plans of the Pope. The odium is taken from Michaelis because of the account he gave to von Lerchenfeld of his trip to Belgium on which he became convinced that Belgium's annexation to Germany would not be an unmixed blessing. The letter of von Kühlmann to Archbishop Pacelli seems to betray a feeling of guilt because the writer expends so much effort in vindicating his every action.

There is not the slightest indication of interdenominational motives. These may have been present, but no mention is made of them. It is known that both Benedict XV and the Nuncio on various occasions spoke of their disappointment at the fate of the peace plan, but they never hinted that it was occasioned by Protestant prejudice.

It should be stated that Deuerlein was not the first Catholic to point out that von Lama's thesis was incorrect. The Irish writer, Denis Gwynn, wrote of von Lama, "He pays little attention to the opposition aroused in France and he assumes that Balfour's reply of August 21 was tantamount to acceptance of the Pope's proposals."[43] Francis Pichon, a French writer, indicts his own nation: "France wanted no premature peace but only a peace resulting from victory won with arms."[44] It is said that after Balfour saw how indignant France felt about being associated with Britain's wired instructions to Count de Salis, the British Secretary of State alleged the wire had been sent by mistake.[45] Perhaps the fairest appraisal of the situation is given by George Seldes in his *The Vatican: Yesterday — Today, Tomorrow,* who distributes the blame over all the belligerents: "The nations were still too blood-thirsty, too land hungry, to accept peace, and each side still was certain of a victory which would gain billions in indemnity, colonies, world trade,

hegemony, the supreme power for future centuries."⁴⁶ It is true that
Germany avoided giving an explicit answer on Belgium, but the
members of the Entente certainly did not distinguish themselves in
their efforts to be cooperative. There is not too much to be said
in their defense on the charge made by Michaelis in his letter of
September 24, "Among our opponents in general, however, a tendency has come to the fore of heaping the blame for the war only
upon the Central Powers and of speaking of them as if a criminal
had to appear before the bench of a strict judge."

When Benedict finally realized that his offer had been rejected
by the principal powers on both sides, he did not hide his disappointment. To Cardinal Csernoch, archbishop of Gran, who
had thanked the Holy Father for his peace plan, the Pope enumerated the reasons that had prompted the note: "paternal love, consciousness of apostolic duty, feelings of commiseration, love of justice, right, and public tranquility." His reward, he wrote, was to
be regarded as "the object of unworthy suspicion." He added wistfully that now he could truly "use that expression of the Apostle:
'We are reviled, and we bless: we are persecuted, and we suffer it;
we are blasphemed, and we entreat.' "⁴⁷

To the hierarchy of Bavaria Benedict wrote a letter of gratitude
for an expression of homage which he had received on the occasion
of a meeting at Freising.

This was no common pleasure, or rather it was a consolation to Us,
a consolation which indeed you see that We greatly need in these
bitter times. For to the other anxieties and cares which afflict Our
soul by the length of this terrible war there is added this, namely that
Our exhortation to restore peace, which in truth sprang from no
other motive than from a sincere desire of public good, not only had
an effect that We hoped for least of all but hatred against Us although
it was a proof of Our love. In this matter We do not so much complain
at the injustice visited upon Us — for We ought to be always ready
to bear insults for the name of Jesus — as We grieve at the loss of so
many lives.⁴⁸

In his annual allocution on Christmas Eve, the Pope expressed to
the assembled cardinals his keen disappointment. In 1914, in the
first of these allocutions, he had spoken of the comforts that he
had mistakenly hoped for at Christmas. By 1917 he had become
much more realistic.

By now accustomed to celebrate, by the Divine Will, with joy tempered by sadness, the most sweet recurrence of the holy feast, we were preparing to give voice to the sorrows of the father and the anguish of the shepherd, in the fourth wartime celebration of the anniversary of the Birth of Our Lord Jesus Christ. . . . We felt, like Paul, a keen sorrow when all Our endeavors to effect a reconciliation among the peoples had failed. We were grieved particularly that the invitation addressed by Us to the chiefs of the belligerent peoples had gone unheeded — not because personal gratification had been denied Us, but because the peace of nations had been delayed.

He explained that all he had done was to gather together points which various "authoritative circles" had presented as "essential principles for discussion." He had meant to hasten the advent of peace but he found that he became merely "the sign which shall be contradicted."[49] "We were comforted," he reflected, "by the hope that Our invitation to peace, since it was not one that looked for immediate effects, might perhaps be likened to the kernel of wheat which our Divine Master says, 'Unless the grain of wheat falling into the ground die, itself remaineth alone; but if it die, it bringeth forth much fruit.' "[50]

Actually, Benedict soon did see the seed which he had planted push its way to the sunlight. On January 8, 1918, Woodrow Wilson delivered an address before the two houses of congress in which he proposed his famous "fourteen points,"[51] all of which were contained implicitly in Benedict's seven points. Wilson rearranged them and proposed them more explicitly. For example, Benedict in his fourth point had spoken of "True liberty and community of the seas." Wilson in his second point spoke of "Absolute freedom of navigation upon the seas." In his second point Benedict spoke of "A simultaneous and reciprocal diminution of armaments according to rules and guarantees." This was handled by Wilson in his fourth point when he alluded to "Adequate guarantees for reduction of national armaments." The sixth point of Benedict, which treats of "Restitution of territories at the moment occupied," was expanded by Wilson into three points, namely, point seven, in which the President spoke of Belgium; point eight, in which he treated of French territory; and point eleven, in which he enumerated the other occupied territories.

Had the war-weary people been asked their opinion, and had they in that era of violent prejudice had the right to speak, Benedict's appeal might have found enthusiastic acceptance. It may be, indeed, that the President's belated use of the papal principles was dictated by the mail received from the people, such as this quaint note from the Quakers:

> We urge thee to accept the great opportunity presented by the Pope's message. Although it does not attempt to set forth detailed and final terms, it at least affords a firm and hopeful basis, in harmony with thy address of the First Month, second, for beginning negotiations leading to permanent peace. We firmly believe that the *growing desire to punish Germany, born of a revengeful spirit,* should be subordinate to the opportunity here offered to safeguard, through liberalism, the future peace of nations.[52]

In this message there is an understanding of Benedict's aims which statesmen and even Catholic journalists failed to reach.

It must have taken great courage for the otherwise shy Della Chiesa to come forward with an official letter addressed directly to the heads of the belligerent nations. He realized that it was an extraordinary act.[53] Since 1870 the popes had deemed it expedient to sit back and suffer the violence done to the Holy See by the *Risorgimento.* But with the world embroiled in the most disastrous war in all history, Benedict XV felt that he must lay aside the reserve practiced by Pius IX, Leo XIII, and Saint Pius X. All of them, it is true, had spoken; but only in apostolic constitutions, encyclicals, *motu proprios,* and consistorial allocutions, always addressed to Catholics. Count Sforza observes that Benedict came forward in the brave spirit of the Gregorys and the Innocents and showed that the Pope was still the universal father, the vicegerent of Jesus Christ whose function it is to save all men.[54]

CHAPTER XV

Benedict, Wilson, and Versailles

IN THE late afternoon of January 4, 1919, some notes lay on the desk of the Pope's *maestro di camera*, ready to be delivered to the editor of *L'Osservatore Romano*. One of the notes had this scrawled comment: "The Holy Father has received in private audience Mr. Woodrow Wilson, the president of the United States." To the casual reader, browsing through the old files of the Vatican newspaper, this announcement is not particularly noteworthy. However, in January, 1919, these two — the Pope and the President of the United States — were the most discussed celebrities in the world. Differing greatly in personal appearance, national background, education, culture, and religion, they were alike in this: both tried to propose a peace plan for the world and both failed.

While in Paris, in December, attending the Peace Conference, Wilson received an unexpected visit from King Victor of Italy, inviting him to include Rome in his itinerary. At this time the President was happy to accept the invitation because it would enable him to pay a visit of state to the Pope.

The idea of visiting the Pope, however, did not receive its first impulse from Victor Emmanuel's invitation. The remote cause was a letter from Cardinal Gibbons of November 27, 1918. In the first part of the letter the Cardinal told Wilson that Benedict thought very highly of the President. Then he went on to say:

> My dear Mr. President, as an American as well as a Catholic, as one who is bound to you by the bonds of patriotism as I am bound to the Holy Father in the bonds of religion, I ask you in the strongest and most affectionate manner of which I am capable not to leave Rome without paying a personal visit to the Pope. I ask you to do this not only because it will be a great consolation to the Holy Father who so admires and trusts you, not only because it will bind the hearts of Catholics to you forever, but because it will delight the hearts of all good men, who whether they agree with the Holy Father in religion or not, at least recognize him as the representative of the greatest

moral authority left in the world, and because you, Mr. President, in the opinion of all men, are the one who raised the late war from the plane of national jealousies into the plane of idealism and made it a conflict and a struggle for justice, for righteousness, for liberty and for nothing else. I say then that this will give delight to all men of good will to know that you have not disregarded or slighted the representative of the moral order.

I feel sure that I have only asked you to do what you have already determined in your heart to do, but which I felt it was nevertheless my duty to put before you.[1]

Only the crassest bigotry could find fault with this approach. Archbishop Giovanni Bonzano, the apostolic delegate to the United States, congratulated Gibbons on his beautiful and thoughtful letter. Wilson's reply is dated three days later, November 30, 1918. He informed the Cardinal that he was deferring pressing matters in order to express personally his appreciation of the prelate's kind words of understanding, words which betokened Gibbons' interest in the welfare of the world at large. He said that he had not worked out the details of his journey to Europe and did not know whether he would visit Italy. He added, "It will give me real pleasure to have your suggestions in mind if I should go to Rome."

January 4 was scheduled for Wilson's audience with the Pope. Despite the fact that the newspapers gave prominent space to the audience, the relations between the Holy See and the House of Savoy, ruptured since 1870, precluded any discussion of this visit. All arrangements were made through the American Embassy. Monsignor Charles O'Hearn, rector of the American College, was to act as ecclesiastical companion to the President. Mrs. Wilson decided not to go but in her memoirs she remarks that several of their attendants were Catholics, and that in their estimation a visit to the Pope constituted "the climax of their lives."[2]

The President's carriage drove into the Court of Saint Damasus, the center of the apostolic palace, where a detachment of gendarmes heralded the President's arrival with bugles. At the foot of the grand staircase he was met by Monsignor Canali, secretary of the Sacred Congregation of Ceremonies.[3] The President was then received by the pontifical court headed by the major domo, the master of the chamber, the grand steward, and the commander of the Swiss Guard.[4] Finally Wilson found himself in the throne room of the Vatican. He had just time to catch a glimpse of two golden chairs when there came forward a small, thin man in a white cassock with a chain and cross twinkling on his breast. Wilson and Benedict XV were face to face.

After Monsignor O'Hearn made the formal introduction, the President stepped forward. He was considerably taller than the Pope. Although he was two years younger, his hair was almost white and contrasted sharply with the jet-black hair of the Pontiff.

The President then introduced the members of his party. The first to be introduced was his personal physician of whom the President said, "This is Admiral Grayson. He is the man who keeps me well."

"Apparently he has done a splendid job," the Pope replied. Then turning to Grayson, he added, "And you have performed a great service to humanity."

Thereafter everyone withdrew, leaving the two world figures to discuss the possibilities of a lasting peace.[5] We know with certainty only one subject which was discussed, and this we have from Benedict's own account. On March 10, 1919, he wrote to Cardinal von Hartmann: "On a solemn occasion we had the opportunity of expressing to a man of exalted rank our lively desire that the hundreds and thousands of prisoners of war who had for so long a time borne the sufferings of captivity be brought back to their native hearths. We had the satisfaction of perceiving that that celebrity shared fully and entirely our ardent wishes and that he was determined to support them."[6] An official communiqué released by the Vatican denied that the Pope had attempted to gain a seat at the peace negotiations. It also branded as untrue the report that Benedict had broached the subject of the Roman Question.[7]

The question may be asked: In what language did the Pontiff and the President converse? Since Benedict had been such an ardent student of French, it was assumed by many that that language was used in the audience. However, the historian Ludwig Pastor records a conversation which he had with Cardinal Gasparri years later in which the latter remarked: "Wilson spoke English only, and an interpreter was necessary."[8]

After the discussion was ended the Pope signaled his intention of saying farewell to the group. Wilson was given a precious mosaic made in the ancient shop of the Vatican. The mosaic, a reproduction of Reni's Saint Peter, measured a yard square. Cardinal Gasparri stepped forward and presented the President with two volumes in rich bindings. They were copies of the newly released *Code of Canon Law*, a major work of Benedict's pontificate. The one volume, bound in white parchment, was autographed by the Cardinal Secretary of State and dedicated to the President. The second was artistically bound in red leather and bore the thoughtful legend: "Homage to Princeton University from Pietro Cardinal Gasparri, Vatican, Rome."

At this point one of the Catholics present, probably Mr. Murphy, the head of Wilson's secret service escort, murmured a request to Monsignor O'Hearn that he and some of his companions receive the papal blessing. Wilson overheard this and, returning to the role of leader of the tour, said briskly, "Very well, how many are Catholics?"

The Holy Father seemed to have understood this question, because he interrupted in Italian, "That doesn't make any difference! This blessing is for you, and for your near and dear ones."[9]

While almost everyone knelt and the President stood with bowed head, the Pope signed himself and began, *"Sit nomen Domini Benedictum!"* The ecclesiastics made the responses. Then, stretching out his arms, the Vicar of Christ said with the stirring reverence for which he was so well known, *"Benedictio Dei Omnipotentis, Patris et Filii et Spiritus Sancti descendat super vos et maneat semper."*

The stone walls echoed the mighty *"Amen!"*

Wilson was visibly touched by the kindness of the Holy Father. Cordially he thanked the Pope and Cardinal Gasparri and took his leave. However, immediately after Wilson left the Square of Saint Peter, his day was somewhat spoiled. He had been told that he could address the people in the Piazza Venezia. But before the President left the Vatican, the police had been given secret instructions to disperse the crowd. Wilson took this as a deliberate slight and, blazing with anger, he spoke his mind to the officials. Mrs. Wilson writes that these latter "tried to explain their action by saying the crowd was so vast that they feared it would get out of hand and cause a riot. Thus they tried to save their faces, but the veneer was too thin to fool anyone."[10] This whole affair seems to have been inspired by anticlerical members in the Italian government, who sought to punish the President for having visited the Holy Father.

Woodrow Wilson left Rome for the Peace Conference in France.

Benedict, who had popularized the expression "a just and lasting peace," had to remain behind.

On December 24, 1915, Benedict learned of the infamous Article 15 in the secret agreement of London of April 25, 1915, which provided unequivocally for the exclusion of the Pope from any peace negotiations.[11]

France, Great Britain and Russia shall support such opposition as Italy may make to any proposal in the direction of introducing a representative of the Holy See in any peace negotiations or negotiations for the settlement of questions raised by the present war.

Even before the facts of this article became fully known, *L'Osservatore Romano* had carried editorials making it plain that Benedict XV would play no part in a peace whose theme would be *vae victis* (woe to the vanquished).[12] In June of 1919 Cardinal Gasparri released the following statement to the press:

It has been repeatedly stated that the Holy See was making efforts to obtain a seat at the Conference, but the truth is nothing was further from our thought. Monsignor Cerretti, who is now in Paris, was merely entrusted by the Holy Father with the task of trying to save flourishing German missions in Africa and Australia.

Several religious orders have been founded by Germany with the sole purpose of evangelizing and civilizing heathen populations. The results have been excellent, and it would be a pity were such good seed thrown in vain. We hope and believe that President Wilson and his colleagues understand the advisability of not wrecking this work of Christian love and sacrifice.[13]

It was on the question of the German missions that Pope Benedict asked the aid of President Wilson and received it. In brief, the reason for the Pope's earnest plea was the following: the Peace Conference attempted to efface all German influence even in so strictly religious an activity as that of evangelizing the heathen. Paragraphs 122 and 438 of the proposed treaty imperiled the freedom of the Church's missionary work. As early as March 25, 1919, the German bishops called the attention of the Holy Father to danger latent in the two paragraphs. Paragraph 122 provided that the local government could expel from its respective district all residents of German origin and fix the conditions of their residence. This was to apply even to missionaries. Paragraph 438 established that the property of the missions in general — Catholic and Protestant — was to be administered by a council composed of Christians nominated by the local government. "The duty of this council is to exercise vigilance that the income finds its way to missions in general."

On June 1, 1919, the leading editorial in *L'Osservatore Romano* explained what violence these two articles in the treaty were doing to the rights of the Holy See. How carefully Benedict controlled the editorial policy of *L'Osservatore Romano* has already been pointed out. If he himself did not write the editorial on the treaty and the missions, he certainly submitted the points to be developed by a staff writer. The article quoted Canon 1350, § 2, of the newly promulgated *Code of Canon Law,* which states that all Catholic missions — as well as property — depend exclusively upon the Holy See. No missionary, the article went on to say, whether he be of a religious order or of the diocesan clergy, may enter the mission field without a diploma or credentials issued by the Sacred Congregation of the Propagation of the Faith. The pope has the right to send out missionaries of every nationality. To exclude any single nationality would be an attempt to restrict divine prerogatives. Property which Catholic missionaries of a given nationality are said to own, is not owned by the nation to which they belong, but by the Sacred Congregation of the Propagation of the Faith. Should a Catholic missionary be so forgetful of his calling as to become a political agent or agitator, the Holy See is to be informed, and the man would be dealt with instantly.

The Pope did not confine his activity to the pen. He sent to Paris one of his foremost diplomats, Monsignor Bonaventura Cerretti. By June 26, Benedict was able to report to the college of cardinals that the clauses had been so revised as to insure freedom to the Catholic missionaries. According to the revision, the various denominations would be able to procure and possess property. The boards empowered to review matters pertaining to the property would not merely be Christians but would be members of the denomination whose property was in question. If it became necessary to exercise some control over personnel in charge of certain missions, no action would be taken without first informing the religious authorities of the missions involved.[14] In a letter to the German bishops in which the Pope described his efforts in procuring these favorable results, he wrote, "Now I am very happy to inform you that owing to the spirit of fairness shown by the personages at the Peace Conference our requests in greater part have been satisfied."[15]

On July 1, 1919, a letter left the Vatican, addressed to "Doctor Woodrow Wilson, President of the United States." The letter is a papal autograph in which Benedict thanks Wilson for his efforts in behalf of the Catholic missions, the details of which had been minutely reported to him by Monsignor Cerretti. However, he has a further request which he would like to make at this time. Would the President use his influence to block the proposed trial of the Kaiser and officers of the German army? This trial, in Benedict's mind, would not only perpetuate hatred and delay the spirit of peace in men's hearts but also create insuperable difficulties which are delineated in an appended clipping.[16]

The clipping from *L'Osservatore Romano,* which the Pope enclosed, bore the dateline, June 2, 1919. Benedict had submitted certain points to a legal expert at the University of Bologna, asking him to develop them in a series of articles. The cutting from *L'Osservatore* was one of these articles and it discussed the determination of the Entente to bring to justice the Kaiser with some nine hundred German generals and officials. The points treated in the articles were the following:

1. That the accusers themselves should constitute the Tribunal of Justice is unprecedented in the history of criminal law.
2. If the allied powers should take action against Holland, which was harboring the Kaiser, it would be a violation of the very principle for which the members of the Entente claimed that they had entered the war, namely, to guarantee the inviolability of the weaker nations.
3. In order to see whether the Kaiser is the sole war criminal, one would have to examine the diplomatic acts from the secret archives of all the belligerents.
4. To force Germany to yield up its generals for punishment would be tantamount to forcing a mother to hand her children over to the enemy for punishment.
5. If Germany should refuse, would the allies reopen the hostilities which they had just concluded?
6. The charge against the Kaiser is that he violated the laws and customs of war. This charge could be pressed only if it could be proved that the leaders of the other nations adhered to these laws and customs.[17]

Wilson replied to the Pope in a letter with a courtesy which contrasted sharply with the tone of his reply to the Peace Note of 1917. The present letter is that of a person writing to a friend whom he cherishes. He said that it was "with the greatest pleasure" that he had used his influence to protect the interests of the missions. He added that he had read with interest Benedict's suggestions that the proposed trial of the Kaiser and German officers be dropped. He graciously complimented Benedict on the clarity with which he had expressed the reason which had motivated his suggestions.[18]

The prudent manner in which Benedict XV presented his request to the President of the United States eventually had the desired effect. Italy was the first to drop her charges against the Kaiser. Japan and the United States speedily followed the example of Italy. For a while France and England stood alone in their efforts to bring him to trial. Gradually even from their ranks the clamor for the Kaiser's life died down.

Benedict XV must not be considered naïvely gullible in regard to the German Emperor's disposition toward the Church. Pastor's diary contains notes of a conversation with Benedict shortly before the latter's death, in which the Pope said that he had never thought of William II as a friend of the Catholic Church. For many years he had known the content of a biting letter which the Kaiser had written on the occasion of Anna von Hessen's conversion to the Catholic faith.[19]

This fact brings into higher relief the Pontiff's example of genuine Christian charity in this loveless world. As usual, Benedict received no thanks for this humanitarian act. In an address given on February 29, 1924, General von Ludendorff, who may well have owed his life to Benedict, excoriated his deceased benefactor for his partiality to France during the war. Whether the Kaiser ever sent a message of gratitude is not known to us. If he did, it was never published.

While Benedict's name was not mentioned expressly in the Treaty of Versailles, his influence was felt. The Peace Note, rejected in 1917, was not forgotten. It is now generally recognized that Wilson's famous "Fourteen Points" were built on Benedict's suggestions. Britain also concurred with the Pope's plea for cancellation of indemnities, but France, Italy, Serbia, and Rumania were determined to exact payment from the vanquished foe. As a result, the Treaty of Versailles imposed insupportable burdens of repayment on the defeated countries.[20] While the treaty made strides in the direction of disarmament, it was not an equitable provision which was finally arranged. But faulty though the clauses were, they reflected that Benedict's point did not go entirely unheeded. The section of disarmament concludes with the words: "Thence must follow a just agreement of all for the simultaneous and reciprocal diminution of armaments." A further influence of Benedict is discernible in the fact that Lloyd George strove hard to obtain the universal abolition of military conscription.

The idea of a League of Nations which Wilson preached so ardently possibly was engendered by Benedict's words advocating "as a substitute for armies the institution of arbitration." Unfortunately, Wilson's own country was the only major one which rejected the League with uncompromising vehemence. Unfortunately also, it was linked in men's minds with the Treaty of Versailles, which was severely criticized the moment its terms became known.

It was Benedict's lot to be continually under fire from his critics. The heads of nations had met to exclude him from the Peace Conference. His Peace Note of 1917 was considered religion's arrogant and unwarranted intrusion into politics, a domain which should be foreign to the papacy. When Benedict followed the only course open to him, that is, of keeping out of the negotiations at Versailles, his silence too was severely criticized.

"Where are the representatives of religion?" asked President Fehrenbach at the Weimar National Assembly.

"The world is again waiting for the voice of revered authority which in times past spoke for justice during international conflicts. The proponents of reconciliation, now standing at the threshold of the greatest and most critical hour, must indeed be waiting for some word from the pope," cried an Augsburg paper in agonizing tones on the eve of the Peace Conference.[21] It certainly was a strange phenomenon that the very ones who had shouted indignation at any of Benedict XV's counsels and proposals for peace during the war, were now loudest in their censure of him for abstaining from active participation in the Peace Treaty.

On June 28, 1919, at three o'clock in the afternoon, the Treaty of Versailles was signed in the Hall of Mirrors. German representatives signed it, designating by their seal that they were accepting the treaty's hard conditions. Yet the world seemed conscience-stricken and demanded a reproof. Through bitter experience Pope

Benedict knew that if he had said one word in protest, that same world would have called down upon him the fire and brimstone of its disorderly thinking. Although Benedict himself kept a discreet silence, *Civiltà Cattolica,* whose editor was in close touch with the Pope, spoke out, sharply indicting the treaty as a travesty of a conciliatory act. The four hundred and forty so-called "Articles of Peace" the periodical denounced as "Articles of War." "In those articles of a treaty promised us for so long a time and given to the world as the very epitome of political sagacity, there is evident a consecration to hatred, a tone inspired by the spirit of revenge, a perpetuation of war."[22] With these all too prophetic words the famed Italian Jesuit publication characterized the Treaty of Versailles.

Before Benedict was to issue his monumental encyclical, *Pacem Dei Munus,* commemorating the long-desired cessation of hostilities, he had to make two pointed appeals for the extinction of hatred. The first, an apostolic letter, *Diuturni luctuosissimi belli,* of June 17, 1919, he addressed to the German hierarchy.[23] He unites his prayers with theirs in thanking God that the great blockade has at last been lifted. He urges them to repair the damages wrought to their country as soon as possible. The heart of the message is an exhortation to them that hate must be banished. It throbs with the very essence of the Gospel.

> It is especially necessary to eliminate every feeling of hatred either toward foreigners, with whom the nation was at war, or toward fellow citizens of other parties; and in the place of hatred put the brotherly love which is of Christ, which knows no barrier or limit or strife of class. And we repeat here the hope We expressed at the last consistory, that "men and people may again be united in Christian charity, because if that be lacking every peace treaty will be vain."[24]

If the Germans smarted at the thought that they, the vanquished, were implicitly accused of harboring hatred, they did not have to feel themselves discriminated against. In due time the French also received their lecture on the abandonment of hatred. The apostolic letter, *Amor ille singularis,* dated October 7, 1919, was written to be read at the dedication of the Church of the Sacred Heart on Montmartre. The church had been built by popular subscription in pursuance of a vow made on the spot just after the defeat of the French armies in 1870. The date for the consecration had been fixed for October, 1914, but the outbreak of the war prevented the ceremony from taking place. The occasion in 1919, therefore, had somewhat of the flush of victory about it. Cardinal Amette, archbishop of Paris, at the Pope's express behest, read in French the autograph letter in the presence of cardinals, archbishops, and bishops, one hundred and twenty-five in number, not counting the hundreds of priests and thousands of laity. After congratulating the Church in France on final realization of their vow, the Pontiff wrote:

> We beg the liberty of pointing out a further design of Divine Providence, namely, as this temple on the Mount of the Martyrs, erected because of a vow taken so many years ago, is a testimony of France's grateful memory toward the Sacred Heart, so its dedication has been delayed until this moment when your nation is bound by the holy task of presenting with grand symbolism a grateful heart to God since it has emerged victorious from the greatest war in man's memory.[25]

In exquisite language Benedict urged prayer to "the Divine Heart which loved and loves the human race and which dowered the French nation with singular favors. Love is repaid only with love." He quotes as the epitome of the Old and New Testaments teaching the words of Christ: " 'Thou shalt love the Lord thy God with thy whole heart, and with thy whole soul, and with thy whole mind.' This is the greatest and the first commandment. And the second is like it, *'Thou shalt love thy neighbor as thyself.'* "[26] "The Sacred Heart," continued Benedict, "shows in a moving manner the immeasurable love of Jesus toward His children so often oblivious of it. This love, however, is destined to be exhibited to all men, even to enemies, because we are all sons of God and have all been redeemed by the blood of Christ."

Again Benedict fingers his worn copy of the New Testament, and the page falls open to one of his favorite texts: "You have heard that it was said, 'Thou shalt love thy neighbor, and thou shalt hate thy enemy.' But I say to you, love your enemies, do good to those who hate you, and pray for those who persecute and calumniate you, so that you may be children of your Father in heaven."[27]

As if aware of the fact that his own entreaties are so inextricably intertwined with those of his Divine Master, Benedict says immediately after the quotation:

This is what our Lord and Master said, this the apostles handed down to us and especially that herald of love, Saint John. We know well enough that a precept of this kind does not please the world. Those who insist on the holiness of this precept find their admonitions interpreted perversely, and are repaid with calumnies. This happened in the case of Jesus Christ; it happens also to His vicar. It cannot be otherwise in the lives of those who preach that injuries should be forgotten and that love must be practiced toward those who have done evil to us and have attacked our fatherland. If we wish to render to the Divine Heart of Jesus the worship most pleasing to Him, we must stimulate in our own hearts this double love of God and of man, irrespective of whether the man is or was our enemy. It is especially *the duty of the clergy* to call the attention of their flock to this work. If we are not reconciled to one another from the bottom of our hearts, there can be no hope of healing such great wounds and of establishing a lasting peace.[28]

Pacem Dei Munus was the encyclical, dated May 23, 1920, which Benedict published at the end of the war. What beautiful words open this magnificent document, *Peace, God's most beautiful gift!* Benedict had mapped out his course in *Ad Beatissimi,* and the world's rejection of him did not make him change his course one iota. Indeed, he worked the more assiduously to make his apostolate of love catch fire in the hearts of men.

John Eppstein, in his monumental work, *The Catholic Tradition of the Law of Nations,* reproduced *Pacem Dei Munus* in full, "since," as he says, "in the midst of the passions bequeathed by a great war, it sets forth the abiding principles of Christian Peace."[29] Eppstein seems to have been one of the few who realized Benedict's greatness as a thinker. This is evident from the fact that, while he usually quotes but a few lines from other papal pronouncements, he quotes every word of this encyclical from the salutation to the conventional conclusion and signature. Francis Pichon says that this encyclical contains the most beautiful thoughts on peace that any pope has ever expressed.[30]

Benedict "prays and exhorts in the mercy and charity of Jesus Christ to strive with all zeal and diligence not only to abandon hatred and to pardon offences but also to promote all those works of Christian benevolence which bring aid to the needy, comfort to the afflicted, and protection to the weak, and to give opportune and appropriate assistance of every kind to all who have suffered from the war."[31]

He repeats what he had said in his letters to the German and the French bishops but with an even greater ardor:

It is Our especial wish that you should exhort your priests, as the ministers of peace, to be assiduous in urging this love of one's neighbor and even of enemies which is the essence of the Christian life, and by *being all things to all men* and giving an example to others, to wage war everywhere on enmity and hatred, thus doing a thing most agreeable to the loving Heart of Jesus and to him, who, however unworthy, holds his place on earth. In this connection Catholic writers and journalists should be invited to clothe themselves as *elect of God, holy and beloved, with pity and kindness.*[32] Let them show charity in their writings by abstaining not only from false and groundless accusations, but also from all intemperance and bitterness of language, all of which is contrary to the law of Christ and does but reopen sores as yet unhealed, seeing that the slightest touch is a serious irritant to a heart whose wounds are recent.

The central paragraph of the encyclical is his summary of the story of the Good Samaritan. "The two cases are similar," he writes: "so too is it necessary that Jesus, of whom the Samaritan was the figure, should lay His hand upon the wounds of society."

The Pope does not mention the League of Nations which Wilson encouraged and fostered but could not induce his own country to accept. Benedict was highly in favor of a league of nations, but not one in which conquerors drunk with power were to favor themselves. Benedict, who was to extend the feast of the Holy Family to the Universal Church, who in order to call attention to the family had written a beautiful encyclical on the fiftieth anniversary of the universal patronage of Saint Joseph, who in his many allocutions spoke so movingly of the beauties of family life, recommended in *Pacem Dei Munus* a "family of peoples."

It is much to be desired, Venerable Brethren, that all states, putting aside mutual suspicion, should unite in one league, or rather a sort of family of peoples, calculated both to maintain their own independence and safeguard the order of human society. What especially, amongst other reasons, calls for such an association of nations, is the need generally recognized of making every effort to abolish or reduce the enormous burden of the military expenditure which states can no longer bear, in order to prevent these disastrous wars or at least to remove the danger of them as far as possible. So would each nation be assured not only of its independence but also of the integrity of its territory within its just frontiers.

The conclusion flows from a heart steeped in meditation of the Divine:

> Meanwhile, trusting in the protection of Mary the Virgin Immaculate, who not long ago We directed should be universally invoked as "Queen of Peace," as also in the intercession of the three Blessed to whom We have decreed the honor of Saints,[33] We humbly implore the Holy Ghost, the Paraclete, that He may "graciously grant to the Church the gifts of unity and peace,"[34] and may renew the face of the earth by a fresh outpouring of His charity for the salvation of all.

CHAPTER XVI

The Apostolate of Charity During the War

BENEDICT'S charitable activities were so varied that it is almost impossible to treat of them all. The chapter dealing with this subject in Father Vistalli's encyclopedic volume is little more than an outline of eight headings with many subdivisions. This outline covers about fifty pages of closely packed print.[1] To give the reader an idea of the multiplicity of the Pope's activities, some of the more interesting of Vistalli's points are here cited: the liberation, exchange, and hospitalization of military and civilian prisoners; the repatriation of tubercular prisoners; the Pope's insistence on Sunday and feast-day rest for interned prisoners; decent burial and individual, marked graves for allied soldiers who were killed at the Dardanelles; material aid of money, food, medicine, and clothing to those rendered destitute by war; the Pope's office or bureau for notifying families as to where their dear ones were imprisoned, and his effort to enable prisoners to write to their families. Only a few of these will be taken up in detail.

EXCHANGE OF PRISONERS

Almost immediately upon his accession to the papal throne, Benedict XV pleaded for an exchange of disabled prisoners. At first it was suggested to him that Spain be made the haven for convalescent French prisoners, and Holland for German prisoners. The efforts to secure the help of Spain, however, were quickly abandoned. Benedict took matters into his own hands and sent his friend, Count Carlo Santucci, a lawyer, to Joseph Motta, the president of the Swiss Federation. In the letter which Count Santucci presented, Benedict said that to him personally Switzerland had occurred first for a number of reasons: (1) its beautiful tradition for hospitality, (2) the peaceful character of its people, (3) its neutrality established now more firmly than ever, (4) its topographical position, and (5) its variety of languages and cultures.[2]

179

The Swiss replied that they were flattered by the Holy Father's kind thoughts toward them and admitted that their government had some thought of offering land for the purposes the Pope had suggested, but they added that the administrative difficulties had seemed too great. Santucci assured them that the Holy Father would assume the responsibility for administration.

On January 11, 1915, Benedict asked all belligerent nations to liberate or exchange civilian prisoners. He made the following classifications: (1) women and girls, (2) boys under seventeen years, (3) adults over fifty-five, (4) physicians and surgeons, (5) ministers of religion, (6) all, regardless of age, who were disabled or otherwise unfit for military service. The appeal was heeded, and almost immediately more than three thousand Belgians were allowed to return home. In one month alone, twenty thousand French returned home.

In May and June of 1916, Benedict suggested to the Allies and the Central Powers that prisoners who were fathers of four children should be released and given hospitality in Switzerland. On April 5, 1917, Germany sent to Constance its first one hundred French prisoners in this classification. A few days later, France sent one hundred German prisoners. The kindly disposed Swiss government took the further step of arranging an equitable repatriation.

SOLDIERS SUFFERING FROM TUBERCULOSIS

Many soldiers had contracted tuberculosis during their service in damp trenches. The Holy Father insisted that these be released without any thought of exchange or compensation. These patients were transferred to the pure air of the mountains of northern Italy.[3] When the shrill whistle of the hospital train sounded, people would leave their work, children would scamper to the stone fences of their property and wave happily to what they termed *il treno del Papa* ("the Pope's train").[4] Through the Pope's efforts 12,376 French, 8594 German, 1822 Belgian, and 964 English prisoners suffering from tuberculosis were transferred to more healthful climes between the end of January, 1916, and November 17, 1917.[5]

ALMSGIVING

When Pius XI ascended the papal throne and caught his first glimpse of the ledger of the Holy See, he was alarmed at what he saw.[6] In fact, Cardinal Gasparri had to borrow money to pay for

THE APOSTOLATE OF CHARITY

Benedict's funeral and the conclave.⁷ The expenditures were clearly recorded. Benedict had spent nothing on himself. He made only the most necessary repairs in the Vatican. He had depleted the treasury in charitable contributions during the war and after. He had asked the world to contribute heroically but he himself always took the initiative in this charity. Louis Bertrand, a journalist, epitomized his impressions of Benedict by saying, "I had the feeling of a sort of perpetual anguish in which the shepherd lives. He seems to suffer cruelly from not being able to act according to his heart."⁸

Benedict kept large sums of money in his desk and would give lavishly to anyone with a sad tale. Sometimes the Pope would exhaust his funds days before they could be replenished. At such times, Cardinal Gasparri used to plead with visitors not to mention their plight in the papal presence because Benedict would be embarrassed to hear of want and yet be unable to alleviate it.⁹

An account of Benedict as almsgiver must be read in the light of money valuations of his day. Methods of distribution also were slower and more primitive than today. Yet Benedict set a pace and fashioned a pattern which made all humanity conscious of its obligation to man. It was fitting that the initiative should come from the "Universal Father" as Benedict liked to term himself.

Belgium was the Holy Father's first concern because from the very beginning he deplored the violation of this little country's neutrality. An American physician who had visited Belgium made the following report:

> Two years of intolerable captivity began to tell their dreadful tale. Tuberculosis is rapidly on the increase, especially among the older children of the working classes. Throughout Belgium, the tuberculosis sanatoria are overcrowded and the waiting lists are increasing. Rickets, among the younger children, is becoming epidemic. The babies born now are pitifully less in weight and measurement. The Belgian mother can barely nurse her child for seven instead of nine months, as heretofore. Hunger, suffering and sickness have fallen upon mother and child.¹⁰

When Benedict was apprised of Belgium's sad plight, he addressed a letter to Cardinal Gibbons, archbishop of Baltimore, and through him to all the bishops of the country, urging them to get all the school children in their respective dioceses to give their mite for their little brothers and sisters in Belgium. In this letter he spoke in the warmest terms of Herbert Hoover, chairman of the Commission for Relief in Belgium. He said of Hoover:

> He has made us see, almost as if they were passing before these very eyes, dimmed with tears, the long file, continuously increasing, of Belgian infants waiting for their daily distribution of bread; unhappy little ones whose bodies, emaciated by lack of proper nutrition bear not infrequently the impress of some deadly sickness brought about by their failure to receive the food which children of their age require.
>
> In view of this condition of affairs, we have considered the work indicated so humanitarian and so holy that, in prompt compliance with the appeal addressed to us by those who are directing the work of the commission, we have decided to approve and recommend it.[11]

Benedict's alms were given in humility and compassion without thought of praise. As with all the facets of his greatness, his charity was taken for granted while he lived. Only at his death did the world realize how much he had done. One of the placards posted alongside the body of Benedict, as he lay in state in the Sistine Chapel read: "Marvelous exemplar of the charity of Jesus Christ. In his soul he embraced all the miseries of his people, and with a lavish generosity he alleviated them."[12]

VISITATION OF PRISONERS

Benedict requested all Italian bishops to visit the prison camps in their dioceses and to relay to prisoners the papal blessing and his good wishes. Outside of Italy he sent special representatives to visit the imprisoned soldiers. Monsignor Raphael Scapinelli and Monsignor Theodore Valfré di Bonzo, successively apostolic nuncios to Vienna, were to visit the Italian prisoners at Mauthausen and Sigmundsherberg. German prisoners were to be visited by Monsignor Eugene Beaupin. French soldiers interned in Germany had Archbishop Pacelli as their visitor. Monsignor Marchetti-Selvaggiani, destined to become the distinguished Cardinal Vicar of Rome during World War II, visited French and German prisoners in Switzerland. Monsignor Angelo Dolci, apostolic delegate to Constantinople, visited the prisoners at Tache Kikla, who for the most part were Protestants. Gifts were to be given in each camp. For example, on Christmas of 1916, about twenty thousand packages were distributed by the papal envoy in Austria.[13]

The visits of these delegates were to be more than the token appearance of a prelate in his robes on a colorfully draped platform to be seen only by a few. Benedict asked the visiting ecclesiastics to move freely among the prisoners and to talk to them without discrimination. They were to see to it that the Catholic prisoners had access to confessors well versed in the language of the prisoners. If there were no such priests in a diocese where, for example, Polish prisoners were interned, the bishop of the see was held responsible for arranging with another diocese the release of a priest who could speak the language.[14] When the papal visitors returned to Benedict to make their reports, he wanted to be informed on incredibly minute details.[15]

Anticlericals, filled with envy and hate, sought a way of rendering the Pope's program odious in the eyes of the people. An Italian paper reported that when Monsignor Scapinelli visited the concentration camp at Mauthausen, he became irked by the discourtesy of an Italian prisoner. The newspaper went on to say that Monsignor Scapinelli recounted the incident to the officer in charge and saw to it that his compatriot was severely punished for his lack of appreciation. The newspaper gleefully asserted that the prisoner was none other than Giulio Aristide Sartorio, the famous painter and notorious anticlerical.

When Monsignor Scapinelli read the account, he was grieved that Benedict's kindness should have been misrepresented in this way and that he himself had been maligned. Therefore, he published an answer saying that he had met many famous men but that he had not encountered Sartorio. The Monsignor pointed out, furthermore, that Sartorio could not have been discourteous to him because no prisoner had ever shown him disrespect.

At about the same time that this incident was said to have occurred, Sartorio, entirely ignorant of the way his name was being used, was repatriated through the efforts of the Holy Father. As an invalid he had been a passenger on the famous *"Treno del Papa."* In 1922, when Benedict XV died, Sartorio wrote, "Is it permissible for an old anticlerical to pronounce judgment on a deceased pope? Benedict XV is a saint."[16]

OFFICE FOR PRISONERS OF WAR

There were many poor people of that era, when radio and television were as yet not known, who could not afford the luxury of a newspaper. They had no conception of the maze of protocol and cordon of functionaries surrounding the person of the Pope. In their minds he was a kind old man living in solitary simplicity like their own rural pastors. When, therefore, they had not heard from their beloved son or husband or father in the armed service, they first tried the ordinary bureaus of information. After receiving the curt *"Je ne sais pas!"* ("I don't know!") from the disgruntled clerk, they were afraid to try a second time.

The next step on the part of the anxious civilians was to write to the kindly pastor of pastors who had spoken so sympathetically to them, the Holy Father himself. The letters were often written in pencil, notes replete with misspellings and grammatical errors, and totally devoid of epistolary form. The tenor of the letters was always the same, "Where is our boy? Please try to find out where he is."

When these letters began to come in, the problem which confronted Vatican clerks was to determine to which division of the Papal Curia they were to be delivered. A secretary may have shown the first of these formless messages to the Holy Father with tongue in cheek. But for Benedict XV there was no humor in messages which came out of the depth of misery.

So moved was the Pope that at first he answered some of these letters personally. When this became known, the volume of this type of correspondence increased fantastically. Mr. Bellamy Storer, the former United States ambassador to Vienna, offered his services in this work of charity. He came twice a week to collect the letters and try to satisfy the agonized inquirers. Benedict read many of them himself and in his own hand made notations on the envelopes or in the margins.[17] In a short time the volume of mail became so great that more personnel had to be enlisted. In the secretariat of state more men were made to share offices and desks were set closer together, so as to make room for a new bureau. It became known as the Provisional Office for Prisoners of War. Monsignor Federico Tedeschini, undersecretary of state, was named the general co-ordinator of the work. "The chief secretary of the bureau," wrote one of the workers at the time, "is really the Holy Father himself."[18]

As soon as a list of prisoners of war could be obtained from a belligerent country, nuns transcribed the names and relevant information concerning the location and physical condition of individuals on colored cards. Requests from anxious relatives were transcribed on white cards. If a colored card was found bearing the name of the person requested on a white card, the two cards were given to a secretary who wrote to the family at once.

Before this time there had been no international office which could pierce the curtains of hostility between warring nations and put prisoners of war in communication with their dear ones so that Benedict's personal acts of kindness at first had very little system or plan. But as soon as a bureau with a staff had been set up in the secretariat of state, the work attained such phenomenal success that the hierarchy of other countries pleaded for branch offices on their own soil. Similar bureaus were established in Germany at Paderborn, in Austria at Vienna, and in Switzerland at Freiburg.

Benedict insisted on one firm rule, namely, that no matter in what country the office happened to be located, under no circumstances was any remuneration to be accepted. In fact, very few of the workers received any salary. It was meant to be an apostolate of charity.

Just as the anticlericals felt obliged to malign Benedict's program of visiting the sick and the imprisoned, they now spewed their venom at the papal bureau of information. The London *Tablet* of July 15, 1916, contained the following comment: "It is pitiable to have to record that one or two Italian papers have endeavored latterly to dissuade people from availing themselves of the Vatican Bureau. That is . . . one of those examples of anticlericalism gone mad."[19] And eventually the anticlericals did succeed. They circulated a rumor that Benedict's bureau was in reality only an agency for espionage. In order to prevent other projects of the Holy Father from being placed in jeopardy, the Holy See reluctantly issued the following notice:

In order to avoid sinister interpretations regarding the charitable transmission of letters for prisoners of war, and especially to prevent the spreading of calumnies about espionage exercised or favored by the Holy See, which some papers have had the audacity to affirm, the Holy See has, to its regret, come to the conclusion that such transmission must be suspended.[20]

Naturally this new sign of his own countrymen's ingratitude grieved Benedict sorely. However, his bitterness found some assuagement in the many letters of gratitude which poured into the Vatican. For example, the children of a Parisian family, whose wounded and tubercular father had been sent to Switzerland through papal efforts, sent an awkwardly penned note to Benedict which said in part: "We feel it our duty to thank Your Holiness for having saved the life of our father."[21] Another letter posted at Constantinople, and signed by twelve men of various faiths, voiced gratitude "for miraculous liberation obtained through your paternal interest." The men expressed themselves as being "deeply moved by such goodness."[22]

It was Turkey, a solidly Moslem country, which erected a beautiful statue to commemorate Benedict's charity toward that country. The statue, made by the Italian sculptor, Quattrini, depicts the Pope, clad in tiara and cope, standing in front of his throne; his foot is poised precariously on the edge of the platform, a shapely hand framed by the rich lace of a rochet is outstretched as far as human equilibrium will permit. Benedict appears desperately anxious to help someone whom he sees in need. In the left hand he holds some document, evidently a list of names of those who in their anguish have made claim on his universal fatherhood. The face is not that of a very old man, but it is deeply lined with fatigue. The eyes seem so very tired. The mouth is set as if to stifle any feelings of fatigue when there is charity to be done. The inscription reads:

To the Great Pope of the World's Tragic Hour
BENEDICT XV
Benefactor of the People
Without Discrimination of Nationality or Religion
A Token of Gratitude From the Orient.[23]

CHAPTER XVII

Benedict the Statesman

THE ROMAN QUESTION

THE multiple activities of Benedict XV during and after World War I give ample proof of his statesmanship. Those who had promised themselves a "political pope," as the newspapers jubilantly called him at his election, were doomed to disappointment. His platform even in the realm of strict politics seemed to be only: "Love one another" and "My kingdom is not of this world." Yet, not in spite of, but because of these formulae he gave to the Holy See in the seven years of his pontificate a prestige in world affairs which it had not enjoyed for over a century.

In this book the terms, Roman Question, Quirinal, Risorgimento, and king of Italy have appeared repeatedly. They all have their roots in papal history of the nineteenth century.

Before 1870, the pope was not only the spiritual leader of the whole world but he was also the temporal sovereign of the Papal States, or the "Patrimony of Saint Peter," as these states were sometimes called. For centuries prior to the unification of Italy in 1870 there was periodic unrest because of the temporal suzerainty of the popes. The hundred years immediately preceding the events of 1870 were especially stormy. Pius VI had died in exile, a victim of the French Revolution. Pius VII had been taken prisoner by Napoleon. In 1848, Pius IX was compelled by Roman revolutionists to flee to Gaeta and did not return to Rome until 1850. Up to the time of his flight, Pius IX had lived in the Quirinal, a magnificent palace built on the Quirinal hill, which the popes had occupied since the time of Paul V (1605–1621). When Pius IX fled in 1848, he left in disguise and had to crawl through a long unused secret passage. From that day the Vatican became the official residence of the popes. In 1870, the Quirinal was chosen as the official residence of the newly declared King of Italy.

Risorgimento is a term which designates the rebirth or remaking of the Italian nation. The term owes its political meaning to the name of a Turinese newspaper founded by Camillo Cavour in 1847, which waged an uninterrupted campaign in favor of political independence and constitutional reform. The term became a battle cry and eventually connoted the literary, academic, and political aspirations of Italy in the nineteenth century. It is now often used synonymously with the coup which unified Italy in 1870.

At the beginning of the nineteenth century, most of northern Italy was under Austrian rule. The rest of the Italian peninsula consisted of the Papal States, the Kingdom of Sardinia, the Kingdom of the Two Sicilies, and a number of smaller states. The various states were caught up in the *Risorgimento* one by one. It was on September 20, 1870, when the forces of the King of Sicily broke through the Aurelian wall near Rome's Porta Pia that Victor Emmanuel II, duke of Savoy and king of Sicily, was acclaimed the king of United Italy. The Vatican lay within the newly created kingdom, and the Pope was regarded as the subject of the king. The fact that the visible representative of Jesus Christ should be the political subject of an earthly king and yet have jurisdiction over the whole earth created a series of thorny problems which constitute the Roman Question.

Italy, however, considered its unification a *fait accompli* and attempted to create the impression that there were no problems and hence no Roman Question. On May 13, 1871, the Italian government issued the *Law of Guarantees* which permitted the pope to continue residence in the Vatican. Some of the "guarantees" or assurances were:

> The person of the pope is to be sacred and inviolable so that any insult or injury to him will be treated on a par with insult or injury to the king's person. (*Articles* 1 and 2) Royal honors are to be paid to the pope, and he has the right to his customary guard. (*Art.* 3) The sovereign pontiff is to be given an annual endowment of 3,225,000 lire (in that era about $622,425) to cover all the needs of the Holy See. (*Art.* 4) The Vatican and Lateran palaces, as well as the summer home of Castel Gandolfo, are to remain the property of the pope. (*Art.* 5) The other articles assure the pope and all engaged in the spiritual government of the Church, as well as the college of cardinals assembled in conclave, complete liberty of communication with the Catholic world, and exemption from all interference.[1]

It was indeed difficult to see how a pope could maintain dignity by accepting terms extended in so condescending a tone. As the perspicacious Leo XIII pointed out:

> The position which is supposed to be guaranteed to Us by law, is not one which *befits* Us and that We require; it is *not a real* independence, but only an *apparent* and *transitory* one, for it is subject to the will of others. This kind of independence can be taken away from Us again by him who gave it to Us; those who conferred it yesterday, can cancel it tomorrow.[2]

Two days after the proclamation of the *Law of Guarantees,* Pius IX made his first official protest. In the encyclical, *Ubi Nos,* dated May 15, 1871, he repudiated these guarantees without qualification. He invoked and re-emphasized a decree of the Sacred Apostolic Penitentiary of February 29, 1868, which opened with the words *Non expedit.* This decree had forbidden Catholics to participate in the elections of the "usurping" kingdom of Italy, which was already threatening the independence of the Holy See.

When Gioacchino Pecci, the camerlengo of Pius IX, ascended the papal throne as Leo XIII, the Church had a ruler who knew how to meet situations with statesmanship and a cool, calculating intelligence. It was not expedient for Leo to deviate from the principles of his predecessor. For that reason he frequently re-emphasized the policies of the *Non expedit.* He yielded no principles for reasons of diplomacy nor did he make any doctrinal compromise.

Pius X did nothing to bring about any new agitation. As a saint of God, permeated with divine charity, he wished well to all, friends and foes alike. When, however, the rights of the Church were impugned, he made his voice heard, and loudly. For example, when Archbishop Andrea Caron was prevented from taking possession of his new see, Genoa, because the *exsequatur* was refused by the Italian government, Saint Pius spoke out openly in an address to the Genoese pilgrims. He said that it was the first time in his ten years as pope that the Italian government "had refused temporal subsistence to a bishop chosen by the Supreme Pontiff for an important see, a bishop long recognized as exemplary in every way, loved by all, recommended even by civil authorities who had had any official relations with him." His protest was formal and unequivocal:

> We cannot accept this new tribulation permitted by the Lord without feeling keenly the grave injury done to the Head of the Church

in his divine mission, and without protesting against the violence perpetrated against this liberty and against this independence which the
Church holds not from men but from God Himself.[3]

As a matter of fact, however, aside from incidents like that
just cited, Italian unity had been accomplished so many years ago
that young men just reaching adulthood could no longer see the
problem which had dismayed their forefathers in 1870. The Church
which had been despoiled was still alive, whereas the men who
had done the despoiling were dead. Therefore, Saint Pius X took
a decisive step in modifying the *Non expedit* in his encyclical, *Il
Fermo Proposito* of June 11, 1905. In it he said very clearly:

> Weighty reasons prevent us from deviating from the rule of con-
> duct bequeathed to us by our predecessors, Pius IX and Leo XIII,
> whereby participation in elections is, generally speaking, forbidden.
> Nevertheless, for other, equally weighty reasons, YOU ARE PER-
> MITTED TO DISPENSE FROM THE LAW IN INDIVIDUAL
> CASES, especially when you are convinced that the salvation of souls
> and the highest interests of your churches are at stake.[4]

With the bishops empowered to permit the faithful to vote, the
strain on Catholic consciences was relieved considerably.

As a private person, Pius X was on friendly terms with the House
of Savoy. He had known the Duke of Genoa, brother of the Queen,
whose flagship had often been anchored at Venice. As pope he
received the Duke and his family in audience. It was the first time
since 1870 that a member of the royal house had entered the
Vatican.[5]

When Giacomo Della Chiesa, the trained diplomat, was elected
to succeed Saint Pius X, many hoped that he would find a way
of solving the Roman Question. On the other hand, those who
regarded him as committed to the policies of Leo XIII and Rampolla feared that he would return to the frigid aloofness of the
Leonine pontificate. Their fears, however, were groundless. In his
relationship to the Italians he continued and expanded the policies
of Pius X. In one of his first allocutions Benedict had said, "To *all*
the children of the Catholic Church the Holy Father owes love,
towards *all* he must extend his shepherding care."[6] He then developed the thought that the pope is the bishop of Rome, and that
on that account he owes a first and special love to the Romans.

As defender of the rights of Peter, he made his first protest in
Ad Beatissimi, November 1, 1914:

We pray with unceasing prayer for the good of Christ's Church, that
it may be left unhindered to bear help and salvation to every part of
the world. Too long has the Church been curtailed in its necessary
freedom of action, ever since the Head of the Church, the Supreme
Pontiff, began to lack that defence of freedom which the providence
of God had raised up during the course of centuries. The loss of that
protection has inevitably caused no light anxiety in the Catholic body;
for all the children of the Roman Pontiff, whether near or living afar,
have a right not to be left in doubt concerning the possession by their
common Father of a true and undeniable freedom in the exercise of
his Apostolic ministry.

While We pray for the speedy return of peace to the world, *We also
pray that an end be put to the abnormal state in which the Head of
the Church is placed* — a state which in many ways is an impediment
to the common tranquillity. Our predecessors have protested, not from
self-interest, but from a sense of sacred duty, against this state of
things; THOSE PROTESTS WE RENEW, and for the same reason
— to protect the rights and dignity of the Apostolic See.[7]

Besides these general endorsements of complaints which had
been made by his predecessors, Benedict registered two protests on
specific incidents which happened during the war. The first incident occurred in connection with Italy's entrance into the war. The
Law of Guarantees had promised personal safety to the diplomats
of embassies accredited to the Holy See even though they should
be of countries at war with Italy. That these embassies function
unhampered two plans were suggested. The diplomats were to
retain their residence and offices. They would have police protection
and would be permitted to communicate with their governments
through Vatican channels. The Holy See, however, was to scrutinize
their *communiqués* to prevent any Italian secret from being shared
with the enemy. Benedict declined this role of censor which he
deemed fraught with too many dangers. The other plan was that
the ambassadors from the Central Powers vacate their embassies
in the city and set up their offices in the rooms of the already
crowded Vatican. Through his secretary of state Benedict made it
known unequivocally that he refused to assume the responsibility of
offering police protection to those whom the state of Italy regarded
as enemy aliens. Should Italy suffer reverses on the battle front
there was always the danger that fanatics would seek revenge
through physical assault on the diplomatic corps or by acts of
vandalism in these temporary offices of the embassies within the

Vatican.[8] The ambassadors, therefore, deemed it wise to withdraw to Switzerland, first to Lugano, later to Bern.

In the consistory of December 6, 1915, the Pope spoke of the inconveniences to which the Holy See was being subjected during time of war. In alluding to the awkward situation of not having the diplomatic corps available for personal consultation, he said:

We limit Ourself to calling attention to the fact that some of the Ambassadors or Ministers accredited to Us by their Sovereigns were constrained to go away in order to safeguard their personal dignity and the prerogatives of their office, which means, for the Holy See, the curtailment of a right proper and native to it and the weakening of a necessary guarantee, as well as the deprivation of the ordinary and by far the most suitable means it is accustomed to use for conducting affairs with foreign governments.[9]

He softened his complaints somewhat when he said, "Certainly those who are governing Italy have not lacked the good intention to eliminate the inconveniences."

The second incident calling for protest was the seizure of the *Palazzo Venezia* on August 25, 1916. Uninterruptedly since 1797 it had been the seat of the Austrian embassy to the Holy See. When the ambassadors from the Central Powers left Rome, the Austrian staff closed the palace and withdrew to Switzerland in the firm hope of reopening the building after the war. After the staff's departure, however, students from the Roman University staged a riotous demonstration, vociferously demanding that Italy should seize the palace. On August 25, in a bombastic decree the Italian government took it over. The Pope was not informed of the fact until 10 o'clock the following morning.[10]

This seizure by Italy of alien property was more than the confiscation of a building of brick and mortar. There were forty rooms to be emptied which contained treasures of art, historic furniture, and age-old archives pertaining to very intimate affairs of the Holy See.

When the news of this action reached him Benedict protested at once through a letter signed by his secretary of state. He argued that the palace was the habitual residence of the Austrian ambassador to the Holy See; that the actual absence of the ambassador from his home did not change the situation; that, in fact, the absence was known to be only temporary because of abnormal circumstances. He called attention to the fact that to his protest of December 6 the Italian government had replied that the ambassador's departure was voluntary on the part of his government and that the Italian state had to disclaim all responsibility for his withdrawal.

This present act of taking possession of the residence of the representative of a foreign power accredited to the Holy See implies in itself an offence to the Holy See, and a violation of that right of representation which belongs to it, and which, moreover, was recognized by the Law of May 13, 1871. Against that act, which furnishes a new proof of the abnormal position of the Holy See, the undersigned Cardinal, by charge of and in the name of His Holiness, has to raise formal and solemn protest.[11]

Benedict's relationship with the kingdom of Italy, however, did not consist solely in written protests against the existing situation. To him belongs the credit for paving the way toward the solution of the Roman Question. It is known that from the very beginning of his pontificate he worked gradually and unobtrusively at formulating a policy for better public relations with the Italian government.[12] His plan did not aim at winning back territory or vindicating material advantages. There were persistent rumors that if the Central Powers should win the war, Austria would be asked to regain the Papal States for the Holy See. Cardinal Gasparri allayed this fear in an interview with a reporter from *Il Corriere d'Italia* on June 28, 1915, when he said:

The Holy See awaits the convenient systematization of its situation, not from foreign arms, but by the triumph of those sentiments of justice which it hopes will spread more and more among the Italian people in conformity with their true interests.[13]

Benedict felt that since the question had originated between the Vatican and the Italian state, it should be settled between them.

Realizing how in Germany, Belgium, Holland, and Switzerland the Church was able to render her social teachings more effective through Catholic political parties, Benedict took another significant step forward in his policy of easing tension. In January of 1919, he permitted Father Luigi Sturzo,[14] a brilliant Sicilian priest, to form a political party, the "People's Party" (*Partito Popolare Italiano*),[15] which would translate the Church's principles of social justice into action. The newly formed party demanded religious, civil, and social liberty, new legislation for labor, reforms in the school system, agrarian reform, proportional representation, and women's suffrage. In short, the party was to make the great encyclicals of Leo XIII functional. So successful was Don Sturzo that in the November elections of the same year, it achieved an astounding victory, with one hundred and one of its candidates elected to parliament. By allowing the party to be organized Benedict tacitly abolished the *Non expedit* which had forbidden all participation in Italian politics. The wisdom of this step is appraised by the *Enciclopedia Cattolica* in these words: "It gave a democratic Christian conscience and a sense of responsibility to Italian Catholics."[16]

A further move, which has not come to light until recently, involved two of the men who were to affix their signatures to the concordat of 1929. Fernand Hayward in his biography of Benedict reveals that Mussolini in the last year of Benedict's life begged Count Carlo Santucci, personal friend of the Pope, to arrange a meeting between himself and Cardinal Gasparri.[17] In his eagerness to leave no stone unturned in anything which pertained to the Roman Question, Benedict urged his Secretary of State to meet with the leader of the Fascist party.

One Sunday, the Santucci family, in order that there would be no one to reveal the slightest detail of the meeting, gave their staff of servants the afternoon off. At a prearranged hour, Cardinal Gasparri rang the doorbell at one entrance of the Santucci home. The future *Duce* was admitted by the Countess at another door. No casual passer-by could have observed the two entrances at the same time and have known that the Santucci's were entertaining the Papal Secretary of State and the onetime anticlerical Mussolini at their home on the same afternoon. The two men were ushered into the salon, and Count and Countess Santucci withdrew. The conversation lasted a long time. Years later, when Count Santucci revealed the story, he said that Mussolini had wanted to ascertain under what conditions the Vatican would conclude a peace with the Italian government. In that interview the first effectual steps were taken for a solution of the Roman Question.

Besides these official approaches to the situation there were many, seemingly casual, kind words uttered by Benedict which made the Italians see that their Holy Father was really their fellow countryman and that he loved them dearly. In the first months of his pontificate he surprised the Italians by using the expression, "beloved Italy" which he employed in his allocutions and documents thereafter. For example, in May, 1915, he expressed fears that "the same terrible conflagration may be in store also for our country, for this Italy so dear to our heart as to that of a Father."[18]

How much Benedict cherished Italy they realized when they heard that he had wept when he learned of Italy's humiliating defeat at Caporetto in December, 1917. More tangible proof of the genuineness of his sorrow when he saw his compatriots in distress is the fact that he ventured out of the strict precincts of the Vatican to visit those injured in the earthquake which shook Rome in 1915.[19]

As soon as Benedict learned that the Austrians had launched an air raid on the city of Ravenna, he sent a note of sympathy, saying that not only were the families of Ravenna plunged into bitter grief but that he himself mourned the innocent victims and that he was sincerely anxious for the irreplaceable architectural monuments of beautiful Ravenna.[20]

It was not only Benedict's thoughtful words and gestures toward the people that engendered hope, but his recognition of the Italian government in a natural and noncondescending manner made the way toward reconciliation easier. When in 1917 he sent copies of the Peace Note to King George of England for distribution to other governments, he wrote that it was his wish that the King relay a copy of the note to "His Majesty, the King of Italy."[21] This was the first time that the Holy See referred to the royal resident in the Quirinal as His Majesty, the King of Italy. Previously, the highest title given him in the official Vatican language was "the Duke of Savoy."[22]

When the armistice was declared, flags of Catholic associations were to be seen among the secular banners in the Quirinal, and those who carried them paid their respects to the King of Italy without fear of censure by ecclesiastical authorities. Benedict also requested the cardinal vicar of Rome to conduct a *Te Deum* service in the Church of Santa Maria in Ara Coeli on Capitol Hill at which the Duke of Genoa was present as the official representative of the King.

One source of repeated embarrassment was the fact that Catholic princes were forbidden to visit the King of Italy, and that the Vatican would not receive any heads of state who had visited the King of Italy first. Saint Pius X, for instance, had refused to receive the prince of Monaco for this reason. This awkward situation Benedict remedied by abrogating the restriction entirely. In *Pacem Dei Munus* he wished to show that the Holy See was doing everything to bring about peace and to allay smoldering hatred. In this connection he wrote:

> And this concord between civilized nations is maintained and fostered by the modern custom of visits and meetings at which the heads of States and princes are accustomed to treat of matters of special importance. So then, considering the changed circumstances of the times and the dangerous trend of events, and in order to encourage this concord, We would not be unwilling to relax in some measure the severity of the conditions justly laid down by Our predecessors, when the civil power of the Apostolic See was overthrown, against the official visits of the heads of Catholic States to Rome.[23]

That within the short seven years of Benedict's pontificate the Vatican's whole approach toward the Roman Question had changed can be seen from the following incident. *L'Osservatore Romano* printed a denial of an Italian newspaper's report that Cardinal Merry del Val had written a protest against the friendly way in which Cardinal Gasparri was consorting with Italian government officials during the illness of Benedict XV. Ludwig Pastor treats this incident in his diary and agrees that the protest of Merry del Val was not a written one. Though his admiration for the Spanish Cardinal was great, Pastor admits that orally Cardinal Merry del Val had objected to the contrast created by his successor in the secretariat of state.[24]

Had Benedict lived longer, it is most probable that he would have found a satisfactory solution. Several sources say that one of the last wishes for the Church, which Benedict expressed before he died, was for a speedy settlement of the Roman Question.[25]

When Achille Ratti became supreme pontiff, as Pius XI, realizing how many steps had already been taken toward reconciliation by his predecessor, he decided to resume the old custom of giving his first apostolic benediction from the balcony jutting out over the square of Saint Peter's. As time went on the indefatigable Cardinal Gasparri blended his deceased master's drafts for a settlement with Pius XI's modifications and the changes necessitated by the Mussolini regime. On February 11, 1929, he brought the document to the Lateran Palace where he and Mussolini affixed their signatures. Pope Benedict's seven years of loving gestures came to fruition in a new era of freedom for the Holy See.

It was not only his "beloved Italy" that caused difficulties. Under Pope Saint Pius X and Cardinal Merry del Val, France had broken diplomatic relations with the Holy See. Benedict had faith that kindness would eventually win back France. To Cardinal Gasparri he said on one occasion, "If France gives me only her little finger, I will hold out to her both my arms."[26] France herself felt keenly her strained relations with the Holy See. As early as May, 1915, Gabriel Hanotaux, a French statesman and stanch Catholic, wrote in the *Figaro*, "France alone has no representative at the Vatican, and it will be readily admitted that by reason of this abstention its authority and even its interests are open to attack."[27] He pointed out the fact that French is the language the Vatican employs in her diplomatic work:

And something of the soul of France passes through the lips of those who speak her tongue there. With joy the Frenchman recognizes this disposition at least of sympathy, whether he considers the sovereign pontiff himself who was brought up in an era which had the world's eyes fixed with kindliness on the "Eldest daughter of the Church," or the cardinal secretary of state who had lived many years among us while he taught in our institutions of higher education.[28]

The canonization of Joan of Arc played no small part in cementing relations between France and the Vatican. This statement must not be construed to mean that the raising of the Maid of Orleans to the dignity of the altar was done with a political end in view. The process had been begun under Leo XIII, and the rite of beatification had been performed by Saint Pius X. However, in the addresses made by the French ecclesiastics on the occasion of the canonization and the replies made by Benedict, desires for reconciliation were being given expression on both sides.

In 1918, the Pope sent Monsignor Bonaventura Ceretti as observer to the peace talks in Paris. In 1919, he returned to defend publicly the rights of the Holy See concerning her missions. A friendship sprang up between Aristide Briand and Monsignor Ceretti. On November 16, 1919, despite sharp opposition, Briand began his campaign for resumption of diplomatic relations with the Holy See. Monsignor Ceretti became the nuncio and Celestin Jonnart was chosen as ambassador to the Holy See.[29] On May 24, 1921, the very day that Jonnart boarded a train from Paris for Rome as official ambassador to the Vatican, Emile Combes died in Paris at the age of eighty-six.[30] Combes was the man who in 1906 had worked so frantically for the severance of France's relations with the Holy See.

Benedict XV showed rare gifts of statesmanship toward many nations, but his work in Poland deserves to be singled out. It is noteworthy particularly because in the course of his activities in connection with Poland's special problems Benedict groomed his successor in the papacy. Benedict undoubtedly worked under divine guidance when he suddenly chose as his emissary a man entirely without experience in the realm of statesmanship. This man, Achille Ratti, proved himself to be the very embodiment of kindness, firmness, and tact.

On March 1, 1918, the Treaty of Brest-Litovsk was signed between Russia and the Central Powers. For the first time since 1815 when Poland had been partitioned, the Poles were free of Russian domination. The bishops of the area which had been under Russian rule for over a century, petitioned the Holy See for an apostolic visitor to renew and intensify the consciousness of the faithful that they belonged to the Church of Rome.

Monsignor Bonaventura Cerretti, then still a member of the staff of the papal secretariat of state, reported the request to the Pope who listened, nodded comprehendingly, and said that he would think about the matter. The next day when Monsignor Cerretti returned, the Pope had already outlined a definite plan of action. He manifested sharp annoyance that the Monsignor had prepared no list of candidates for the office of apostolic visitor. Benedict drummed the desk nervously, and his penetrating eyes looked expectantly at the embarrassed secretary. In his confusion, Cerretti could think of only one name, and that was the name of the prefect of the Vatican Library, Monsignor Achille Ratti.[31]

The reason why Ratti's was the only name that came to Monsignor Cerretti's mind is interesting. A few days before this conversation with the Pope, Cerretti had given a dinner at which the name of Achille Ratti happened to come up. Someone expressed regret that Ratti, prefect of the Vatican Library, had never been given the opportunity of using his rare intellectual gifts in public life. He was humorously dubbed the "library mouse" and "bookworm." Therefore, when the Pope reproved Cerretti for not having prepared a slate of candidates, this conversation about Ratti came to mind.

When Monsignor Cerretti blurted out the name of Achille Ratti, Benedict, to the secretary's surprise, did not seem at all amazed. The Pope had great respect for the librarian's talents, and, of late, had made it a practice of calling him to his study in order to discuss matters of state on which Benedict desired the past history. True, Ratti had no experience in the field of diplomacy but he had at his finger tips a wealth of details on world history.

The Holy Father discussed the matter with his Secretary of State, and in a few days, Cardinal Gasparri broached the matter to Achille Ratti. The librarian protested that he could not think of accepting so great a responsibility in a field for which he had not been trained. He felt, however, that he knew the Pope well enough to tender his refusal in person. With the reasons well arranged in his orderly mind, he entered the study of His Holiness. As soon as Ratti began to introduce the subject of his visit, Benedict tapped the desk impatiently and interrupted with the brisk question, "When do you leave for Poland?"[32] The question was stated so peremptorily that the librarian could do nothing else but accept. He went to Monsignor Cerretti's office and announced that Benedict had decided for him. He said that, in the Pope's words, he heard the voice of God.

Although Achille Ratti had the facts of Polish history well in hand, he needed proximate preparation for his task. He was given a desk in the secretariat of state where he was to pore over dossier upon dossier of diplomatic material pertaining to Poland. He summarized whatever he read and finally returned a list of recommendations of what in his estimation ought to be done in Poland. Cardinal Gasparri was most enthusiastic about this list because its succinct formulation showed an uncanny grasp of the situation and augured well for an excellent relationship between the Holy See and Poland.[33]

Monsignor Ratti left for Poland on Pentecost, May 19, 1918. The Pope penned a letter of introduction in which he wrote of the apostolic visitor:

> As a mark of Our benevolence we have resolved to send you in Our place Our dear son Achille Ratti, Protonotary Apostolic and Prefect of the Vatican Library. We can recommend him as a man whose piety, zeal for religion, experience, and knowledge are known to all. It is he who, as Apostolic Visitor, will deal with affairs belonging to the ecclesiastical order.[34]

The papal visitor made a good impression on both clergy and faithful. He met with the bishops, traveled continually, and visited the most outlying places. He participated in and preached at the national shrine of Our Lady of Częstochowa. In this way he rallied the people around the image of Mary and she created new hope in their hearts. When the glorious reports of Poland's renewed loyalty to the Holy See began to reach the Vatican, Pope Benedict happened to be in consultation with a French diplomat. As if speaking to himself, he said, "If you resolve to act unswayed by political feeling, that is to say, if you act only to follow justice and truth, and to be a faithful instrument of Divine Providence, then you are never entirely without illumination from above."[35]

The Pope's acquiescence to the Polish hierarchy's request, to name Achille Ratti as papal nuncio, terminated other interesting plans that were in the making. Pope Benedict had conceived the idea of entering into communication with Lenin. Since Monsignor Ratti was working in an area which had once been under Russian domination, he decided to visit Kerenski, Trotsky, and Lenin to learn what he could of their intentions. He had already taken the first steps in obtaining a visa when he received a telegram from Cardinal Gasparri, informing him that he was to prepare for episcopal consecration. He was to be the titular archbishop of Lepanto.

It is easy to see that Benedict XV and Achille Ratti saw eye to eye on the situation in the new Russia. In his letter to the Pope, explaining his intention of visiting the new Soviet state, Ratti had written: "I believe that to save his immense territory we need more than prayers; we need the blood of Catholics, the blood of priests."[36]

On October 28, 1920, Achille Ratti received episcopal consecration in Warsaw from the hands of Cardinal Kakowski, archbishop of that see. The newly consecrated Nuncio began work at once. There was a bitter dispute between the Poles and the Germans concerning Upper Silesia. Archbishop Ratti prepared a letter in German and in Polish to be read from every pulpit. In this document the spiritual policy of Benedict XV was sharply in the foreground. He wrote that the faithful were "to endeavor to understand the position of the other side and to remember that, Poles or Germans, they were to the Holy Father first of all Catholics and equally his children." This was a favorite thought of Benedict which he had expressed in *Ad Beatissimi*, in *Pacem Dei Munus*, and in his many allocutions during the war.

The wording of messages to the faithful was not the only thing in which there was a parallel between Achille Ratti and Benedict XV. The Nuncio's reward was the same as Benedict had received during the war: vituperation, ingratitude, and false accusation. Achille Ratti was now indeed sharing in the mysteries of the papacy. While still apostolic visitor, he had made a report to Benedict, remarking that his new work gave him many consolations, that mingling among the people gave him an ever greater awareness of being God's instrument. Benedict answered, "Very well, and now consider the fact that this is the experience which is Our privilege daily."[37] The reverses which he was soon to experience as nuncio gave him more opportunity to taste the experiences which were the Pope's daily bread. Later, in recounting his experiences in Poland, he said, "When only the Germans were against me, I did not know whether I was on the right track; but when also the Poles expressed their feelings against me, I was certain that I was doing the right thing."[38] That was the gauge which Benedict had always applied when he wished to see whether he was really impartial.

The heat of anger rose so high among the factions that they went to the extent of demanding the Nuncio's abrupt recall. But Benedict was not a man to be coerced. He examined the claims of both Germans and Poles, and replied that if he were to recall Archbishop Ratti, he would never send them another nuncio.[39] The Nuncio was not recalled until his erstwhile superior, Cardinal Ferrari, archbishop of Milan, died. Archbishop Ratti was notified of his promotion to the historic see of Milan and of his elevation to the college of cardinals. For bestowing this honor, Benedict was naturally criticized. When this was brought to the Pope's attention, he said tersely, "In this nomination only God and myself have had a part."[40] When on June 13, 1921, Achille Ratti received the red hat with Camillo Laurenti and Giovanni Tacci, Pope Benedict seated before the three pronounced this enigmatic statement, "There has been a generous distribution of red during the past few days, but soon there will be a distribution of white, and the white robes will surely fall upon one of you."[41]

Cardinal Ratti did not take possession of his see until September 8. Barely five months later he emerged from the conclave as Pius XI.

CHAPTER XVIII

Benedict XV, Pope of Canon Law and Sacred Scripture

THE HALL OF CONSISTORIES was ablaze with light and color. The day was June 28, 1917, the vigil of the feast of Saints Peter and Paul. This day was to mark the publication of the Code of Canon Law. Benedict XV was seated on the throne surrounded by the cardinals, bishops, members of the pontifical court, consultors for the compilation of the Code, and many others who had contributed to the completion of the Code. Cardinal Gasparri, after a brief address, presented the Pope with a preciously bound copy of the Code of Canon Law.

Benedict XV had the ability of the great orator to be inspired by setting and audience. On that day in 1917, he delivered an allocution as colorful as the hall in which it was delivered. Referring to the Church in time of war, he said, "under a head crowned with thorns it is not good for members to garland themselves with roses." Today, however, he felt that an exception was justified.

> The great work of the codification of canon law has reached the end at last; the actual proof of it We hold in the volume just given Us. With the presentation of this volume the most eminent president of the commission for the codification has placed a worthy crown on the work entrusted to him by Our venerated predecessor.

Only one thing, said Benedict, marred the day. Pius X, who had inaugurated the codification, "could not with his own hands set the crown on the work which he had initiated." Benedict felt that the words once spoken by Christ now had special reference to himself: "Others have labored and you have entered into their labors" (Jn. 4:38). Nevertheless, Benedict said that he derived comfort from the thought that in heaven Pius X would now be rejoicing in the work, and by his intercession would insure the daily increase of its fruit.[1]

In return for the copy of the Code, the Pope gave Cardinal Gasparri the decree of publication, *Providentissima,* in which he traced the history of canon law. In the decree as in the allocution, Benedict XV gave all credit to his predecessor. He pictured himself as one who had entered where another had labored, who had but reaped what another had planted and watered. A few days later, July 16, he wrote to Cardinal La Fontaine, patriarch of Venice, in answer to a note of congratulations:

> You are to rejoice for a very special reason, namely Pius X was the author of the code, in whom you justly rejoice as the beneficent founder of your Institute of Canon Law. In this way, therefore, may you regard yourselves as having received the distinguished work from the hands of Our predecessor of happy memory, Pius X, that the more accurately and the more perfectly you explain the code to your students, the greater will be the honor which you may consider yourselves as having paid to your father of immortal memory.[2]

At this point it is well to quote once more the remark about Benedict made by the Anglican clergyman who wrote under the name *Diplomaticus*, "Recently we have observed the Vatican's peculiar inability to advertise itself."[3] The world was too interested in itself, too plagued by war, to investigate whether Benedict really did no more than place the seal on the work of Saint Pius X. The learned Monsignor Batiffol, in close touch with the situation, wrote of Benedict's own valuable contribution to the Code, "He follows his own line with infinite discretion, more disposed to impersonal and silent decisions. How instructive would be a study of the *Ius Canonicum* published in 1917, so rich in decisions of this kind, corrections often infinitesimal, but which reveal the same persevering spirit."[4]

Before Benedict's personal contribution to the codification is evaluated, the magnitude of the task which confronted Saint Pius X must be understood. Christ in His teaching throughout the land of Palestine had made prescriptions, and the Apostles continued the work of legislation. The Church through the supreme pontiffs and through ecumenical and provincial councils passed laws whenever needs arose. In the course of time, however, there were so many isolated laws that no one could know them all. "The laws of the Church had so increased in number, and were so separated and scattered, that many of them were unknown, not only to the people, but to the most learned scholars as well," is Benedict's terse appraisal of the situation in his constitution of promulgation.

On one occasion Cardinal Gasparri remarked, "Even lifelong students of canon law were oftentimes at a loss to know whether there existed a canonical prescription covering a particular case, or whether a previously existing law was still in force."[5]

Over the centuries a number of attempts had been made to organize the unwieldy mass. The first collection of importance was undertaken by a monk named Gratian about the year 1150, at Bologna, the see of the two great jurist popes, Benedict XIV and Benedict XV. He tried to harmonize the material and reconcile apparently contradictory decrees. His work, which became known as the Decree of Gratian, was used widely but was not given official recognition by the Church. Appendixes, corrections, glosses, and "compilations" began to appear almost immediately. Among the supreme pontiffs who made contributions in the form of the so-called "compilations" and collections were Innocent III (1216), Honorius III (1226), Gregory IX (1234), Boniface VIII (1298), Clement V (1313), John XXII (1317), Gregory XII (1580), Sixtus V (1586), Clement VIII (1590), and Benedict XIV (1740–1758). The confusion engendered by these scattered and abortive attempts at codification which spanned eight centuries, that is from Gratian (1150) to Saint Pius X (1903), gave rise to a general desire for one compact code of canon law.

One day, shortly after his accession to the papacy, Saint Pius X asked Pietro Gasparri, an outstanding canonist, how long a codification of law would take. Gasparri answered that in his opinion, provided that he would have a sufficient number of able assistants, it could be done in twenty-five years. "Then do it," was the short answer of the Pontiff.[6] On March 19, 1904, Saint Pius X published the *motu proprio, Arduum sane munus* ("a difficult task indeed"), in which he decreed the work of codification and prescribed the general norms to be followed. A commission of cardinals was named, consultors were selected from among the Church's most outstanding theologians and canonists, and a presiding officer was chosen. It was no matter of surprise that the presiding officer chosen was Pietro Gasparri, who had risen to a position of pre-eminence in canon law during his years on the faculty of the *Institut Catholique* in Paris.

Besides these experts whom the Pope summoned to Rome, all the bishops in the world and the superior-generals of all religious orders were consulted periodically by letter. Every bishop had the right to keep a representative in Rome so that he could have a voice at the meetings.[7] It was the duty of all assistants and consultors, whether resident in the Eternal City or not, according to Pope Benedict's constitution of promulgation, "To gather together and to digest with order and clarity all the laws of the Church issued down to our own day, removing all that were abrogated or obsolete, adapting others as far as needful to the necessities and customs of the present time, and making new ones according as the need and opportunity should direct."[8]

Quietly the work went forward, and by the winter of 1912 the whole span of the Code was complete, and a provisional text was printed. It was sent to all bishops and superior-generals for comment. The notations which were received were in turn printed and distributed so that they could be carefully examined by all the members. In 1916, a second trial copy of the Code was printed and distributed to a very restricted group of consultors, most of whom were resident in Rome. This volume differed considerably from that of 1912, and it differed but little from the final printing in 1917. There were some corrections, but they did not affect the canons substantially. These emendations were based on the suggestions made by those who had scrutinized the edition of 1916.[9] On December 4, 1916, in a secret consistory Pope Benedict XV was able to tell the Sacred College that he would soon be able to grant the request which Cardinal Agliardi had voiced immediately after the coronation ceremony when he had said: *"Da nobis codicem"* ("Give us the Code"). In the consistory of 1916, the Pontiff said in part:

> Divine Providence had ordained that the glory of rendering this immense service to the Church should fall to Pius X, Our predecessor of saintly memory. You are aware, Venerable Brethren, with what alacrity he set himself to this truly gigantic task at the very beginning of his pontificate, and with what zeal and perseverance he pursued it during the whole time that he held the reigns of government. And though it was not granted to him to complete his undertaking, nevertheless, *he alone must be accounted to be the author* of the Code, and therefore will his name be handed down to posterity by the side of those pontiffs of greatest fame in the annals of canon law, such as Innocent III, Honorius III, and Gregory IX. *For us it is enough to be able to promulgate* that which he accomplished.[10]

On Pentecost Sunday, May 28, 1917, Benedict promulgated the

Code in the monumental constitution, *Providentissima Mater Ecclesia*. In it he gave the history of canon law, a masterpiece of condensation. The *vacatio legis* or "nonenforcement of the law" was applied for a year; that is, the laws would not be binding until Pentecost Sunday of the following year, namely, May 19, 1918.

However, at the request of Pope Benedict, Cardinal Gasparri issued a document on August 20, 1917, which provided for the immediate observance of five articles of legislation.[11]

Pope Benedict himself made suggestions and changes before the final revision went to print. He had a keen legal mind, he had achieved a doctorate in civil law at the University of Genoa, he had earned a doctorate in canon law at the Gregorianum. His many years in the Curia had trained him to see loopholes in legal wording which seemed impregnable to others. Seven years in a large diocese bristling with difficult situations had taught him to appreciate the practical requirements of those in the sacred ministry and to detect the impracticality of certain clauses in the law. All these factors contributed to make him eminently capable in ironing out imperfections in the Code.

One example that is attributed to Benedict XV personally is Canon 245 which appeared for the first time in the final edition of the Code. It assumes that a doubt arises as to which sacred congregation is competent to deal with a case that has been presented. There is to be no permanent or standing commission which decides the congregation or tribunal which is to adjudicate the matter. Each time a case of this kind is submitted to the Curia, the supreme pontiff himself is to appoint a new commission of cardinals expressly for that case.[12] Formerly the *Signatura Apostolica* made the decision. Canon 245 is new and no source for it is cited because none is known.[13]

In an allocution to the Sacred College on March 22, 1917, Benedict announced suppression of the Congregation of the Roman Index as an independent congregation.[14] The Index would now be in the competency of the Holy Office whose prime duty it was to watch over the preservation of the Faith. He made it clear, however, that he was not the innovator but that this plan had occurred to his keen-minded predecessor.[15] He said that he knew this from the lips of those illustrious men who had assisted Saint Pius X in his work. In order that the Holy Office be not overburdened because of this extra work, he transferred all questions regarding the granting of indulgences to the Sacred Penitentiary. To this rule there was to be one exception. For example, if a prayer which had been submitted for an indulgence carried some dogmatic implication of doubtful character, the Holy Office was to pass judgment on the matter, since that congregation had the duty of guarding against all doctrinal errors.

On the other hand, in his *motu proprio* of November 4, 1915, *Seminaria Clericorum*,[16] instead of suppressing a congregation, Benedict erected a new one, the Congregation of Seminaries and Universities. In 1824 Leo XII had established a Congregation of Studies to function in the nature of a federal office of education for the Papal States. In 1870, when the Papal States ceased to be, the competency of this office ceased for the land once governed by the pope, but it continued to serve the Catholic universities in other parts of the world. Benedict, in creating a new congregation, placed both seminaries and universities within its competency.

It must not be thought that Benedict XV felt himself bound to execute all implicit wishes of his predecessor. For example, in the matter of the so-called "suburbicarian sees," he reversed the plan of Saint Pius X. The word "suburbicarian" is not a synonym for "suburban." Surrounding Rome in a radius of about fifteen miles there are six ancient suffragan sees with colorful histories which are of great interest to the lover of Christian antiquity. They are: (1) Albano, (2) Frascati, (3) Palestrina, (4) Sabina, (5) Ostia and Velletri, (6) Porto and Santa Rufina. These sees are called "suburbicarian."

The cardinal bishops in the Sacred College, who held positions in the Curia, were the bishops of these sees. If the cardinal bishop of one see died, e.g., Frascati, and the cardinal bishop of Sabina wanted a transfer to the vacant diocese, he would resign the see of Sabina and "opt" or apply for the see of Frascati. In an apostolic constitution, *Apostolicae Romanorum*,[17] Saint Pius X decreed that because of their work in the Curia, the cardinals should have auxiliary bishops who would actually reside in the suburbicarian sees. This meant that the cardinal would have little more than a title and position of honor.

In an apostolic constitution, *Ex actis tempore*,[18] issued February 1, 1915, Benedict XV praised Saint Pius X for terminating the practice of "opting" for one suburbicarian see after another. "What great inconveniences and detriment this frequent changing of sees inflicted on the care of souls, the Pontiff in his vigilance aptly pointed out and legislated so as to meet the difficulty directly." But Benedict reversed the precept of Pius that the cardinals were to have auxiliaries to do their work for them in the suburbicarian sees. In Benedict's opinion the territory of these sees is so small, they are so near to Rome, and modern travel has become so easy that there is no need for auxiliary bishops. If, because of bad health or old age or some other reason, the cardinal should not be able to perform his duty in the suburbicarian see, he could always petition the Holy See for help.

Canonists surmise that Benedict's reason for the abolition of the auxiliaries may have been prompted by several considerations. First, he wished to lighten the financial burden of the faithful in the suburbicarian sees. It would be difficult for them to support both cardinal and auxiliary, the latter of whom would be entirely dependent on what he received from the people of the diocese. Second, the arrangement by which the cardinal, a member of the Curia, would take personal charge of his see goes back to a tradition of almost apostolic times. Third, it focuses attention on the dignity and historic importance of "cardinal bishops."[19] Outside of reasons which Benedict himself enumerated, he adds, "There are other reasons of no small moment for it."[20] He makes no further explanation.

One might make a conjecture to explain the reason for Benedict's action. For seven years Giacomo Della Chiesa had been active as an archbishop in a very difficult diocese. Perhaps with his experience as a member of the Papal Curia and more recently as an active ordinary, he realized that the cardinals in the Curia did not always give practical problems submitted to them the sympathetic treatment they deserved. If the members of the Curia were to have firsthand experience in the care of souls, they would be more likely to appreciate the difficulties of the bishops in charge of sees.

It would seem that Cardinal Merry del Val remained true to the spirit which had dictated Saint Pius X's provision for auxiliary bishops to be in actual residence in the suburbicarian sees and to carry out all the duties of a bishop. Benedict had offered the former Secretary of State a suburbicarian see, most likely Albano, which was left vacant by the death of Cardinal Agliardi.[21] He refused with thanks, giving as his reason that, were he to do all the work required in the see, his efficiency in the Curia would suffer.[22]

It was not only his predecessor's legislation that Benedict reversed. If he saw that his own regulations did not accomplish what he intended, he had the humility to reverse his own legislation.[23] For example, on December 31, 1914, shortly after his coronation, Benedict issued a *motu proprio, Non multo post,*[24] which provided for changes in the curriculum of the Roman Academy of Saint Thomas to insure more intensive and fruitful work. On February 11, 1916, he met with the cardinals presiding over the Academy and they drew up a new set of statutes. These returned almost entirely to the laws laid down by Leo XIII in 1895.[25]

In the diary of Cardinal Gasquet another instance of Benedict's reversal of his own legislation is found.

> Cardinal Vico came to tell me that the Holy Father having read my memorial about the change of the rubric in the Missal about the abbots, had given an order that the old rubric was to be restored. This is a remarkable instance of the Pope better informed going back on his former decision.[26]

The Code of Canon Law arranges all the laws in numerical succession from Canon 1 to Canon 2414. Previously, a canonist would have to read through long case histories before he would come to a knowledge of the legal principle involved. In wonderful contrast, the canons of the Code are couched in direct, brief, imperative sentences which definitely reveal the mind of the legislator.

Archbishop (now Cardinal) Amleto Giovanni Cicognani, brilliant canonist and for many years apostolic delegate to the United States, writes of the Code:

> The Code of Canon Law was not intended, therefore, as a book of cases or case law. Nor would such presentation of Church law be suitable for the clergy, since they are undoubtedly much more learned than the populace to whom civil codes are directed. Consequently, the Code contains certain canons that are merely doctrinal or even dogmatic in character, for example, canons 108, 218, 329, 737, 801, 803, 1012, 1322, #1. As regards its foundation, canonical legislation in the Code is based on doctrine that is *immutable* and *eternal,* while civil legislation, according to the common opinion of the legislators, is *positive* in character, and depends upon the legislative will, popular customs and the like.[27]

Immediately after publishing the Code, Benedict XV made three major pronouncements concerning it: (1) he established rules for teaching the Code; (2) he founded a Commission for the Interpretation of the Code; (3) he determined that the numbers of the canons should always be kept intact.

In the decree, *Cum novum,* of August 7, 1917, Benedict stipulated that the canons of the Code would be studied not only synthetically but also analytically. In other words, the canons are to be taught in their numerical sequence, and each canon is to receive its interpretation and commentary point by point. The words of the mandate read: "Adhering strictly to the order of the code, and careful to preserve the strict sequence of titles and chapters, in teaching canon law, the professors must interpret the individual canons with a thorough explanation." The instructors are told, furthermore, to give a fitting comprehensive history of the legislation by showing how the matter came to be a problem, and what its development and changes were in the course of time. This was to prevent the student of canon law from falling into lax habits. The Code was not intended to do half the work for him. Through a series of texts from the past the student should see the history and the purpose of law unfolding itself.[28]

For the future of the Code Benedict foresaw two dangers. The first one was that there would be too many disputes about its meaning. The second one was that too much new legislation would soon render the Code obsolete.[29]

The first danger he obviated by establishing the Commission for the *Authentic Interpretation of the Canons of the Code.* This he did even before the Code went into effect. In answer to those who felt that the Code should make canonists and commentators superfluous, Benedict in his *motu proprio, Cum iuris canonici*[30] of September 17, 1917, pointed out that he was not doing something without precedent. The Congregation of the Council, still in existence today, had been established by Pope Pius IV in 1564 as the official organ for the correct interpretation and practical application of the acts of the Council of Trent. In like manner also is the Code to be authentically interpreted by a permanent staff of experts.

The second danger, that of too much legislation, Benedict met by curtailing the legislative powers of the various congregations. Their function henceforth was not so much to make new general decrees, but to issue instructions designed to put the laws of the Code into effect.

In the same *motu proprio, Cum iuris,* Benedict decreed that if a sacred congregation should make a new universal law which enlarges on an already existing law or should institute legislation on which the Code is silent, the commission with the approval of the pope must determine where the new canon is to be added. If the new legislation is on a point not treated by the Code at all, it is to be cast into canon form, and the commission will determine the place where it will fit best, but the numbers of the canons must under no circumstance be shifted. The preceding number will be used again with the annotation *bis* (a second time) or *ter* (a third time). For example, if we assume that the commission has ruled that a new law should be placed after Canon 1315, it would again be Canon 1315, but it would have the annotation *bis*. This obviates the necessity of learning a new number for a canon each time such an addition would be made. Benedict's words are very plain: "So that no canon may ever be moved from its place or that the series of numbers may in any way be disturbed."[31]

Outside of the changes of legislation which Benedict made or more precise wording which he added to certain canons, there were certain points of law which caused him concern because they were almost universally forgotten or disregarded. Francis Pichon mentions Canon 336, paragraph 3, as a canon which Benedict surely desired to be retained. Pichon recounts that when Monsignor Della Chiesa was in the secretariat of state under Leo XIII and Saint Pius X, he used to be amused at the great number of vicars-general in the sees of France. The limitation of one vicar-general to a diocese goes back to the Fourth Lateran Council in the year 1215. When a representative from a diocese in France would come to the desk of Monsignor Della Chiesa to fulfill the preliminaries of protocol, the Monsignor would with mock seriousness interpose the question, "And how many vicars-general do you have in your diocese?" When the unsuspecting priest would answer, "Six," "Seven," or "Eight," the Undersecretary with an enigmatic smile would enter the answers on the sheet before him.[32] Canon 366, paragraph 3 reads: "Only one vicar-general may be appointed, unless a diversity of rites, or the size of the diocese, should require more."

It was during the pontificate of Benedict that the Holy See changed the method of selecting bishops for the United States, where a very lengthy and cumbersome method had been in use. Only after a diocese was vacated by death or transfer did the process of looking for a new bishop begin. Many ecclesiastics had to be consulted, and ratifications had to be obtained. The Holy Father, who had the final word, often desired further confirmation. All this took time, and the result was that a diocese might be left widowed for a long time to the detriment of religion. The periodical *Rome* pointed out a further disadvantage.

> Americans are so anxious to have a good bishop that they often leave no stone unturned to secure the best one possible by writing to the Holy See directly to point out the merits of their favourite candidate. Sometimes they go a little farther and seek to advance his cause by dwelling on real or imaginary deficiencies of the other candidates.[33]

A new method of selecting bishops was ordered in the decree, *Ratio pro candidatis ad episcopale ministerium,*[34] of July 25, 1916. The decree summarized the essential changes in the following words,

> It does not seem wise that a matter, than which hardly any other in the Church can be regarded as more important, should be treated in a hurried manner and only under the spur and impulse of necessity; while on the other hand, seeing that the vacancy of dioceses is certain to occur, even though the time of its occurrence is uncertain, it would be better to provide for it in due season, and to present to the Apostolic See, at least generically, in anticipation the names of those whom the bishops consider to be worthy and suited for the pastoral charge.[35]

The new rules provide for greater secrecy under oath, a biennial meeting of the bishops of a province for a discussion of candidates, and a personal knowledge about the candidate's qualifications. Benedict found the new method proposed for use in America so successful that he extended it to Canada in 1919[36] and to Scotland in 1921.[37]

Despite Benedict's personal contribution to the study of canon law, the credit for the general work of codification belongs to Pius X. To Benedict XV, however, ultimately belongs the credit for the growing and enlightened interest in Sacred Scripture perceptible throughout the world today. In fact, it has been said that just as Pius IX is known in history as the pope of the Immaculate Conception, Leo XIII as the pope of the Rosary, and Pius X as the pope of Holy Communion, Benedict XV should be known as the pope of Holy Scripture.[38]

The leaning of Giacomo Della Chiesa toward the study of Scripture manifested itself early in his life. When still a layman enrolled in the school of law at the University of Genoa, he organized an extracurricular program of apologetics in which the New Testament played an important role. As a seminarian at the Capranica, he imparted religious instruction to the children in the Church of Santa Maria in Aquiro with special emphasis on Bible history.

In 1902, Monsignor Giovanni Mercati,[39] an employee in the Vatican Library, in collaboration with Pasquale Scotti, who was in charge of the Vatican printing press, conceived the idea of a society which would distribute the New Testament in an inexpensive edition. Because of Monsignor Della Chiesa's known interest in acquainting the laity with the treasures of Holy Writ, it was to him that Mercati and Scotti revealed their project before presenting it to Leo XIII for approval. Furthermore, the Undersecretary of State enjoyed the reputation of knowing the mind of Leo better and of possessing greater persuasive powers with him than many of the cardinals. It surprised no one, therefore, when the Pope approved the plan wholeheartedly. Monsignor Della Chiesa became the first president of the newly founded "Pious Society of Saint Jerome for the Diffusion of the Holy Gospel." The patriarch of Venice, Cardinal Sarto, who within a year was to succeed Leo as pope, sponsored the new project warmly in his own see.[40]

When 500,000 copies of a popularly priced New Testament were placed in the hands of the people, Pius X wrote a letter of congratulation to the cardinal protector of the society. The saintly Pope called this achievement "a splendid proof of the extraordinary zeal displayed by the members."[41] During the seven years that he was archbishop of Bologna, Giacomo was regularly re-elected president of the society. But when he himself became pope, he appointed as his successor in the office of president Cardinal Cassetta, bishop of the suburbicarian see of Frascati, who for many years had been active in the society and its cardinal protector.[42]

In February, 1915, Benedict received the professors and students of the Pontifical Biblical Institute. As is customary in audiences granted to a whole school, the rector delivered an address in which he traced the interest of the supreme pontiffs in this institute of scriptural studies. Leo XIII had conceived the idea of founding it but had died before his plans could be realized. Pius X had executed the designs of his predecessor. At this point Benedict made it clear that he was no less interested than his predecessors. He said:

In Our breast also burns brightly the desire to ensure that the prestige of the Apostolic See be kept aloft, that from Rome may ever go forth the Word which is to be guide and norm for all men of science. To Rome must people turn for the sure and authentic interpretation of all doctrine in any way connected with dogmatic truth, and from Rome must be sent the doctrine which may be described as cognate to strictly theological studies, and in especial the direction of studies in matters akin to sacred theology, that is, biblical studies.

But with regard to biblical studies a special note is to be found in the fact that in a camp other than ours men have been working, and it is necessary that Rome weigh it, that Rome tell the Catholic world what is the truth, what is the value to be assigned to the productions put forth by those in the other camp. Thus the Pontifical Biblical Institute has come to be a necessity of our time.[43]

In the same year Benedict suggested to Cardinal Cassetta that leaflets containing the text of the day's Gospel with a short homily on the passage be distributed at all the Sunday Masses in Rome's churches.[44] People who attended a Mass at which there was no reading of the Gospel or sermon could take the leaflet with them and read it later.

On June 15, 1917, Benedict published his monumental encyclical, *Humani Generis,*[45] in which he stated that a knowledge of Sacred Scripture was the *conditio sine qua non* of an effective sermon. He always reserved the "encyclical form" of document for subjects on which there was some current error. Among the abuses he condemned in *Humani Generis,* he mentioned "those frequent allusions to profane and non-Catholic literature to the exclusion of Sacred Scripture." Further on in the letter he remarked, "We see that not a few of our sacred preachers overlook in their sermons the Sacred Scriptures."

In order that the encyclical might not be laid aside with a sigh of admiration and then be immediately forgotten, Benedict saw to it that the Sacred Congregation of the Consistory issued a decree which concretely embodied the norms proposed in the encyclical.[46] Rule Twenty-One of that document reads:

> May the preacher ever have before his eyes, and may he put into practice what Saint Jerome recommended to Nepotianus, "Read Sacred Scripture again and again: in fact, never allow Sacred reading matter to be put out of your hands." The sermon of a priest is founded on the reading of the Scriptures.

In the annual allocutions to the Lenten preachers of Rome, Benedict's message was always that of a fiery evangelist. One year, he chose as his text the blessing the celebrant gives to the deacon before the reading of the Gospel: "The Lord be in thy heart and on thy lips that thou mayest worthily and competently announce His Gospel." Benedict analyzed each word but his emphasis was on the word "Gospel" and especially on "His" (Christ's) Gospel.[47]

Benedict's allocutions never failed to delight his hearers. No matter what the occasion was, he could find some incident in Holy Writ which would serve as a counterpart of the present instance. At times he would find one of those charming Old Testament stories that are seldom used. For example, when he was urging the Sunday of general Communion for the children,[48] he proved the efficacy of a child's prayer from the story of Agar and Ismael. The verse which served as his text was the angel's word to Agar: "Fear not, for God has heard the boy's cry in this plight of his" (Gen. 21:17). At other times, it would be a phrase which he used as a refrain, as he did in the famous *Clama ne cesses* allocution.

However, Benedict's greatest claim in the realm of Sacred Scripture is derived from his encyclical, *Spiritus Paraclitus*.[49] September 30, 1920, the fifteenth centenary of St. Jerome's death, prompted Benedict to issue an encyclical which would set forth the saint's illustrious service to the Church in the field of scriptural studies. The encyclical was published September 15, two weeks before the saint's feast, to insure its timely arrival in all parts of the world.

Unlike Benedict's other writings, which were known for their brevity, *Spiritus Paraclitus* is one of the longest encyclicals in history. In it he extolled St. Jerome for the impetus he gave to biblical studies and for his rigorously orthodox teaching concerning the inspiration, authority, and inerrancy of Sacred Scripture. The Pope proceeded to point out the dangerous tendencies which were again creeping into biblical studies, such as unwarranted distinctions between "relative and absolute truth," "primary and secondary elements," the denial of historic truth in the Bible, and the misuse of principles which had been suggested by Leo XIII with prudence and caution.[50] Benedict gave practical counsels as to the manner in which these errors could be counteracted. A lengthy and very inspiring part of the encyclical deals with the Bible's place in priestly education.

Before closing his encyclical, Benedict referred to the "Pious Society of Saint Jerome for the Diffusion of the Holy Gospel." One can detect a justifiable flush of pride in his words:

> Our thoughts naturally turn just now to the Society of Saint Jerome, which We Ourselves were instrumental in founding; its success has gladdened us, and we trust that the future will see a great impulse given to it. The object of this society is to put into the hands of as many people as possible the Gospels and Acts, so that every Christian family may have them and become accustomed to reading them. This We have much at heart, for We have seen how useful it is. We earnestly hope, then, that similar societies will be founded in your dioceses and affiliated to the parent society here.

Spiritus Paraclitus gave new impetus to the study of the Bible.[51] The clergy took to heart the directives on preaching the Bible. Discussion clubs for the study of the New Testament began to spring up everywhere.

Benedict did not live to see his hope reach the extraordinary realization which it did in the United States. The attractively printed translation of the New Testament published by the Confraternity of Christian Doctrine,[52] sold over a million copies. It is not a gratuitous assumption to say that this success is a flowering of Benedict's efforts. The late Archbishop Edwin O'Hara,[53] founder of the Catholic Biblical Association of America and the moving force behind the new translation, had been a military chaplain in France during World War I. He had been deputed to report to Pope Benedict on religious life in the trenches.[54] The chaplain was deeply impressed by the spiritual aspect of the Holy Father and edified by the gracious hospitality which the Pope extended to him. He listened carefully and then inquired whether any attempt had been made to provide the soldiers with a pocket-sized volume of the Gospels. Benedict then spoke with great seriousness of the necessity of reading and meditating on the Gospel. His sentiments in private conversation were the same as those with which he closes his encyclical, "This We have much at heart, for We have seen how useful it is."

CHAPTER XIX

The Piety of Benedict XV

TODAY few advert to the fact that it was during the pontificate of Benedict XV that the apparitions at Fatima occurred. Mary's first appearance to the children occurred on May 13, 1917, at the very hour that the Holy Father was consecrating a young man to the episcopate. That young man was Eugenio Pacelli, who twenty-five years later as Pius XII was to dedicate the human race to the Immaculate Heart of Mary.

Very seldom, however, is the consecrator of that day, Benedict XV, mentioned in this connection. It seems to be part of "the inscrutable design of Divine Providence" — to borrow one of Benedict's favorite expressions — that after his death he should have gone through a period of all but complete oblivion. One revelation in that frequently retold story of Fatima is usually passed over, namely, that Mary definitely did call attention to her faithful client, Giacomo, by the grace of God destined to go down in history as Benedict XV.

One day the children were discussing the apparitions among themselves. Jacinta abruptly asked Lucy, "Have you ever seen the Holy Father?" Before Lucy could answer, Jacinta, with the beautiful naïveté of a child, answered her own question:

"I do not know how it happened, but I saw him in a very large house, kneeling before a little table, weeping, with his head between his hands. Outside there was a crowd. . . . Poor Holy Father."[1]

The unstudied simplicity of Jacinta's statement lends credence to the story. Had she described Benedict XV carried through St. Peter's on the *sedia gestatoria,* one could say that descriptions or newspaper pictures had imbedded themselves in the child's imagination so that any thought of the Pope would have had to clothe itself in some coloring of glory. Instead she describes a small, grief-stricken priest on his knees at a table. The infrequently photographed Benedict had never been pictured in this pose.

In reality, it is known that in those days Pope Benedict did fre-

quently seek refuge on his knees at a table in his room. Friedrich
von Lama gives an account of a German priest who in a private
audience asked the Pope whether he really hoped for peace through
his incessant admonitions. Benedict ushered his visitor to his inner
chamber. He went to a table on which was a statue of Our Lady
of Protection (*Madonna della Guardia*). Slowly he sank to his
knees, and, as though entirely alone, remained in this posture for
a long time. Then he arose, blessed his visitor, and, with a look
of deep introspection, dismissed him.[2] Perhaps the priest visitor
was disappointed. From a "diplomatic Pope" one would have expected a brilliant analysis of the political situation. Instead he was
given a practical application of the etymological meaning of "pontiff" which means "bridgebuilder." Benedict showed his visitor that
the supreme pontiff's chief task was prayer to bridge the gap
between God and man.

The old saying, "Each new pope must in some respect be the
opposite of his predecessor,"[3] did much harm to a fair appraisal of
Benedict XV. Some, such as the Modernists, who had fared ill
under Saint Pius X, disparaged his piety and pointed hopefully to
the diplomatic skill, the humanistic interests, and the aristocratic
origin of the new Pope. Others, who had thrown in their lot with
the Integralists, characterized Benedict as worldly, haughty, and
vain, in contrast to the simple, humble Sarto. One Italian priest,
Antonio Oldrà, a well-known admirer of Pius X, burst out in anger
when he heard Benedict accused of hauteur and vanity. One day
Father Oldrà had an audience with him, and after that day he
never grew tired of sharing with others his admiration for Benedict's
apostolic simplicity. "I can assure you with absolute certainty,"
he said, "that no pope has ever been simpler, more unaffected
and modest in his demeanor and conversation than Benedict XV."[4]
Still, the protests of individuals did little to overcome the harm
done to the reputation of Benedict XV by those who thought that
by contrasting Saint Pius X favorably with his successor, they were
doing Pius a service.

On the occasion of the unveiling of the monument to Benedict XV,
Pius XI paid a beautiful tribute to his predecessor's piety. "In
the scale of things that were beautiful, pure, holy, sublime, and
edifying in the life of Benedict XV, his piety occupies the highest
rung."[5] Benedict's piety showed itself not only in his private devotions but also in his daily striving for the attainment of Christian

perfection, in his external demeanor and internal recollection at liturgical functions, and in the prayerful thoughts manifested in his documents and allocutions.

All through life Benedict had to fight against his volatile temper. Over the years, he attained a high degree of self-discipline but on occasion his tendency to anger would still assert itself. The suffering of the person on whom he vented his temper was infinitesimally small compared to Benedict's sorrow when he realized that he had hurt the feelings of another. An example of his contrition and act of reparation came to light in an anecdote told by the aged Jacchini who had served five pontiffs in the capacity of coachman.

As has been said earlier, Benedict did not derive much joy from recreating in the Vatican gardens. Those who had his welfare at heart pleaded with him so urgently to take some recreation that he would at times give in to them. One summer day when news of the war was especially gloomy, Benedict decided to go for a solitary ride so that he might set his thoughts in order. For a man who had once owned an automobile, primitive though it may have been in 1912, this ride in a historic carriage constituted a retrogression. He who had traversed the Pyrenees on his journeys to Spain, who had been in the Tyrolese mountains on his missions to the Viennese court, who had crossed the Swiss Alps on his pilgrimage to Lourdes, who had been through all the mountain areas of Italy, must have been bored with this "make-believe" ride in the gardens, which, though beautiful, had been seen by him thousands of times. The ride must have been no less boring to old Jacchini who knew every shrub along the route.

On this particular afternoon, the coachman was nodding and dozing over his reins, and the horses aware of the situation, accelerated their pace so as to return as quickly as possible to their cool stables. As a result the carriage rattled over the cobblestone roads with uncomfortable speed. It was not so much the jogging which angered Benedict as the memory of an earlier ride when Jacchini's carelessness had more serious results. Besides, Benedict always felt that the hot stifling atmosphere was too hard on the horses bred in a cooler climate.[6] And so, on this summer day, the cumulative effect of Benedict's reluctance to go for a ride, of his annoyance at Jacchini's lack of attention to the one task for which he was retained, the thought of the world's lack of co-operation with him in the war, the memory of an accident that might have been fatal, all conspired to make him release his wrath. Like a spring in a clock which breaks suddenly and recoils loudly, Benedict scolded Jacchini with all the sharpness and stridency at the command of the true Italian temperament.

The poor old man could hardly believe that this was the gentle Della Chiesa whom he had learned to love under Leo XIII and Pius X. Deeply hurt, Jacchini had only one thought when the coach returned to the spot where the guards helped Benedict to alight. He wanted to escape to the privacy of his home to be alone in his grief and humiliation. As Benedict alighted, however, he asked Jacchini to come to his private apartments. Jacchini had terrible fears of a summary dismissal as his bony hand grasped the bannister of the stairs. Benedict meanwhile gave orders to the guards to leave him alone with the coachman. When Jacchini entered the papal apartments, Benedict came from an adjoining room, looking very weary and sad. In his hand he was clutching a bottle of choice wine and two glasses. With an embarrassed smile he asked Jacchini to do him the favor of drinking a glass of wine with him, the only refreshment the Pope was accustomed to take.[7] Until his dying day, the simple old coachman was the envy of his colleagues when he told the story of Benedict's having invited him to drink a glass of wine with him. The Holy Father lived literally by the evangelic precept, "Let not the sun go down upon thy anger."[8]

Examples of Benedict's favorite form of reparation, almsgiving, have been given in previous chapters. He was genuinely sad when he could not give to everyone who asked him. He felt that the Church lost in some way if he, the universal father, did not donate to every worthy cause. Benedict's example infiltrated even the students in the Roman colleges who as a rule were not in affluent circumstances. Yet in that postwar era they shared their superfluous goods and money with everyone in need.[9]

Giacomo Della Chiesa's habit of making a half hour's meditation before Mass in the Church of San Eustachio has already been described. Elderly priests who had been students in Rome during Benedict's pontificate still describe the quiet piety with which he said Mass. A renowned bishop who prefers that his name be not mentioned recalls how Benedict gave the absolution over the catafalque on an anniversary of the death of Saint Pius X. The bishop was commenting on the thought that, since the Church is the Mystical Body of Christ, then every gesture of the liturgy is a gesture of

Christ. He said that whenever he hears or sees this thought expressed, there comes to his mind the picture of Benedict XV, walking slowly around the catafalque with censor in hand, eyes closed, lips moving, as with great deliberation he recited the *Pater Noster* in silence. He avers that at the time the thought struck him that Christ would have performed this ceremony in precisely that manner. He recalls how awed he was and how happy to be a priest, an instrument of the Mystical Christ. Among all Pius X's writings, Benedict's favorite was the *Exhortation to the Catholic Clergy*, written to commemorate Pius' golden jubilee as a priest.[10] The whole tenor of that exhortation is that the priest must have a "sense of Christ." This Benedict showed forth in his every word and deed.

That Benedict's liturgical piety caught fire can be seen from an article that appeared in *The Tablet* in the last year of his life. It called attention to a recent increase in piety among the faithful.

> Unmistakable signs have been furnished lately in many processions with the Blessed Sacrament through the streets of Rome. . . . The celebrations for the beatification of the Trinitarian Tertiary, Blessed Anna Maria Taigi, had given opportunity for a display of devotion not the least remarkable feature of which was the exemplary behaviour of the regiment of Bersaglieri as the procession passed their barracks — and there have been others. To such as remember the Romans' conduct only a few years ago, the people of Rome on their knees in the streets before the Blessed Sacrament is a cheering sight.[11]

It would be difficult to collect and arrange all the beautiful thoughts that Benedict wrote and uttered, which show his deep piety. A number of instances have been given to exemplify his striving toward perfection in his own life. In order not to protract this chapter unduly, only a few devotions which were dear to Benedict will be singled out — his love of the Sacred Heart, his reverence for the Holy Eucharist, his filial devotion to Mary, and his unusual interest in the lives of the saints.

Several times this book has raised the question as to why Benedict XV should have been forgotten so quickly and on the very points in which he was so intensely interested. One of these points was devotion to the Sacred Heart of Jesus. True, Benedict wrote no encyclicals expressly on the Sacred Heart but many of his briefs, official epistles, private letters, and allocutions contained some exhortation that the Heart of Jesus should receive greater honor.

In Benedict's first years as archbishop of Bologna, his favorite project was the completion of the splendid Church of the Sacred Heart, the construction of which had been begun by his immediate predecessor, Cardinal Svampa. The magnificent edifice was dedicated on October 15, 1912, and on the following day the remains of Cardinal Svampa were transferred from the local cemetery to the church for burial. Archbishop Della Chiesa on that occasion made the point that Cardinal Svampa had lived and died "in the Sacred Heart of Jesus." The new Archbishop now wanted him literally buried in the Sacred Heart.[12]

In the electrifying *Clama ne cesses* allocution on the first Christmas Eve of Benedict's pontificate, the core of the message was, "Cry out, and do not stop, and We praise the pastors and single individuals who have determined to promote or multiply public or private prayers *to do sweet violence to the Most Sacred Heart of Jesus* to obtain that an end may come to the terrible scourge which now grips and throttles such a great part of the world."[13]

The beautiful prayer which Benedict composed and published on January 10, 1915, began with the words, "Dismayed by the horrors of a war which is bringing ruin to peoples and nations, we turn, O Jesus, *to Thy most loving Heart as to our last hope.* . . . From Thy sacred Heart Thou didst shed forth over the world Divine Charity, so that discord might end and love alone might reign among men."

It was Benedict XV who canonized Saint Margaret Mary Alacoque, the Visitation nun to whom our Lord appeared and asked that she be the missionary of the devotion to the Sacred Heart. Her cause had been introduced not long after her death in 1690. Pius IX had beatified her in 1864. Benedict XV was pleased to put the final seal of approval on this disciple of the Sacred Heart by canonizing her on the feast of the Ascension, May 13, 1920.

Pope Benedict's homily in Saint Peter's on that occasion was especially impressive. He pointed out how applicable were the complaints of ingratitude and irreverence voiced by the Sacred Heart to Saint Margaret Mary Alacoque. He called attention to the fact that Jesus showed Margaret Mary His heart which had as its decoration a cross, a crown of thorns, and a lance, all reminders of His Passion. It was not accidental, the Pope said, that he was canonizing Saint Margaret Mary and Saint Gabriel of Our Lady of Sorrows on the same day. Both saints were again calling men to a contemplation of the Passion of Christ. In His Passion Christ had showed His greatest love for us. The world is ailing because of wounds, and these wounds need the motherly hand of Mary and the medicine of Jesus' loving Heart.[14]

Benedict's letter to Cardinal Amette on the occasion of the dedication of the Church of the Sacred Heart on Montmartre in Paris contains in capsule form the whole theology of the devotion that Saint Margaret Mary was to preach. "While the most Sacred Heart of Jesus shows in a sensible manner His boundless love for His children, who too often, alas, are forgetful, at the same time it reminds us of this great duty whereby we ought to love God above all things and our neighbor as ourselves."[15] He hammered home the point that the French could not sincerely dedicate this church and themselves to the Sacred Heart if they continued to harbor hatred against the enemy.

In October, 1919, Father Gemelli, O.F.M., a convert to Catholicism, a former physician of renown and war hero, came to Benedict XV with a request for permission to found a Catholic university in Milan, dedicated to the Sacred Heart. The idea of a university for laymen under the patronage of the Sacred Heart appealed to Benedict and he readily gave his permission. Later he wrote to Father Gemelli, "And We are absolutely convinced that under the auspices of the Most Sacred Heart to whom under a pious impulse you consecrated this academy of learning, and in whom are all the treasures of wisdom and knowledge, you will quickly and successfully bring this work to its desired perfection."[16]

Benedict XV did not only allude to the Sacred Heart in his public pronouncements. In his private thinking he was much preoccupied with devotion to the Sacred Heart. One day a pontifical institution requested his approval on a diploma embellished — or more correctly cluttered — with various symbols and devices. It had pictures of the Immaculate Conception and of Saints Agnes, Rose, and Joan of Arc. Because of his shortsightedness, the Pope held the document very close to his eyes, peered intently, and seemed to search for something. Finally he returned the page with anything but enthusiasm. "We find one thing lacking," he said with disappointment, "and that is the emblem of the Sacred Heart." A few days later, when the diploma was returned with signs of having undergone a rigorous revision, the Sacred Heart had a place of honor. Benedict handed back the certificate with a gracious compliment.[17]

Father Mateo Crawley-Boevey became the apostle of "The Enthronement of the Sacred Heart" because of a miraculous cure when he first crossed the threshold of Paray-le-Monial in 1907. Paray-le-Monial is the site of the apparitions of the Sacred Heart to Saint Margaret Mary Alacoque. In 1915, Father Mateo was granted an audience with Benedict XV, who humbly requested the privilege of assisting at Father Mateo's Mass. The scene must have been reminiscent of Raffaello's mural, "The Miracle of Bolsena" in the Vatican Museum, which depicts the Supreme Pontiff kneeling at a faldstool while the Bohemian priest, in whose favor a Eucharistic miracle had been wrought in 1563, offers Mass at the Pope's altar.

Benedict handed Father Mateo a lengthy autographed letter in which he stated that he looked forward to a great increase of true Christian spirit in family life as a consequence of the devotion of the Enthronement.[18] When Father Mateo began to thank His Holiness for this unexpected sign of favor, Benedict said, "Do not thank me, my son. Do you not say that you are the apostle of the great King Jesus?"

"Oh yes, indeed, Your Holiness," interjected Father Mateo, "that I wish to be with my whole soul!"

"Well then," replied Benedict with a smile, "you preach the King. I am His prime minister, and must look to His interests. Is it not I then who am to thank *you* for what you are doing for the King of Love?"[19]

Maria di Pietro, a noblewoman and personal friend of Benedict XV, describes poetically the influence which Benedict's personal devotion to the Sacred Heart began to exert.

> He is a sovereign who prepares the way, "ordering all things mightily and sweetly." The Sacred Heart finds Its way into families, institutions, schools, and armies. The image of the Sacred Heart is worn over the hearts of young people, over the beds of the dying, over cradles and beside coffins, is enthroned in the golden cornices and is inlayed amidst the rosettes in the salons of patricians, watches with anxious tenderness from the grimy, smoky walls of a farmer's kitchens.[20]

From his earliest childhood, Giacomo Della Chiesa had been intimately associated with the Blessed Virgin Mary. He was born about two weeks before Pius IX defined the Immaculate Conception. When little Giacomo was brought home, his mother paused for an instant before the ancient statue of Mary above the portal of their home. His parish church was Saint Mary of the Vineyards. The place of pilgrimage which literally watches over Genoa was the shrine of Our Lady of Protection.

A devotion in which Benedict XV was especially interested was the rosary. On December 21, 1914, he granted an audience to a representation from the "Pious Union of the Family Rosary." Benedict was asked for a renewal of endorsement of this religious society which Saint Pius X had approved during his pontificate. Benedict replied, "Of course, of course, gladly do I give my name to this pious sodality. I have always recited the rosary in common with the people with whom I lived. Even now, in the evening when the day's work is done, we assemble in my private chapel, and in unison we recite the blessed beads of Our Lady."[21]

Benedict was always eager to recommend the rosary. On January 10, 1915, when he decreed the day of exposition of the Blessed Sacrament to implore God for peace, the public recitation of the rosary and the prayer of his own composition formed the core of the day's exercises. Incidentally, in that prayer he had written: "And do thou, O most holy Virgin, as in other times of sore distress, be now our help, our protection, and our safeguard." Most of his letters and addresses closed with some exhortation that Mary be made the refuge of those in need. On May 5, 1917, he decreed that the invocation, "Queen of peace," be added to the Litany of the Blessed Virgin Mary.[22]

Shortly after Benedict's elevation to the papacy, the people of Genoa began to make plans to honor this most illustrious son of their city. After some deliberation they concluded that they would make Benedict happiest by gathering money for a shrine in honor of Our Lady of Protection. The sculptor, Antonio Canepa, was engaged to make a statue of the *Madonna della Guardia*. The shrine was erected in the gardens of the Vatican not far from the Grotto of Lourdes so dear to Leo XIII. On May 2, 1917, Benedict XV was carried to his coach on the *sedia gestatoria* amid happy cheers of the populace. A procession preceded by the famous silver trumpets marched to the new shrine, and there Benedict was to bless the statue. Before the solemn blessing took place, Benedict sat on a throne facing the statue and delivered an address. The gift, the presence of so many Genoese, the spontaneous joy of the people at a time when the press tried to make him unpopular touched the Pope's heart, and he was visibly moved.

In tenderest terms he expressed his gratitude to the Genoese. He called attention to the fact that he was fortunate to have been born in the shadow of the *Madonna della Guardia* in Genoa. Providence, however, did not leave him without Mary's special protection. He said,

When out of the kindness of the heart of that holy and unforgettable Pius X, We were assigned to the see of Saint Petronius at Bologna, in Our first pastoral letter We expressed Our pleasure and hope that just as from a mountain, the ornament and crown of Our fatherland, the Mother of Protection had smiled on Our cradle, so from another mountain, from the Hill of Protection, which dominates the city of Bologna, and over which stands the majestic temple of Our Lady of Saint Luke, the Celestial Guardian would bless Our new mission.

However, after seven years in Bologna, Archbishop Della Chiesa went to Rome for the conclave and was destined never to return. As a member of the Della Chiesa family, he found a certain poignancy in this thought. If people, especially sailors, had been away on a voyage and all went well, they made a pilgrimage to the shrine of *Madonna della Guardia*. Pietro Antonio Della Chiesa, who in 1590 was named General of the Galleys of the Republic of Genoa, was famous for his pilgrimages of thanksgiving to the lofty chapel in Genoa. Alluding to the fact that he, Giacomo Della Chiesa, had ascended the chair of Peter, he continued:

But then when Our Lord wanted to raise the least of His bishops to the first of His sees, We were sad to leave Our flock in whose midst We were firmly convinced that We would die. We ought to be able to draw joyous auspices for Our pontificate from the solicitude which the Virgin has shown in wanting Us under her protection even when We thought We would have to stand far away from her shrine. And now, at last, We can glory in the holy thought that We have in common with the Evangelist Saint John the privilege of taking into Our own home the Mother of Jesus. Of Saint John alone was it said, "and from that hour the disciple took her into his home." That prerogative confirmed his title of "beloved disciple." And, O what an intimacy of devotion must have drawn the virgin disciple to the Virgin Mother, what riches of comforts the apostle of love must have drawn from the heart of Mary! Surely, We shall not be wrong if We say that the parallel in the privilege of taking the Mother of Jesus into Our home here at the Vatican, places in Our heart the hope that We also can have a more intimate communication of love with Holy Mary, that We can recognize her counsels better, that We shall have a more ready aid and a more efficacious comfort.[23]

Giacomo Della Chiesa's reputation as a Mariologist with *Maria della Guardia* as his specialty must have gone back many years. On August 29, 1900, when the Sacred Congregation of Rites granted the feast of Our Lady of Protection a proper office in the breviary, Monsignor Della Chiesa, Undersecretary of State, was selected to be the preacher and to do the honors at the shrine in Genoa. This sermon was printed at the time and was quoted in print whenever there was further discussion of the glories of Our Lady of Protection. In 1917, *Civiltà Cattolica* printed an impressive list of books and periodicals where the address of 1910 could be found and also reprinted part of the sermon.[24] The allocution of 1917 is much less academic, the style is less studied than in 1900. In seventeen years, Giacomo Della Chiesa's mingling with people and their problems, the anguish imposed by the war, greater spiritual maturity which only years of meditation can give, conspired to lend warmth and pathos to the papal allocution.

In the pontifical letter, *Inter sodalicia,* addressed to the Sodality of Our Lady of a Happy Death, Pope Benedict gave a clear and succinct exposition of Mary's office as coredemptrix. In the past, supreme pontiffs had alluded to that office of the Blessed Virgin, but surely never so poetically.[25]

In 1921, on the political front there was a struggle for power in Italy. Communists and other minor liberal forces were opposing Fascists, Socialists, and, of course, the People's Party. Hardly a day passed without riots and loss of civilian life in the streets throughout the cities of Italy. On July 25, 1921, the feast of Saint James, the Pope's patron saint, Benedict published a prayer which he himself had composed and indulgenced richly. The first part is built on the evangelic precept of the forgiveness of enemies, the second places the cause in Mary's hands.

> O God of goodness and forgiveness, with lacerated heart we surround Thy altars and implore pity. After the horror of war, the most terrible scourge is this fierce hatred which makes men of the same family persecute and kill each other in party strife. The land most famed for Christian piety, cradle of civil kindness, is becoming once again a bloodstained field of civil war.
>
> Have pity, O Lord! Thou who hast revealed the noble law of pardon

of offences and love of enemies, cause those who are not even enemies but are indeed brothers to embrace again, cause arms by which blood is shed to be laid down, and all may repeat in the beloved mother tongue the prayer that Thou dost teach: Our Father who art in Heaven; and that all who have seen Thy Son open His heart and His arms to those who crucified Him may feel their souls flooded with burning love and may say with humility and trust: Forgive us our trespasses as we forgive them that trespass against us.

Virgin Immaculate, Queen of Hearts, come down among thy children and make them hear thy Mother's voice. Thou alone by thy intercession canst reconcile them with Almighty God and reconcile them among themselves; thou alone canst give them taste of the sweetness of the peace that is prelude of eternal life. Amen.[26]

Mention has already been made of the saints whom Benedict canonized and of the blessed whom he beatified. His allocutions on those occasions were always gems of information and seeds of contemplation. Five of his encyclicals were written on saints: St. Jerome, St. Dominic, St. Francis of Assisi, St. Boniface, and St. Ephrem. In each case Benedict first recounted the main points in the saint's life and then selected some special incident which served as an occasion for developing a particular point of theology applicable as an antidote against some current error or abuse.

To this list should be added the *motu proprio* on St. Joseph entitled *Bonum sane,* in which Benedict designated naturalism as the greatest plague in man's thinking. "The effect of [naturalism], wherever it takes root," he wrote, "is to lessen the desire for celestial blessings, quench the flame of divine charity, and withdraw man from the healing and sanctifying grace of Christ. In the end the light of Faith is taken from him, only the corrupt forces of nature are left, and he is delivered to be the prey of the very worst passions." Benedict showed how this has crept into family life and into social life in general. As a remedy he suggested a contemplation of Saint Joseph who had led a life like ours. "Let us learn from Saint Joseph how to look on passing events in the light of eternal things to come, and seeking the consolation for the inevitable troubles of human life in the hope of celestial blessings, aspire to those with all their strength, resigned to the will of God, living soberly according to the rules of piety and justice."[27]

One more example of Benedict's study of the lives of saints should be cited. He was personally very interested in the cause of

Thérèse of Lisieux, "The Little Flower." It was he who exempted her cause from the fifty years' delay imposed by canon law between the death of the person and the examination of the process. On August 14, 1921, he promulgated the decree concerning Thérèse's heroic virtues and delivered an allocution on "Spiritual Childhood."

Bishop Stefano Ferrando[28] of Shillong, India, a native of Genoa, in commenting on his illustrious fellow citizen, mentioned the allocution on "Spiritual Childhood" first. In his estimation the Pope's theological development of this point, so seldom touched upon, yet so vital a part of the Gospels, gave Benedict XV a true claim to fame.

In the allocution, Benedict pointed out that spiritual childhood was "the result of trust in God and complete abandonment to Him." In Thérèse Martin, Benedict XV saw spiritual childhood in an extraordinary degree. Of spiritual childhood he said,

> It knows nothing of self-pride, or the thought of being able to attain by purely natural means a supernatural end, or those spurious notions of self-reliance in the hour of danger and temptation. On the other hand, it presupposes a lively faith in the existence of God, a practical homage to His power and mercy, a confident recourse to the providence of Him who alone can give us grace to avoid evil and seek good.

The Pope quoted in full all the texts from the Gospel in which Christ enjoined spiritual childhood. Of Christ and His insistence on spiritual childhood, Benedict said, "He went so far as to exclude from His kingdom those who did not become as little children." The Pontiff reviewed the life of Thérèse Martin and verified the points necessary for the concept of spiritual childhood.

Happily he dwelt on the famous pilgrimage which Thérèse and her saintly father made to Rome on the occasion of Leo XIII's jubilee in November, 1887. The incident has been celebrated in painting[29] and in literature. Incidentally, at the time of Thérèse's visit to Leo XIII, Giacomo Della Chiesa had just returned from Spain to begin work in the secretariat of state as an apprentice.

The audience of Thérèse Martin was memorable because of the fact that she broke the strict rule enjoined on pilgrims which forbade speaking to Leo XIII during an audience. Instead, young Thérèse blurted out her request that the Pope give her a dispensation to enter Carmel. Luckily, Leo, who usually took a grim view of infringements of protocol, did not become angry but merely placed

his thin finger over his lips to indicate silence, and said in French, *"Allons ... allons ... vous entrerez si le bon Dieu le veut"* ("Well, well, you will enter if it be God's will").
Benedict said of the incident,

> What a useless journey it seemed! . . . Thérèse could have acted upon the advice given her by Pope Leo XIII, who told her to "do whatever her superior should enjoin in the matter," for among her superiors she placed foremost her bishop. However, this assiduity in seeking to gain her object, though quite lawful in itself, might nevertheless have given rise to the belief that Thérèse relied upon human means; her confidence in God might have seemed diminished, her abandonment less complete. She preferred to remain silent under this new disappointment, and continued to maintain her peace of mind in the firm belief that God rewards in His own time those who trust in Him.

His wish was that the world imitate her abandonment and trust in God. "Duplicity and crafty stratagem are only too characteristic of the day. It is not, therefore, to be wondered at that piety toward God and charity toward one's neighbor, should be so wanting. May all this soon be changed! To the deceits, the fraud, the hypocrisy of the world, may there be opposed the sincerity of a child."[30]

There was indeed a Benedict whom the world did not know — a man of deep personal piety — a true man of God. Since, thanks to the troubled era in which he reigned, relatively few people were able to be received by him in audience, the world learned but little of his piety. Hilaire Belloc who was granted an audience with the Pope on June 5, 1916, has left us a frank and interesting confession of surprise that Benedict was "a thoroughly good man" and that there was "holiness in his expression." Belloc wrote:

> I had a long, long talk with him. He is a *thoroughly good man,* which is not what I had been led to expect! I had thought to see one of those rather subtle and very *bornés* Italian officials — *bureaucrates.* Instead of that he has something like Holiness in his expression and an intense anxious sincerity. He spoke of individual conversion as opposed to political Catholicism in a way which — with my temperament all for the Collective Church — profoundly impressed me. I was exceedingly glad to have seen him and to have gotten his blessing.*

* From *The Life of Hilaire Belloc* by Robert Speaight, copyright 1957 by J. B. Morton. Used by permission of the publisher, Farrar, Straus and Cudahy, Inc.

CHAPTER XX

Benedict and Christian Life

PIETY cannot remain hidden long in any man. Eventually it manifests itself externally in word and act. In a pope this is especially true because his official acts which are performed for the sanctification of his people spring ultimately from his own piety.

One category of public acts comprises the canonizations and beatifications which Benedict performed. Actually he canonized only three saints, a very small number in contrast to the thirty-four canonized by his successor, Pius XI. World conditions, however, and not personal inactivity explain the disparity. An immense concourse of people from the saint's native land is expected in the Eternal City for the canonization rite, and Benedict's brief pontificate took place under conditions which rendered travel impossible. In addition, Pius X had revised the liturgical calendar so as to emphasize Sunday and the temporal cycle; the sanctoral cycle was not to overshadow the day of the Lord. Therefore, Benedict did not immediately replenish the purged Church calendar with newly canonized saints.

On Ascension Thursday, May 13, 1920, Saints Margaret Mary Alacoque and Gabriel of Our Lady of Sorrows were canonized in a single ceremony, and on Sunday, May 16, Joan of Arc was elevated to the altar. These saints were chosen with care. Each was to teach a truth and to exemplify a virtue particularly necessary at that time.

SAINT MARGARET MARY ALACOQUE

Saint Margaret Mary Alacoque, born July 22, 1647, in France, entered the convent of the Visitation Order at Paray-le-Monial at the age of 23. The mysteries of the Sacred Heart, best known through the First Friday devotions, were revealed to her in three special manifestations. Christ told her that she must tell her director to spread devotion to the Sacred Heart. The Sisters did not believe her, and she was made to suffer many humiliations. However, peace came after her many trials, and she died on October 17, 1690.

At the time of the canonizations, Father C. C. Martindale, S.J., wrote a searching article on Margaret Mary's purpose in God's plan.[1] He traced the re-Christianization of France through four great movements: "The *Catholic Calvinism* of the Jansenists; the *Catholic Buddhism* of the Quietists; the active charity of Vincent de Paul; the lofty speculative devotion of Bérulle's Oratory." The first two movements sinned by excess. To the rigorism of the Jansenists, Margaret Mary Alacoque's devotion offered Christ Compassionate; to the Quietists, absorbed in a nebulous mysticism, she offered the *human* Heart; to Saint Vincent's workers who spent themselves in physical activity for the poor, she taught that their hearts must be Christ's. The Jesuit theologian pointed out that in his day there were intellectuals absorbed in what he called "discarnate, self-emptied, annihilated devotion to the Word." He believed that devotion to the Sacred Heart as preached by Margaret Mary Alacoque and now brought into sharper focus by her canonization, would have the stabilizing effect which they needed.

In his allocution at the canonization, Pope Benedict said:

> The apostolate of Margaret Mary Alacoque, in general, has not yet found among the faithful the response and favor that it should have. Oh, with what effrontery and with what frequency, do we not in everyday life observe the continuation of that cry, "We do not wish this man to be king over us!" (Luke xix, 14.) It seems to us that the full glorification of Margaret Mary has been reserved by God for such a time in which the mission entrusted to her to propagate the cult of the Sacred Heart will appear more extended and more accepted in the world, and on that account richer in fruit.

SAINT GABRIEL OF OUR LADY OF SORROWS

St. Gabriel is not well known in the United States of America. If he were better known and revered, perhaps through his intercession, the wave of juvenile delinquency might be less appalling. Unlike many saints Gabriel is an appealing model for boys and young men.

Gabriel of Our Lady of Sorrows — Francis Possenti before he took the religious habit — was born at Assisi on March 1, 1838. He was educated in the school of the Christian Brothers and later in the Jesuit College at Spoleto.

A description of Francis Possenti's character and temperament is found in the process of his canonization. "He was gay and witty, and his fine intellectual gifts and manly, open nature made him the most popular boy in the college with his masters and fellow students. He was a handsome, healthy, truthful, fun-loving lad." Apparently he was not different from other boys. He was fond of well-tailored and fashionable clothes, no great problem for his father who was a successful lawyer.

He applied for entry into the Society of Jesus, and the Jesuit provincial accepted him. However, he asked for time to prepare himself. September 5, 1856, was "prize day" at the Jesuit college. As valedictorian, Francis delivered an address, and in the presence of the apostolic delegate, was awarded the gold medal for the highest general average in the whole college. After the ceremony, Francis made his farewell to the world and entered the monastery of the Passionists at Morrovalle. On November 21, he received the habit and took the name of Gabriel of the Sorrowful Mother, whom from childhood, as his brothers inform us, he loved with special tenderness. His motto was "Charity which is fond of restrictions is not charity." By this motto he lived and spent himself for God and for his brothers. On February 27, 1862, scarcely five years after his religious profession, he died of tuberculosis.

It was the expressed wish of Pope Leo XIII and Saint Pius X that Gabriel be regarded the chief patron of modern youth. Benedict XV underscored this wish and extolled him as a credit to the education imparted in the schools of the Christian Brothers. In his allocution, he pointed out how fittingly Margaret Mary and Gabriel belonged together as devotees of Christ's Passion. Margaret Mary pointed to the Heart of Jesus pierced with a lance; Gabriel was devoted to the heart of Mary pierced with a figurative sword as she suffered with Jesus in His Passion and Death.

SAINT JOAN OF ARC

On Sunday, May 16, 1920, Benedict XV on the *sedia gestatoria* again entered the basilica of Saint Peter. The huge church was packed with French ecclesiastics, statesmen, and many people who came as humble pilgrims for the canonization of their national heroine.

Joan of Arc, a young peasant girl who was born at Domremy in 1412, received an extraordinary assignment. Saint Michael, Saint Catherine, and Saint Marguerite appeared to her while "their voices" came from heaven and exhorted her to help the king of France. This she did. On April 29, 1429, at the head of the army, she entered Orleans forcing the English to lift their siege. On July 17, the king was crowned at Rheims, thanks to her victories. On May 23, 1430, she was taken prisoner and her long Calvary began. Imprisoned, maltreated, accused of sorcery, judged for political motives before a religious tribunal, she was condemned to death. On May 30, 1431, she was burned alive at Rouen. She never desisted from protesting her innocence, her fidelity to God, and her submission to the Church. The purity of her life, her integrity, her piety, her charity even in battle are proofs of her sincerity and the genuineness of her sanctity.[2]

Pope Calistus III quashed the foul verdict of 1431, Pope Leo XIII allowed the process of her canonization to be opened, and Saint Pius X declared her "blessed."

Most of the articles in the periodicals of the time extol Joan of Arc as a patroness of justice.[3] More specifically Benedict looked upon her as an exemplar of the true patriotism which Thomas Aquinas treated under the "potential parts" of justice.

Benedict was a pacifist, yet in no way did he disparage patriotism. "On the contrary," wrote the editor of Stimmen der Zeit in his obituary of Benedict XV, "in the Maid of Orleans, Benedict elevated Christian patriotism to the altar."[4]

For Benedict patriotism connoted "an understanding of those near us, which then spreads to those situated more remotely. In the same way love for fellow men should grow. Love emanates from us, spreads, extends itself first to our parents, our relatives, our home, then to the people about us and finally to all mankind. In this love for some more than for others there should be no conflict but subordination and Christian solidarity. To favor one people and to oppress the other is to distort the natural order. All must be inflamed by the same fire. There are those who say that they love the whole world but not their own country. That too is an illusion. True patriotism must steer a middle course between a fanatical exclusiveness and a vague, fuzzy, philanthropy." Joan of Arc was a true patriot in Benedict's estimation. From his admiration for this saint one can see that Benedict, in spite of his love of peace, did not condemn all war unconditionally. In Catholic theology war is not always immoral. It is no more immoral than the maintenance of military forces. For Benedict, war was the cause of great physical evil, but at times war must be tolerated to repair or prevent moral evil. Benedict's words must be understood correctly, not as a political maneuver to court the French as he was accused of doing.

In his own conduct during the war Benedict was accused of lack of patriotism. He had tried to dissuade Italy from entering the war. By the Treaty of 1882 Italy really belonged to the Central Powers, and Benedict was pleased that the terms of the pact did not force Italy to enter the war against France and Great Britain. In his estimation, Italy's entry into war was not justified. Why then did he weep when he heard of Italy's crushing defeat at Caporetto? He wept because of his patriotism, he wept because one of his spiritual children had been hurt needlessly. He was human and, therefore, because of his patriotism, he felt more pain when his own people were crushed and beaten.

The canonization of Joan of Arc was to teach the principles of patriotism. Certain Germans and Italians were angered by Benedict's allocution in which he praised the French and expressed the thought that he could be French at heart even though he could not be French by blood. Benedict made no apologies for what he had said. He believed, as every good Catholic believes, that one of the highest honors that can come to a country is the elevation of one of its children to the Catholic altar. France had this honor. As father of all children of the Church, Pope Benedict was as happy that this honor came to France, one of his children, as though it had come to him personally.

Benedict XV also beatified several servants of God. On April 29, 1917, he beatified Joseph Benedict Cottolengo who in 1828 founded the "Little House of Divine Providence" at Turin for sheltering the poor. With his facile use of Sacred Scripture, Benedict on that occasion delivered a stirring allocution.[5]

In 1920, besides canonizing the three saints, Benedict beatified four other servants of God. The series began on May 9 with the beatification of Louise de Marillac (1591–1660), foundress of the Ladies of Charity. She had been under the direction of Saint Vincent de Paul and her heroic work and perseverance had been a great consolation to Vincent in his trials and hardships.

On May 23, the people of Ireland were made very happy because of Benedict's beatification of Oliver Plunket, Archbishop of Armagh (1629–1681). Benedict said,

It was not without a special decree of Divine Providence that the beatification of the Venerable Oliver Plunket has been celebrated in these days. For is not the present moment one in which Ireland has most need of help from on high that she may realize her legitimate desires, without, however, neglecting any part of her duties? Most opportunely, therefore, does the beatification of the Venerable Oliver Plunket come at the present moment, for it is to be hoped that now that he is raised to the glory of the blessed he will be a more powerful intercessor than ever on behalf of his countrymen.[6]

On May 30, the beatification of Anna Maria Taigi (1769–1837) took place. Benedict had spoken frequently about her, stressing the point that one need not be in a cloister or belong to a celebrated religious order, or be in a special or remarkable walk of religious life to gain the honors that the Church decrees. All that is needed is the performance of duty in heroic degree in the state of life to which each individual Catholic has been called.[7]

On June 6, the series of festivities was closed with the beatification of twenty-two martyrs of Uganda. In 1880, only twenty years after the discovery of Uganda and two years after Catholicism was brought to Uganda by five White Fathers of Cardinal Lavigerie, twenty-two natives valiantly died for their Faith. Among those who were to be put to death had been a few little boys who were spared because of their youth. At the rite of beatification there was a hush as two Negroes entered the basilica, walking in a prominent division of the procession. They were two of those who had been spared. Their large eyes scanned the painted canvas in the "Glory of Bernini" on which the martyrs were depicted as the artist imagined them to have been on the day of their martyrdom. Had intercession not been made with the savage King Mwanga, this too would have been their day, and they would also have been on the painting with martyrs' palms in their hands.

Another facet of Benedict's piety was displayed by the changes which he introduced in the liturgy. Already in boyhood Giacomo Della Chiesa was known for the practice of the fine Christian virtue of fidelity. On August 10, 1915, he issued the apostolic constitution, *Incruentum Altaris Sacrificium,*[8] in which he extended to priests of the whole world the privilege of saying three Masses on All Souls' Day.

In his humility, Benedict says that the idea of permitting three

Masses did not originate with him. It had its origins in the piety of the people. Benedict wrote:

Indeed, that very ancestral piety became so intense that, many centuries ago, in the kingdom of Aragon, by a custom gradually introduced, secular priests celebrated twice, and regulars three times, on the day of Solemn Commemoration of all Souls: this privilege Our predecessor of immortal memory Benedict XIV not only, for just reasons, confirmed, but also, at the request of Ferdinand VI, Catholic King of Spain, and likewise John V, King of Portugal, by an apostolic letter dated August 26, 1748, so extended, that to every priest whomsoever in the dominions subject to either prince he granted the faculty of celebrating three times on the same Solemn Commemoration.[9]

It must be remembered that Benedict XIV had been the last archbishop of Bologna to become pope. Benedict XV had frequently expressed his admiration for his predecessor's work in the sees of Bologna and Rome. The very fact, therefore, that it was Benedict XIV who had given approval for the saying of three Masses on All Souls' Day in the Iberian peninsula was enough to incline Benedict favorably toward the practice. Furthermore, he had become a specialist on the history of piety in that country. In his apostolic constitution, therefore, one can see some of his personal interests.

Benedict explained that the third Mass of that day had a twofold aspect. First, he felt that the Church owes a debt to the departed. In England and other Protestant countries there are many buildings, turned to profane use or converted into Protestant churches, which were built from funds donated on the condition that Masses be said daily for the souls of the donors. The pious founders died peacefully in the assurance that, though their descendants might not remember them in prayer, the daily Masses of the clergy would not cease to intercede with God for the repose of the testators' souls. However, the Protestant Revolt seized these houses with the result that the Masses were never said.

"We are strongly impelled," he wrote, "to supply in some wise, as far as in us lies, the suffrages omitted." In other words, Benedict XV wished to make restitution to those donors who had died many years ago. He reasoned that the Church had spread, that there are many more priests saying Mass today than would have said Mass in those profaned houses. If all these thousands of priests say a

Mass for the repose of the souls of the defrauded donors, the debt will gradually be paid off.

In this apostolic constitution Benedict gave us a glimpse into his past. He wrote that charity toward those souls had already "inflamed" him "in boyhood."

The second aspect of the Pope's intention was the repose of the many soldiers dying during the war. "We perceive," he wrote, "almost before our eyes such a multitude of men, in the flower of their age, succumb to premature death in battle; to purify their souls, though the piety of kindred be not lacking, who will say nevertheless that it is equal to the need?"

This apostolic constitution teaches a beautiful truth — the complete control of Christ's Vicar on earth over the spiritual goods in the Church's treasury. It taught the solidarity of the Communion of Saints. Benedict was four centuries removed from the day of the outrage against the donors, yet in virtue of the power of the keys, he could now make good their loss.

Benedict made but four changes in the calendar of the Church. They were all published in the same decree[10] on October 26, 1921. The Sunday within the octave of the Epiphany was dedicated to Jesus, Mary, and Joseph, and became the feast of the Holy Family. The feasts of Saint Gabriel Archangel, March 24, and of Saint Raphael, October 24, were raised to the rank of major double. In the mind of the Supreme Pontiff, the three feasts were associated. Gabriel had announced to both Mary and Joseph the mystery of the Incarnation. The liturgical status of the Archangel Raphael was elevated because he had conferred great favors on the family of Tobias, model of Old Testament family life. The idea of the family motivated the three changes.

The same decree gave Saint Irenaeus a place in the calendar of the universal Church, setting June 28 as his feast day. Irenaeus was first a most important link in tradition. The decree refers to him as "that famous disciple of Saint Polycarp, the bishop of Smyrna," who in turn was the favorite disciple of John the Evangelist, "that disciple whom Jesus loved."[11] In addition, Saint Irenaeus wrote words which prove that from the beginning it was taken for granted that the see of Rome enjoyed the primacy of jurisdiction. The decree quotes the famous passage, "Every church throughout the world should bring itself into line with the Roman Church because of that Church's surer guarantees." And since Saint Irenaeus was concerned with the whole Church's consolidation in the family of Rome, he was to be honored by the whole Church and not merely in his own see of Lyons.

Benedict XV increased the number of Prefaces in the Mass by two additions.[12] The *Requiem*, which hitherto employed the common Preface, was to have its proper Preface in which occur the beautiful words,

> . . . through Christ our Lord. In whom the hope of a blessed resurrection is shown to us: that they who are saddened by the certain necessity of dying, be comforted by the promise of eternal life to come.
>
> For the life of Thy faithful, O Lord, is changed, not destroyed: and when the home of this earthly life is dissolved, an everlasting dwelling in heaven shall be gained.

The text of this Preface was not a new composition. It is an old Preface found in the Mozarabic rite of Spain.[13]

In the same decree, the feast of Saint Joseph was also given a proper Preface.

Training of the clergy was one of Benedict's great preoccupations. His very first encyclical, *Ad Beatissimi*, recommended to all clerics a rereading of Saint Pius X's *Exhortation to the Clergy*. In an audience, a visitor regretted that a certain seminary had so few aspirants to the priesthood. "It is not the number that matters, but the quality," was the Pope's terse comment.[14]

Benedict's creation of the Congregation of Seminaries and Universities attests his interest in the formation of the clergy. In his apostolic letter on missions, his extraordinarily high standards in missionary seminaries were discussed. Annually, he held a contest for the students of the Roman Seminary to see who had the greatest proficiency in memorizing the Gospels. In 1919, he conducted a seminar under the open sky in the Vatican gardens. The participants were students from all the seminaries in Rome. The subject of the discussion was an exegesis of passages in Chapters 11 to 21 of Saint John's Gospel. The Pope led the discussion, asked the questions, and distributed twenty-five prizes.[15]

In his encyclical, *Humani Generis*, Pope Benedict reminded priests of their obligation to preach not politics, not strange philosophies, but the Word of God. He pointed out in plain language how sermons reflect the state of the preacher's own interior life. If his spiritual life is a desert, his sermons will not inspire his hearers even though for a time they may please the ear. In this encyclical the Pope outlined the prerequisites of the preacher: (1) complete and full submission to God's will; (2) a preparation of the soul to support every kind of pain and grief; (3) possession of what Saint Paul defines as the "Spirit of Prayer."

Annually he addressed the Lenten preachers of Rome before they began their series of sermons. Since he himself had always borne in mind the holiness of the preacher's task, he had new admonitions year after year, but his insistence on Holy Writ was constant and unvaried. Thus, for example, he exhorted the preachers:

> We are pleased first of all to recall to you what must be the matter of your sermons. We will not do you the wrong to suppose that you are ignorant of your duty to preach "the word of God"; and therefore We would not admit even the possibility that any one of you is preparing to take into the pulpit arid questions of philosophy, history, or politics. The sacred orator must aim chiefly at the spiritual profit of those who listen to him; but the rule of Christian life is drawn from that "word of God, written and revealed," which forms the deposit of the faith, and which is authoritatively interpreted by the infallible magisterium which Christ Himself has put in the Church. To this most pure source, therefore, let the sacred orators have recourse for the saving water wherewith they are to satisfy the people thirsting for truth.[16]

In the field of education Benedict XV advanced no revolutionary ideas. However, he expressed himself on the subject frequently. It is unfortunate that anthologies of papal pronouncements on education carry no reference to Benedict XV.[17] Reticent by nature, he did not repeat in new encyclicals what had been said by his predecessors except in a brief summary. He did, however, speak of education in his allocutions. What he gave his hearers were not opinions or theories but authentic expressions of the Church's teaching.

For Benedict XV, the home was the starting point of all education. The mother especially was to be personally active in the education of her child. The woman of the nobility is not to rest content that a governess is taking charge of the education of her child.[18] A mother in the plebeian ranks is not to leave the matter solely to the school. Women should insist on religious instruction. They should make all parents aware of this obligation and see that it is part of the school's curriculum. Benedict was, of course, speaking of conditions in a thoroughly Catholic country like Italy.[19]

Pope Benedict, who himself had attended a high school conducted by priests, believed that older boys should be taught by men consecrated to God. Therefore, he was always most gracious to the Christion Brothers founded by Saint John Baptist de La Salle. When Christian Brothers were among the pilgrims in an audience, Benedict invariably asked about their work and expressed satisfaction with the important work they were doing for the Church.[20]

Even though Benedict had written no encyclicals which had to do with social questions, he gave his messages on social questions to representatives of Catholic Action whom he summoned frequently.[21] In an audience granted to diocesan committees of Catholic Action he said:

> The child represents for us the future of society. The society of the future is being formed by the children of today, and it will have just that amount of good in it as is represented by the education which the children of today receive. Therefore, it is pre-eminently important that children and young people today should receive an education founded on principles of religion and honesty. To that end is required generosity on the part of the rich, patience on the part of teachers, care on the part of all, in order that out of a religious foundation of education today may arise an improved state of society in the future.[22]

Benedict XV was seen and known so little that hardly anything is recorded concerning his personal magnetism. One would be inclined to think that his physical deformities — slight though they were — would have presented a barrier between himself and Nature-loving youth. On the contrary, however, his slim, youthful appearance and his fine scholarly face, his elegant language and charismatic gift of oratory made Benedict XV so popular with young people that, had he lived longer, he could have become a menace to Mussolini and his efforts to win over the hearts of Italian youth.

Before the opening of school, the first week of September, 1921, there was a congress of young people from all over Italy. Benedict XV said Mass for them in Saint Peter's. Thirty thousand teen-agers crowded into the great basilica. It was a low Mass and the young people were allowed to recite the *Gloria, Credo,* and *Pater Noster* with the Holy Father, a foretaste of the *Missa recitata* or "dialogue Mass" which has become quite general in our day. After Mass, there was Benediction of the Blessed Sacrament, at which the Pope himself performed the incensation. He led the congregation in reciting the act of consecration to the Sacred Heart, and then he addressed them. His return to the chapel of the Blessed Sacrament was greeted with so much cheering and shouting that the situation almost went out of hand.[23]

After the Mass, both in the square of Saint Peter and in the Colosseum, amid the cheers of "Long live the Pope," there was heard the cry, "Long live the Pope King," *Papa-Re,* a cry that had not been heard since 1870. It was thought to have been dead long ago. Newspapers magnified the incident so that it created some unrest in the provinces. Both the Italian government and Catholic leaders issued statements insisting that the Society of Catholic Youth was loyal and patriotic, but that youthful enthusiasm at having seen the Holy Father carried them to this extreme.[24]

The incident, unimportant though it may seem, shows what an influence the personality of Benedict XV might have exerted on educational policies of Italy had he lived longer. At the canonization of Saint Joan of Arc, the Pope stopped before the division of white-clad French girls and said a few words of encouragement to them. They too became wildly enthusiastic for Benedict XV. Saint Augustine had taught that only that teacher is really successful who can create a love for him in his students. This gift in Benedict was a great asset for the supreme teacher of Christendom.

CHAPTER XXI

Benedict the Universal Father

IN BENEDICT's first encyclical, the blueprint for his whole pontificate, he wrote, "Immediately We began to regard with unspeakable affection the flock committed to Our care: a flock truly immense, for in one way or another it embraces all mankind. For all, without exception, have been delivered by Jesus Christ, at the price of His blood, from the slavery of sin: nor is anyone shut out from the benefits of His Redemption."[1] Benedict was very conscious of his universal fatherhood, and there is hardly a country which did not receive some favor from him. One of the first segments of Christendom to claim his attention was that which falls within the compass of the Oriental Churches.

During the academic year, a visitor to Rome will see young bearded men in cassocks, wearing a woolen headdress resembling a black stovepipe hat without brim. These clerics will walk briskly, ten or twelve in a group, double file. The language they speak is Arabic. They are students in one of the Oriental colleges in Rome. All too often the question which slips from the visitor's lips is, "But they aren't Catholics, are they?"[2] Had it been possible, Benedict would gladly have placed shielding hands over the ears of those students to prevent their hearing a question so charged with suspicion. Not only are they Catholics but they are Catholics with a rich and noble heritage. Orientals in union with the Holy See are often called "Uniats," although to some members of the Oriental Church the term is opprobrious. They prefer to be called Eastern Rite Catholics.

Their interests were supervised and safeguarded by the Congregation for the Propagation of the Faith, a congregation primarily concerned with the mission fields in foreign lands. True, in 1862 Pope Pius IX had created a special division in the congregation which had the lengthy title of "Sacred Congregation of the Propagation of the Faith for Matters of Oriental Rite," but even this arrangement did not flatter the Eastern Rite Catholics. That their interests were ultimately watched over by an office for foreign missions, they felt,

243

carried the insinuation that they stood in need of evangelization and conversion.

Once upon the papal throne, Benedict was able to give free rein to that "wonderful impulse of zeal" as he called it in *Ad Beatissimi*. In the *motu proprio, Dei Providentis,* of May 1, 1917, he reminded the world that it was his duty to conserve and foster all the churches which form the Mystical Body of Christ.[3] "Since We embrace all churches in paternal charity, We do so especially in the case of the Oriental churches which in ancient times gave forth so bright a beam of light that even now, after so long an interval, We see the other regions of Christianity still glittering in their splendor." It was his wish to do all in his power to bring about an amelioration of their condition. This he proposed to do by instituting the new Congregation for the Oriental Churches.

Benedict made it clear that he wished nothing to carry over from the past which had created the impression that the popes cared less for the Orientals or that they wished them to be subservient to the Latins.

> When our Churches of the East shall see the supreme pontiff watching in person over their interests, they will without fail understand that it is impossible for the Holy See to give any greater sign of affection for them. Moreover, We may hope that the Latins will not again be represented to Christians of the East as objects of suspicion, for the present act will make it still clearer that the Church of Jesus Christ, because it is neither Latin, Greek, nor Slavonic, but Catholic, makes no distinction between its sons, and that all these, be they Greek, Latin, Slavonic, or of other national groups occupy the same place before this Apostolic See.

The sentence which spoke of "the supreme pontiff watching in person over their interests" was to be taken absolutely literally. The *motu proprio* establishing the new congregation provided that its prefect was to be the Pope himself. The original staff was carefully selected and included the most learned and renowned ecclesiastics of the day.[4]

On October 15, 1917, Benedict issued another *motu proprio, Orientis Catholici,* in which he provided for the erection of an Institute for Oriental Studies.[5] It was to be open to priests of the Latin rite who wished to exercise their ministry in the Balkans and Middle East among Orientals in communion with Rome, by Oriental Catholics, and by Orientals of the schismatic rites. This provision must have seemed shockingly liberal to some. Benedict invited the schismatics to put aside their prejudices long enough to pursue studies in the new institute where both doctrines could be examined, that is, those of the churches in union with Rome and of the dissidents. Every student was to be given the opportunity of comparing for himself the sources of doctrines of his sect with those of the church united under Rome. The rest of the document is brief and can be quoted verbatim.

1. An institute for the carrying on of studies in Oriental matters shall be established in Rome, which, being under the special vigilance and care of the supreme pontiff, shall be adorned with the title "pontifical."
2. It shall be directly subject to the Congregation for the Oriental Church, and through that to Ourself and Our successors.
3. The institute shall have its own distinct seat in the house near the Vatican where up to now has been the *Hospitium de Convertendis,* commonly called, but We desire that that shall take place without any detriment to the said hospice.
4. There shall be taught in this institute:
   a) Orthodox theology which touches the various doctrines of the Christians of the Orient on divine things, with lectures on Oriental patrology, historic theology, and patristics.
   b) The canon law of all the Christian peoples of the Orient.
   c) The different Oriental liturgies.
   d) Sacred and profane history of Byzantium and the rest of the Orient to which shall be added lectures on ethnographic geography, sacred archaeology, the civil and political constitution of those peoples.
   e) Oriental liturgy and preaching.
5. The course of all these studies shall be completed in two years.
6. The schools of the Institute shall be attended by priests of Latin Rite who are going to enter on the sacred ministry in the Orient, and they may be attended not only by our Oriental clerics, but also by such of the Orthodox as desire instructions in the higher truth.
7. That there may be nothing wanting for the studies, We add to the Institute a library well equipped both with an abundant selection of books and suitable periodical literature.

And what We have here constituted We order to be valid in perpetuity, all things to the contrary, even those worthy of very special mention, notwithstanding.[6]

Today we realize how explosive the situation in the Middle

East can be and how it can affect the whole world. Since 1950, universities and colleges, both secular and sectarian, are instituting departments of Middle Eastern studies.

Besides the two *motu proprios,* Benedict showed his benignity toward the Orientals in many other ways. In Rome he reopened the Coptic College for Ethiopian students at the Church of Saint Stephen of the Abyssinians. At the scenic abbey of Grottaferrata he established a minor seminary which he placed in the hands of Greek Basilian monks. It was to house youths of the Greek rite aspiring to the priesthood in order that they might serve Albanians of that rite, resident in Italy. To the Syrian Patriarch of Antioch he gave the historic Church of Santa Maria in Campo Marzio so that his people might also have a national church in Rome. In 1921, the last year of Benedict's life, on the feast of Saints Peter and Paul, patronal feast of the great basilica and of Rome, he granted an audience to over two hundred people from the Middle East who came to thank him. After the exhausting ceremonies he was so fatigued that he could hardly stand, yet he insisted on walking about the hall to extend his hand to each member of the delegation.[7]

The third great step in winning the confidence of Eastern Rite Catholics was the publication of the encyclical, *Principi Apostolorum,* on October 5, 1920. This document elevated Saint Ephrem, the Syrian monk and deacon of Edessa, to the rank of Doctor of the Church.[8] In order to qualify for this title, a saint must not only have been endowed with profound learning, but he must also have taught Christian doctrine or defended it against heretics in an extraordinary manner. Saint Ephrem is the only deacon to be named a Doctor of the Church, which he shares with two popes, eighteen bishops, and eight priests. The latest addition to the list of Doctors is the Capuchin, St. Lawrence Brindisi (March 19, 1959).

On September 15, 1920, Benedict XV had published the great encyclical, *Spiritus Paraclitus* in which he developed the life of Saint Jerome and his influence on Christian learning. In the encyclical, *Principi Apostolorum,* which he published twenty days later, Benedict developed the life of Saint Ephrem and showed how this Syrian saint influenced Christian culture.

It is advantageous, Venerable Brethren, that this encyclical should follow so closely upon the heels of the one which We have just recently given you on the fifteenth centenary of the death of Saint Jerome because these two distinguished men possess similar attributes in more than one respect. If you reflect for a moment, you will realize that Jerome and Ephrem were practically contemporaries. Both were monks, both inhabitants of Syria, both specialists in the knowledge and study of the Sacred Books. One is inclined to compare them to the two candlesticks that stand before the Lord of the earth, destined by God so that one would illuminate the West and the other the East. As far as what is contained in their writings, both are of the same excellence, both of the same spirit.

In his conclusion Benedict refers to the Eastern schismatics with fatherly kindness. "Oh, may with the grace of God and the protection of Saint Ephrem, those barriers finally fall, which, we regret, hold so large and distinguished a portion of the Christian flock estranged from the mystical rock upon which Christ built His Church."

Benedict's intercession in behalf of the Greek Orthodox clergy is an act of love, which fits into the mosaic of resolutions found in *Ad Beatissimi*. Mistakes of intransigence have been made on both sides since the days of Photius and Michael Cerularius, the architects of the schism, and a coolness, if not hostility, on the part of the Greek Orthodox clergy toward Rome has always characterized the relationship.[9]

In 1919, the lot of the Greek Orthodox Church under the Bolsheviks became so unbearable that the Orthodox Archbishop Sylvester of Omsk, president of the Supreme Administration of the Orthodox Church, and Archbishop Benjamin of Simbirsk sent a telegram to Pope Benedict in which they called attention to the crimes committed and the cruelty perpetrated by communists. They complained that cities had been sacked, churches profaned and despoiled, more than twenty of their bishops and a number of priests had been murdered. Some victims were first mutilated and then killed; others were buried alive. Nuns were violated. Other outrages were mentioned. Benedict replied at once by telegram that he would storm heaven so that God would alleviate their misery, and he promised to come to their rescue with all other means at his disposal.

On March 12, at the behest of Pope Benedict, Cardinal Gasparri addressed Vladimir Lenin directly, "The Holy Father implores you to issue a strict order that the ministers of religion, no matter of what persuasion they are, to be shown respect. Humanity and religion will be grateful to you."[10]

An insulting letter came by way of response from Tchitcherine, Commissioner of the People for external affairs, which said:

> In Russia, separation of church and state is an established fact. Religion is treated as a private affair. Therefore, it is absolutely mendacious to speak of persecution of ministers of religion. In our country nothing occurs which is comparable to the things to which the Roman Church has recourse regularly in districts where that Church has the greater number of adherents.

The letter became more angry in tone and the writer informed Cardinal Gasparri:

> The Church which up to now has been termed by the Roman Church as *schismatic* and *heretical,* you today suddenly qualify as *orthodox.* I assure you that there has been no persecution of its clergy because of their religious convictions. If they were found guilty of conspiracy against the Soviet government, they were punished like any laymen.

Tchitcherine pointed to atrocities committed against the Russian people in Poland and Czechoslovakia and accused the Catholic hierarchy of having been the leaders. He closed with the bitter complaint that the ideals of humanity for which the Russian Revolution had struggled had never received a word of praise from the Vatican.

After 1919 famine and disease began to rage in Russia. Patriarch Tychon did not wish to humble himself to the extent of appealing to the Pope. Instead, he decided to ask the Protestant churches for help. He appealed to the Episcopalians in England, and convinced that the United States was a Protestant country, he addressed another letter to "The Archbishop of New York." The only archbishop of New York whom the postal department knew was Cardinal Hayes. The good Cardinal instead of being offended, was gently amused at the error and responded generously.[11]

Rising above the slight intended against Rome, Benedict sent a message to Cardinal Gasparri on August 5, 1921, calling his attention to the reports on the critical situation of the Russians.

> As far as can be gathered from the first short and reserved accounts, We are faced with one of the most appalling catastrophes in history. Masses of human beings at the very last stage of exhaustion and ravaged by hunger, typhus and cholera, are wandering desperately through a land now barren, and seeking to reach the more populous centers where they hope to find bread, and whence they are being driven

back by force of arms. It is the case of a people already terribly tried
by the scourge of war; a people over whom gleams the sign of Christ,
and a people always firm in its determination to belong to the great
Christian family. Separated, indeed, as they are from Us by the
barriers which long centuries have raised, they are the nearer to Our
fatherly heart in proportion to the greatness of the trials through which
they are passing. My Lord Cardinal! We feel the duty laid on Us
to do all that Our poverty makes possible to help Our far off children.
. . . Therefore, We ask you, my Lord Cardinal, to use all the means
at your disposal to bring home to the governments of the different
nations the need for prompt and efficacious common action.[12]

The foreign missions were likewise objects of Benedict's predilection. He was never too busy or too fatigued to receive a missionary in audience. Many a missionary priest, still alive today, speaks
of his audience with Benedict XV. He would place a chair next to
his own, so that Pontiff and missionary would converse, sitting side
by side. The reason for this arrangement was really not quite so
flattering as some of the missionaries seem to have thought. The
Pope was becoming increasingly hard of hearing, and if he had
his visitor on his "good" side, he could converse in a more chatty
manner. But even if this manner of granting an audience was not
meant to inflate the pride of the missionary, it was, nevertheless,
a sign of his intense interest in missionary work. It showed that
he was interested in more than bare statistics which could have
been submitted on paper. By chatting with the missionary he was
able to absorb some of the atmosphere of mission life.

On November 30, 1919, Benedict issued a very important apostolic epistle, *Maximum Illud*,[13] which mission societies at the time
hailed as the greatest pontifical pronouncement on missions in the
modern era. This document is popularly called an "encyclical."
Technically, it is not an encyclical, and the *Acta Apostolicae Sedis*
does not list it among the encyclicals in its table of contents. As
will be seen from several quotations, it is written in a forceful,
straightforward style — not in the ornate "curia form" in which
encyclicals are usually written.

As in his encyclicals, in which Benedict was wont to introduce
his subject with a historical sketch, he opens *Maximum Illud* with
the story of the great missionary saints of antiquity, such as Gregory the Illuminator in Armenia and Victorinus in Styria. The successors of these giants of the Faith are the priests in the mission

fields today. He then makes a direct appeal to the various classes of missionaries and has words of admonition for each.

First he speaks to the bishops and vicars and prefects apostolic, reminding them of their special fatherhood. They must be the *soul* of their territory. They must be vigilant, diligent, full of charity, ready to sympathize. Missionaries must never be satisfied with the mere fact that they have made converts, but must watch that none of them lapse back into paganism. They must never be narrow or provincial in their views, but should be friendly with their colleagues of other societies, for all are working toward the greater glory of Christ. His great call is for a native clergy.

> The main care of those who rule the missions should be to raise and train a clergy from amidst the nations among which they dwell, for on this are founded the best hopes for the Church of the future. Linked to his compatriots as he is by the bonds of origin, character, feelings and inclinations, the indigenous priest possesses extraordinary facilities for introducing the Faith to their minds, and is endowed with powers of persuasion far superior to those of any other man. It thus frequently happens that he has access to places where a foreign priest could not set foot.[14]

The bishops, vicars, and prefects apostolic are to foster and thoroughly form a native clergy. "A raw and unfinished preparation, such as will allow one to be ordained, will not do by any means; but the training should be full, adequate in extent of studies and length of years, such as is given to priests of civilized nations."

The missionary is to spread the glories of the Kingdom of God, not of his own native land. The missionary is to be a priest of more than ordinary learning. It is not true to say that a rich store of virtue is more important. He will be in places where he has no access to libraries, where he cannot consult with the learned. Objections to the Faith will be made, and the missionary must be prepared to answer. Therefore, seminaries which train missionaries are to have special courses in missiology. "This We command," wrote Benedict with vehement finality.

Benedict reminds the missionary that he must *know* the language of the natives. By this he does not mean a slight knowledge of everyday parlance but a knowledge of the language which will enable him to speak it easily and grammatically.

The missionary must excel in personal sanctity. If he is endowed with extraordinary talents, if he is schooled in all the intellectual disciplines, if he is conversant with every canon of urbanity, but lacks innocence of morals, his efficacy is nil. The natives can sense this because they are affected more by instinctive feeling than by arguments of reason.

For those not in the mission fields, Benedict has a serious word.

> All who have the gift of Faith owe God a debt of gratitude. This debt can be paid in no better way than in helping the missionary. 1) The missionary and his work can first of all be helped by prayer. This aid is within the reach of every Catholic. 2) As the mission field is pitifully undermanned, We urge all bishops to cultivate missionary vocations.

Bishops are not to grant permission grudgingly to seminarians to go into the foreign mission fields, as if by doing so they were impairing the work of the diocese at home. The Pope makes a promise:

> In the place of the one whom you send forth, God will raise up two very able priests for you. 3) Today more than ever we need greater financial support for the missions, and We appeal to all the faithful to give generously according to their means. We ask all Catholics to assist those organizations that take care of the support of the missions.

He recommended three organizations to the liberality of the people: (1) the Propagation of the Faith whose principal role is to supply funds for the support of missions already in existence or for the founding of new ones; (2) the Holy Childhood whose task is to see that baptism be administered to the dying children of infidels; and (3) the Work of Saint Peter which provides for the education and the upkeep of the indigenous clergy.

The encouragement which *Maximum Illud* gave to missionary societies can never be fully appreciated. However, it was Pius XI who became known as the "Pope of the Missions." It was he who harvested where Benedict had planted. Pius XI was the first to consecrate Chinese, Japanese, and Indian bishops who had been trained in the superior seminaries which Benedict had prescribed. Early in his pontificate, Pius XII in a single dramatic ceremony consecrated twelve missionary bishops, natives of the countries which they were to evangelize.

When, after seven war-harassed years, Benedict died, the Congregation of the Propaganda had seventy-nine new jurisdictions, that is, nine archbishoprics, twenty-seven bishoprics, five abbeys and prelatures nullius, two delegations, twenty-eight vicariates apostolic and eight prefectures apostolic.*

Many countries experienced intimately Benedict's universal fatherhood. Mexico, perhaps because of his love for Spain, had from the earliest days of his priesthood[15] held a particular attraction for him. On June 15, 1917, the feast of the Sacred Heart, Benedict wrote a touching letter to the Mexican bishops who had published a protest against the new antireligious constitution. He said that he had read their letter over and over, and that he found what he had expected, "your deep-seated love of your country, whose prosperity, as you rightly assert, cannot be separated from the reverence due to the ancient religion." He commended them to

---

* Past and present have come together rather strangely in the story of the Propaganda. Bishop Radini-Tedeschi before his elevation to the episcopate had been in the secretariat of state with Giacomo Della Chiesa under Leo XIII. Bishop Radini-Tedeschi chose Angelo Giuseppe Roncalli to be his own secretary, placed him in charge of the office of Propagation of the Faith in Bergamo, and arranged it so that Angelo Roncalli should meet Benedict XV. In 1921, when Benedict began to execute his aggressive campaign in the mission fields inaugurated in his apostolic letter, *Maximum Illud,* he summoned Angelo Roncalli to Rome to reorganize the Sacred Congregation for the Propagation of the Faith. Monsignor Roncalli set to work with his usual energy, aggressiveness, and genius for systematizing and organizing his work. It was Benedict XV, who, as he did with Achille Ratti and Eugenio Pacelli, put the foot of Angelo Roncalli on the first rung of the ladder which led him to the chair of Peter in the person of him whom we now hail as John XXIII.

A staff writer of *Osservatore Romano* listed Angelo Roncalli's encounters with Giacomo Della Chiesa, which culminated in a warm friendship and in the present Holy Father's great admiration for Benedict XV.

Angelo Roncalli saw Monsignor Della Chiesa for the first time when the latter was still a *minutante* in the secretariat of state. They met for the first time on January 30, 1905, when another employee in the secretariat of state, Giacomo Radini-Tedeschi, was consecrated by Pius X. At the consecration banquet, Roncalli and Della Chiesa were seated together in friendly conversation.

In 1909, Bishop Radini-Tedeschi decided to spend a few days with Archbishop Della Chiesa, now in charge of the metropolitan see of Bologna. The Bishop of Bergamo brought his young secretary, Don Angelo, as his traveling companion. While the two ordinaries discussed diocesan problems, Father Roncalli had the opportunity of learning more about his admired host through conversations with Countess Persico, Giacomo's sister, Julia, who did her best to make the young priest feel at home.

In 1921, Benedict was looking for a priest to reorganize the Congregation of the Propagation of the Faith. On the list of possible candidates, his quick eye lit on the name of Roncalli first. He is said to have exclaimed excitedly, *"Questo, questo!"* ("This one, this one!") The author of the article adds that the Pope acted "with that nervous energy which was characteristic of him when he wanted to put an end to any uncertainty in his own mind and to forestall any possible objections to a decision which he was determined to make." — "Benedetto XV nei ricordi di Giovanni XXIII," *L'Osservatore Romano* (January 22, 1959), p. 3.

Our Lady of Guadalupe, promising to offer his own Mass on her feast day, December 12, for the people of Mexico.[16]

The explosive situation in the Middle East which has caused so much nervous tension in recent years had its origins during the pontificate of Benedict XV. The Balfour Declaration, expressing Britain's favorable view on "the establishment in Palestine of a national home for the Jewish people,"[17] was published in 1917 and endorsed in 1918.

Benedict observed silence on the subject until June 13, 1921, when in a secret consistory he expressed his anxiety in these words:

> However, inasmuch as the situation in Palestine is not yet definitely regulated, We now raise Our voice that, when the time comes to establish a permanent condition of things, to the Catholic Church and to all Christians shall be assured the inalienable rights they hold. Certainly We have no desire that any damage shall be done to the rights of the Jewish element; what We mean is that they must in no way be put above the just rights of the Christians.[18]

In 1917, when the British under General Allenby were victorious in Palestine, Italy was jubilant. Benedict did not join in the civic demonstrations. He did not rejoice in political victories achieved through bloodshed. He was criticized for not having permitted the ringing of the bell on Saint Peter's when the bell on the Italian Capitol boomed out the message, *"Gerusalemme Liberata."*[19] Benedict waited silently for the religious celebration which marked the restoration of the Holy Sepulcher to Christian hands. Then he sent a message to be read to the assembled populace by the Cardinal Vicar.

> Over our joy, our transport, strictly religious, *there is still a cloud:* that the new liberators of the Holy Sepulcher do not all carry in their hearts, as did the mighty crusaders of the pious Godfrey, the holy unity of the Faith as willed by Christ. Now that the Holy Sepulcher returns into Christian hands, may it say to all believers that One is the Redeemer, therefore one the Faith, one the baptism, one the doctrine, One our Head Invisible, Jesus Christ, one our head visible, His Vicar on earth. . . . Open your hearts, then; let the holy love of Jesus Christ open them wide, and *pray for those, too, who have been conquered today,* that all infidels may lay aside old errors, and may be soon found again as brothers in the city consecrated by the infinite love of Jesus Christ, who sacrificed Himself to the Father on behalf of all.[20]

As universal father, Benedict insists that neither Jew nor Arab may be excluded from his charity.

Fortunately, the United States of America suffered no period of persecution, famine, or devastation, and hence did not stand in need of Benedict's pity. He looked upon the United States as a country upon which he could rely if he stood in need of support — moral no less than financial. For Herbert Hoover and his work of alleviating starvation in Europe, the Pope had the highest praise. Unlike many Europeans, he did not regard America only as the land of financial opportunities automatically bound to dispense alms, but viewed with joy the freshness of outlook which came from American spirituality, culture, and learning.

The bishops who came for their *ad limina* visits found in Benedict an interested and understanding shepherd. It was he who in 1921 provided the people of the United States with a national church, a privilege which other countries had enjoyed for centuries. The Church of Santa Susanna was entrusted to the Paulist Fathers who were charged with caring for the citizens of the United States who were working or were making a pilgrimage in Rome.[21]

Benedict XV was interested also in church edifices in America. When the imposing Cathedral of Saint Paul was being dedicated, he wrote to Archbishop Ireland, "We have been informed that a temple has been raised which in size, magnificence, and beauty is really remarkable. In our pleasure on learning this We cannot but highly praise all who have contributed to the success of the work."[22] In 1918, he wrote a warm letter urging the people of the United States to complete their national shrine in honor of their patroness, Mary Immaculate. He alluded to the pleasure he had experienced in hearing from Archbishop Bonaventure Cerretti about his visit to the United States on the occasion of Cardinal Gibbons' silver jubilee. The professions of loyalty on the part of the people of the United States, which Archbishop Cerretti relayed to him, bound the people of America more closely to the Pope's heart. To show that his encouragement was not merely confined to words, Benedict promised to send a statue of Mary of the Immaculate Conception which he was having executed in the workshops of the Vatican museum of art. He hoped that the statue would find its place on the high altar of the national shrine when it would be completed.[23]

When the Catholic University of America celebrated its silver jubilee, he wrote, "We love — nay, We have ever before Our eyes the American nation, strong in its youth, and *second to none in its energy of hand and brain.*"[24]

CHAPTER XXII

Benedict XV, the Writer

WHEN Monsignor Anton De Waal wrote the life of Benedict XV up to the time of his coronation, he remarked wistfully, "Monsignor Della Chiesa has left us no learned treatises."[1] As a matter of fact, the routine work in the secretariat of state did not leave Monsignor Della Chiesa any time for creative writing. The only works from his pen which appeared in print prior to 1914 are to be found in *Il Bolletino*, a diocesan paper which he had founded as archbishop of Bologna. These articles, however, merely clarify points of canon law, rubrics, and policies of the Archbishop for his clergy and flock.

Had Giacomo Della Chiesa had the time and opportunity, he could have enriched Catholic literature with the fruit of his pen.

One of the prized possessions of the Academy of Noble Ecclesiastics is the portfolio of lectures on diplomatic style which he had delivered while he was a professor at that school. The lectures are written in longhand in perfect French. Insistence on precise vocabulary was one of his favorite preoccupations. He knew the rhetorical devices of the Latin classicists, and he employed them. Perhaps he was too conscious of the figures of Latin rhetoric with the result that his writings at times seem to lack life and freshness. His allocutions, however, were an entirely different matter. In them it was an inspired Benedict who spoke.

Ludwig Pastor remarks in his diary how he had looked forward to the first allocution of Pius XI, for whom he had always felt an unbounded admiration. However, when he had heard him, he contrasted him unfavorably with Benedict XV. In speaking of the contrast, he jotted in his diary that Pius XI replied *"nicht so lebhaft sprudelnd wie Benedict XV"* ("not in the lively, sparkling manner of Benedict XV").[2]

The German verb, *sprudeln,* is onomatopoeic and colorful. It means to splash like a fountain, like the fountains in front of Saint Peter's. Fountains have a pleasant pattering sound as the windswept spray at times passes beyond the rim on the catch bowl and falls on the flagstones of the pavement. The air passing through the spray cools and refreshes the passing pilgrim. The sun takes on every color of the spectrum when its reflection is seen in the spray. No single English word can express all these impressions. For *sprudeln* the dictionary has "bubble forth, overflow, splash, sparkle, murmur." In this one word the genius of the German language has gathered many connotations. In Pastor's view, Benedict XV did all these things in his allocutions.

That Benedict himself felt that he could deliver an interesting address can be gleaned from the following anecdote. Monsignor Alberto Arborio-Mella di Sant'Elia, like Rudolf Gerlach, had been appointed a secret chamberlain on active duty on the day of Benedict's election. Besides his reputation for enjoying the confidence of the Holy Father, Monsignor Arborio-Mella di Sant'Elia soon was acclaimed as an interesting and eloquent preacher. One day, a member of the Swiss Guards asked him whether he would address them on their feast day. The Monsignor brusquely refused. The guard, piqued at what he considered a snub, happened to be on duty in the Pope's presence the following day. Since Benedict was always very pleasant to the personnel about the throne, the guard told him about the Monsignor's unceremonious refusal.

Later in the day, Benedict summoned his chamberlain and with a display of great seriousness said to him:

"I have a problem on my hands. The Swiss Guards are very anxious to have a speaker for their feast day. Now, it is a sad thing that in this huge staff at the Vatican we have only two priests who can deliver an address of which we do not have to feel ashamed. The one speaker is you, and the other happens to be myself. But since you have already been asked to speak and have refused, the Holy Father himself will have to do it."

To the delight of the Swiss Guards, Benedict himself graced the occasion and delivered a beautiful sermon.

Arborio-Mella di Sant'Elia loved to relate the anecdote and point out how neatly he had been rebuked and at the same time complimented by the Holy Father.[3] Benedict always felt that if a man possessed special talents, he had a duty, even though it entailed inconvenience, to employ them in the service of religion.

Like Benedict himself, his twelve encyclicals have sunk into what Philip Hughes calls an "unintelligent oblivion."[4] It is doubtful whether he required the aid of the secretaries usually employed for the preparation of encyclicals because Latin literature was his hobby and curial style the subject he had taught in the Academy of Noble Ecclesiastics. It is also thought that the development of the subject matter was the fruit of his own labors. The Roman correspondent of *The Tablet* wrote in 1920, "The Holy Father's encyclicals and other important pronouncements are his own; otherwise we should never be able to see what is so luminous, the wonderful continuity of his important utterances from November 1, 1914, to Pentecost, 1920.[5]

Ad Beatissimi,[6] Benedict's first encyclical, was issued on All Saints' Day, 1914. Its theme was "Love one another." It began with the words, "When, by the unsearchable counsel of God's providence, and without any merit of Our own, We were called *to* the Chair *of the most blessed* Prince of the Apostles. . . . We began to regard with unspeakable affection the flock committed to Our care."* As has been said in the chapter devoted to this encyclical, it served as the blueprint for Benedict's pontificate.

In 1916, Benedict issued no encyclical, but on June 15, 1917, he wrote the valuable encyclical on preaching, *Humani Generis*.[7] It began, "It is the desire of Jesus Christ, once He had wrought the redemption *of the human race* by His death on the cross, to lead men to obey His commands, and thus win eternal life." This encyclical has been analyzed in an earlier chapter. Benedict is outspoken about errors committed by priests in their preaching. He writes, "They may be reduced to three: for either the one chosen to preach is not the right person, or his office is not performed with the right intention, or it is not done in the right way."

Benedict was very firm in the matter. If the candidate for the priesthood does not have the character or the talent necessary to preach with authority, he "must without any consideration whatever be debarred from a function for which he is not qualified." The greater part of the encyclical is devoted to an insistence on prepara-

---

* The Latin language has a word order of greater flexibility than that of the modern vernaculars so that words can be concentrated at the beginning of a sentence and can therefore convey meaning with added emphasis. In English a similar grouping of words would be meaningless. Therefore, in the first sentence of each encyclical, which will be quoted in full, certain words will be found printed in italics. This is done to make those readers who do not know Latin aware of the English equivalents of the opening phrases in the Latin original. These phrases have come to serve as the titles of the encyclicals.

tion, both remote and proximate. The preacher must know the Bible, he must study, he must meditate.

In 1918, Benedict XV wrote but one very brief encyclical. It was *Quod Iam Diu*,[8] issued on December 1. It followed upon the armistice of November 11. *"That* which the entire world has *so long* sighed for, what Christianity implored with so much fervent prayer, and what We, the interpreter of the sorrow of all, with the heart of a father, continually kept asking for, has come in a moment." The purpose of the encyclical is clearly stated, "It will be your care to announce public prayers in each parish of your respective dioceses in that form which you will consider timely, to implore for the approaching peace conference the light of the Heavenly Father."

Contrary to what is customary in papal letters, *Quod Iam Diu* does not at the outset enumerate the false concepts which occasioned the encyclical. That an unwholesome attitude toward the coming peace conference is perceptible, Benedict implies in his remark that without heavenly guidance the delegates from the various nations will act under the impulse of hatred and vindictiveness.

The first encyclical to make its appearance in 1919 was that of May 14, on the twelfth centenary of Saint Boniface, the apostle of Germany. The encyclical, *In Hac Tanta*,[9] *"In this so great* a weight of calamities," lauds the work of Boniface and quotes at great length from a medieval biography of the saint. However, the purpose of the encyclical is not merely hagiographical. As always there are erroneous notions which must be corrected. "We have recently followed," he wrote, "with greater solicitude and more anxious care the sudden calamities and most disturbing public events which have occurred among your nation and neighboring nations and which still hold our minds in suspense in expectation of what is to come." That year, 1919, Kurt Eisner, a Jewish idealist from Bavaria who exerted powerful influence in Germany, was assassinated by Count von Arco, a monarchist. Religious and national hatred flared up threateningly during the period of readjustment between a monarchy and a democratic form of government. It was these events that Benedict watched "in suspense in expectation of what is to come." This hatred constituted the error which *In Hac Tanta* set out to condemn. The Pontiff appealed to the example of Saint Boniface whose "charity was not circumscribed by the boundaries of Germany alone. Boniface embraced absolutely all nations though they were most hostile to one another." He pointed out that Boniface "with even greater love embraced the neighboring nation of the Franks. To the Angles he, as a member of the same race, commended the propagation of the Catholic Faith." It was a condemnation of the racism preached by the Nazis long before their day of power.

In 1919, Benedict XV also made an appeal for the impoverished and famished children of war-torn Europe, especially of the Central Powers. One may wonder why the Pope should have cast this request for funds and provisions into encyclical form, if an encyclical is to be a papal action against a rampant error. The error consisted in the refusal to see the human race as one big family under the Fatherhood of God.

Benedict's first attempt to break down the world's provincialism was made in the encyclical, *Paterna Iam Diu*[10] of November 24, 1919. The opening words in English are, "It has *long* been the expectation and hope of Our *paternal* heart that, once the terrible conflict was ended, and the spirit of Christian charity restored, the regions desolated by famine and misery, especially in Central Europe, might little by little improve their condition, thanks to the united efforts of all good men." The Pope referred to his earlier request addressed to the hierarchy of the United States, and praised the generous response of that country. He designated the coming feast of the Holy Innocents, December 28, as a day of prayer and alms. "In order to help on a larger scale so many poor children in this most noble competition of charity, in addition to money it will be necessary to gather food, medicines, and clothing, all of which we are so greatly wanting in these regions."

After the encyclical had said in beautiful language that the situation of "these innocent children . . . recalls the image of the Divine Infant, suffering for love of all men in the cave at Bethlehem the rigor of winter and the want of all things," certain Catholics still could not understand why they should be asked to help the children of Germans, for they steadfastly refused to banish their hatred toward them.

To show how deep-seated this hatred was, one example can be quoted. After reading Benedict's moving encyclical, a correspondent for one of the world's leading Catholic papers wrote that the former appeal to the United States for Belgian children was an entirely different situation from the present request for the children of "the culprits now begging the mercy of the world, but never breathing a word of confession of their guilt!" Writing in a most sardonic tone, the Catholic correspondent continues:

> In the eyes of the common Father such things would pale into insignificance, *even if he thought of them at all*, before the spectacle of starving children. . . . Is it too much to ask that those in Germany who are spending money in riotous living shall pay their share? Otherwise we shall have a return of the old conditions: the Allies, innocent of "the deadly struggle which has put half the world in mourning" will be impoverishing themselves — and with thousands of their children suffering too — to help the children of the guilty party, who blatantly impenitent, can thus spend the money on himself.[11]

We who read these words today are appalled at the effrontery of this critic of the Holy Father who dared to quote Benedict's own words with unveiled sarcasm. That writer was unacquainted with God's word: "My son, to your charity add no reproach, nor spoil any gift by harsh words. . . . Only a fool upbraids before giving."[12]

On May 23, 1920, Benedict wrote *Pacem Dei Munus*,[13] "*Peace, the beautiful gift* of God." Francis Pichon called it the most elegant document on peace ever written by a pope.[14] The word *munus* can mean duty, gift, or privilege. The ordinary ecclesiastical writer would have written *Pacem Dei Donum*. The ancient glossaries inform us that *donum* can mean any kind of gift. *Munus*, however, means a gift which comes to us in virtue of the giver's office. Only God, because He is God, can give true peace. Hence, God's peace under Benedict's precise pen becomes a *munus* and not a *donum*. *Civiltà Cattolica* hailed the document as a true encyclical in every sense of the word because in its tone and sentiments it is addressed to all men, "to the small and the great, to men in public life and in private life, to subjects and to rulers, to individuals and to nations."[15] The first error it condemns is a peace built on a vindictive spirit. The same article in *Civiltà Cattolica* sees in it a condemnation of Socialism and Communism because the encyclical "preaches a very different and pure fraternity, an international family of peoples, and finally an elevation of the proletariat of a different sincerity and importance than that paraded by utilitarian and materialistic socialism."[16]

On September 15, 1920, came the great encyclical on Sacred Scripture, *Spiritus Paraclitus*[17] ("The Spirit Comforter") to which

Pius XII referred in *Divino Afflante Spiritu*[18] as a document "never to be forgotten." One of the errors which occasioned *Spiritus Paraclitus* was "the appearances of history theory" propounded by those who feigned to misunderstand certain principles in Leo XIII's *Providentissimus Deus*.

On October 5, 1920, Benedict published the encyclical, *Principi Apostolorum Petro*,[19] which proclaimed the fact that Saint Ephrem had been selected to join the roster of the Doctors of the Church. Its opening sentence is too long to quote in full. *"To Peter, the Prince of the Apostles* it was entrusted by the Divine Founder that he . . . should feed the flock of Christ." In this encyclical Benedict wishes to put Saint Ephrem before the world as "a splendid examplar of sanctity, doctrine, and patriotism." In his biographical sketch of St. Ephrem, he depicts him as an Arab of singular erudition and culture, proficient in theology, philosophy, and music. In view of the fact that in modern times a lack of appreciation of the Arab's potentialities constitutes one of the main obstacles to a proper meeting of Eastern and Western minds, Benedict wishes to pave the way for such an understanding. This he does by honoring St. Ephrem, a representative of Arab stock.

On December 1, 1920, Benedict once more decided to make an appeal in behalf of the impoverished children of belligerent nations. The encyclical is known as *Annus Iam Plenus*,[20] *"A whole year* has *now* passed since We called upon all Christians to turn their hearts in pity toward the children of Central Europe." The reason for the repetition of the message, he said, is manifold. "The general scarcity and the high cost of living, which the war has brought in its train" made the assistance given in the previous year less than was anticipated. In some parts of Europe hostilities and even massacres have arisen so that "numberless families have been reduced to penury."

On January 6, 1921, the feast of the Epiphany, Benedict XV issued the encyclical, *Sacra Propediem*,[21] "We think it very fitting," the encyclical begins, "to celebrate the *sacred* jubilee in the *near future* which marks the seven hundredth anniversary of the founding of the third order." Benedict strikes a personal note as he recalls that when the centenary of the birth of Saint Francis of Assisi was being celebrated during his days as a member of the secretariat of state, and he heard Leo XIII praise the Third Order in a stirring allocution, he was so edified that he went to the Church of Santa Maria in Capitolio and asked to be enrolled that very afternoon as a tertiary of Saint Francis. He feels that at this time precisely it is necessary to preach the glories of Saint Francis in order to refute "something which has been fabricated in the workshop of the Modernists." They had taught that "the man from Assisi had shown but little devotion to the Holy See, that he was an example of a certain vague and empty religiosity and that, therefore, you could not really call him "Francis" or "Saint." He also refers to the crime of which he could not rid his mind, "a world aflame with a horror-laden war." "The conflagration," he writes, "is not totally extinguished, rather its embers are smoking everywhere and in some places even flaring." In what he says next, he undoubtedly had Socialism and Communism in mind, even though he does not mention them by name. "Coupled with this mischief is an ailment in the vitals of our government — brought on by long-standing oblivion and contempt of Christian principles — namely, class struggling so bitterly with class about the distribution of wealth, that the world is threatened with ruin." The charity, meekness, and spirit of poverty exemplified by the gentle Francis are to act as an antidote against those tendencies.

The only real departure from papal tradition which Benedict appears to have made in the realm of encyclicals was *In Praeclara Summorum*,[22] dated April 30, 1921, an encyclical commemorating the sixth centenary of the death of Dante Alighieri. Because of it, Benedict was referred to as the "humanistic Pope."[23] It is true, he loved the classics and art, but, usually the term "humanist," when applied to popes, brings up Renaissance names like Leo X and Julius II, or the Avignon popes.

As usual, the first sentence of the encyclical strikes the keynote. *"On the distinguished list* of men of the *greatest* talents, who are the pride of the Catholic faith, and who, besides in other fields, left particularly in that of literature and art the immortal fruits of their genius well deserving of recognition by religion and civilization, supreme arises Dante Alighieri, of whose death the sixth centenary is on the eve of being celebrated."

That Benedict XV was personally very fond of reading Dante can be seen from exclamatory sentences which make their appearance throughout the encyclical, such as, "It is impossible, then, to express the intellectual enjoyment procured by the study of the supreme poet!"

There was, however, more purpose to the encyclical than an encomium of Dante. As a matter of fact, the correct view of Dante was necessary, and certain errors connected with Dante were growing up in Benedict's day which, if left unchecked, eventually would have had grave consequences.

The encyclical praises Dante for the use of the writings of Saint Thomas Aquinas as source material for the theology taught in the *Divine Comedy*. The Pope extols Dante for his clear teaching on the divine inspiration of Sacred Scripture and for his masterful exposition of the authority of Tradition and the Magisterium of the Church. He does not deny that it is regrettable that Dante wrote insultingly about certain supreme pontiffs whom he believed to have been politically on the side of those who had driven him out of his beloved city. However, with his characteristic understanding, Benedict wrote, "But one must pity a man, so battered by fate, if sometime, with ulcerated mind, he broke into invectives which exceeded all limits." Despite this resentment voiced by Dante against the political actions of a medieval pope, Benedict points out that the poet never for an instant called into question the supreme power of the keys entrusted to the supreme pontiff.

Toward the end of the encyclical Benedict alludes briefly to the errors which a right and thorough study of Dante could dissipate. (1) "Those who dare to deny this glory to Dante, and reduce the religious substratum of the *Divine Comedy* to a vague ideology, without any foundation of truth, disown in Dante what is his characteristic and inspiration of all his other merits." In time of stress and turmoil men like to turn to the mystical and occult for answers not conceded to man in the ordinary plan of human existence. There had been those who, like Michelangelo Caetani,[24] a close friend of Stendhal, had tried to make of Dante an "esoteric poet." The Rosicrucians in their literature at the present time list Dante as one of their number. According to them he is supposed to have known how to tap "cosmic streams of knowledge," a privilege of the initiates. The same type of hazy, fuzzy mysticism was attributed to Dante as had been done to Saint Francis of Assisi. There were men like Luigi Valli,[25] who attempted to show that Dante had been permeated with the heretical ideas of the Albigensians, who in turn reflected an ancient Persian teaching of a god of good and a god of evil.

(2) Benedict was intent on showing that the very person of

Dante, the theologian, could disprove some of the tenets of the philosophy taught by the *Risorgimento*. "Let this one example suffice to show how untrue it is that the homage of mind and heart to God clips the wings of genius, when on the contrary, it elevates it." (3) He struck at the confiscation of religious schools and their subsequent complete secularization. "How wrongly opposed to the progress of culture and refinements are those who want to banish from public instruction any idea of religion." (4) Against such movements as the anti-God campaigns carried on in the newly born communistic Russia or the attitude of the conference at Versailles, which refused to invoke the name of God, Benedict showed how Dante emphasized without ceasing "the creating and preserving action of God Almighty. . . . Very deplorable is, indeed, the method reigning today, of educating the student's youth as if God did not exist, and without the smallest allusion to the supernatural."

Benedict's last encyclical, issued on June 29, 1921, was *Fausto Appetente Die*,[26] on Saint Dominic, founder of the Order of Preachers. It begins with the words, "Since *the joyous day is drawing near* on which seven hundred years ago that torch of sanctity, Dominic, bade adieu to the woes here below in order to enter the abode of the saints, it has fallen to the happy lot of Us who for a long time were among his most devoted clients, but even more so since the day on which We assumed the rule of the church at Bologna which jealously guards his ashes. It has fallen to Our happy lot, We repeat, to be enabled from this Chair of Peter to exhort the Christian people to venerate the memory of that very holy man."

Benedict proceeds to praise the Order of Preachers for three great contributions. (1) They curbed the spread of heresy. He pays tribute to the great and learned preachers of the past, who, by their preaching, stemmed the tide of erroneous thinking. As examples he singles out Saints Hyacinth, Peter the Martyr, and Vincent Ferrer. Among the theologians of the order he lists Saints Albert the Great and Thomas Aquinas. As a codifier of law he singles out Raymond of Penafort. (2) By their devotion to the see of Peter, the Dominicans had heroically defended the rights of the Church. In this connection, Benedict alludes to the persuasive powers of the Dominican tertiary, Saint Catherine of Siena, who had convinced the Pope of the necessity of returning to Rome after the Avignon residence which had lasted seventy years. He points to the fact that the Dominicans had produced four supreme pontiffs,[27] of whom he singles out only Saint Pius V because he had attributed the defeat of the Moslems to the intercession of Mary and had on that account given her the title, "Help of Christians." This consideration leads Benedict to the third point. (3) The Dominicans preached the rosary and love of our Lady.

Benedict concludes by offering this remedy: "To heal the ills of this century, how much do we not need the maternal patronage of Mary! Here the third order has an immense field of labor. We wish this to be the special task of all followers of Father Dominic: that the Christian people everywhere become accustomed to praying the rosary."

How much Benedict wrote in his student days is not known. The locked room of his student days in the ancestral home in Pegli which contains all his private papers and books is said to hold that secret. Once only was the curtain lifted on his ambitions to write imaginative literature for publication, but the evidence is very flimsy.

In 1952, newspapers[28] carried a brief notice that in the archives of a small church in Bologna the manuscript of a play written by Giacomo Della Chiesa in 1873 had been found. It is said to be a murder mystery, a romantic drama in blank verse, recounting the murder of Duke Alessandro de Medici by an assassin hired by his relative, Lorenzino. In 1873, Giacomo Della Chiesa would still have been a student at the University of Genoa. Why the play should have been filed in the archives of one of the smaller churches in Bologna is a mystery.[29]

One might, however, conjecture a situation similar to the following. On the occasion of an administration of confirmation, the Archbishop sat in conversation with his priests. The conversation might have drifted to the subject of a priest's dabbling in the art of creative writing or the group might have discussed the Medici family in Florence. Archbishop Della Chiesa might have said that in his youth he had had ambitions to publish a play. Thereupon the priest of the unnamed "little church" might have been the one to ask to examine the manuscript since the topic was of especial interest to him. One can assume that the Archbishop saw to it that the manuscript was duly delivered to the priest. As happens so often, the priest kept it longer than he intended. Meanwhile the Archbishop of Bologna was elected to the papacy, and the return of the manuscript was rendered all the more difficult. It lay safely stowed away in the archives of the church until it was uncovered in 1952.

Benedict's reputation for facility of expression, felicity in the use of allusion, and readiness to make his hearers feel their human dignity rests on his allocutions, especially those that were not delivered from a prepared manuscript. Perhaps he had been a professor of diplomatic style too long so that, when he wrote, he rearranged and polished his work until his painstaking care became a little too obvious. It was in his extemporaneous discourses, when he had to rely on his spontaneous impulses, that he showed himself an inspired orator.

CHAPTER XXIII

The Death of Benedict XV

WHEN Cardinal Della Chiesa became Pope, the papers predicted a long pontificate because the age of 60 was considered relatively young for election to the Chair of Peter.[1] Although his appearance had always been delicate, his health actually had been good. He himself, however, seemed to have had presentiments concerning his untimely death.

On April 24, 1920, the papers carried the headline: POPE SELECTS TOMB.[2] For no apparent reason he had called for Cardinal Merry del Val, archpresbyter of Saint Peter's, to accompany him to the crypt of the mighty basilica. There, without much ado, he pointed to a spot opposite the tomb of Saint Pius X, where he desired to be laid at rest. It was but another indication of Benedict's great regard and affection for his saintly predecessor.[3]

When, on June 13, 1921, Achille Ratti was created cardinal, Benedict murmured as if to himself, "There has been a generous distribution of red during the past few days, but *soon* there will be a distribution of white, and the white robes will surely fall upon one of you."[4] Polite contradiction of the proximity of a conclave evoked no comment from Benedict. He merely smiled but as one who possesses knowledge which he cannot share with others.

In his diary Ludwig Pastor jotted down notes of some interesting conversations he had with visitors who passed his desk in the Vatican archives. One of these conversations was with Bishop Schmid-Grüneck of Chur, who recounted something which a Novalis, Ludwig Tieck, or Edgar Allan Poe would have utilized to the fullest. It concerned a "double" of Benedict XV whose life span coincided with the Pope's. During various audiences Bishop Schmid-Grüneck would tell the Pope of a canon in Chur who was born on the same day in 1854 as Benedict. His name also was Jacob, the German equivalent of Giacomo. He, too, had been ordained in 1878. In many respects his physical appearance resembled that of Giacomo Della Chiesa.

Benedict was always amused by this strange coincidence. However, in November, 1921, the Bishop, who was in Rome on business, told Benedict that the similarity had run its course, that his counterpart lay critically ill. Benedict looked off into space, and, blanching a little, said, *"È tempo che il suo coetaneo à Roma pensi alla sua fine!"* ("It's time that his double at Rome also think of his own end!") A week later, the Bishop of Chur in his final audience before departing for his see, informed the Pope that the canon had died. Pensively Benedict repeated the statement which he had made the week before. After taking his leave, the Bishop stopped suddenly on the stairs, and a pang of anguish shot through his innermost parts as the thought struck him, "You have seen Benedict XV for the last time!" Two months later the Holy See was vacant.[5] How these incidents remind one of the phrase which occurs in the breviary so frequently, *"tempore mortis suae admonito"* ("having been advised as to the time of his death").

The strangeness of the coincidence is heightened when we read another anecdote. At about the same time — it was in November, 1921 — the Sisters at the Hospice of Saint Martha asked the Pope to say Mass for them in their chapel on the last day of their retreat. Benedict's *maestro di camera* consulted his calendar and refused because the day interfered with Benedict's own retreat. When the Pope learned of this, he sent word that he would say Mass for the Sisters at the beginning of their retreat, adding good-humoredly, "provided that We shall be authorized to do so by the mother superior."

The Mass was to be said very early so that the Pope could pass through Saint Peter's privately before people would be in the church. Benedict, true to his habit of punctuality, was there at the appointed time, but the janitor or *sanpietrino* was not there to unlock the door. The Pope had left a warm bed and had to stand in an unheated drafty passage for over half an hour before the door was opened.

Chilled to the marrow, the Pope vested. Once at the altar, he regained his composure and said Mass in his usual edifying manner. He enjoyed his breakfast with the delighted nuns hovering about him. He visited every part of their hospice and chatted with everyone. It was noticed that he was in excellent humor and visibly delighted. He received some object of piety from them as a gift and then gave his blessing. It was the last recreation that Benedict XV had on earth.[6]

A day or two later the Pope was observed to be suffering from a cold which held him in its grip with dogged tenacity. Early in January of 1922, Vatican personnel began to comment on his hacking cough. The winters in Rome may be mild in comparison with those of other places, but in Pope Benedict's pontificate very few buildings had central heating plants. Normally the Romans carried a blanket or shawl with them whenever they caught a slight cold. Because of the dampness, the buildings offered little or no protection consequently, quite often such a cold would last all winter.

On January 5, 1922, the Roman aristocrats and patricians had paid their annual New Year's visit, and Benedict addressed them pleading for his favorite cause, the missions. He suggested that the ladies of the aristocracy employ their time in sewing for the missions, that they contribute generously to finance the noble work of the missionary. As he withdrew to his private apartments, comments were made about the apparent physical discomfiture of the Pontiff. Involuntarily, a strangely prophetic remark escaped him, *"La tosse è il tamburo della morte!"* ("A cough is the herald of death!")[7]

At 7:30 on January 12, he said Mass for the students of the College of the Propaganda and personally gave Holy Communion to more than a hundred people. Someone remarked how hot and feverish the Pontiff's hand felt as he kissed the ring before the reception of Holy Communion.[8] As was his cherished custom, Benedict made his thanksgiving by attending another Mass offered immediately after his own, fusing his thanksgiving with participation in the Eucharistic Sacrifice. In this way he bore out in his own prayer life the etymological meaning of *Eucharist*, which literally means *Thanksgiving*. He addressed the students, but his remarks were punctuated by violent seizures of coughing. However, he worked all day and retired to his bedroom no earlier than ten in the evening. The next few days he continued to rise at five. Everyone who heard the excruciating cough sympathized with the Pope as he held audiences and worked with astounding intensity.

On January 16, Dr. Battistini, his physician, finally won a point. He induced Benedict to retire at eight o'clock instead of at ten. Small though this concession was, it occasioned the general comment that the Pope must feel very much indisposed to make such a radical change in his routine.

The following day he again rose at five, made his long meditation and preparation for Holy Mass. He received the undersecretary of state in a lengthy audience, then his old friend Cardinal Valfrè' di Bonzo, the papal delegate from the Ukraine, and finally five state dignitaries. At six o'clock that evening he dragged himself to his bedroom and retired.[9] The next day was January 18, the feast of Saint Peter's Chair, the opening day of the Chair of Unity Octave to which he had given so universal a status. Benedict, however, was unable to rise from his bed. He allowed Dr. Battistini to be called early. That day the first official medical report was released: "The Supreme Pontiff is suffering from bronchitis."[10] He rested comfortably all day, and Dr. Battistini was well satisfied with his patient's docility.

On January 19, he attended Mass from his bed. Monsignor Migone, who had served his master at so many turns and crises, offered Mass in an adjoining room where the altar was so placed that the Pontiff could see and hear everything from his bed.

The rest of the day Benedict's gentle, though, as usual, somewhat cynical humor manifested itself. For example, he told Cardinal Gasparri that in his sixty-seven years the sum total of his medical expenses had been two and a half lire.[11] He wanted some trifle from a drawer and with an amused smile watched the Secretary of State awkwardly rummaging about amid Benedict's symmetrically placed possessions. Finally he said, "Please bring me the whole drawer, I should have known that you cannot see through my eyes."[12] Every action, every word, was engendered by the same spirit of love and sympathy.

During the night his condition worsened alarmingly. In the morning he again attended Mass from his bed, but his breathing was very labored. After Mass he asked for Holy Viaticum. This task of love was performed by Monsignor Zampini, the sacristan of the Vatican. While arrangements were being made, he begged for absolute solitude so that he could prepare for that which for the Supreme Pontiff as well as for the simplest heir of heaven is a very important step in his mortal life. Soon the bell heralded the advent of the Eucharistic Lord. Monsignor Zampini was accompanied by Cardinals Vincenzo Vanutelli, dean of the Sacred College; Merry del Val, archpresbyter of Saint Peter's; Pietro Gasparri, Secretary of State and Camerlengo; and Oreste Giorgi, grand penitentiary; and sixteen other cardinals.

First Cardinal Giorgi read the profession of Faith formulated by the Tridentine and Vatican Councils. The Pope's rochet, pectoral cross, and stole were put over his night clothes, but he was too weak to sit up and read the formula. Therefore, it was read a few words at a time, and the dying Pope repeated it. What the ritual demands is that the dying pontiff with what is almost his last breath prove that he holds securely to the deposit of Faith of which he was the supreme guardian. The grand penitentiary, to whom the key to the spiritual treasury of the Church is granted for immediate use, granted general absolution and the final indulgence.

After the reception of Holy Viaticum Benedict rested more easily. Someone said to him in all kindness, "Holy Father, now just don't worry about anything. Do just as your doctors tell you."

It was at this point that he made the response which has become so famous, "If it pleases my Lord that I should work a little longer for His Church, I am at His service; but if He says, 'that's enough' (basta!), then may His holy Will be done!"[13] He turned to Cardinal Silj and with childlike humility asked him to entrust his lot to the Blessed Virgin Mary.

Ludwig Pastor who was waiting in an outer room records how awesome it was to see the otherwise jovial Gasparri now red and swollen-eyed from weeping.[14] Thomas Morgan records how touched he was to see Monsignor Pizzardo weeping bitterly.[15]

Benedict's hand was laid on a scarlet velvet cushion edged in gold. Each cardinal passed and kissed the aristocratic hand, now appearing to be of delicately wrought alabaster. During the lengthy ceremony the Pope seemed to be in a comatose state and unaware of those whose lips touched his ring, but when Cardinal Merry del Val knelt to do so, he opened his eyes, looked into those of the Cardinal, and murmured, "Alive or dead, pray for me."[16]

As evening came, in all simplicity Benedict asked his nephew, Count Persico, the son of his beloved sister Julia, whether people were praying for him. This was remarkable for a man who always seemed so self-sufficient in his relationship with God and apparently never craved any sentiment from the populace.

"Holy Father," replied the Count, "not only Rome, but all of Italy, in fact the whole world is praying for you!"[17]

Dr. Battistini was heard to murmur, "Take me away, O Lord, but save the Pope."

As is so often the case with the dying who hear the barest whisper, Benedict, otherwise somewhat hard of hearing,[18] caught this sigh of the good doctor. "It is you who should go to bed," he said. "You are older than I. Go to bed!"[19]

At two o'clock in the morning on January 21, Benedict asked for Extreme Unction. Monsignor Zampini administered it, and the Pope with his usual grace thanked him for having rendered him this sacred service also.[20] One Mass after the other was being celebrated in the adjoining room. For a while, Extreme Unction lent that almost universally observable effect of an increase of bodily strength. Benedict took a little breakfast and then entered into one of his pleasant conversational moods. He requested that Archbishop Nasalli-Rocca of Bologna be admitted. He wanted to know many details concerning the see which he had ruled so lovingly before his elevation to the papacy. He congratulated this prelate on the excellent work he was doing. He asked that several bishops whom he mentioned by name be admitted. Count Lombardo of Genoa presented greetings from that city. Benedict, always pleased to hear from the see of his birth, clearly pronounced his apostolic benediction over Genoa.

After four o'clock in the afternoon Benedict's mind began to wander. During a lucid interval he was told gently but unequivocally by Dr. Battistini that he must gird himself for his last journey. Loudly and clearly, so that his voice was heard not only by those in the adjoining room, but also in the corridor, he cried out, *"Offriemo volentieri la vita per la pace del mondo!"* ("Gladly do We offer Our life for the Peace of the World").[21] It was spoken in the plural, that is, in the language of the Papal Curia. It was Benedict's last official pronouncement, his last, though unwritten *motu proprio* for the universal Church.

Then he dug the back of his head into the pillow as though to make himself comfortable for the last time. He called for Fra Celidonio, his male nurse, and said to him in Spanish that Cardinal Vico would say Mass in place of the *maggiordomo*, who was also ill. He gave explicit orders that the *maggiordomo* was not to be awakened in the morning, but was to get as long a rest as possible. Precise as ever, he was still the father of the household, the head of Vatican Palace, and was issuing the final instructions before retiring for the night.

Curiously, he asked his other nephew, Marchese Giuseppe Della Chiesa, whether prayers were really being offered for him. Even though Benedict was a man of most intensive prayer, his anxiety as to whether the Church was really praying for him was a symbol of something much more deeply imbedded in the spiritual strata of this otherwise so self-contained man. In most dioceses the oration for the Pope was being added in every Mass as an *Oratio pro re gravi* (an oration in time of crisis).

Suddenly Benedict asked what time it was. He was told that it was half past nine in the evening. "Oh, well," he said apparently with great satisfaction, "there is still plenty of time until six o'clock."[22] At the time no one knew what he meant. The bystanders shrugged their shoulders, thinking it was delirium. During the night he would suddenly open his eyes wide, impulsively throw back the covers, trying desperately to leave his bed.[23] When those about the bed restrained him, he would say, "Let me dress, let me rise, I have much to do. There is important mail that I must take care of."[24] Did he remember the accusation of himself to his predecessor that he is said to have found unopened on the desk of Saint Pius X when he came to take the helm of Peter's boat?[25]

At two o'clock the hand of death was laid in earnest upon Pope Benedict. His face began to take on that final nobility which can come only from the signet ring of death. His waxen face glistened, his nose became pointed, his cheeks collapsed, his mouth opened so that the unmistakable death rattle began to be heard.

Cardinal Giorgi moved forward to perform his final task as grand penitentiary. Slowly, loudly, and firmly he said, "Your Holiness, bless your relatives!"

The Pope kept his eyes closed but with his right hand made a tiny gesture, signifying the triple sign of the cross.

"Your Holiness," continued the Cardinal, "now bless your household!" Weakly and wearily the Pope responded with the same gesture.

"Your Holiness," said the almost cruelly persistent Cardinal, "bless the people who are expecting peace!"

At this point something like a prodigy occurred. Benedict XV threw back the covers from about his shoulders, tried to raise himself as though he wanted to view a great area of upturned faces and to throw off a web in which the accouterments of death were entangled. With a mighty gesture he traced the sign of salvation three times, and with extraordinary volume said, "May the Blessing of God Almighty, the Father, the Son, and the Holy Spirit, descend upon you and remain forever!"²⁶ In that last act he restated in word and deed the whole *motif* of his pontificate!

At the very stroke of six Benedict took a deep breath and solemnly exhaled it. The terse bulletin in *Acta Apostolicae Sedis* reads: *"Summus Pontifex Benedictus XV die xxii Ianuarii hora VI sanctissime obdormivit in Domino!"*²⁷ ("The supreme pontiff, Benedict XV, on the 22nd day of January at the hour of six, with great holiness fell asleep in the Lord!")

Notes

CHAPTER I   *Birth and Childhood*

1. About the Pope's father we can only conjecture. From the aged clergy in Rome and Genoa the writer learned that Benedict XV said very little about his father. Once he is said to have remarked, "My poor father acted according to his lights," in obvious reference to his sternness.
2. Anton De Waal, *Der neue Papst, unser heiliger Vater Benedikt XV* (Hamm: Breer und Thiemann, 1915). Cf. the picture facing page 56. Francesco Vistalli, *Benedetto XV* (Roma: Tipografia Poliglotta Vaticana, 1928). Cf. the picture facing page 16.
3. De Waal, *op. cit.*, p. 4; Vistalli, *op. cit.*, p. 16.
4. Antonio Durante, *Benedetto XV* (Roma: A. V. E., 1939), p. 3.
5. The residence at Pegli was intended only as a summer residence, though the home in the city of Genoa itself receives no mention in the anecdotes concerning Giacomo's youth. In fact, the residence in Genoa is no longer standing. The house at Pegli has been turned into an apartment house. One room, however, is said to contain the personal belongings of Benedict XV. The room is locked and permission to enter must be obtained from the Della Chiesa family, no longer in residence at Genoa.
6. De Waal, *op. cit.*, p. 3.
7. P. Ansgar Pöllmann, *Benedikt XV aus der Familie Della Chiesa. Ein helles Bild auf dunklem Hintergrunde* (Diessen vor München: Jos. C. Huber, 1915), pp. 168 f and 173. Pöllmann claims that several characters of history were among the *Campiones Sanctae Ecclesiae Romanae.* He says that the word *Campio* is not derived from *campus,* the Latin word for "battlefield," but is a late Latin word derived from *Kämpfer,* "fighter."
8. William Barry, "Benedict XV: Pontiff of Peace," *Dublin Review,* CLXX (1914), 162.
9. De Waal, *op. cit.*, p. 3.
10. Barry, *op. cit.*, p. 162.
11. Leo P. Schlegel, *Papst Benedikt XV* (Freiburg, Schweiz: Kanisiuswerk, 1932), p. 6.
12. The only writer who expresses his debt of gratitude for these incidents is Josef Schmidlin, *Papst Geschichte der neuesten Zeit* (München: Kösel und Pustet, 1953, III.
13. Ludwig Freiherr von Pastor, *Tagebücher, Briefe, Erinnerungen, herausgegeben von Wilhelm Wühr* (Heidelberg: F. H. Kerle, 1950), pp. 119, 127.
14. De Waal, *op. cit.*, p. vi.
15. *Ibid.;* Schlegel, *op. cit.*, p. 6; Vistalli, *op. cit.*, p. 18 f.
16. Vistalli, *op. cit.*, p. 18.
17. De Waal, *op. cit.*, p. 6.
18. *Ibid.*, p. 7.
19. *Ibid.*, p. 6; Schlegel, *op. cit.*, p. 7.
20. De Waal, *op. cit.*, p. 6 f; Durante, *op. cit.*, p. 16.
21. Cf. the picture facing page 8 in De Waal, *op. cit.*
22. Vistalli, *op. cit.*, p. 15.

CHAPTER II   *Candidate for a Doctorate in Three Faculties*

1. De Waal, *op. cit.*, p. 12.
2. Schlegel, *op. cit.*, p. 2.
3. De Waal, *op. cit.*, p. 12.
4. *Ibid.*, p. 10.
5. Schlegel, *op. cit.*, p. 10.
6. De Waal, *op. cit.*, p. 9 f.
7. *Ibid.*, p. 10.
8. Schlegel, *op. cit.*, p. 11.
9. De Waal, *op. cit.*, p. 14.
10. *Ibid.*, p. 17.
11. Giambattista Migliori, *Benedetto XV* (Milano: La Favilla, 1932), p. 11. Throughout his pontificate, the Pontiff had his visitors sit on a chair beside him so they could speak into his "better ear."
12. Frances Minto Elliot, *Roman Gossip* (Leipzig: Tauchnitz, 1896), p. 47.
13. Pastor, *op. cit.*, p. 77 ff.
14. De Waal, *op. cit.*, p. 19.
15. *Ibid.*, p. 21. Monsignor De Waal is indebted to Bishop Leonard Baumbach, a Passionist, Bishop of Nocopolis, for this anecdote.
16. *Ibid.*
17. Encyclical, *Humani Generis*, June 15, 1917.
18. Schlegel, *op. cit.*, p. 13.
19. *Ibid.*, p. 14; Vistalli, *op. cit.*, p. 44.
20. Quoted in Vistalli, *op. cit.*, p. 43.
21. Francesco Zanetti, *Nella Città del Vaticano* (Roma: Sallustiana, 1929), p. 233.
22. De Waal, *op. cit.*, p. 20.
23. *Ibid.*, p. 23.
24. *Ibid.*, p. 24.

CHAPTER III   *In the Service of the Holy See*

1. De Waal, *op. cit.*, p. 20.
2. Schlegel, *op. cit.*, p. 15.
3. Horace, *Odes*, ii, ode 2:19 f.
4. "The blood that flowed in the veins of Spaniards was Phoenician, Iberian, Celtiberian, Greek, Carthaginian, Roman, Visigoth, Vandal, Moslem. The Iberians had brought the culture of the Orient; the Celts, their knowledge of iron and metals; the Romans, law and administration; the Goths, agriculture and more warfare; the Moslems, the compass, paper, and Greek learning, but also love of pleasure." — Joseph H. L. Schlarman, *Mexico, A Land of Volcanoes* (Milwaukee: Bruce, 1950), p. 14.
5. Schlegel, *op. cit.*, p. 16.
6. *Ibid.;* Vistalli, *op. cit.*, p. 51.
7. Thomas B. Morgan, *A Reporter at the Papal Court* (New York: Longmans, 1938), p. 15.
8. Schlegel, *op. cit.*, p. 18; Vistalli, *op. cit.*, p. 52.
9. Leo Schwering, "Benedikt der Fünfzehnte, ein Versuch zur Würdigung seiner Politik," *Deutsche Rundschau*, CLXXXIV (July-September, 1920), 307.
10. *Ibid.*, p. 48; Vistalli, *op. cit.*, p. 52.

11. Vistalli, *op. cit.*, p. 52.
12. *Ibid.*, p. 46.
13. *Ibid.*, p. 53.
14. It will be remembered that the mother of the Sons of Zebedee came to the divine Master and said to Him, "Command that these my two sons may sit, one at thy right hand and one at thy left hand, in thy kingdom" (Mt. 20:21).
15. Schmidlin, *op. cit.*, p. 183 *n.*
16. Durante, *op. cit.*, p. 13.
17. Francis A. MacNutt, *A Papal Chamberlain* (London: Longmans, Green & Co., 1936), p. 312.
18. Maria di Pietro, *Benedetto XV* (Milano: Societa Editrice Vita e Pensiero, 1941), p. 35.
19. Schlegel, *op. cit.*, p. 22.
20. De Waal, *op. cit.*, p. 39.
21. Schmidlin, *op. cit.*, p. 182.
22. Schlegel, *op. cit.*, p. 20.
23. *Ibid.*
24. Di Pietro, *op. cit.*, p. 31 f.
25. William Cardinal O'Connell, *Recollections of Seventy Years* (Boston: Houghton Mifflin Co., 1934), p. 340.
26. James H. Moynihan, *The Life of Archbishop John Ireland* (New York: Harpers, 1953), p. 100.
27. Jan Olav Smit, *Angelic Shepherd* (New York: Dodd, Mead and Co., 1950), p. 58.
28. De Waal, *op. cit.*, p. 58.
29. *Ibid.*, p. 57.
30. Pastor, *op. cit.*, p. 376.
31. *Ibid.*, p. 58.
32. Moynihan, *op. cit.*, p. 358.
33. De Waal, *op. cit.*, p. 60.
34. Vistalli, *op. cit.*, p. 68.
35. E. J. Dillon, "The Pope and the Belligerents," *Contemporary Review,* CVII (May, 1915), 554 f.
36. Ernst Lieber (1838–1902), expert in jurisprudence and leader of the Center Party in Germany.
37. De Waal, *op. cit.*, pp. 25–27.

CHAPTER IV   *Restoring All Things in Christ*

1. Bernard O'Reilly, *Leo XIII, seine Zeit, sein Pontificat und seine Erfolge* (New York: John S. Winston Co., 1903), p. 706.
2. Hilaire Belloc, *Charles II* (New York: Harpers, 1939), p. 273. Belloc frequently refers to the public nature of a king's death bed. "Kings . . . must die as they were born, in public, for they were not individual men but the State itself — the nation incarnate. All must be witness to their coming and their going."
3. Francis Pichon, *Benoit XV* (Paris: Editions Spes, 1940), p. 214; De Waal, *op. cit.*, p. 60.
4. *Ibid.*, p. 710.
5. Charles Williams, *James I* (New York: Roy, 1953), p. 300.
6. Frances Alice Forbes, *Rafael Cardinal Merry del Val* (London: Longmans, Green & Co., 1932), p. 64 f. This book mentions Benedict XV but twice and in the coldest of terms. Cf. also MacNutt, *op. cit.*, p. 244.

7. Orazio M. Premoli, *Contemporary Church History* (London: Burns, Oates and Washbourne, 1932), p. 33.
8. Thomas B. Morgan, *Speaking of Cardinals* (New York: Putnam, 1946), p. 52 f.
9. Forbes, *op. cit.*, p. 29.
10. Maria Longworth Storer, *In Memoriam Bellamy Storer* (privately printed, 1923), pp. 87, 96, 100, 104.
11. Thomas B. Morgan, *The Listening Post* (New York: Putnam, 1944), p. 133.
12. One morning a stir was caused in San Pietro when Cardinal Merry del Val was saying Mass. An Italian lady who saw him for the first time cried out, *"Dio mio, com' è bello!"* ("My God, but he's handsome!") — René Bazin, "Le Cardinal Merry del Val," *Revue des Deux Mondes*, January 15, 1931, p. 298.
13. Morgan, *Speaking of Cardinals*, p. 49. Used by permission.
14. Martin Doherty, *The House on Humility Street* (New York: Longmans, Green & Co., 1942), p. 206.
15. Forbes, *op. cit.*, p. 19 f.
16. *Ibid.*, pp. 79–81.
17. Morgan, *Speaking of Cardinals*, p. 49.
18. Emilio Bonomelli, *I Papi in Campagna* (Roma: Gherardo Casini, 1953), p. 352.
19. Friedrich Schiller, *Ueber naive und sentimentalische Dichtung* (1795).
20. Schlegel, *op. cit.*, p. 20.
21. *Ibid.* "Als ich ihn zum erstenmal sah, machte er auf mich den Eindruck eines *von der Natur etwas stiefmütterlich* behandelten Menschen."
22. John L. Bonn, *The House on the Sands* (New York: Doubleday, 1950), p. 211. The present writer is aware that he is quoting from fictionalized biography. However, Father Bonn explains that he had visited with Francis MacNutt repeatedly and that much of what he adds over and above what can be found in *A Papal Chamberlain*, he gleaned from his conversations with MacNutt. At least the remark attributed to Benedict is not out of character.
23. De Waal, *op. cit.*, p. 80; Vistalli, *op. cit.*, p. 85.
24. Giovanni Pioli, "Benedict XV: The Significance of his Election," *Contemporary Review*, CVI (October, 1914), pp. 506–514.
25. Walter Lowrie, *Saints Peter and Paul in Rome* (London: Oxford University Press, 1940), p. 49.
26. Forbes, *op. cit.*, p. 127.
27. *Ibid.*, p. 134.
28. *Ibid.*, p. 156.
29. Pio Cenci, *Il Cardinale Raffaele Merry del Val* (Roma: Berruti, 1933), p. 456 f.
30. *Ibid.*, p. 448.
31. L. J. S. Wood, "Benedict XV, Pontiff of Peace," *Dublin Review*, CLXX (1922), 179.
32. Forbes, *op. cit.*, p. 157.
33. Cardinal Merry del Val, *Memories of Pope Pius X* (Westminster: Newman, 1941), p. xiii.
34. *AAS*, XL (1956), 596.
35. Hartwell de la Garde Grissell, *Sede Vacante, Being a Diary Written During the Conclave of 1903* (Oxford: Parker, 1903), p. 4.
36. Merry del Val, *Memories*, p. 1.
37. *Ibid.*, p. 2 f.
38. According to Schmidlin, when the members of the conclave expostulated, *Pudeat te, pudeat te!* ("You ought to be ashamed of yourself!") Cardinal Puszyna seems to have shown that he took pride in his action, for he retorted, *"Non, est honor meus. Honori mihi duco!"* ("No, it is an honor. I deem it an honor!") — *op. cit.*, p. 17 *n.*

39. Katherine Burton, *The Great Mantle* (New York: Longmans, Green & Co., 1950), p. 142.
40. Merry del Val, *Memories,* p. 7.
41. Frances Forbes and Professor Cenci render Cardinal Merry del Val a disservice by their avoidance of the name of Benedict XV. Giacomo Della Chiesa was closely associated with Merry del Val for many years before he became pope, and after his accession to the papacy he honored the Spanish Cardinal frequently by appointing him to various posts and by asking him to represent the supreme Pontiff at different functions.

R. P. Dal-Gal (*Le Cardinal Merry del Val* [Paris: Nouvelles Editions Latines, 1955]) and Hary Mitchell (*Le Cardinal R. Merry del Val* [Paris: Paris-Livres, 1956]) ignore the existence of Benedict XV completely. Marie Cecilia Buehrle, *Rafael Cardinal Merry del Val* (Milwaukee: Bruce, 1957), avoids this error of silence.
42. Merry del Val, *Memories,* p. 59.
43. Morgan, *Speaking of Cardinals,* p. 50. Besides his winning appearance and refinement of demeanor, Merry del Val possessed the gift of learning languages easily and well. Although Spanish was spoken in the intimate family circle, Rafael frequented English schools, and English became his favorite language. When his father became minister to Belgium, Merry del Val attended two schools in Brussels where French was the spoken language. His parents had their summer villa in Austria where Rafael learned German — a spoken German pronounced in the soft, pleasant accent of Austria. His many years in Italy enabled him to speak Italian in such a way that but few could detect that it was for him an acquired language.
44. Count Carlo Sforza, *Contemporary Italy,* trans. Drake and Denise De Kay (New York: Dutton, 1944), p. 200.
45. De Waal, *op. cit.,* p. 92.
46. Durante, *op. cit.,* p. 29 f.
47. *Ibid.,* p. 30.
48. Merry del Val, *Memories,* p. 43.
49. Durante, *op. cit.,* p. 30.
50. Vistalli, *op. cit.,* p. 70 f.
51. *Ibid.,* p. 71.
52. Sforza, *op. cit.,* p. 201.
53. Pioli, *op. cit.,* p. 506.
54. J. S. Barnes, "Benedict XV: An Impression," *Dublin Review,* CLV (1914), 376.

CHAPTER V   *Modernists and Integralists*

1. Francis X. Seppelt and Clement Löffler, *A Short History of the Popes,* trans. from the German by Horace A. Frommelt (St. Louis: Herder, 1932), p. 492.
2. Francis T. Furey, *Life of Leo XIII and History of His Pontificate* (Philadelphia: Catholic Educational Company, 1904), p. 191.
3. Leo XIII, "Saepenumero," *Acta Sanctae Apostolicae Sedis,* XVI (1883), p. 54.
4. "Qu'est-ce que l'Intégrisme?" *La Vie Intellectuelle,* XXIV (Août-Septembre, 1952), 136. For a more recent survey of the situation, cf. Robert A. Graham, "Ends and Means in Controversy," *America,* XC (April 14, 1956), 54–56.

There are those, who, in an almost fanatic loyalty to Merry del Val, make a heated defense of Integralism without grasping what it meant. For example, Hary Mitchell, *op. cit.,* p. 147 f., writes that, in 1955, "one of the dignitaries of the episcopacy" [sic] gave a retreat in one of the major seminaries of France and warned the seminarians against certain liberal movements. Then this retreat master added, "But there is another evil which rages among us, Integralism." Mitchell, who confesses that he is "neither a philosopher, nor a theologian," and that he is "entirely unskilled in subtleties of this baffling casuistry," says that he "modestly had recourse to a good old dictionary of student days." There he looked up the following words: *integral,* used as a noun to designate a person. The meaning Mitchell found was, "A man of absolute, incorruptible probity." To be more completely informed, he now looked up *integrity.* He found, "State of a thing which has all its parts without alteration. Virtue, quality of an integral person." Mitchell therefore concludes that to say that a man is "integral" is the highest praise one can speak of him.

5. Herbert Spencer (1820–1903).
6. Georg Wilhelm Friedrich Hegel (1770–1831).
7. Seppelt-Löffler, *op. cit.,* p. 518.
8. *Catholic Encyclopedia,* X, 415.
9. *Acta Apostolicae Sedis,* XL (1907), 268.
10. *Ibid.,* 470–478.
11. *Ibid.,* 593–650.
12. "Ad Beatissimi," *Acta Apostolicae Sedis* (Romae: Typis Polyglottis Vaticanis), VI (1914), 657. The abbreviation of this newer series of the acts of the Holy See will be *AAS.*
13. Barry, *op. cit.,* p. 164.
14. Ludwig Pastor, *Tagebücher,* p. 383.
15. Michael De La Bedoyere, *The Life of Baron Von Hügel* (London: J. M. Dent and Sons, 1951), p. 181.
16. "Qu'est-çe que l'Intégrisme?" *loc. cit.,* p. 138 f.
17. Schmidlin, *op. cit.,* p. 163.
18. *Ibid.,* p. 167.
19. "Qu'est-çe que l'Intégrisme?" *loc. cit.,* pp. 14, 143.
20. *Ibid.,* pp. 144, 150.
21. Joseph Clifford Fenton, "Two Currents in Contemporary Catholic Thought," *American Ecclesiastical Review,* CXIX (October, 1948), 297.
22. Durante, *op. cit.,* pp. 149–152.
23. Sforza, *op. cit.,* p. 201.
24. *Ibid.;* Pastor, *Tagebücher,* pp. 695–697.
25. De Waal, *op. cit.,* p. 63; Migliori, *op. cit.,* p. 56 f.
26. Migliori, *op. cit.,* p. 75 f.
27. Pöllmann, *op. cit.,* p. 121.
28. Durante, *op. cit.,* p. 152.
29. Schmidlin, *op. cit.,* p. 163.
30. *Ibid.,* p. 168.
31. *Enciclopedia Cattolica,* II, 1347.
32. Francis Beauchesne Thornton, *The Burning Flame, the Life of Pope Pius X* (New York: Benziger, 1952), p. 180 f.
33. De La Bedoyere, *op. cit.,* p. 153.
34. Schmidlin, *op. cit.,* pp. 163, 166, 169.
35. Adrien Dansette, *Histoire religieuse de la France contemporaine* (Paris: Flammarion, 1951), p. 464. Cf. also Alois Hudal, *Die Österreichische Vatikanbotschaft, 1806–1918* (München: Pohl, 1952), p. 289. Bishop Hudal, an Austrian prelate, for many years rector of Santa Maria del Anima, relates that Archbishop Piffl of Vienna had registered a vehement protest when Monsignor Benigni wanted to open a branch office of *Correspondance de Rome* in Vienna. He claimed it would destroy the united Catholic front in his see.

36. Pastor, *Tagebücher*, p. 548.
37. Thornton, *op. cit.*, p. 180; *Enciclopedia Cattolica*, II, 1347.
38. Rome, *A Weekly Record of Everything Worth Knowing About the Eternal City*, XV (April 25, 1914), 197 f.
39. Dansette, *op. cit.*, p. 463.
40. The part of the *Ad Beatissimi* which has been perhaps most frequently mentioned in the years since its original appearance is that in which the Sovereign Pontiff asked his people to refrain from "using distinctive names by which Catholics are marked off from Catholics." From the context there can be hardly any room for doubt that the term to which the Pope objected was "integralist." And, for this reason, some Catholic lecturers and writers have professed to see in this a condemnation of the group to which the name "integralists" has been applied.... The *Ad Beatissimi* definitely and clearly objects to the use of the name. In no way does it state or even imply any dissatisfaction with the persons to whom that name had been applied. — Joseph Clifford Fenton, "Pope Benedict XV and the Rules for Theological Discussion," *The American Ecclesiastical Review*, CXXXV (July, 1956), 50 f.
41. *Ibid.*, p. 470; Schmidlin, *op. cit.*, p. 168.

CHAPTER VI   *Archbishop of Bologna*

1. Vistalli, *op. cit.*, pp. 75–77.
2. Durante, *op. cit.*, pp. 30–32.
3. The picture is found in De Waal, *op. cit.*, opposite p. 66; in Vistalli, *op. cit.*, p. 79.
4. De Waal, *op. cit.*, p. 70 f.
5. *Ibid.*, p. 74 f.
6. Vistalli, *op. cit.*, pp. 78–80.
7. De Waal, *op. cit.*, p. 76.
8. Vistalli, *op. cit.*, p. 80.
9. Schmidlin, *op. cit.*, p. 183 *n*.
10. De Waal, *op. cit.*, p. 72 ff; Schmidlin, *op. cit.*, III, 83.
11. De Waal, *op. cit.*, p. 77.
12. *Ibid.*, p. 79 f.
13. *Ibid.*, p. 80.
14. *Ibid.*
15. *Ibid.*, p. 96. This official visitation of inspection dated back to the fifth century. It was confirmed by the Council of Trent as mandatory for all dioceses.
16. Vistalli, *op. cit.*, p. 81.
17. De Waal, *op. cit.*, p. 80; Vistalli, *op. cit.*, p. 85.
18. De Waal, *op. cit.*, p. 96.
19. Schlegel, *op. cit.*, p. 31; Vistalli, *op. cit.*, p. 86.
20. De Waal, *op. cit.*, p. 102.
21. *Ibid.*, p. 93.
22. *Ibid.*, p. 97.
23. Vistalli, *op. cit.*, p. 93.
24. De Waal, *op. cit.*, p. 9; Zannetti, *op. cit.*, p. 236.
25. De Waal, *op. cit.*, p. 91.
26. *Ibid.*, p. 105.
27. *Ibid.*, p. 93.
28. *Ibid.*, p. 107 f.
29. *Ibid.*, p. 93.

30. Migliori, *op. cit.*, p. 63.
31. De Waal, *op. cit.*, p. 102.
32. *Ibid.*, p. 94 f.
33. *Ibid.*, p. 109.
34. *Ibid.*, p. 98.
35. *Ibid.*, p. 94.
36. *Ibid.*, p. 119.
37. *Ibid.*, pp. 94, 101.
38. Migliori, *op. cit.*, p. 89.
39. De Waal, *op. cit.*, p. 101.
40. *Ibid.*
41. *Ibid.*, p. 120.
42. Durante, *op. cit.*, p. 60.
43. Burton, *op. cit.*, p. 77.
44. Francis MacNutt was wont to say that the only topic of conversation in which Della Chiesa showed vivid interest was Mexico. Cf. Bonn, *op. cit.*, p. 149.
45. Vistalli, *op. cit.*, p. 94 f.
46. *Ibid.*
47. *Ibid.*
48. Burton, *op. cit.*, p. 85.
49. Pierre Fernessole, *Pie X* (Paris: Lethielleux, 1952), I, 95 f.
50. De Waal, *op. cit.*, p. 28.
51. Durante, *op. cit.*, p. 42 ff.
52. De Waal, *op. cit.*, pp. 31 ff, 121.
53. *Ibid.*, p. 121.
54. *Ibid.*

CHAPTER VII   *The Cardinal*

1. De Waal, *op. cit.*, p. 72; Pöllmann, *op. cit.*, p. 115 ff; Schmidlin, *op. cit.*, p. 183; Hudal, *op. cit.*, p. 286.
2. Barry, *op. cit.*, p. 163.
3. Shane, Leslie, *Cardinal Gasquet* (London: Burns, Oates, 1953), p. 190. Italics are the writer's.
4. Burton, *op. cit.*, p. 211.
5. De Waal, *op. cit.*, p. 110.
6. MacNutt, *op. cit.*, p. 313.
7. Leslie, *op. cit.*, p. 190.
8. De Waal, *op. cit.*, p. 111.
9. *Ibid.*, p. 72.
10. *Ibid.*, p. 116.
11. *Rome*, XV (May 30, 1914), 253.
12. *Ibid.*, p. 206.
13. De Waal, *op. cit.*, p. 112 f; Vistalli, *op. cit.*, p. 98.
14. H. Marucchi, "Santi Quattre Coronati," *Rome*, XV (February 14, 1914), pp. 80–82.
15. De Waal, *op. cit.*, p. 113; Vistalli, *op. cit.*, p. 102.
16. Thomas à Kempis, *The Imitation of Christ*, Bk. I, xx, 5 and 7.
17. Schlegel, *op. cit.*, pp. 28–30; De Waal, *op. cit.*, p. 93.
18. Merry del Val, *Memories*, p. 73.
19. *Ibid.*, p. 75.

CHAPTER VIII   The Conclave

1. Ps. 140:5.
2. Schmidlin, *op. cit.*, p. 184.
3. *Ibid.*
4. *Ibid.*
5. Schmidlin, *op. cit.*, p. 184.
6. De Waal, *op. cit.*, p. 129.
7. Cenci, *op. cit.*, p. 266.
8. Premoli, *op. cit.*, p. 32.
9. Moynihan, *op. cit.*, p. 329.
10. Migliori, *op. cit.*, p. 87 f.
11. Aurelio Galli, Latin stylist, created cardinal in 1923, died in 1929.
12. *AAS*, VI (1914), 481.
13. Schmidlin, *op. cit.*, III, 185.
14. *Ibid.*, p. 188.
15. Georges Seldes, *The Vatican: Yesterday-Today-Tomorrow* (New York: Harper, 1934), p. 112.
16. Sforza, *op. cit.*, p. 199.
17. Humphrey J. T. Johnson, "Pope Benedict XV: 1854–1954," *Tablet*, CCIV (November 20, 1954), 495.
18. Schmidlin, *op. cit.*, p. 189.
19. Sforza, *op. cit.*, p. 199.
20. Zanetti, *op. cit.*, p. 208.
21. *AAS*, XXXVIII (February 4, 1946), 65–99.
22. The translation is taken from *The Tablet*, CLXXXVII (March 9, 1946), 124.
23. *Ibid.*
24. David Lathoud, *Avec le Pape au Vatican* (Paris: Centurion, 1955), p. 25.
25. Schmidlin, *op. cit.*, p. 189.
26. Cenci, *op. cit.*, p. 127.
27. Achille Ratti answered, "During the pontificate of Pius IX, I was made an active member of the Catholic Church and took the first steps in my ecclesiastical career. It was Pius X who called me to Rome. Pius is a name of peace. Therefore, desirous as I am of dedicating my efforts to the work of world pacification, to which my predecessor Benedict XV consecrated himself, I choose the name of Pius XI." — Morgan, *A Reporter at the Papal Court*, p. 36.
28. Eugenio Pacelli answered, "My name will be Pius, because most of my life has been passed during the pontificate of a Pope of that name, and especially because of my grateful memory of Pius XI, who always showed me such extraordinary affection." — Smit, *op. cit.*, p. 106.
29. *AAS*, VI (1914), 494.
30. Schmidlin, *op. cit.*, p. 189.
31. *Ibid.*
32. One is reminded of Frederick Rolfe's (Baron Corvo) *Hadrian VII*, that delightful tongue-in-cheek novel on the papacy. It was first published in 1903, a full decade before the election of Benedict XV. The casual reader, not adverting to this chronological priority, might conclude that the story of Benedict's choice of a name inspired Rolfe's story of Hadrian's choice of a name and the subsequent objections. In Rolfe's novel, the newly elected pontiff is asked what pontifical name he would choose.

"'Hadrian the Seventh,' the response came unhesitatingly, undemonstratively.

"'Your Holiness would perhaps prefer to be called Leo, or Pius, or Gregory, as is the modern manner?' the Cardinal-Dean inquired with impervious suavity. "'The previous English pontiff was Hadrian the Fourth; the present English pontiff is Hadrian the Seventh. It pleases Us; and so, by our own impulse, We command!' "There was no more to be said." — Frederick Baron Corvo, *Hadrian the Seventh* (New York: Knopf, 1925), p. 73.

33. Vistalli, *op. cit.,* p. 111; Johnson, *Tablet,* CCIV (November 20, 1954), 495.
34. Emmanuel Heufelder, *Der heilige Benedikt von Nursia* (Augsburg: Christkoenigsverlag vom Weissen Kreuz, 1934), pp. 5–7.
35. Zanetti, *op. cit.,* p. 208; Smit, *op. cit.,* p. 33.
36. John Farrow, *Pageant of the Popes* (New York: Sheed and Ward, 1942), p. 365 f.
37. Schmidlin, *op. cit.,* III, 198, n. 23.
38. This writer is indebted for this anecdote to a Franciscan whom he chanced to meet in the Middle East, who had been a student in Rome at the time of Benedict's election.
39. *AAS,* XIV (1922), 71.
40. Some of the anecdotes were invented by wags with the Roman student's genius for caricature. For example, at the time of Benedict's coronation a story made the rounds which said that at the ceremonial embrace of peace, Benedict quoted Ps. 117:23 to Merry del Val, *"Lapidem, quem reprobaverunt aedificantes; hic factus est in caput anguli"* ("The stone which the builders rejected; the same is become the head of the corner"). With equal gravity, according to the story, Merry del Val is said to have responded by quoting from the next verse, *"Et es mirabile in oculis nostris"* ("And it is a wonder in our eyes").
41. Merry del Val, *op. cit.,* p. 67.
42. *Enciclopedia Cattolica,* II, 1286.
43. Pichon, *op. cit.,* p. 32; Durante, *op. cit.,* p. 41.
44. Schmidlin, *op. cit.,* III, 189.
45. E. Vercesi, *Tre Papi* (Milano: Edizioni "Athena," 1929), p. 246.

CHAPTER IX   *Coronation and First Acts*

1. Camille Cianfarra, *The Vatican and the War* (New York: Dutton, 1945), p. 87.
2. Zanetti, *op. cit.,* p. 209.
3. *Ibid.,* p. 210.
4. De Waal, *op. cit.,* p. 140.
5. Robert Garland, "The Coronation of Benedict XV," *The Outlook,* CVIII (November 25, 1914), 698–707.
6. *Ibid.,* 707.
7. H. V. Morton, *In the Steps of Saint Paul* (London: Rich and Cowan, 1936), p. 338.
8. Garland, *op. cit.,* p. 707.
9. De Waal, *op. cit.,* p. 151.
10. Vistalli, *op. cit.,* p. 387.
11. *AAS,* VI (1914), 372. The last words are from Jeremias, 29:11.
12. *Ibid.,* 501 f.
13. Lord Clonmore, *Pope Pius XI and World Peace* (New York: Dutton, 1938), p. 18.
14. Vercesi, *op. cit.,* p. 246.
15. Authors speak of the fact that Benedict "rejected" Merry del Val as though the fact that Benedict did not reappoint the secretary of the former pontificate were

something tantamount to a public display of personal feeling. Quite to the contrary, it was not customary for a pope to reappoint his predecessor's secretary of state. Saint Pius X did not choose Rampolla. In fact, it was resented that Saint Pius X kept Della Chiesa as undersecretary. When Pius XI reappointed Gasparri, who had been Benedict's secretary of state, it was considered as something almost without precedent.

16. Seppelt and Löffler, *op. cit.*, p. 523.
17. Pastor, *Tagebücher*, p. 598.
18. Vercesi, *op. cit.*, p. 247 f.
19. Morgan, *Speaking of Cardinals*, p. 53.
20. Thomas B. Morgan, *The Listening Post, Eighteen Years on Vatican Hill* (New York: G. B. Putnam's Sons, 1944), p. 137.
21. Zanetti, *op. cit.*, p. 220.
22. Durante, *op. cit.*, p. 35.

CHAPTER X   The Human Benedict

1. *Westminster Gazette,* quoted in *Catholic Bulletin* (St. Paul, Minnesota), September 25, 1914, p. 1.
2. Pichon, *op. cit.*, p. 35 f.
3. *Rome,* XVII (February 27, 1915), 95 f.
4. Zanetti, *op. cit.*, p. 225.
5. *Ibid.*, p. 220.
6. *Ibid.*, p. 238 f; Sforza, *op. cit.*, p. 201; Durante, *op. cit.*, p. 42.
7. Zanetti, *op. cit.*, p. 222.
8. *Ibid.*
9. Leo XIII had given a very enthusiastic allocution to the Franciscans, which impressed Giacomo Della Chiesa so much that he went to a Franciscan house that very afternoon and applied for admission to their chapter of tertiaries. He always took pride in fostering the spirit of St. Francis.
10. Lathoud, *op. cit.*, p. 121.
11. *Ibid.*
12. John P. McKnight, *The Papacy* (New York: Rinehart, 1952), p. 236.
13. Zanetti, *op. cit.*, p. 221.
14. *Ibid.*, p. 227 f.
15. Smit, *op. cit.*, p. 132.
16. *Ibid.*
17. Migliori, *op. cit.*, p. 137 f.
18. Durante, *op. cit.*, p. 77 f.
19. Migliori, *op. cit.*, p. 62.
20. Zanetti, *op. cit.*, p. 234.
21. *Ibid.;* Durante, *op. cit.*, p. 95 f.
22. Zanetti, *op. cit.*, p. 236.
23. *Ibid.*, p. 233.
24. Lk. 12:22. The translation may be found in James A. Kleist, S.J., and Joseph L. Lilly, C.M., *The New Testament* (Milwaukee: Bruce, 1954).

CHAPTER XI   The First Encyclical, Ad Beatissimi

1. Robert Dell, "The Vatican and the War," *The Fortnightly Review,* CIII (Old Series), XCVII (New Series) (1915), 290.

2. William Kay Wallace, *Greater Italy* (New York: Charles Scribner's Sons, 1917), p. 176.
3. *Tablet,* CXXVI (July 31, 1915), 152.
4. Wood, *op. cit.,* p. 178.
5. Pichon, *op. cit.,* p. 87.
6. *Rome,* XVI (December 12, 1914), 64–71. The official Latin version appears in *AAS,* VI (1914), 565–581.
7. Pichon, *op. cit.,* p. 73.
8. Dell, *op. cit.,* p. 286 f.
9. The *Catholic Encyclopedia* (X, 415) opens the discussion of theological Modernism with the terse remark, "A full definition of modernism would be rather difficult."
10. Benedict was always most gracious to Catholic societies which he received in audience. The various subordinate societies of Catholic Action were objects of his predilection. His allocutions to them were always carefully prepared. The Knights of Columbus of the United States were received by him with great enthusiasm.
11. As will be pointed out in the chapter which treats of Benedict's writings, he carefully avoided repeating what had been set down by his predecessors. He always urged a rereading of what his predecessors had written.
12. *L'Osservatore Romano,* November 19, 1914.

CHAPTER XII   *The Incessant Cry for Peace*

1. J. Mattern, "The Pope and His Critics," *The Open Court,* XXX (1916), 262.
2. Robert Dell, *op. cit.,* p. 287.
3. *AAS,* VI (1914), 567.
4. Mattern, *op. cit.,* p. 264.
5. Mt. 5:11 f.
6. Fernand Hayward, *Un Pape Méconnu, Benoit XV* (Tournai: Castermann, 1955), p. 71.
7. *Ibid.,* p. 70.
8. Smit, *op. cit.,* p. 36.
9. Vercesi, *op. cit.,* p. 247 f.
10. Denis Gwynn, *The Vatican and War in Europe* (Dublin: Browne and Nolan, 1940), p. 66.
11. Pastor, *Tagebücher,* p. 877.
12. Gwynn, *op. cit.,* p. 66.
13. Pichon, *op. cit.,* pp. 120–143; *Rome,* XVII (May 29, 1915), 258.
14. *Rome,* XVII (June 26, 1915), 302.
15. Gasquet, *op. cit.,* p. 244.
16. *Rome,* XVII (July 3, 1915), 8. All subsequent quotations of the interview are taken from *Rome's* coverage of the situation.
17. Gasquet, *op. cit.,* p. 244 f. The entry in Gasquet's diary for June 24 mentions but a few of the many periodicals which participate in the verbal fray after the publication of the interview.
18. *Op. cit.,* p. 261.
19. Wood, *op. cit.,* p. 192.
20. Anne O'Hare McCormick, *Vatican Journal 1921–1954* (New York: Farrar, Straus and Cudahy, 1957), p. 19.
21. Pichon, *op. cit.,* p. 82.

22. *Rome,* XVI (January 2, 1915), 4–6.
23. *Ibid.,* (January 23, 1915), 41.
24. *AAS,* VI (1914), 668 f.
25. *Rome,* XVII (January 23, 1915), 41.
26. "Diplomaticus," *No Small Stir, What the Pope Really Said About the Great War* (London: The Society of SS. Peter and Paul, 1917), p. 14.
27. *Ibid.,* p. 13.
28. *Ibid.,* p. 14.
29. *AAS,* VII (1915), 254.
30. *Ibid.,* 365–368.
31. Benedict's sentence seems inspired by a line from Tacitus. "Metus ac terror sunt infirma vincla caritatis; quae ibi removeris, qui timere desierint, odisse incipient." — P. Cornelius Tacitus, *Vita Iulii Agricolae,* xxxii.
32. Adolph Hitler, *Mein Kampf* (New York: Reynal and Hitchcock, 1941), p. 920.
33. Premoli, *op. cit.,* p. 41.
34. The wording of the prayer is that of the official translation found in *AAS,* VII (1915), 13 f.
35. *Scritti e Discorsi di Benito Mussolini* (Milano: Ulrice Hoepli, 1934), I, 53.
36. Pichon, *op. cit.,* p. 96.
37. Schmidlin, *op. cit.,* p. 267; *Rome,* XVII (February 6, 1915), 62.
38. Pichon, *op. cit.,* p. 151.
39. Luigi Sturzo, *Church and State* (New York: Longmans, Green and Co., 1939), pp. 469–471. Permission to quote was granted by Messrs. Geoffry Bles, LTD., London, who now hold the rights.

CHAPTER XIII *Treason*

1. *New York Times,* August 16, 1916, p. 3.
2. "The Vatican and the Germanic Powers," *Contemporary Review,* October, 1917, p. 407.
3. *New York Times,* December 3, 1921, p. 1.
4. *Ibid.,* June 27, 1917, p. 3; *Scotsman,* June 7, 1915, p. 1.
5. E. J. Dillon, "Italy's New Birth," *Fortnightly Review,* LXXXIII (July 1, 1915), 1–15.
6. Mattern, *op. cit.,* 258–277.
7. Dillon, "Italy's New Birth," *op. cit.,* p. 11 f.
8. *Codex Iuris Canonici,* Canon 2351. Cf. also Canon 984, 5°, and Canon 985, 5°.
9. "The Vatican and the Germanic Powers," *op. cit.,* p. 407; *New York Times,* January 9, 1917, p. 1; London *Times,* August 8, p. 5; December 3, 1921.
10. *Times* (London), August 8, 1917, p. 5; *New York Times,* January 9, 1917, p. 1.
11. Pöllman, *op. cit.,* p. 276.
12. This writer was in Rome in 1939, when Eugenio Cardinal Pacelli was elected pope, and also went to the *Stazione* in Rome to see the prelates arrive.
13. On June 21, 1954, this writer had a lengthy visit with Monsignor Gallinetti who had been the vicar-general of Archbishop Della Chiesa. He related that he had been surprised to read of the selection of a German as papal chamberlain, and even though he had lived with the Archbishop in his residence during the years he was vicar-general, he had never seen Gerlach nor had any correspondence been carried on with him.
14. *AAS,* VI (September 17, 1914), 511.
15. *L'Osservatore Romano,* September 7, 1917, p. 1.

288 NOTES

16. *AAS,* VI (September 17, 1914), 507. How different was the career of Gerlach's co-chamberlain, Camillo Caccia-Dominioni! He was made *maestro di camera,* and later created cardinal by Pius XI in 1935. It was he who announced the election of Pius XII and it was he who crowned the new Pope on the balcony of San Pietro on March 12, 1939. He died November 12, 1946, two days before Gerlach.
17. One of the few German ecclesiastics who were allowed to remain was Monsignor Anton De Waal, on whose life of Benedict the present writer drew so heavily in the first part of this biography. He was beloved by Italians and foreigners without discrimination. Even Father Francis Ehrle, S.J., accepted the suggestion that he resign his post as Vatican librarian and return to his own country. From this it can be seen that Gerlach's request to remain in Rome was something exceptional.
18. Wood, *op. cit.,* 198.
19. *Times* (London), August 8, 1917, p. 5.
20. *Ibid.*
21. *Ibid.*
22. Jean Neuvecelle, *The Vatican, Its Organization, Customs, and Way of Life* (New York: Criterion, 1955), p. 97.
23. *Times* (London), August 8, 1917, p. 5.
24. Wood, *op. cit.,* 202.
25. The source of information was a member of a religious order who had been a member of one of the sacred congregations at the time of the Gerlach defection. He cleared his own thinking on the matter by reminiscing and musing aloud and bringing to the fore the rumors of that time. He admitted that he had no direct information. He had seen Gerlach at various times but knew nothing directly about his trial or dismissal from the Vatican. His sources were the newspaper reports and the stories that were circulating at the time.
26. Monsignor Louis Duchesne's letter to Archbishop Ireland, February 1, 1917, is to be found in the Archives of the Archdiocese of Saint Paul. It is quoted by Moynihan, *op. cit.,* p. 270.
27. *New York Times,* June 27, 1917, p. 3.
28. Wood, *op. cit.,* 202 f.
29. *New York Times,* June 27, 1917, p. 3.
30. Gal. 5:22.
31. *Tablet,* CXXX (July 7, 1917), 17.
32. *New York Times,* January 11, 1917, p. 1.
33. *Tablet,* CXXX (July 7, 1917), 17.
34. Alois Hudal, *op. cit.,* p. 299.
35. *Ibid.*
36. *Tablet,* CXXX (July 7, 1917), 17.
37. *Ibid.*
38. *L'Osservatore Romano* (June 27, 1917).
39. *Civiltà Cattolica,* LXVIII, iii (1917), 92. The translation is taken from *Tablet,* CXXX (July 7, 1917), 17.
40. *Times,* August 8, 1917, p. 5a.
41. *Tablet,* CXXX (July 7, 1917), 18.
42. *Ibid.,* p. 17.
43. Edward L. Heston, *The Holy See at Work* (Milwaukee: Bruce, 1950).
44. *Tablet,* CXX (July 7, 1917), 17.
45. Ps. 108:13.
46. Schwester Teresia Renata de Spiritu Sancto, *Maria Erzberger* (Köln, 1953); J. N. I. Van Hilsum, *Maria Erzberger, Zr. Gertrudis* (Antwerp: Nelissen, 1956); Hilda C. Graef, "A Life for a Soul," *Cross and Crown,* VII (June, 1955), 208–217.
47. Teresia Renata, *op. cit.,* p. 11 f.

48. Van Hilsum, *op. cit.*, p. 98 f.
49. The reply (June 7, 1956) to a letter addressed to the Academy of Noble Ecclesiastics brought only this information about Gerlach's death: "Er starb tatsachlich in England, im November, 1946, versöhnt mit der Kirche, wie das der dortige Bischof (ich weiss nicht, wer) dem Presidenten geschrieben hatte."
50. Rom. 5:20.

CHAPTER XIV   *The Papal Peace Note of 1917*

1. J. Daniel Chamier, *Fabulous Monster* (New York: Longmans, 1934), p. 299.
2. France and Russia came to an understanding in 1891, and formed the Franco-Russian Alliance in 1894. The purpose was mutual protection against Germany. Great Britain began to be alarmed, and, dropping her previously unfriendly attitude toward France, in 1904 established an Entente Cordiale with France. In 1907, Great Britain and Russia signed an agreement, composing their differences in the Middle East. The three countries, Great Britain, France, and Russia were designated the Triple Entente or simply the Entente. On the other side, Germany and Austria-Hungary were united in a dual alliance in 1879. Later an agreement was made with Italy, so that there was a triple alliance of Germany, Austria-Hungary, and Italy. On paper Italy belonged to the latter alliance, but by a secret treaty made in London in 1915, Italy joined the Entente. On August 28, 1916, Italy was to enter the war on the side of the Entente. Germany and Austria-Hungary were called the Central Powers because they were hemmed in by England, France, and Russia.
3. Arnold Struker, *Die Kundgebungen Papst Benedikts XV zum Weltfrieden* (Freiburg: Herder, 1917), p. 115 f.
4. Seppelt and Löffler, *op. cit.*, p. 528.
5. A. J. P. Taylor, *The Struggle for Mastery in Europe, 1848–1918* (Oxford: Clarendon Press, 1854), p. 555.
6. Benedict's immediate successor was also present in the Sistine Chapel. Monsignor Achille Ratti, prefect of the Vatican Library, left his work in the library to be present for the ceremony. — Oscar Halecki, *Eugenio Pacelli: Pope of Peace* (New York: Creative Age Press, 1951), p. 51.
7. *Peace Action of Pope Benedict XV* (Washington: Catholic Association for International Peace, n.d.), p. 4.
8. Taylor, *op. cit.*, p. 564.
9. Frederic William Wile, *Men around the Kaiser* (Indianapolis: Bobbs-Merrill, 1914), p. 20.
10. Kaiser Wilhelm II Hohenzollern, *Ereignisse und Gestalten aus den Jahren, 1878–1918* (Leipzig: K. F. Kochler, 1922), p. 225. In his slender autobiographical account the Emperor, who was not in the habit of employing many words of adulation for others, shows that he had been very favorably impressed by the papal representative. He wrote of him, "An aristocratic, likable, and distinguished appearance, with great intelligence and impeccable manners, the perfect model of a high prelate of the Catholic Church."
11. Struker, *op. cit.*, p. 129.
12. Seldes, *op. cit.*, p. 265.
13. Hohenzollern, *op. cit.*, p. 177.
14. *Peace Action*, p. 6.
15. *Ibid.*
16. Gwynn, *op. cit.*, p. 48 ff.

17. *Ibid.*, p. 53.
18. Pichon, *op. cit.*, p. 165.
19. *Ibid.*, p. 166 f.
20. J. Jusserand, "Letter to the Editor," *American Historical Review*, XXXVII (July, 1932), 818.
21. *U. S. Congressional Record*, 65th Cong., *1st* Sess., 1917, *LV*, Part 6, 6407 f.
22. Ernst Deuerlein, "Zur Friedensaktion Papst Benedikts XV, 1917," *Stimmen der Zeit*, CLV (January, 1955), 241–256.
23. Friedrich Ritter von Lama, *Die Friedensvermittlung Papst Benedikts XV und ihre Vereitlung durch den deutschen Reichskanzler Michaelis* (München: Kössel, 1932), p. 193.
24. *Ibid.*, p. 193.
25. *Ibid.*, p. 194.
26. Von Lama, *Der Vereitelte Friede* (Augsburg: Haas und Grabherr, 1926), p. 25.
27. Von Lama, *Die Friedensvermittlung*, pp. 221–224.
28. *Peace Action*, p. 21.
29. Von Lama, *Die Friedensvermittlung*, p. 227 f.
30. Wood, *op. cit.*, p. 190.
31. Migliori, *op. cit.*, p. 126 f.
32. Schmidlin, *op. cit.*, p. 214.
33. *Peace Action*, p. 20.
34. Von Lama, *Der Vereitelte Friede*, p. 40.
35. Von Lama, *Die Friedensvermittlung*, p. 267.
36. *Ibid.*, pp. 271–273.
37. Von Lama first published his accusations in periodicals. In *Papst und Kurie* (1925) he gives a brief review of the question. *Der vereitelte Friede* (1926) has the subtitle, "My accusation against Michaelis and the Evangelical Brotherhood." *Die Friedensvermittlung* (1932) in its lengthy title lays the blame for the shipwreck of the papal peace plan at the feet of Michaelis.
38. Deuerlein's article in *Stimmen der Zeit, loc. cit.*, was occasioned by a reading of Konstantin, Prince of Bavaria, *The Pope, a Portrait from Life* (New York: Roy, n.d.). In this book the Prince alleges that Pius XII recounted the fate of Benedict's peace plan in a series of private audiences. Deuerlein asserts that the purported narration is gleaned from the works of von Lama.
39. Richard von Kühlmann, *Erinnerungen* (Heidelberg: 1948), p. 475.
40. Deuerlein, *op. cit.*, p. 250.
41. *Ibid.*, p. 251 f.
42. *Ibid.*, p. 253 ff.
43. Gwynn, *op. cit.*, p. 54.
44. Pichon, *op. cit.*, p. 167.
45. Taylor, *op. cit.*, p. 565.
46. Seldes, *op. cit.*, p. 268.
47. *AAS*, X (1917), 14. The English translation is taken from Harry C. Koenig, *Principles for Peace, Selections from Papal Documents* (Washington: N.C.W.C., 1943), p. 240. The quotation from Sacred Scripture within the letter is from 1 Corinthians, 4:12 f.
48. *AAS*, X (1917), 15; Koenig, *op. cit.*, p. 240.
49. Lk. 2:34.
50. Koenig, *op. cit.*, pp. 240–253. The quotation from Sacred Scripture is from Jn. 12:24 f.
51. *U. S. Congressional Record*, 65th Cong., 2nd Sess., 1918, LVI, Part I, 680 f.
52. *Catholic Bulletin*, September 22, 1917, p. 4.
53. Dansette, whose treatment of Benedict is not sympathetic, terms his peace action

an exhibition of *orgueil* (arrogance), *op. cit.*, p. 488. An understanding of Benedict's character would certainly exonerate him from that charge.

54. Sforza, *op. cit.*, p. 206.

CHAPTER XV   *Benedict, Wilson, and Versailles*

1. John Tracy Ellis, *The Life of James Cardinal Gibbons* (Milwaukee: Bruce, 1952), II, 281 f.
2. Gerald W. Johnson, *Woodrow Wilson* (New York: Harper, 1944), p. 196.
3. Nicola Canali, close friend and companion of Cardinal Merry del Val, was transferred from the secretariat of state to the Congregation of Ceremonies by Benedict XV in 1914. He was elevated to the Sacred College by Pius XI in 1935. Now he is the Grand Penitentiary of the Church.
4. Camille Cianfarra, *op. cit.*, p. 90, tells an amusing anecdote about Wilson who became so very nervous in the presence of the Vatican officials that he suddenly handed his hat to a monsignor and would have entered the throne room in his overcoat had not an old attendant tapped him imperiously upon the shoulder.
5. Robert J. Bender, "W. W.," *Scattered Impressions of a Reporter who for Eight Years "Covered" the Activities of Woodrow Wilson* (New York: United Press Associations, 1924), p. 51 ff.
6. Friedrich Ritter von Lama, *Papst und Kurie in ihrer Politik nach dem Weltkrieg* (Illertissen: Martinusbuchhandlung, 1925), p. 15.
7. *Ibid.*
8. Pastor, *Tagebücher*, p. 877.
9. *New York Times*, January 5, 1919.
10. Edith Wilson, *op. cit.*, p. 217.
11. Friedrich Engel-Janosi, "The Roman Question in the First Years of Benedict XV," *Catholic Historical Review*, XL (October, 1954), 282.
12. *Rome*, XIX (February, 19, 1916), 86.
13. *Catholic Bulletin*, June 21, 1919, p. 1.
14. Von Lama, *Papst und Kurie*, p. 149.
15. *The Catholic Bulletin*, August 2, 1919.
16. Joseph P. Tumulty, *Woodrow Wilson as I Know Him* (Garden City: Doubleday, Page and Co., 1921), pp. 117–119.
17. Von Lama, *Papst und Kurie*, pp. 117–119.
18. Tumulty, *op. cit.*, p. 483.
19. Pastor, *Tagebücher*, p. 717.
20. Gwynn, *op. cit.*, p. 69.
21. Von Lama, *Papst und Kurie*, p. 126.
22. "La Guerra Sociale dopa la Pace di Versailles," *Civiltà Cattolica*, LXX, iii (August 30, 1919), 271.
23. *AAS*, XI (1919), 307 f.
24. *Ibid.*
25. *Ibid.*, pp. 412–414.
26. Mt. 22:37–39.
27. Mt. 5:43–45.
28. *AAS*, XI (1919), 308.
29. Eppstein, *op. cit.*, p. 235.
30. Pichon, *op. cit.*, p. 200.
31. All quotations are taken from Eppstein, *op. cit.*, pp. 236–242.
32. Col. 3:12.

33. The three saints whom Benedict canonized are Joan of Arc, Margaret Mary Alacoque, Gabriel of the Sorrowful Mother.
34. It is the *Oratio secreta* from the Mass of Corpus Christi.

CHAPTER XVI   The Apostolate of Charity During the War

1. Vistalli, *op. cit.*, pp. 237–284.
2. "L'opera del S. P. Benedetto XV in favore dei prigionieri di Guerra," *Civiltà Cattolica*, LXIX (1918), iii, 399.
3. Vistalli, *op. cit.*, p. 240.
4. *Ibid.*, Migliori, *op. cit.*, p. 142; Hayward, *op. cit.*, p. 76.
5. Thomas Ewing Moore, *Peter's City* (New York: Macmillan, 1930), p. 195.
6. Seldes, *op. cit.*, p. 250.
7. Cianfarra, *op. cit.*, p. 57.
8. Durante, *op. cit.*, p. 130.
9. Cianfarra, *op. cit.*, p. 130.
10. Francis Pichon, *op. cit.*, p. 232 f.
11. *Tablet*, CXXVIII (November 11, 1916), 646.
12. *AAS*, IX (1917), p. 11 f.
13. Vistalli, *op. cit.*, p. 497; Migliori, *op. cit.*, p. 139.
14. Hayward, *op. cit.*, p. 78.
15. Migliori, *op. cit.*, p. 146.
16. *Ibid.*, p. 146 f.
17. Vistalli, *op. cit.*, pp. 240, 272.
18. Hayward, *op. cit.*, p. 75.
19. *Tablet*, CXXVIII (July 15, 1916), 81.
20. *Ibid.* (October 21, 1916), 538.
21. *Civiltà Cattolica*, LXIX (1918), iv, 283 f.
22. *Tablet*, CXXVIII (August 26, 1916), 274.
23. Vistalli, *op. cit.*, p. 28.

CHAPTER XVII   Benedict the Statesman

1. *Catholic Encyclopedia*, VII, 48. For a translation of all the guarantees, cf. John Carrere, *The Pope* (New York: Henry Holt, 1926), pp. 251–255.
2. René Füllöp-Miller, *Leo XIII and Our Times* (London: Longmans, 1937), pp. 104 f.
3. *AAS*, V (1913), 58.
4. *AAS*, XXXV (1905), 745–761.
5. Not long after this formal audience a tall feminine figure, heavily veiled, was seen entering for a papal audience. Rumor said that it was Elena, queen of Italy. Burton, *op. cit.*, p. 154.
6. *Rome*, XVI (December 12, 1914), 71.
7. *AAS*, VI (1914), 659 f.
8. Hudal, *op. cit.*, p. 298.
9. *Rome*, XVIII (December 11, 1915), 281 f.
10. *Tablet*, CXXVIII (October 14, 1916), 505 f.
11. *Ibid.*, 506.
12. Friedrich Engel-Janosi, "The Roman Question in the First Years of Benedict XV," *Catholic Historical Review*, XL (October, 1954), 280.

13. *Ibid.*, 278.
14. See *Time*, March 8, 1954, p. 35 f., for the interesting story of Father Sturzo who came out of his retirement long enough to address the senate in a brief message delivered in Ciceronian eloquence.
15. The People's Party must not be confused with the People's Union because both employed the adjective *Popolare*. The People's Union (L'U.P.), founded by Pius X to be an instrument of Catholic Action, was strictly religious and under the supervision of the Holy See. The Popular or People's Party (P.P.I.) was political and autonomous except insofar as it was guided by Catholic principles. The two organizations were not subordinated, one to the other. They worked side by side. Alcide De Gaspari (d. 1954) was one of the Party's first presidents.
16. *Enciclopedia Cattolica*, IX, 875.
17. Hayward, *op. cit.*, pp. 131–134.
18. *Rome*, XVII (May 29, 1915), 258.
19. Zanetti, *op. cit.*, p. 236.
20. *Rome*, XIX (February 26, 1916), 103.
21. Von Lama, *Die Friedensvermittlung*, p. 80 f.
22. Füllöp-Miller, *op. cit.*, p. 106.
23. Eppstein, *op. cit.*, p. 240.
24. Pastor, *Tagebücher*, p. 728 f.
25. Engel-Janosi, *op. cit.*, 285.
26. Schmidlin, *op. cit.*, 268; Pichon, *op. cit.*, p. 129.
27. *Rome*, XVII (June 5, 1915), 266.
28. *Ibid.*
29. Cardinal Merry del Val, however, thought these efforts futile. Once he had expressed himself in these words, "France is much too grand a lady to condescend to set foot in the Vatican over the steps of an embassy." Von Lama, *Papst und Kurie*, pp. 176–181.
30. Pichon, *op. cit.*, p. 226.
31. Morgan, *A Reporter at the Papal Court*, pp. 144–148.
32. Hughes, *op. cit.*, p. 68; Morgan, *A Reporter at the Papal Court*, p. 147.
33. *Ibid.*, p. 148.
34. Benedict Williamson, *The Story of Pope Pius XI* (London: Alexander-Ouseley, 1931), p. 49 f.
35. Von Lama, *Pius XI*, p. 20.
36. Clonmore, *op. cit.*, p. 55.
37. Von Lama, *Pius XI*, p. 46 f.
38. *Ibid.*, p. 47.
39. Morgan, *A Reporter at the Papal Court*, p. 154.
40. *Ibid.*, p. 60.
41. *Ibid.*, p. 160.

CHAPTER XVIII   *Benedict XV, Pope of Canon Law and Sacred Scripture*

1. *Tablet*, CXXX (July 7, 1917), 18 f.
2. *AAS*, IX (1917), 381 f.
3. "Diplomaticus," *No Small Stir, What the Pope Really Said About the Great War* (London: Society of Saints Peter and Paul, Publishers to the Church of England, 1917), p. 16.

4. Pierre Henri Battifol, "Pope Benedict XV and the Restoration of Unity," *The Constructive Quarterly*, VI (1918), 211.
5. Heston, *op. cit.*, p. 163.
6. Vistalli, *op. cit.*, p. 386.
7. T. Lincoln Bouscaren and Adam C. Ellis, *Canon Law: Text and Commentary* (Milwaukee: Bruce, 1957), p. 5.
8. P. Charles Augustine, O.S.B., *A Commentary on the New Code of Canon Law* (St. Louis: Herder, 1918), I, 64–68.
9. Arcadius Larraona and Servus Goyeneche, "De SS. Congregationum tribunalium et officiorum constitutione et interna ordinatione," *Apollinaris*, XXV (1952), 103.
10. Merry del Val, *Memories*, p. 59 f. Italics are mine.
11. *AAS*, IX (1917), 475. These articles are: (1) Canon 859, § 2, which provides for the length of the Easter season; (2) Canon 1108, § 3, concerning the authorization of the solemnity of matrimony in "closed times" under certain conditions; (3) Canon 1247, § 1, concerning the holydays of obligation; (4) Canons 1250–1254, concerning the days of fast and abstinence; (5) Canons 239, § 1; 240; 600, 3°; 1189; 1401, which treat of privileges of cardinals which they can use at once.
12. Augustine, *op. cit.*, II, 249.
13. Larraona and Goyeneche, *op. cit.*, 104.
14. *AAS*, IX (1917), 167.
15. *Ibid.*, 162.
16. *Ibid.*, VII (1915), 493–495.
17. *Ibid.*, II (1910), 277 ff.
18. *Ibid.*, VII (1915), 229 ff.
19. Nikolaus Hilling, "Die Gesetzgeberische Tätigkeit Benedikts XV," *Archiv Für katholisches Kirchenrecht*, XCVIII (1918), 223–239, 398–406, 561–574.
20. *AAS*, VII (1915), 230.
21. Antonio Cardinal Agliardi, bishop of Albano, subdean of the College of Cardinals, chancellor of the Holy Roman Church, died March 19, 1915.
22. Cenci, *op. cit.*, p. 523 f.
23. Hilling, *op. cit.*, p. 224 f.
24. *AAS*, VII (1915), 6 f.
25. *Ibid.* (1916), 364 ff.
26. Leslie, *op. cit.*, p. 246.
27. Amleto Giovanni Cicognani, *Canon Law* (Philadelphia: The Dolphin Press, 1934), p. 428.
28. Lawrence McReavy, "The Silver Jubilee of the Code of Canon Law," *Clergy Review*, XXIII (November, 1943), 485.
29. *Ibid.*, 284.
30. *AAS*, IX (1917), 483.
31. *Ibid.*, 484.
32. Pichon, *op. cit.*, p. 78 f.
33. *Rome*, XX (November 11, 1916), 227.
34. *AAS*, VIII (1916), 400–404.
35. *Rome*, XX (November 11, 1916), 230.
36. *AAS*, XI (1919), 124–128.
37. *Ibid.*, XIII (1921), 13–16.
38. Hayward, *op. cit.*, p. 116.
39. Giovanni Mercati, an international authority on paleography especially of the patristic period, was born in Gaida in 1866. After teaching for some years in the diocesan seminary, he was appointed to the Ambrosian Library in Milan where he met Dr. Achille Ratti, the future Pius XI. In 1936, he was created cardinal and made archivist of the Holy Roman Church. He died in August, 1957.

40. Hayward, *op. cit.*, p. 116.
41. Durante, *op. cit.*, p. 68.
42. *AAS,* VI (1914), 539.
43. *Rome,* XVII (February 27, 1915), 101.
44. *Ibid.*, XVIII (September 4, 1915), 118.
45. *AAS,* IX (1917), 305–317.
46. *Ibid.*, 335–341.
47. *Rome,* XIX (March 11, 1916), 125–128.
48. *Ibid.*, XX (August 5, 1916), 64–66.
49. *AAS,* XII (1920), 385–422.
50. After Leo had given suggestions for interpreting passages which describe natural phenomena, he proceeded to a discussion of historical references in the Bible. He opened this new section with the words, "The principles here laid down will apply to cognate sciences and especially to history." This sentence opened the door to the theory which bore the label, "the appearances of history theory." Benedict deplored the theory as "rash and false deduction."
51. Hayward, *op. cit.*, p. 20.
52. *The New Testament* (Paterson, N. J.: St. Anthony Guild Press, 1941).
53. Archbishop O'Hara died on September 11, 1956, in Milan on his way to the Assisi conference.
54. A few weeks before he died, he told of his audiences with Saint Pius X, Benedict XV, Pius XI, and Pius XII. The conference with Benedict was carried on in French without an interpreter. Archbishop O'Hara had learned this language to some extent when he was a chaplain in France but Pope Benedict sensed what he wanted to say and helped the young priest without manifesting any spirit of condescension.

CHAPTER XIX   *The Piety of Benedict XV*

1. Montes De Oca, C.S.Sp., *More About Fatima and the Immaculate Heart of Mary* (Westminster, Md.: The Newman Bookshop, 1947), p. 65.
2. *Peace Action,* p. 22.
3. Luigi Salvatorelli, *Pio IX e la sua Eredita Pontificale* (Turin: Enaudi, 1939), p. 13.
4. Durante, *op. cit.*, p. 48.
5. *Ibid.*, p. 44.
6. On a warm September afternoon in 1915, one of the fine Irish horses, a gift to Benedict from Cardinal Bauer, suddenly dropped dead while harnessed to the papal carriage. — *New York Times,* September 23, 1915, p. 13.
7. Durante, *op. cit.*, p. 49.
8. Eph. 4:26.
9. Albert Oesch, *P. Michael Hofmann, S.J.* (Innsbruck: Verlag Felizian Rauch, (1951), p. 161.
10. In the encyclical *Ad Beatissimi* he urges all to review his predecessor's exhortation to the clergy.
11. *Tablet,* CXXXVIII (July 9, 1921), 49.
12. Durante, *op. cit.*, p. 51 f.
13. *Rome,* XVII (January 2, 1915), 5.
14. *AAS,* XII (1920), 222–225.
15. *Ibid.*, XI (1919), 413.
16. *Ibid.*, XIII (1921), 196.

17. Di Pietro, *op. cit.,* p. 95.
18. *AAS,* VII (1915), 203 f.
19. Mateo Crawley-Boevey, *Jesus, King of Love* (Fairhaven, Mass.: National Center of the Enthronement, 1943), pp. 249, 277 f.
20. Di Pietro, *op. cit.,* p. 64.
21. Durante, *op. cit.,* p. 57.
22. *AAS,* VII (1915), 498.
23. *Civiltà Cattolica,* LXVIII (1917), iii, 420 f.
24. *Ibid.,* p. 409 f.
25. *AAS,* X (1918), 181–184.
26. *Ibid.,* XIII (1921), 369 f.
27. *Ibid.,* XII (1920), 313–317.
28. Bishop Stefano Ferrando, once a Salesian missionary, is the bishop of Shillong, India. He visited the Saint Paul Seminary in 1956. Since Giacomo Della Chiesa visited Genoa but rarely, Bishop Ferrando had never seen him. He was, however, well acquainted with biographical details and especially those things which Benedict did in favor of the missions.
29. The picture painted by Thérèse's sister Celine appears in the first edition of the autobiography, and has been reproduced many times. It is a remarkably good likeness of Leo XIII, gaunt and awesome, yet with a whimsical look upon his face. Thérèse kneels unabashed at his side, with her folded hands on the aged Pope's right knee. Two Noble Guards with looks of consternation on their faces advance from an archway.
30. *Saint Thérèse of Lisieux,* trans. and ed., Thomas Nimmio Taylor (New York: P. J. Kennedy, 1927), pp. 256–267.

CHAPTER XX   *Benedict and Christian Life*

1. *Tablet,* CXXXVI (May 22, 1920), 681 f.
2. *Missel Quotidien des Fidéles* (Tours: Maison Mame, 1953), p. 1141.
3. Di Pietro, *op. cit.,* p. 62.
4. Heinrich Sierp, "Benedikt XV," *Stimmen der Zeit,* LXX (1922), 407.
5. *Tablet,* CXXIX (May 12, 1917), 602; CXXXVI (May 15, 1920), 645 f.
6. *Ibid.,* CXXXVI (June 5, 1920), 763.
7. *Ibid.*
8. *AAS,* VII (1915), 401–404.
9. *Rome,* XVIII (August 21, 1915), 90.
10. *AAS,* XIII (1921), 543 f.
11. Jn. 21:20.
12. *AAS,* XI (1919), 190 f.
13. Josef A. Jungmann, *Missarum Sollemnia* (Wien: Herder, 1949), II, 148.
14. Durante, *op. cit.,* p. 77.
15. *Tablet,* CXXXIV (December 13, 1919), 803.
16. *Rome,* XVII (February 20, 1915), 89.
17. Pierre Fernessole, *La Sainteté Pie XII et l'Education de la Jeunesse* (Paris: Lethielleux, 1955), pp. 28–31.
18. "Allocution to the Roman Patriciate and Nobility," *Tablet,* CXXVII (January 15, 1916), 43. The allocution was delivered on January 4, 1916.
19. *Ibid.,* CXXXIV (November 1, 1919), 570.
20. *Rome,* XVIII (October 23, 1915), 194.
21. Di Pietro, *op. cit.,* p. 1 f.

22. *Tablet,* CXXXIII (March 15, 1919), 311.
23. *Ibid.,* CXXXVIII (September 17, 1921), 374 f.
24. *Ibid.* (September 24, 1921), 405.

CHAPTER XXI   *Benedict the Universal Father*

1. *Rome,* XVI (December 12, 1914), 64.
2. This is not a hypothetical question. The present writer has had frequent occasion to lecture on the various religions in the Middle East. He has praised the Maronites for their stanch loyalty to the Holy See. Invariably there is a question from the floor as to whether they are Catholics in the real sense of the word.
3. *AAS,* IX (1917), 529–531.
4. *Tablet,* CXXX (December 15, 1917), 802.
5. *AAS,* IX (1917), 531–533.
6. *Tablet,* CXXX (December 1, 1917), 705.
7. *Civiltà Cattolica,* LXXII (1921), ii, 177 f.
8. *AAS,* XII (1920), 457–471.
9. Donald Atwater, "Facts That Make Reunion With the Orthodox Church Difficult," *Catholic Mind,* XLII (October, 1944), 616–619.
10. Von Lama, *Papst und Kurie,* p. 367 f.; Hayward, *op. cit.,* p. 105 f.
11. Von Lama, *Papst und Kurie,* p. 369 n.
12. *Tablet,* CXXXVIII (1921), 245.
13. *AAS,* XI (1919), 440–455.
14. The translation is taken from *Two Encyclicals on the Foreign Missions* (New York: America Press, 1944), p. 35.
15. Bonn, *op. cit.,* p. 149.
16. *AAS,* IX (1917), 376 f.
17. James Parkes, "The British Mandate," *Land Reborn,* VI (May–June, 1956), 3.
18. *Tablet,* CXXXVIII (June 25, 1921), 821 f.
19. *Ibid.,* XXX (December 29, 1917), 875 f.
20. *Ibid.*
21. Frank Brutto, "Santa Susanna, Church of the Two Houses," *Catholic Digest,* XX (September, 1956), 117 f.
22. *AAS,* VII (1915), 167 f.
23. *Ibid.,* XI (1919), 173.
24. *Ibid.,* VII (1915), 166. A translation is found in *Rome,* XVI (May 1, 1915), 209.

CHAPTER XXII   *Benedict XV, the Writer*

1. De Waal, *op. cit.,* p. 124.
2. Pastor, *Tagebücher,* p. 775 f.
3. For this anecdote the author is indebted to Archbishop Romolo Carboni, apostolic delegate to Australia, who visited Saint Thomas College on April 13, 1957. Archbishop Carboni had worked side by side with Arborio-Mella di Sant'Elia. This is his family name; his Christian name is Alberto. He had a gift for telling anecdotes about the supreme pontiffs with whom he had been associated. He had been appointed a secret chamberlain on active duty by Saint Pius X, and was reappointed to that position by Benedict XV on the very day of his election.

Benedict was very fond of this chamberlain but expected of his subordinates the same precision that he himself practiced. In this connection Archbishop Carboni told another of Arborio-Mella di Sant'Elia's anecdotes.

One day, Arborio-Mella di Sant'Elia came to Cardinal Gasparri very crestfallen. He told the Secretary of State that he was sure that his days at the Vatican were numbered, that undoubtedly he would soon be dismissed. Gasparri asked what indications he had of this. Arborio-Mella di Sant'Elia replied that he had made a slight error in a task which the Pope had asked him to perform. Benedict noticed it at once and said sharply, "Oh, why don't you go to bed and sleep?" The Pope had accented the word "bed." Gasparri began to laugh in his characteristic choking, almost apoplectic manner until all in the room turned from their desks to learn the reason for the outburst. When the rotund Gasparri finally recovered his poise, he said, "Don't let that worry you. How would you like to be in my shoes? He tells me that every day."

Pius XI made Monsignor Arborio-Mella di Sant'Elia *maestro di camera*. He was elected governor of the conclave in 1939. He retained his position of *maestro di camera* until his death. He was also president of the Heraldic Court of the Pontifical Commission, a bureau which Benedict XV had established in 1916. Alberto Arborio-Mella di Sant'Elia died on March 20, 1953, at the age of seventy-three. He was a Sardinian by birth.

4. Hughes, *op. cit.*, p. 177.
5. *Tablet*, CXXXVI (June 19, 1920), 825.
6. *AAS*, VI (1914), 565–581.
7. *Ibid.*, IX (1917), 305–317.
8. *Ibid.*, X (1918), 473 f.
9. *Ibid.*, XI (1919), 209–221.
10. Wendell Willkie, *One World* (New York: Simon and Schuster, 1943); *AAS*, XI (1919), 437–439.
11. *Tablet*, CXXXIV (December 6, 1919), 767 f.
12. Sir. 18:14, 17.
13. *AAS*, XII (1920), 209–218.
14. Pichon, *op. cit.*, p. 200.
15. *Civiltà Cattolica*, LXX (1920), ii, 503.
16. *Ibid.*
17. *AAS*, XII (1920), 385–422.
18. *Ibid.*, XXXV (1943), 297–326.
19. *Ibid.*, XII (1920), 457–471.
20. *Ibid.*, 553–556.
21. *Ibid.*, XIII (1921), 33–41.
22. *Ibid.*, 209–217.
23. Hayward, *op. cit.*, p. 153.
24. *Ibid.*, p. 155.
25. *Ibid.*
26. *AAS*, XIII (1921), 329–335.
27. The Dominican popes were: Innocent V (1276), Benedict XI (1303–1304), Pius V (1566-1572), and Benedict XIII (1724–1730).
28. *Register*, November 23, 1952.
29. Letters to obtain definite information written by this author to members of the clergy in Bologna did not receive an answer. A research student in Rome made inquiries as recently as 1956, but was unable to obtain further information. A visit to Bologna by the present writer to inquire about the manuscript brought no further results.

CHAPTER XXIII   *The Death of Benedict XV*

1. Barnes, *op. cit.*, 376 f.
2. *Catholic Bulletin,* April 24, 1920, p. 1.
3. Durante, *op. cit.*, p. 36.
4. Clonmore, *op. cit.*, p. 68; Morgan, *A Reporter at the Papal Court,* p. 160.
5. Pastor, *Tagebücher,* p. 746 f.
6. Durante, *op. cit.*, pp. 178–180.
7. Premoli, *op. cit.*, p. 49.
8. *Civiltà Cattolica,* LXXIII (1922), i, 194.
9. Schmidlin, *op. cit.*, p. 331.
10. *AAS,* XIV (1922), 53.
11. Vistalli, *op. cit.*, p. 430.
12. *Der Wanderer* (Saint Paul, Minn.), January 26, 1922, p. 1.
13. Vistalli, *op. cit.*, p. 427.
14. Pastor, *Tagebücher,* p. 720.
15. Morgan, *A Reporter at the Papal Court,* p. 11.
16. Buehrle, *op. cit.*, p. 207.
17. Vistalli, *op. cit.*, p. 430.
18. Migliori, *op. cit.*, p. 11.
19. Morgan, *A Reporter at the Papal Court,* p. 13.
20. Schlegel, *op. cit.*, p. 56.
21. Zannetti, *op. cit.*, p. 251.
22. Schlegel, *op. cit.*, p. 58.
23. Vistalli, *op. cit.*, p. 430.
24. Zannetti, *op. cit.*, p. 240.
25. Sforza, *op. cit.*, p. 202.
26. Migliori, *op. cit.*, p. 12.
27. *AAS,* XIV (1922), 55.

Bibliography

BOOKS

Augustine, P. Charles, O.S.B. *A Commentary on the New Code of Canon Law.* 8 vols. St. Louis: Herder, 1918.

Bender, Robert J. *"W. W.," Scattered Impressions of a Reporter who for Eight Years "Covered" the Activities of Woodrow Wilson.* New York: United Press Associations, 1924.

Bonn, John L. *The House on the Sands.* New York: Doubleday, 1950.

Bonomelli, *I Papi in Campagna.* Roma: Gherardo Casini, 1953.

Bourassa, Henri. *Le Pape Arbitre de la Paix.* Montreal: Devoir, 1918.

Bouscaren, T. Lincoln, S.J., and Ellis, Adam C., S.J. *Canon Law: A Text and Commentary.* Milwaukee: Bruce, 1958.

Brennan, Richard. *A Popular Life of Our Holy Father Pope Pius the Ninth.* New York: Benziger, 1877.

Buehrle, Marie Cecilia, *Rafael Cardinal Merry del Val.* Milwaukee: Bruce, 1957.

Burton, Katherine. *The Great Mantle, the Life of Giuseppe Melchiore Sarto Pope Pius X.* New York: Longmans, Green and Co., 1950.

Carrere, Jean. *The Pope.* Translated by Arthur Chambers. New York: Henry Holt and Co., 1926.

Cenci, Pio. *Il Cardinale Raffaele Merry del Val.* Roma-Torino: Berruti, 1933.

Chamier, J. Daniel. *Fabulous Monster.* New York: Longmans, Green and Co., 1934.

Cianfarra, Camille. *The Vatican and the War.* New York: Dutton, 1945.

Cicognani, Amleto Giovanni. *Canon Law.* Philadelphia: Dolphin Press, 1934.

Clonmore, Lord. *Pope Pius XI and World Peace.* New York: Dutton, 1938.

Corvo, Baron Frederick (Frederick Rolfe). *Hadrian the Seventh.* New York: Knopf, 1925.

Crawley-Boevey, Mateo, SS.CC. *Jesus, King of Love.* Fairhaven, Mass.: National Center of the Enthronement, 1943.

Dal-Gal, R. P. *Le Cardinal Merry Del Val.* Paris: Nouvelles Editions Latines, 1955.

Dansette, Adrien. *Histoire Religiouse de la France Contemporaine sous la troisième Republique.* Paris: Flammarion, 1951.

De la Bedoyere, Michael. *The Life of Baron von Hügel.* London: J. M. Dent and Sons, 1951.

De Oca, Montes, C.S.Sp. *More about Fatima and the Immaculate Heart of Mary.* Translated by J. da Cruz. Westminster, Md.: Newman Bookshop, 1947.

De Waal, Anton. *Der neue Papst: Unser heiliger Vater Benedikt XV.* Hamm: Breer und Thiemann, 1915.

Di Pietro, Maria. *Benedetto XV.* Milano: Società editrice Vita e Pensiero, 1936.

Doherty, Martin. *The House on Humility Street.* New York: Longmans, 1942.

Dubly, Henry Louis. *The Life of Cardinal Mercier, Primate of Belgium.* Herbert Wilson, trans. London: Sands and Co., 1928.

Durante, Antonio. *Benedetto XV.* Roma: Editrice A.V.E., 1939

Elliot, Frances Minto. *Roman Gossip.* Leipzig: Tauchnitz, 1896.

Ellis, John Tracy. *The Life of James Cardinal Gibbons.* 2 vols. Milwaukee: Bruce, 1952.

Eppstein, John. *The Catholic Tradition of the Law of Nations.* Washington, D. C.: Catholic Association for International Peace, 1935.

Farrow, John. *Pageant of the Popes.* New York: Sheed and Ward, 1942.

Fernessole, Pierre. *Pie X.* 2 vols. Paris: Lethielleux, 1952.

——— *Sa Sainteté Pie XII et l'Education de la Jeunesse.* Paris: Lethielleux, 1955.

Forbes, Frances Alice Monica. *Rafael, Cardinal Merry del Val, a Character Sketch.* London: Longmans, Green and Co., 1932.

Füllöp-Miller, Rene. *Leo XIII and Our Times.* London: Longmans, Green and Co., 1937.

Furey, Francis T. *Life of Leo XIII and History of His Pontificate.* Philadelphia: Catholic Educational Company, 1904.

Gannon, David. *Father Paul of Graymoor.* New York: Macmillan, 1951.

Gonella, Guido. *The Papacy and World Peace.* London: Hollis and Carter, 1945.

Goyau, Georges. *Papauté et Chretienté sous Benoit XV.* Paris: Perrin et Cᵗᵉ, 1922.

Grissell, Hartwell de la Garde. *Sede Vacante, Being a Diary Written during the Conclave of 1903.* Oxford: Parker, 1903.

Gwyn, Denis. *The Vatican and War in Europe.* Dublin: Browne and Nolan, 1940.

Halecki, Oscar. *Eugenio Pacelli: Pope of Peace.* New York: Creative Age Press, Inc., 1951.

Hayward, Fernand. *Un Pape méconnu Benoît XV.* Tournai: Castermann, 1955.

Heston, Edward L. *The Holy See at Work.* Milwaukee: Bruce, 1950.

Heufelder, Emmanuel. *Der heilige Benedikt von Nursia.* Augsburg: Christkoenigsverlag vom Weissen Kreuz, 1934.

Hitler, Adolf. *Mein Kampf.* New York: Reynal and Hitchcock, 1951.

Hudal, Alois. *Die Österreichische Vatikanbotschaft 1806–1918.* München: Pohl and Co., 1952.

Hughes, Philip. *Pope Pius the Eleventh.* New York: Sheed and Ward, 1937.

Johnson, Gerald W. *Woodrow Wilson, the Unforgettable Figure who Has Returned to Haunt Us.* New York: Harper, 1944.

Kay-Smith, Sheila. *Quartet in Heaven.* New York: Harper, 1952.

Koenig, Harry C. *Principles for Peace, Selections from Papal Documents, Leo XIII to Pius XII.* Washington, D. C.: N.C.W.C., 1943

Konstantin, Prince of Bavaria. *The Pope, a Portrait from Life.* New York: Roy, n.d.

Kürenberg, Joachim von. *The Kaiser, a Life of Wilhelm II, Last Emperor of Germany.* Translated by H. T. Russell and Herta Hagen. New York: Simon and Schuster, 1955.

Lama, Friedrich Ritter von. *Die Friedensvermittlung Papst Benedikts XV und ihre Vereitlung durch den deutschen Reichskanzler Michaelis.* München: Kösel und Pustet, 1932.

———— *Papst Pius XI, sein Leben und Wirken dargeboten zu seinem goldenen Priesterjubiläum.* Augsburg: Institut Haas und Grabherr, 1929.

———— *Papst und Kurie in ihrer Politik nach dem Weltkrieg.* Illertissen: Martinusbuchhandlung, 1925.

———— *Der vereitelte Friede. Meine Anklage gegen Michaelis und den Evangelischen Bund.* Augsburg: Institut Haas und Grabherr, 1926.

Lathoud, David. *Avec le Pape au Vatican.* Paris: Centurion, 1955.

Leslie, Shane. *Cardinal Gasquet.* London: Burns, Oates, 1953.

Lowrie, Walter. *Saints Peter and Paul in Rome.* London: Oxford University Press, 1940.

Ludwig, Emil. *Wilhelm Hohenzollern, the Last of the Kaisers.* New York: Putnam, 1927.

McKnight, John P. *The Papacy, a New Appraisal.* New York: Rinehart, 1952.

MacNutt, Francis Augustus. *A Papal Chamberlain*. London: Longmans, 1936.

Merry del Val, Rafael. *Memories of Pope Pius X*. Westminster, Md.: Newman Press, 1951.

Migliori, Giambattista. *Benedetto XV*. Milano: "La Favilla," 1932.

Mitchell, Hary. *Le Cardinal R. Merry del Val, Secrétaire d'État de Saint Pie X*. Paris: Paris-Livres, 1956.

Moore, Thomas Ewing. *Peter's City, an Account of the Origin, Development and Solution of the Roman Question*. New York: Macmillan, 1930.

Morgan, Thomas B. *The Listening Post, Eighteen Years on Vatican Hill*. New York: G. P. Putnam's Sons, 1944.

—————— *A Reporter at the Papal Court, a Narrative of the Reign of Pope Pius XI*. New York: Longmans, 1938.

—————— *Speaking of Cardinals*. New York: G. P. Putnam's Sons, 1946.

Morton, H. V. *In the Steps of Saint Paul*. London: Rich and Cowan, 1936.

Moynihan, James H. *The Life of Archbishop John Ireland*. New York: Harper, 1953.

Mussolini, Benito. *My Autobiography*. New York: Scribner, 1928.

Neuvecelle, Jean. *The Vatican, its Organization, Customs, and Way of Life*. New York: Criterion, 1955.

O'Connell, William Cardinal. *Recollections of Seventy Years*. Boston: Houghton Mifflin Co., 1934.

Oesch, Albert. *P. Michael Hofmann, S.J.* Innsbruck: Felizian Rauch, 1951.

O'Reilly, Bernard. *Leo XIII, seine Zeit, sein Pontificat und seine Erfolge*. New York: John S. Winston Co., 1903.

Pastor, Ludwig Freiherr von. *Tagebücher — Briefe — Erinnerungen*. Edited by Wilhelm Wühr. Heidelberg: F. H. Kerle, 1950.

Pichon, Francis. *Benoît XV*. Paris: Éditions Spes, 1940.

Pöllmann, P. Ansgar. *Benedikt XV aus der Familie der Della Chiesa, ein helles Bild auf dunklem Hintergrunde*. Diessen vor München: Jos. C. Huber, 1915.

Premoli, Orazio M. *Contemporary Church History*. London: Burns, Oates and Washbourne, 1932.

Saint Thérèse of Lisieux. Translated and edited by Thomas Nimmo Taylor. New York: P. J. Kennedy, 1927.

Salvatorelli, Luigi. *Pio IX e la sua Eredità Pontificale*. Turin: Enaudi, 1939.

Schlarman, Joseph H. L. *Mexico, a Land of Volcanoes.* Milwaukee: Bruce, 1951.

Schmidlin, Josef. *Papstgeschichte der neuesten Zeit.* Vol. III. München: Kösel und Pustet, 1953.

Scritti e Discorsi di Benito Mussolini. Vol. I. Milano: Ulrico Hoepli, 1934.

Seldes, George. *The Vatican: Yesterday — Today — Tomorrow.* New York: Harper, 1934.

Seppelt, Francis X., and Löffler, Clement. *A Short History of the Popes.* Translated by Horace A. Frommelt. St. Louis: Herder, 1932.

Sforza, Count Carlo. *Contemporary Italy.* Translated by Drake and Denise De Kay. New York: Dutton, 1944.

Sheen, Fulton J. *Communism and the Conscience of the West.* Indianapolis: Bobbs-Merrill, 1948.

Smit, Jan Olav. *Angelic Shepherd, the Life of Pope Pius XII.* New York: Dodd, Mead and Co., 1950.

Speaight, Robert. *The Life of Hilaire Belloc.* New York: Farrar, Straus and Cudahy, 1957.

Storer, Maria Longworth. *In Memoriam Bellamy Storer.* Boston: privately printed, 1923.

Struker, Dr. Arnold. *Die Kundgebungen Papst Benedikts XV zum Weltfrieden.* Freiburg: Herder, 1917.

Sturzo, Luigi. *Church and State.* New York: Longmans, Green and Co., 1939.

Taylor, A. J. P. *The Struggle for Mastery in Europe, 1848–1918.* Oxford: Clarendon Press, 1954.

Teresia Renata de Spiritu Sancto, Schwester. *Maria Erzberger.* Köln: privately printed, 1953.

Thornton, Francis Beauchesne. *The Burning Flame, the Life of Pope Pius X.* New York: Benziger, 1952.

Tumulty, Joseph P. *Woodrow Wilson as I Know Him.* Garden City: Doubleday, Page and Company, 1921.

Van Hilsum, J. N. I. *Maria Erzberger, Zr. Maria Gertrudis.* Antwerp: Nelissen. 1956.

Van Paassen, Pierre. *Days of Our Years.* New York: Hillman-Curl, Inc., 1939.

Vercesi, P. *Tre Papi: Leone XIII — Pio X — Benedetto XV.* Milano: Edizioni Athena, 1929.

Vernadsky, George. *Lenin, Red Dictator.* Translated by Malcolm Waters Davis. New Haven: Yale University Press, 1931.

Vistalli, Francesco. *Benedetto XV.* Roma: Tipografia Poliglotta Vaticana, 1928.

Wallace, William Kay. *Greater Italy.* New York: Charles Scribner's Sons, 1917.
Wheeler-Bennett, John W. *Wooden Titan.* New York: William Morrow, 1936.
Wile, Frederic William. *Men around the Kaiser.* Indianapolis: Bobbs-Merrill, 1914.
Williamson, Benedict. *The Story of Pope Pius XI.* London: Alexander-Ouseley, 1931.
Wilson, Edith Bolling. *My Memoir.* Indianapolis: Bobbs-Merrill, 1938.

Zanetti, Francesco. *Nella Citta del Vaticano: Cinque Papi attraverso gli annedoti da Pio IX a Pio XI.* Roma: Tip. Edit. Sallustiana, 1929.

PUBLIC DOCUMENTS

Acta Apostolicae Sedis. Vols. VI (1914)–XIV (1922).
Acta Sanctae Apostolicae Sedis, XVI (1883), "Saepenumero"; XL (1907), *"Pascendi."*

U. S. Congressional Record, 65th Cong., 1st Sess. (1917), LV, Part 6; 2nd Sess. (1918), LVI, Part 1.

ARTICLES

Atwater, Donald. "Facts that Make Reunion with the Orthodox Church Difficult," *The Catholic Mind,* XLII (October, 1944).

Barnes, J. S. "Benedict XV: an Impression," *The Dublin Review,* CLV (October, 1914), 373–377.
Barry, William. "Benedict XV: Pontiff of Peace," *The Dublin Review,* CLXX (1922), 161–178.
Battifol, Pierre Henri. "Pope Benedict XV and the Restoration of Unity," *The Constructive Quarterly,* VI (1918), 209–225.
Bloch, Jean-Richard. *"Conte de Noel,"* Europe, XXX (1932), 603–609.
Brutto, Frank. "Santa Susanna, Church of the Two Houses," *The Catholic Digest,* XX (September, 1956), 117–120.

Dalla Torre, Giuseppe. "Benedetto XV," *Enciclopedia Cattolica,* II, 1286–1294.
Dell, Robert. "The Vatican and the War," *The Fortnightly Review,* CIII (Old Series), XCVII (New Series), (February, 1915), 286–295.
Deuerlein, Ernst. "Zur Friedensaktion Papst Benedikts XV. (1917)," *Stimmen der Zeit,* CLV (January, 1955), 241–256.

Dillon, E. J. "Italy's New Birth," *The Fortnightly Review*, LXXXIII (July, 1915), 1–15.
———— "The Pope and the Belligerents," *The Contemporary Review*, CVII (May, 1915), 553–571.

Engel-Janosi, Friedrich. "Osterreich-Ungarn und der Vatikan während des Pontifikats Pius' X und der Wahl Benedikts XV," *Mitteilungen des österreichischen Staatsarchivs*, V (1952), 278–301.

Fenton, Joseph Clifford. "The Semicentennial of the *Lamentabili* and the *Pascendi*," *The American Ecclesiastical Review*, CXXXVI (January, 1957), 42–54.
———— "Two Currents in Contemporary Catholic Thought," *The American Ecclesiastical Review*, CXIX (October, 1948), 293–301.

Garland, Robert. "The Coronation of Benedict XV," *The Outlook*, CVIII (November 25, 1914), 689–707.
Graef, Hilda C. "A Life for a Soul," *Cross and Crown*, VII (June, 1955), 208–217.
Graham, Robert A. "Ends and Means in Controversy," *America*, XC (April 14), 54–46.

Hale, William Harlan. "Thus Spoke the Kaiser, the Lost Interview which Solves an International Mystery," *The Atlantic Monthly*, CLIII (May, 1934), 513–523.
Hilling, Nikolaus. "Die Gesetzgeberische Tätigkeit Benedikts XV bis zur Promulgation des Codex iuris canonici," *Archiv für katholisches Kirchenrecht*, XCVIII (1918), 223–239, 298–406, 561–574.

Johnson, Humphrey J. T. "Pope Benedict XV: 1854–1954," *The Tablet*, CCIV (November 20, 1954), 495 f.
Jusserand, J., "Letter to the Editor," *American Historical Review*, XXXVII (July, 1932), 817–819.

Larraona, Arcadius, et Goyeneche, Servus. "De Sacrarum Congregationum, Tribunalium et Officiorum Constitutione et Interna Ordinatione post Constitutionem 'Sapienti Consilio,' " *Apollinaris*, XXV (1952), 85–139.
Linder, Josef. "Die absolute Wahrheit der heiligen Schrift nach der Lehre der Enzyklika Papst Benedikts XV 'Spiritus Paraclitus,' " *Zeitschrift für katholische Theologie*, XLVI (1922), 254–277.

McReavy, Lawrence. "The Silver Jubilee of the Code of Canon Law," *The Clergy Review*, XXIII (November, 1943), 481–486.

Mattern, J. "The Pope and His Critics," *The Open Court*, XXX (May, 1916), 258–277.

Parkes, James. "The British Mandate," *Land Reborn*, VI (May-June, 1956), 3–16.

Pioli, Giovanni. "Benedict XV: the Significance of his Election," *The Contemporary Review*, CVI (October, 1914), 506–514.

"Qu'est-ce que l'Intégrisme?" *La Vie Intellectuelle*, XXIV (Août-Septembre, 1952), 136–152.

Schwering, Leo. "Benedikt der Fünfzehnte, ein Versuch zur Würdigung seiner Politik," *Deutsche Rundsachau*, CLXXXIV (July-September, 1920), 306–315.

Sierp, Heinrich, S.J. "Benedikt XV," *Stimmen der Zeit*, LXX (1922), 401–409.

Vermeersch, Arthur, S.J. "Modernism," *The Catholic Encyclopedia*, X, 415–421.

"The Vatican and the Germanic Powers," *The Contemporary Review*, CXII (October, 1917), 402–412.

Wood, L. J. S. "Benedict XV, Pontiff of Peace," *The Dublin Review*, CLXX (April, 1922), 161–212.

PAMPHLETS

"Diplomaticus." *No Small Stir, What the Pope Really Said about the Great War*. London: Society of Saints Peter and Paul, Publishers to the Church of England, 1917.

Peace Action of Pope Benedict XV, a Summary by the History Committee of Friedrich Ritter Von Lama's "Die Friedensvermittlung Papst Benedikt XV." Washington, D. C.: The Catholic Association for International Peace, n.d.

Schlegel, P. Leo. *Papst Benedikt XV*. Freiburg, Schweiz: Kanisiuswerk, 1932.

Sheen, Fulton J. *The Philosophy of Communism*. Washington, D. C.: N.C.W.C., 1947.

Simon, M. *Quand le Pape est mort*. Rome: Pages Romaines, 1938.

Two Encyclicals on the Foreign Missions. New York: America Press, 1944.

OTHER SOURCES

The Catholic Bulletin (Saint Paul, Minn.). Vols. IV (1914)–XII (1922).

La Civiltà Cattolica (Rome). Vols. LXV (1914)–LXXIII (1922).

The New York Times. 1914–1922.

L'Osservatore Romano. 1914–1922.

Rome, a Weekly Record of Everything Worth Knowing about the Eternal City. Vols. XV (1914)–XXI (1917).

The Tablet. Vols. CXXIV (1914)–CXXXIX (1922).

Index

Before Della Chiesa became pope, he is referred to as Giacomo except in such cases where, for example, a character trait is mentioned. This will appear under Benedict XV.

Cassetta, Francesco de Paolo, president of Society of St. Jerome, 213

Catholic Biblical Association of America, 216

Catholic University of America, Benedict and, 254

Cavour, Camillo, philosopher of *Risorgimento,* 188

Celidonio, Fra, Benedict's nurse, 272

Central Powers, definition of, 140, 289 *n.* 2

Cerretti, Bonaventura, and Achille Ratti as visitator to Poland, 198 f; Benedict's messenger to Versailles, 169 f; friendship with Briand, 197

Charles I, Emperor of Austria-Hungary, and Benedict's peace note, 157

Children of Europe, Benedict's appeal for, 259 f; collections for, 261

Christian Brothers, Benedict's interest in, 241

Chur, Canon in diocese of, Benedict's double, 267 f

Cicognani, Amleto Giovanni, on code of Canon Law, 209

Clama ne cesses, see Benedict XV, Allocutions, *Di accogliere*

Code of Canon Law, *see* Canon Law, Code of

Combes, Emile, death of, 197 f

Communism, condemned in *Pacem Dei Munus,* 260; and study of St. Francis, 262

Coptic College reopened, 246

Corrigan, Michael A., Archbishop of New York, impression of Giacomo, 25

Cottolengo, Joseph Benedict, St., *see* Benedict XV, Beatifications

Crawley-Boevey, Mateo, audience with Benedict, 223 f

Csernoch, Janos, Archbishop of Gran, on Integralists, 52 f

Cum de fidelibus, see Benedict XV, pope, Letters

Cumiuris, see Benedict XV, *Motu Proprios*

Cum novum, see Benedict XV

Dante Alighieri, encyclical on, 262–264

De Lai, Gaetano, Cardinal, Prefect of Consistorial Congregation, 50; Giacomo's warning to, on anti-modernist measures, 40; and La Sapiniére, 51

Dell, Robert, on Benedict, 106

Della Chiesa, Giovanna, Marchesa (Giacomo's mother), 3; death of, 40; Giacomo's consideration toward, 24

Della Chiesa, Giovanni (brother of Benedict), visits in Vatican gardens, 97 f

Della Chiesa, Giuseppe, Marchese (Giacomo's father), death of, 21; description of, 3; postpones Giacomo's studies for priesthood, 9

Della Chiesa, Julia (Benedict's sister), *see* Persico, Julia, Countess

Della Chiesa, Marchese Giuseppe, Jr., nephew, in sickroom, 272

Della Volpe, Francesco Salesio, Camerlengo of Pius X, 69; and senior Cardinal Deacon announces election of Benedict XV, 82

de Marillac, Louise, St., *see* Benedict XV, Beatifications

de Medici, Alessandro, Duke, drama supposedly written by Giacomo, 265

de Salis, John Francis Charles, Count, British minister to Holy See, and Benedict's peace note, 145, 147

Deuerlein, Ernst, historian, on von Kühlmann and Benedict's peace note, 160; on Michaelis and Benedict's peace note, 159

De Waal, Msgr. Anton, on delay of Giacomo's *exsequatur,* 56; first biographer of Benedict, 6 *n;* on Giacomo before Leo XIII, 26; on Rampolla's routine, 28 f

Dialogue Mass, 241

Dillon, E. J., on Gerlach, 127–130; on Giacomo's diplomatic tactics, 28; on Giacomo and Rampolla, 28

Diuturni luctuosissimi belli, see Benedict XV, Letters

Divino afflante Spiritu, see Pius XII, pope

Dolci, Angelo, Apostolic delegate to Constantinople, 182

Dominic, St., encyclical on, 264 f

Drama, supposedly written by Giacomo, 265

Duce, Il, see Mussolini, Benito,

Eisner, Kurt, assassination of, 258

Embassies to Holy See, status during war, 191 f

Entente, definition of, 140, 289 *n.* 2